631 Rapid Recipes At Your Fingertips

FOR HOMEMADE FOOD with all of the "from scratch" flavor but none of the fuss, you can rely on this eighth edition of the cookbook containing recipes from *Quick Cooking* magazine.

2006 Quick Cooking Annual Recipes conveniently gathers every speedy recipe published in *Quick Cooking* during 2005—that's 631 recipes in all—and combines them in one reader-friendly collection. This recipe-packed volume is filled with hundreds of mouth-watering photos so you can see what many of the dishes look like before you prepare them for your family.

Here's what else you'll find inside:

Chapters That Meet Your Needs. With 21 chapters that correspond to popular features in *Quick Cooking* magazine, it's a snap to find a recipe that matches your family's taste and timetable. (See page 3 for a complete list of chapters.)

For example, when you have a mere 10 minutes to spare in the kitchen, rely on Roast Beef Barbecue, Split-Second Shrimp, Green Chili Tomato Soup, Loaded Tortillas, Mousse Tarts or any of the 21 other timeless recipes in the "10 Minutes to the Table" chapter.

Or on busy weeknights when your family is eyeing the table and you're watching the clock, see the "30 Minutes to Mealtime" chapter for 18 complete meals that go from start to finish in half an hour or less.

Mix and Match 30-Minute Meals. Our food editors provide even more entrees and other dishes you can fix in a half hour or less. Just group any of these recipes you like to create a 30-minute menu. (This time-saving tool appears on page 4.)

Award-Winning Recipes. You'll get all the palate-pleasing, quick-to-prepare foods that earned top honors in the six national recipe contests we held last year: Swift Skillet Side Dishes, Beat-the-Clock Breads, Speedy Brunch, 10-Minute Mainstays, Swift After-School Snacks and In-a-Dash Desserts.

Easy-to-Use Indexes. To make all 631 recipes easy to find, we've listed them in two indexes. (See page 316.) The general index lists every recipe by category and/or major food ingredient. The alphabetical listing is great for folks who are looking for a specific family favorite. In both indexes, you'll find a bold red checkmark (✓) in front of all recipes that use less fat, sugar or salt and include Nutritional Analysis and Diabetic Exchanges.

Every rapid recipe and helpful hint in this *2006 Quick Cooking Annual Recipes* cookbook was specifically selected with the busy cook in mind. You're sure to enjoy this timeless treasury for years to come...and you'll be able to treat your loved ones to comforting, wholesome home cooking without spending all of your precious time in the kitchen.

2006 Quick Cooking Annual Recipes

Editor: Michelle Bretl
Art Director: Lori Arndt
Executive Editor/Books: Heidi Reuter Lloyd
Senior Editor/Books: Julie Schnittka
Proofreader: Julie Blume Benedict
Graphic Art Associates: Ellen Lloyd,
Catherine Fletcher
Editorial Assistant: Barb Czysz

Taste of Home Books
©2005 Reiman Media Group, Inc.
5400 S. 60th St., Greendale WI 53129

International Standard Book Number:
0-89821-474-2
International Standard Serial Number:
1522-6603
All rights reserved.
Printed in U.S.A.

PICTURED ON THE COVER: Raspberry Lemon Torte (p. 218), Grilled Vegetable Medley (p. 126) and Grilled Pork Chops (p. 156).

Taste of Home's
QUICK COOKING

Editor: Julie Kastello
Associate Editors: Mary Spencer, Mary Hanson, Mark Hagen
Copy Editor: S.K. Enk
Editorial Assistants: Ursula Maurer, Mary Ann Koebernik
Creative Director: Ardyth Cope
Art Director: Julie Wagner
Contributing Designers: Jim Sibilski, Monica Bergwall
Food Editor: Janaan Cunningham
Associate Food Editors: Coleen Martin, Diane Werner RD
Recipe Editor: Mary King
Test Kitchen Director: Mark Morgan RD
Senior Home Economist: Amy Welk-Thieding RD
Home Economists: Tina Johnson, Peggy Fleming RD, Nancy Fridirici, Ann Liebergen, Pat Schmeling, Wendy Stenman
Contributing Home Economist: Susan Guenther
Test Kitchen Assistants: Rita Krajcir, Suzanne Kern, Kris Lehman, Sue Megonigle, Megan Taylor
Food Photographers: Rob Hagen, Dan Roberts, Jim Wieland
Photographers' Assistant: Lori Foy
Food Stylists: Kristin Arnett, Sarah Thompson, Joylyn Trickel
Contributing Food Stylists: Diane Armstrong, Suzanne Breckenridge, Mary Franz, Lorene Frohling, Julie Herzfeldt, Jim Rude
Set Stylists: Julie Ferron, Stephanie Marchese, Sue Myers, Jennifer Bradley Vent
Graphic Art Associates: Ellen Lloyd, Catherine Fletcher
Senior Vice President and Editor in Chief: Catherine Cassidy
Vice President and Advertising Sponsorship Director: J.P. Perkins
President: Barbara Newton
Chairman and Founder: Roy Reiman

⏱ *Contents*

Mix and Match 30-Minute Meals

WITH the *2006 Quick Cooking Annual Recipes* book, planning weekday dinners for your family is as easy as can be. And you can start today by taking advantage of the handy guide on these two pages.

Here's how to use it: Our food editors selected various recipes from this book that can be fixed in only a half hour or less. Begin by choosing an "Effortless Entree" on this page, whether it's a beef, poultry, pork, seafood or meatless main dish.

Next, pair that entree with one or more "Easy Accompaniments" on the opposite page. Customizing a swift family supper has never been easier!

Effortless Entrees

Easy Accompaniments

Recipe Contests Yield Quick Winning Dishes

EVERYONE KNOWS that *Quick Cooking* magazine readers have the best rapid recipes around. Many of those dishes come to light when readers enter them in our national recipe contests...and our judges reveal their top picks among those entries.

Want to find out which tasty and time-saving dishes in this book were deemed tops in a *Quick Cooking* contest? It's easy—just check the special section here.

On these two pages, we've featured the six talented cooks who took home Grand Prize honors in the 2005 contests. We've also let you know where to find their Grand Prize recipes in this book, so you can turn to those celebrated dishes right away...and even prepare them for your family tonight!

Plus, we've listed the 11 other winning recipes in each contest. It's a complete list of dishes—all 72 of them—that received awards during the past year.

Because we've included the page numbers for the runner-up recipes, too, you'll easily be able to locate each contest winner. Dozens of top-honor dishes are right at your fingertips!

A Wide Range of Winners

The contest topics during the past year yielded a variety of reader recipes, but all of those dishes have one thing in common—they're fast-to-fix foods that fit into busy cooks' lifestyles.

In the "Swift Skillet Side Dishes" contest, readers submitted easy meal accompaniments that will complement many main courses. And "Beat-the-Clock Breads" resulted in plenty of baked delights that are fresh from the oven in a flash.

Do you need early-day fare for your family or guests? Check out the eye-opening winners of the "Speedy Brunch" contest. Or see "10-Minute Mainstays" for pleasing recipes that require only moments to get on the table.

On hectic nights during the week, "Swift After-School Snacks" are sure to tide both kids and adults over until dinner. And "In-a-Dash Desserts" will give your family taste-tempting treats any time you like.

So choose your favorites among these prize-winning recipes—or put them all in your upcoming menu plans. Either way, you'll have stand-out sensations you and your family are sure to love.

Her Tomatoes Stole the Side-Dish Show

THERE'S ALWAYS room for one more at Phyllis Shaughnessy's table in Livonia, New York. And her guests often enjoy Tomatoes with Horseradish Sauce, the recipe that garnered Phyllis first place in *Quick Cooking's* "Swift Skillet Side Dishes" contest.

"When tomatoes are plentiful, I make this dish regularly for my husband, Tom, and me," she says. "But regardless of the season, it's a wonderfully fresh-tasting treat that's nice enough for company."

Swift Skillet Side Dishes Contest Winners

Tomatoes with Horseradish Sauce *(Grand Prize)*.........p. 121
Creamy Zucchini *(2nd Place)*.......................................p. 121
Bacon Mashed Potatoes *(3rd Place)* ....p. 122
Spicy Asparagus Spears *(4th Place)*..............................p. 122
Country Corn *(Runner-Up)*...p. 125
Blue Cheese Green Beans *(Runner-Up)*.......................p. 122
Herbed Rice *(Runner-Up)*...p. 123
Spanish Squash Medley *(Runner-Up)* ....p. 122
Cranberry Apple Saute *(Runner-Up)*............................p. 124
Skillet Sausage Stuffing *(Runner-Up)* ....p. 126
Ginger Garlic Linguine *(Runner-Up)* ....p. 128
Golden Diced Potatoes *(Runner-Up)* ....p. 125

Baker Rose to the Top with Quick Bread

WHEN it comes to making recipes like her Marmalade Monkey Bread—the Grand Prize winner in the "Beat-the-Clock Breads" contest—Delia Kennedy has had lots of practice. She cooks 7 days a week at her home in Deer Park, Washington.

"In fact, my husband and I rarely go to restaurants because Gary prefers home cooking," relates Delia. "Sometimes I experiment by mixing together a few of my favorite recipes. That's how I created this sweet pull-apart bread."

Beat-the-Clock Breads Contest Winners

Marmalade Monkey Bread *(Grand Prize)*....................p. 134
Chocolate Chip Muffins *(2nd Place)*...........................p. 137
Sweet Potato Quick Bread *(3rd Place)* ....p. 134
Garlic Herb Twists *(4th Place)*......................................p. 140
Oregano-Swiss Bread Slices *(Runner-Up)*.....................p. 137
Coconut-Chip Coffee Cake *(Runner-Up)*.....................p. 136
Spiced Walnut Loaf *(Runner-Up)*.................................p. 140
Lemon Blueberry Muffins *(Runner-Up)*........................p. 136
Pumpkin Coffee Cake *(Runner-Up)*.............................p. 140
Mini Italian Biscuits *(Runner-Up)*................................p. 141
Cinnamon-Nut Coffee Cake *(Runner-Up)*...................p. 136
Berry Bread with Spread *(Runner-Up)*..........................p. 141

Cook's Brunch Bake Proved Irresistible

FOR Patricia Harmon of Economy Borough, Pennsylvania, spending time in the kitchen is a favorite pastime. "I thoroughly enjoy creating recipes," she relates. "And I love quick brunch foods, whether they're for guests or just my husband, Paul, and me."

After sampling Florentine Egg Bake—Patricia's entry in the "Speedy Brunch" contest—our judges gave it top honors. "My family likes Italian food," she says, "and this bake has a lot of Italian flavor."

Judges Picked Her Garden-Fresh Salad

WORKING as an adoption social worker means Kati Spencer of Taylorsville, Utah spends several nights a week interviewing families. To make dinner for her and husband Ryan easy, she turns to recipes like Fiery Chicken Spinach Salad—the Grand Prize winner in the "10-Minute Mainstays" contest.

"I love this main-dish salad because nearly everything that goes into it is canned, packaged or already cooked, so it's ready in a flash," Kati relates.

Her After-School Snack Got High Marks

SINCE Lisa Renshaw's children are no longer school-aged, she's found someone new to try her PB&J Spirals. "I recently made them for my grandson, Nicholas," she writes from the home she shares with husband Warren and son Jacob in Kansas City, Missouri.

Awarded the top prize in the "Swift After-School Snacks" contest, Patricia's recipe wins over kids of all ages. "I've found that the combination of peanut butter and jelly is a hit with adults, too," she says.

Cook's Cool Pie is a Dessert Favorite

BOTH Arletta and Keith Slocum of Venice, Florida have a love of cooking, and the couple share sit-down meals nearly every night of the week.

"We try to have healthy dinners that include salad and veggies," Arletta explains. "But we also like to have dessert."

One treat they particularly enjoy is Butter Pecan Pumpkin Pie...and the *Quick Cooking* judges loved it, too. After tasting Arletta's frosty dessert, they awarded it top honors in the "In-a-Dash Desserts" contest.

Chapter 1

8

EVERY BUSY COOK has a favorite dinner menu that can be relied on again and again. This memorable meal not only beats the clock when time is tight, it has all the homemade taste and hearty goodness that a hungry family craves.

Here, six on-the-go cooks just like you share their top choices —meals they turn to when dinnertime is mere moments away. Each of these winning recipes can be prepared in only 30 minutes...or less.

You'll find a mouth-watering main course, stand-out side dish and delectable dessert or beverage with every menu. After tasting these delicious dishes, your family is sure to request them regularly—even on days when you have time to spare.

SPEEDY SUPPER. Pasta Beef Soup, Savory Cheese Bread and Hard-Shell Ice Cream Sauce (all recipes on pp. 12 and 13).

Delicious Dinner is Sure To Satisfy

PEOPLE who know Nella Parker will tell you that she's always on the go. The active cook from Hersey, Michigan enjoys gardening, sewing, river rafting and making handcrafts when she's not volunteering with Meals on Wheels or helping the elderly.

"I've always enjoyed living a busy lifestyle—whether it involves outdoor activities or things done indoors," Nella explains. "That's why I rely on easy menus that I can prepare in a hurry."

No matter how full her days are, Nella still finds time to prepare a sit-down meal four to five times a week for as many as 12 people.

"Although I don't have children or grandchildren, I have lots of nieces and nephews who often drop by and stay for dinner," she reports. "That's when I dig into my recipe files to find a fast menu.

"The delicious meal I'm sharing here can be on the table in a matter of minutes," Nella relates.

To speed preparations, the experienced cook fixes pretty Strawberry Yogurt Trifle first. "This dessert is a family favorite," notes Nella. "Since it requires only five ingredients, it's a breeze to assemble."

After preparing and refrigerating the trifle, Nella starts on her Flavorful Fish Fillets. "I like to make this entree whenever there's a special occasion in my large family. The fish has great taste without time-consuming preparation."

While the fillets cook, Dilled Green Beans are a snap to make. "I serve this versatile side dish quite often," Nella says. "For extra flavor, I crumble bacon on top."

Strawberry Yogurt Trifle

Prep/Total Time: 20 min.

✓ Uses less fat, sugar or salt. Includes Nutritional Analysis.

  5 cups cubed angel food cake
  1 carton (8 ounces) vanilla yogurt
  1 cup whipped topping, *divided*
  3 cups sliced fresh strawberries
  1 tablespoon flaked coconut, toasted

Place cake cubes in a 2-qt. bowl. Combine the yogurt and 3/4 cup whipped topping; spoon over the cake. Top with strawberries and remaining whipped topping.

Sprinkle with coconut. **Yield:** 4-5 servings.

Nutritional Analysis: 1-1/4 cups (prepared with reduced-fat yogurt and reduced-fat whipped topping) equals 230 calories, 3 g fat (2 g saturated fat), 3 mg cholesterol, 367 mg sodium, 45 g carbohydrate, 3 g fiber, 5 g protein.

Flavorful Fish Fillets

Prep/Total Time: 15 min.

  1 package (18.7 ounces) frozen breaded fish fillets
  3 tablespoons olive oil
  1 jar (26 ounces) spaghetti sauce
  3 tablespoons prepared horseradish
  1 cup (4 ounces) shredded mozzarella cheese

In a large skillet, cook fish in oil for 4 minutes on each side or until crisp and golden brown. Meanwhile, in a large saucepan, combine the spaghetti sauce and horseradish; cook until heated through. Spoon over fish; sprinkle with cheese. Cover and remove from the heat. Let stand for 5 minutes or until cheese is melted. **Yield:** 4-5 servings.

Dilled Green Beans

Prep/Total Time: 20 min.

✓ Uses less fat, sugar or salt. Includes Nutritional Analysis and Diabetic Exchanges.

  1 cup water
1/4 cup chopped green pepper
  2 tablespoons chopped onion
  2 teaspoons beef bouillon granules
1/2 teaspoon dill seed
  2 packages (9 ounces *each*) frozen cut green beans

In a large saucepan, combine the water, green pepper, onion, bouillon and dill. Bring to a boil. Reduce heat; cover and simmer for 5 minutes. Add the beans. Cover and simmer 8-10 minutes longer or until beans are crisp-tender; drain. **Yield:** 5 servings.

Nutritional Analysis: 3/4 cup (prepared with reduced-sodium bouillon) equals 39 calories, trace fat (trace saturated fat), trace cholesterol, 240 mg sodium, 8 g carbohydrate, 3 g fiber, 2 g protein. **Diabetic Exchange:** 1-1/2 vegetable.

Easy Options for Trifle

SIMPLE RECIPES like Strawberry Yogurt Trifle offer lots of flexibility. Let your family's tastes—or your imagination—dictate easy substitutions.

For example, you could replace the angel food cake with pound cake or use another type of fruit in place of the strawberries. Or, instead of using vanilla yogurt, try lemon or a different flavor.

In-a-Hurry Menu Warms Hearts

THERE IS ALWAYS someone coming or going at Brenda Jackson's home in Garden City, Kansas.

Brenda's husband, Michael, works long hours as a physician, and the couple's daughter, Stephanie, stays on the run with her college classes.

"Michael, Stephanie and I come and go at different times of the day, but we always try to eat dinner together," says Brenda. "There are usually just the three of us at the table, unless our son, Matthew, pays a visit."

Brenda likes to keep busy by testing recipes for a popular cookbook author. "I love cooking and baking, so it's a perfect pastime for me," notes the stay-at-home mom. "I also prepare meals for fellow church members."

In her free time, Brenda attends Bible study groups, volunteers with her church, reads and takes walks. Her hobby, however, is happily cooking up a storm in her kitchen.

"I make an average of six sit-down dinners each week," says Brenda. "However, due to our varied schedules, I rarely prepare main courses that need to be served right away, because I don't always know when we'll all be home and ready to sit down to dinner."

It comes as no surprise, then, that the satisfying supper Brenda shares here is ready in 30 minutes and reheats well.

She begins by preparing hearty Pasta Beef Soup. "Convenient canned goods, tomato juice and a frozen pasta-vegetable medley make it flavorful and fast," she writes.

"But it's also flexible because you can use other ingredients, such as a different frozen pasta-vegetable blend," Brenda adds. "On occasion, I stir in shredded zucchini or yellow squash, too."

As the soup simmers, Brenda whips up Hard-Shell Ice Cream Sauce. "I keep the ingredients for this chocolate sauce on hand so I can make it any time I need an easy dessert," she says. "It's very rich and delicious. People like that it forms a crunchy shell over the ice cream...much like a treat from an old-fashioned ice cream parlor.

"Once the sauce has cooled a bit, I transfer it to a microwave-safe container and set it in the refrigerator. Then, when it's time for dessert, I just warm it up in the microwave."

With the chocolate sauce complete, Brenda quickly creates Savory Cheese Bread. "This golden bread is a recipe I made up years ago when I wanted something simple that complemented several dishes," she explains. "These cheese-topped slices are perfect with chunky soup or most any entree.

"Like everyone, I need to throw something together quickly on many nights," Brenda relates. "This dinner tastes great and is ready in a flash."

Pasta Beef Soup
Prep/Total Time: 25 min.

✓ Uses less fat, sugar or salt. Includes Nutritional Analysis and Diabetic Exchanges.

- **1 pound ground beef**
- **2 cans (14-1/2 ounces *each*) beef broth**
- **1 package (16 ounces) frozen pasta with broccoli, corn and carrots in garlic-seasoned sauce**
- **1-1/2 cups tomato juice**
- **1 can (14-1/2 ounces) diced tomatoes, undrained**
- **2 teaspoons Italian seasoning**
- **1/4 cup shredded Parmesan cheese, optional**

In a large saucepan, cook the beef over medium heat until no longer pink; drain. Add the broth, frozen pasta with vegetables, tomato juice, tomatoes and Italian seasoning; bring to a boil. Reduce the heat; cover and simmer for 10 minutes or until vegetables are tender. Serve with Parmesan cheese if desired. **Yield:** 6 servings.

Nutritional Analysis: 1-1/2 cups (prepared with lean ground beef and reduced-sodium beef broth and tomato juice; calculated without Parmesan cheese) equals 253 calories, 9 g fat (4 g saturated fat), 46 mg cholesterol, 680 mg sodium, 21 g carbohydrate, 3 g fiber, 20 g protein. **Diabetic Exchanges:** 2-1/2 lean meat, 1 starch, 1 vegetable.

Savory Cheese Bread
Prep/Total Time: 10 min.

- **1/4 cup butter, softened**
- **1/4 to 1/2 teaspoon lemon-pepper seasoning**
- **1/4 teaspoon garlic powder**
- **1/4 teaspoon dried basil**
- **1/4 teaspoon dried oregano**
- **12 slices French bread (1 inch thick)**
- **2 cups (8 ounces) shredded Italian-blend cheese**

In a small bowl, combine the butter, lemon-pepper seasoning, garlic powder, basil and oregano. Spread mixture over one side of each slice of bread.

Place butter side up on an ungreased baking sheet. Sprinkle with cheese. Broil 4 in. from the heat for 2-3 minutes or until cheese is melted and edges are golden brown. **Yield:** 6 servings.

Hard-Shell Ice Cream Sauce

Prep/Total Time: 10 min.

1 cup (6 ounces) semisweet chocolate chips
1/4 cup butter, cubed
3 tablespoons evaporated milk
Vanilla ice cream
1/2 cup sliced almonds

In a heavy saucepan, combine the chocolate chips, butter and evaporated milk. Cook and stir over low heat until the chocolate chips are melted and the mixture is smooth.

Serve chocolate sauce warm over vanilla ice cream (the sauce will harden). Sprinkle with sliced almonds. Refrigerate any leftovers. The sauce can be reheated in the microwave. **Yield:** about 1 cup.

Chicken and Rice Get a Tasty Twist

IF YOU'RE looking for Lucille Gendron from Pelham, New Hampshire, chances are you'll find her in the kitchen. "It's 24-hour cooking for me," the busy wife and mother says with a laugh.

Not only does Lucille spend her days planning and preparing meals as an assistant manager chef for a corporate cafeteria, but she also owns a small catering business.

"I started cooking when I was 5, working alongside my mom," Lucille explains. "As I grew, I would cook to celebrate anything and everything. If the sun was shining, I'd make something special."

Nowadays, Lucille cooks fast dishes to fit her family's schedule. Her husband, Derek, is a police officer, and daughters Alicia and Kara are on the go with school, sports, church activities and Scouting, but the family eats together as often as possible.

"Quick and nutritious recipes are important to me because I like to have our family gather around the table for supper," she says. "We always seem to have a lot to talk about, and sharing our daily events over a hot meal is soothing to the mind and soul."

Rather than shopping for special convenience products, Lucille makes the most of what's in her pantry. "Coming from an old-fashioned Sicilian household, I prefer to make everything from scratch. So I often create dishes from ingredients we have on hand," Lucille notes.

One of Lucille's favorites is the swift-to-fix combination she shares here. "Oriental Chicken was originally a recipe from another family member, but one night I added some ingredients I had on hand," Lucille says. "Everyone really enjoyed it."

As an accompaniment, Lucille serves Fruited Rice Pilaf. "I'm always trying to get fruit into our menus. I stirred some into plain rice pilaf one night, and it was a hit!"

Although both of Lucille's creations were greeted with cheers, Pistachio Cream Pie is known by a slightly less flattering name in her extended family.

"Once, I was making a pudding and coconut pie for my mother's uncle and decided to toss in some pineapple and cream cheese. Though everyone else really liked it, he didn't, and called it the 'Yucka Pie,'" Lucille laughs. "My husband and kids love it, though. And I'm happy because they're getting even a little more fruit without realizing it!"

Oriental Chicken

Prep/Total Time: 20 min.

    4 boneless skinless chicken breast halves
        (4 ounces *each*)
    2 tablespoons butter
    1 cup teriyaki sauce
    1/2 cup water
    1/2 cup orange marmalade
    1/2 to 1 teaspoon minced garlic

In a large skillet, brown chicken on both sides in butter. Combine the teriyaki sauce, water, marmalade and garlic; pour over chicken. Bring to a boil. Reduce heat; cover and simmer for 10-15 minutes or until juices run clear. **Yield:** 4 servings.

Fruited Rice Pilaf

Prep/Total Time: 15 min.

    1 package (6 ounces) rice pilaf
    2 tablespoons butter, softened
    1/2 cup pineapple chunks
    1/2 cup raisins
    1/4 cup prepared Italian salad dressing
Toasted coconut, optional

Cook rice pilaf according to package directions. Stir in the butter until melted. Add the pineapple, raisins and salad dressing. Top with toasted coconut if desired. **Yield:** 4 servings.

Pistachio Cream Pie

Prep/Total Time: 15 min.

    1 package (8 ounces) cream cheese, softened
    1 cup milk
    1 package (3.4 ounces) instant pistachio
        pudding mix
    1 can (8 ounces) crushed pineapple, drained
    1 graham cracker crust (9 inches)
    2 cups whipped topping
Toasted coconut

In a small mixing bowl, beat the cream cheese, milk and pudding mix until smooth. Fold in the pineapple. Spoon into the crust. Spread with the whipped topping; sprinkle with coconut. Cover and refrigerate pie until serving. **Yield:** 6-8 servings.

Time-Saving Technique

To get dinner on the table in a flash, I keep meals as quick and easy as I can. On Sundays, I like to make all of my meats and main courses for the week. Then, on a busy night, all I have to do is heat the meat and add a side dish. Meat loaf and roast are good choices because it's easy to use the leftovers to make new dishes like tacos or stew.

—Lucille Gendron

Sandwich Supper Has Family Appeal

FAMILY comes first for Krista Collins of Concord, North Carolina. Married to husband Andy for 13 years, the former middle school teacher works part-time at a preschool so she can spend more time with children Jared and Olivia.

"We recently moved to 2 acres outside of the city limits, so I could garden and can the fresh vegetables we grow," she explains. "Our yard has a creek and woods for the kids to explore. We also enjoy going on family camping trips."

When planning dinner menus and preparing the food for her family, Krista always keeps several considerations in mind.

"Andy works for an equipment rental company until late evening and looks forward to a warm meal every night," she relates. "So I need to cook dishes that remain delicious until he gets home. Also, our kids can be picky eaters, so whatever I cook must meet their tastes as well.

"We're on a budget," Krista adds. "Since it's more economical to cook at home than eat at a restaurant, I fix dinner at least 6 nights a week. I also try to incorporate items that are buy-one-get-one-free at the grocery store or beans or tomatoes that I canned over the summer."

The minute-saving menu that Krista shares here is inexpensive and enjoyed by the whole family. "I fix the salad first, the sandwiches next and the punch last, so it retains its fizz," she explains.

"I've made Ranch Pasta Salad for years—it's a recipe from a high school friend's mom. Any time I serve a sandwich meal like hamburgers, hot dogs or sloppy joes, I have this flavorful salad alongside," she notes.

"It is very satisfying and healthy because of the variety of vegetables it calls for. If you like, you can use low-fat ranch dressing or substitute vegetables of your choice to match your family's tastes or dietary needs," Krista suggests.

Only ground beef and three other convenient ingredients are needed to make the filling for sure-to-please Salsa Sloppy Joes.

"I created these sandwiches when I realized I did not have a can of sloppy joe sauce," Krista recalls. "The sweet brown sugar in this recipe complements the tangy salsa."

To round out the meal, Krista stirs up refreshing Strawberry Spritzers. "My grandma Naomi Beller served this tangy beverage in a punch bowl every year at Christmas, and we all looked forward to that tradition," she says.

"It also is great on hot summer days when the grill is fired up. Plus, it's an easy way to get my picky kids to eat their fruit...I have to be creative!"

Ranch Pasta Salad

Prep/Total Time: 25 min.

✓ Uses less fat, sugar or salt. Includes Nutritional Analysis and Diabetic Exchanges.

  3 **cups uncooked tricolor spiral pasta**
  1 **cup chopped fresh broccoli florets**
3/4 **cup chopped seeded peeled cucumber**
1/2 **cup chopped seeded tomato**
  1 **bottle (8 ounces) ranch salad dressing**
1/2 **cup shredded Parmesan cheese**

Cook pasta according to package directions; drain and rinse in cold water. In a large bowl, combine the pasta, broccoli, cucumber and tomato. Drizzle with salad dressing; toss to coat. Sprinkle with Parmesan cheese. **Yield:** 8 servings.

Nutritional Analysis: 3/4 cup (prepared with fat-free dressing) equals 192 calories, 2 g fat (1 g saturated fat), 4 mg cholesterol, 445 mg sodium, 36 g carbohydrate, 1 g fiber, 7 g protein. **Diabetic Exchanges:** 2 starch, 1 vegetable.

Salsa Sloppy Joes

Prep/Total Time: 20 min.

1 **pound ground beef**
1 **jar (11 ounces) salsa**
1 **can (10-3/4 ounces) condensed tomato soup, undiluted**
1 **tablespoon brown sugar**
8 **hamburger buns, split**

In a large skillet, cook beef over medium heat until no longer pink; drain. Stir in the salsa, soup and brown sugar. Cover and simmer for 10 minutes or until heated through. Spoon 1/2 cup onto each bun. **Yield:** 8 servings.

Strawberry Spritzers

Prep/Total Time: 10 min.

1 **package (10 ounces) frozen sweetened sliced strawberries, thawed**
2 **liters lemon-lime soda, chilled**
1 **can (12 ounces) frozen pink lemonade concentrate, thawed**

Place the strawberries in a blender; cover and process until pureed. Pour into a pitcher; stir in the soda and lemonade concentrate. Serve immediately. **Yield:** 2-1/2 quarts.

Planning Ahead Pays Off for Busy Cook

The weekly menus that I create for my family help mealtime run smoothly on busy nights. I use the recipes in *Quick Cooking* and other resources to plan a complete 7-day menu.

I write every ingredient that I need for the week's meals on my grocery list, and I post a list of all the recipes I've chosen on the refrigerator. The recipe list comes in handy as a quick reference tool for me. It also gives me flexibility by making it easy for me to mix and match main courses, side dishes and desserts.

I mostly choose recipes that use my oven and stovetop, but I usually include at least one slow cooker recipe, too. That way, if it looks like one of my days is going to be extra busy, I can plan to use the slow cooker recipe that day and maybe a more time-consuming recipe the next.

—*Krista Collins*

Pork Chop Feast Pleases In a Jiffy

SINCE retiring from the University of Oregon's Business Office, Betty Jean Nichols of Eugene, Oregon spends more time in her kitchen. "I enjoy cooking and have been working up recipes for years," she says.

While she also devotes time to other pastimes such as painting and writing her memoirs, Betty Jean has garnered the most recognition for her culinary talents. She has won several state and national recipe contests, including a dessert competition that featured a free trip to New York City to present her winning creation on the television show *Good Morning America*.

Whether she's fixing dinner for herself or for her three grown children and their families, Betty Jean serves dishes that are simple but special, like the three recipes featured in the mouth-watering meal for four shared here.

Moist Cider Pork Chops are flavored with a sensational combination of garlic, green onions, celery, dried thyme and apple cider. "If you have fresh thyme from your garden, use that," Betty Jean recommends. "And boneless chops cook even faster."

To complement the pork, she serves Asparagus with Mushrooms. "This side dish is not fussy, but looks and tastes special," she notes. "People say it's delicious."

With just three ingredients, Broiled Blueberry Dessert makes an easy, yummy ending. "My daughter and her husband grow blueberries, so we like to try new ways to prepare them," she relates.

Cider Pork Chops

Prep/Total Time: 25 min.

✓ Uses less fat, sugar or salt. Includes Nutritional Analysis and Diabetic Exchanges.

- 2 tablespoons all-purpose flour
- 1/2 teaspoon salt
- 1/4 teaspoon pepper
- 4 bone-in pork loin chops (1/2 inch thick)
- 1 tablespoon canola oil
- 1 cup sliced celery
- 1/2 cup sliced green onions
- 2 teaspoons minced garlic
- 1/4 teaspoon dried thyme
- 1 cup apple cider *or* unsweetened apple juice

In a large resealable plastic bag, combine the flour, salt and pepper. Add pork chops and toss to coat. In a large skillet, brown chops in oil over medium heat for 3-4 minutes. Remove and keep warm.

In the same skillet, saute the celery, onions, garlic and thyme for 2-3 minutes or until crisp-tender. Return pork to the pan. Add cider. Bring to a boil. Reduce heat; cover and simmer for 7-8 minutes or until the meat juices run clear. Serve with a slotted spoon. **Yield:** 4 servings.

Nutritional Analysis: 1 serving equals 290 calories, 12 g fat (4 g saturated fat), 86 mg cholesterol, 393 mg sodium, 13 g carbohydrate, 1 g fiber, 31 g protein. **Diabetic Exchanges:** 4-1/2 lean meat, 1 fruit.

Asparagus with Mushrooms

Prep/Total Time: 15 min.

- 1 pound fresh asparagus, trimmed and cut into 2-inch pieces
- 2 teaspoons ground ginger
- 2 tablespoons vegetable oil
- 3 cups sliced fresh mushrooms
- 1 teaspoon salt
- 1/8 teaspoon sugar
- 1/8 teaspoon pepper

In a large skillet, saute asparagus and ginger in oil for 2-3 minutes or until asparagus is crisp-tender. Add the mushrooms, salt, sugar and pepper. Cook and stir 2-3 minutes longer or until mushrooms are tender. **Yield:** 4 servings.

Broiled Blueberry Dessert

Prep/Total Time: 10 min.

- 3 cups fresh blueberries
- 1/2 cup sour cream
- 2 tablespoons brown sugar

Divide blueberries among four ovenproof 8-oz. custard cups. Spread with sour cream; sprinkle with brown sugar. Place on a baking sheet. Broil 4-6 in. from the heat for 3-4 minutes or until bubbly and sugar is melted. **Yield:** 4 servings.

Tips for Great Garlic

DO YOU like to cook with fresh garlic? To keep it fresh, store it in an open container in a cool, dark place. Stored this way, unbroken garlic bulbs will keep for up to 8 weeks; unpeeled individual cloves will keep up to 1 week.

A green sprout in a garlic clove indicates that the garlic is past its prime. Some garlic lovers believe that a green shoot imparts a bitter flavor. If you find a green shoot in a clove, it's all right to use the garlic in a pinch. Simply halve the clove, cut out and discard the shoot and use the garlic as desired.

Easy Steak Dinner's Made For Two

AFTER more than 50 years of marriage and raising two sons of her own and three children of relatives, busy freelance writer Jeanette Cakouros has quick cooking down to a science.

"At first I was often caught at the end of the afternoon with nothing ready for dinner. Now, in order to write as long as I can, I set my alarm clock for 45 minutes before I want to serve dinner. This gives me time to finish my sentence, paragraph or thought before heading to the kitchen," she explains from Brunswick, Maine.

With her family now grown, one of the most important considerations when planning meals for husband John and herself is "not cooking too much—or the two of us will be eating leftovers for weeks," Jeanette says with a laugh.

The menu for two Jeanette shares here uses the microwave and stovetop. "It's one of my favorites because everything can be cooking at once," she says. "None of the recipes takes longer than 25 minutes from start to finish."

The Greek-style Spinach Rice makes a tasty complement to juicy Steaks with Mushrooms. "I cut the small steaks off a good roast purchased on sale, then individually wrap and freeze them so just the number needed can be taken out," Jeanette notes.

For a sweet ending, luscious Maple Syrup Pudding whips up in just 10 minutes in the microwave. "The pudding will still be warm at dessert time, which makes it an especially good addition to a winter supper," Jeanette adds.

"While preparing this meal keeps me hopping, the result is an elegant dinner that can be doubled for guests. Everyone loves the combination."

Steaks with Mushrooms

Prep/Total Time: 25 min.

    2 boneless beef sirloin steaks (5 ounces *each*)
1/2 teaspoon salt
1/4 teaspoon pepper
    2 tablespoons butter
    1 cup sliced fresh mushrooms

Rub both sides of steaks with salt and pepper. In a large skillet, cook steaks in butter until meat reaches desired doneness (for medium-rare, a meat thermometer should read 145°; medium, 160°; well-done, 170°). Remove and keep warm. In the same skillet, saute mushrooms until tender. Serve with steaks. **Yield:** 2 servings.

Spinach Rice

Prep/Total Time: 20 min.

1/2 cup chopped onion
    2 tablespoons olive oil
    2 cups torn baby spinach
3/4 cup water
    1 tablespoon dried parsley flakes
1/2 cup uncooked instant rice
1/4 to 1/2 teaspoon salt
1/8 teaspoon pepper

In a saucepan, saute onion in oil until tender. Add the spinach, water and parsley. Bring to a boil. Stir in the rice, salt and pepper. Cover and remove from the heat; let stand for 7-10 minutes or until rice is tender and liquid is absorbed. **Yield:** 2 servings.

Maple Syrup Pudding

Prep/Total Time: 10 min.

1-3/4 cups milk
    1 package (3 ounces) cook-and-serve vanilla pudding mix
1/4 cup maple syrup
Whipped topping, optional

In a microwave-safe bowl, whisk the milk, pudding mix and syrup until combined. Cover and microwave on high for 5-6 minutes or until the mixture comes to a full boil, stirring every 2 minutes. Pour into dessert dishes; cool slightly. Garnish with whipped topping if desired. Refrigerate leftovers. **Yield:** 4 servings.

Editor's Note: This recipe was tested in a 1,100-watt microwave.

Here's the Plan

TO PUT this marvelous meal on your dinner table quickly, follow Jeanette's step-by-step plan for preparing all three recipes.

1. Whisk the ingredients for the pudding and put it in the microwave to cook. (This does a superb job and doesn't require constant stirring.)
2. For the side dish, chop the onion while the pan is heating. Add the oil and saute the onion while tearing the baby spinach.
3. Add the spinach, water and parsley to the pan, bring it to a boil and then add the rice, salt and pepper. Cover it and let it stand.
4. In another pan, cook the steaks to the desired doneness, then saute the mushrooms.
5. Pour the pudding into dessert dishes and allow it to cool slightly.

Chapter 2

CELEBRATING special times of the year by serving special food doesn't have to mean hours of effort in the kitchen.

Thanks to all the speedy seasonal recipes here, you can easily delight friends and family with delicious, festive dishes at holiday dinners, school functions, parties and more.

You'll find a merry mix of Christmas desserts...Halloween sweets...a memorable meal for St. Patrick's Day...Valentine's Day treats...Easter goodies... and a super summer picnic.

No matter how busy your schedule is, these timely recipes will help you make the most of special occasions all year long.

FESTIVE FARE. Halloween Poke Cake, Marshmallow Witches and Two-Layer Silk Pie (all recipes on pp. 30 and 31).

Dazzle Your Valentine Tonight

IF THE WAY to a loved one's heart is through the stomach, these beyond-compare bites are sure to win affection. The delicious desserts featured here are smothered with gooey caramel, drenched in rich chocolate or brimming with luscious fruit, so they're sure to satisfy a sweet tooth.

Best of all, each of these no-fuss sweetheart treats can be assembled in minutes with only a few items from your local grocery store.

So bring one to the table tonight to amaze special dinner guests, surprise your spouse or celebrate Valentine's Day with your family.

You're sure to be sweetly rewarded with genuine smiles and heartwarming compliments...as well as requests for second helpings.

Devilish Valentine's Cake

(Pictured at right)

Prep: 10 min. **Bake:** 25 min.

Valentine's Day doesn't get much sweeter than when this fudge-covered creation makes an appearance. Prepared by our Test Kitchen home economists, the masterpiece starts with a cake mix, so preparation is a snap.

  1 package (9 ounces) devil's food cake mix
3/4 cup semisweet chocolate chunks
1/2 cup hot fudge ice cream topping
1-1/2 cups fresh raspberries

Grease a 9-in. heart-shaped baking pan. Line with waxed paper; grease and flour the paper. Set aside. Prepare cake batter according to package directions; stir in chocolate chunks. Pour into prepared pan.

Bake at 350° for 25-30 minutes or until a toothpick inserted near the center comes out clean. Cool for 5 minutes before inverting onto a serving platter. Spread warm cake with hot fudge topping. Arrange raspberries over the top. **Yield:** 6-8 servings.

Blackberry Cherry Cobbler

Prep: 15 min. **Bake:** 25 min.

This is a very good dessert that's easy to make and calls for only a few ingredients. Refrigerated biscuits form the golden topping over ruby-red cherries and blackberries.
—June Cunningham, Carsonville, Michigan

  1 can (21 ounces) cherry pie filling
  2 cups frozen blackberries, thawed
1/4 teaspoon ground cinnamon
TOPPING:
1/3 cup sugar
1/4 teaspoon ground cinnamon

  1 tube (7-1/2 ounces) refrigerated buttermilk biscuits
  3 tablespoons butter, melted
1/4 cup sliced almonds

In a large saucepan, combine the pie filling, blackberries and cinnamon. Cook over medium heat until mixture is bubbly, stirring occasionally. Pour into a greased 11-in. x 7-in. x 2-in. baking dish.

In a small bowl, combine the sugar and cinnamon. Dip biscuits in butter and then in cinnamon-sugar. Arrange biscuits around edges of dish; sprinkle with almonds. Bake, uncovered, at 350° for 25-30 minutes or until golden brown. Serve warm. **Yield:** 10 servings.

Dressed-Up Cheesecake

(Pictured at right)

Prep/Total Time: 5 min.

Our Test Kitchen home economists take advantage of convenience products to transform plain store-bought cheesecake into a delectable dessert.

1/2 cup milk chocolate toffee bits
1/4 cup caramel ice cream topping
  1 frozen New York-style cheesecake (30 ounces), thawed
Chocolate syrup

In a small bowl, combine toffee bits and caramel topping; spread over cheesecake. To serve, drizzle chocolate syrup on dessert plates; top each with a slice of cheesecake. **Yield:** 6-8 servings.

German Chocolate Fondue

(Pictured at right)

Prep/Total Time: 15 min.

Just a handful of ingredients and a microwave make this fondue a fast favorite. Use dippers such as cookies and strawberries. —Helen Phillips, Horseheads, New York

2/3 cup light corn syrup
1/2 cup heavy whipping cream
  2 packages (4 ounces each) German sweet chocolate, chopped
Shortbread cookies *and/or* assorted fruit

In a microwave-safe bowl, combine corn syrup and cream. Cover and microwave on high for 2 to 2-1/2 minutes or until mixture comes to a boil, stirring twice. Stir in chocolate until melted. Transfer to a fondue pot and keep warm. Serve with cookies and/or fruit. **Yield:** 2 cups.

Editor's Note: This recipe was tested in a 1,100-watt microwave.

Devilish Valentine's Cake
German Chocolate Fondue
Dressed-Up Cheesecake

St. Pat's Day Meal Is Magically Easy

IRISH EYES will surely be smiling with these fast and fun recipes that mark the holiday.

Whether you're proud to be Irish or just Irish for the day, you'll enjoy this minute-saving menu that offers a taste of the Emerald Isle. While we can't promise it will give you the luck of the Irish, it certainly will make St. Patrick's Day more festive.

Start out this theme meal by assembling swift corned beef sandwiches and spiced fries. Then finish things off with cute shamrock-shaped snacks that will leave the whole family doing a joyful jig.

Best of all, it won't keep you in the kitchen for hours yet will surely draw plenty of compliments—and that's no blarney!

Hot Corned Beef Buns

(Pictured at right)

Prep/Total Time: 30 min.

It wouldn't be St. Pat's Day without corned beef...and folks will love these savory sandwiches. My mother-in-law gave me this recipe. I've also placed the filling between slices of bread and cooked the sandwiches like grilled cheese.
—Toni Keyworth, Yale, Michigan

> 1 pound deli corned beef, chopped
> 1 cup (4 ounces) shredded cheddar cheese
> 2/3 cup mayonnaise
> 2 tablespoons dried minced onion
> 1 tablespoon dill *or* sweet pickle relish
> 2 tablespoons butter, softened
> 6 hamburger buns, split

In a bowl, combine the corned beef, cheese, mayonnaise, onion and relish. Spread butter over cut side of buns. Spoon corned beef mixture over bottom halves; replace tops. Place in an ungreased 13-in. x 9-in. x 2-in. baking pan. Cover with foil. Bake at 425° for 15-20 minutes or until heated through. **Yield:** 6 servings.

Irish Spud Strips

(Pictured at right)

Prep/Total Time: 30 min.

I came up with this recipe by sheer luck when I was trying to create a good-tasting yet different side dish. I toss the crisp fries with Cajun seasoning and Parmesan cheese.
—Naomi Kay Smith, Canandaigua, New York

> 3 tablespoons grated Parmesan cheese
> 4-1/2 teaspoons Cajun seasoning
> 2-1/2 cups vegetable oil

> 3 medium potatoes, peeled and sliced
>   lengthwise into 1/4-inch strips
> Additional Parmesan cheese, optional

In a large resealable plastic bag, combine the Parmesan cheese and Cajun seasoning. In an electric skillet, heat oil to 375°. Pat potatoes dry with paper towels; place a third of the strips in bag and shake to coat. Cook in hot oil for 3-4 minutes or until golden brown, turning occasionally. Drain on paper towels. Repeat with remaining potato strips. Sprinkle with additional Parmesan cheese if desired. **Yield:** 4-6 servings.

Clover Crispies

(Pictured at right)

Prep: 30 min. + cooling

These sweet snacks whipped up by our Test Kitchen home economists are like the pot of gold at the end of your family's St. Patrick's Day feast. With their yummy peppermint and marshmallow flavor, they'll make even those without Irish hearts happy.

> 3 tablespoons butter
> 4 cups large marshmallows (about 40)
> 1/4 teaspoon peppermint extract
> 6 cups crisp rice cereal
> 6 ounces white candy coating, chopped
> 4 drops green food coloring, optional
> Green sprinkles

In a large saucepan, melt the butter. Add marshmallows; cook and stir over low heat until melted. Remove from the the heat; stir in extract and cereal; mix well. With buttered hands, press mixture into a greased foil-lined 13-in. x 9-in. x 2-in. pan. Cool completely on a wire rack.

Turn onto a cutting board; remove foil. Cut with a 3-in. shamrock cookie cutter; reshape shamrock stem if needed (save scraps for another use). In a microwave, melt candy coating.

Stir in food coloring if desired. Spoon over cutouts and spread evenly. Decorate with sprinkles. Let stand until set. **Yield:** 15 servings.

Speedier Spuds

TO CUT PREP when fixing the Irish Spud Strips, use 3-3/4 cups frozen french fries instead of peeling and cutting fresh potatoes. Try crinkle-cut, shoestring or steak fries. Because the cooking time will vary based on the kind of fries you choose, follow the package directions for best results.

Clover Crispies
Hot Corned Beef Buns
Irish Spud Strips

Easter Treats Bring Baskets of Joy

YOU may just outshine the Easter Bunny when you share these sweet holiday goodies with friends and family.

For your Sunday dinner, prepare a heavenly angel food cake flavored with lemon pie filling. The recipe requires only four ingredients, so you'll be hoppin' in no time.

Whip up a cool strawberry pie as another wonderful dessert option for your special meal. Want to cut down kitchen work on the holiday? Feel free to make this pie ahead of time—just store it in the freezer.

To fill Easter baskets, you'll be on a roll when you present luscious candy eggs. They feature the popular blend of chocolate and peanut butter...so they're sure to be a treat every "bunny" will love.

Lemon Angel Cake

(Pictured at right)

Prep/Total Time: 30 min.

I rely on tangy lemon pie filling and a few other ingredients to quickly dress up a store-bought angel food cake. If there's time, I use a boxed mix to bake the cake.
—*Debbie Segate, Grande Prairie, Alberta*

  1 **cup heavy whipping cream**
  1 **tablespoon confectioners' sugar**
  1 **can (15-3/4 ounces) lemon pie filling**
  1 **prepared angel food cake (14 ounces)**

In a small mixing bowl, beat cream until it begins to thicken. Add the confectioners' sugar; beat until stiff peaks form. Place pie filling in a bowl; fold in whipped cream.

Split cake into two horizontal layers. Place bottom layer on a serving plate; top with 1 cup lemon mixture. Top with the second cake layer. Frost top and sides of cake with remaining lemon mixture. Chill for 15 minutes or until serving. Refrigerate leftovers. **Yield:** 10-12 servings.

Creamy Strawberry Pie

(Pictured at right)

Prep: 25 min. + chilling

I like to end a nice company meal with this easy make-ahead dessert. The eye-catching pie has a big strawberry flavor and extra richness from ice cream. —*Dixie Terry Marion, Illinois*

  1 **package (10 ounces) frozen sweetened**
    sliced strawberries, thawed
  1 **package (3 ounces) strawberry gelatin**
  2 **cups vanilla ice cream**
  1 **pastry shell (9 inches), baked**
Sliced fresh strawberries, optional

Drain strawberries into a 1-cup measuring cup and reserve juice; set berries aside. Add enough water to juice to measure 1 cup; pour into a large saucepan. Bring to a boil over medium heat. Remove from the heat; stir in gelatin until dissolved. Add ice cream; stir until blended. Refrigerate for 5-10 minutes or just until thickened (watch carefully).

Fold in reserved strawberries. Pour into pastry shell. Refrigerate until firm, about 1 hour. Garnish with fresh strawberries if desired. Refrigerate leftovers. **Yield:** 6 servings.

Peanut Butter Eggs

(Pictured at right)

Prep: 35 min. + standing

This recipe came from my mother-in-law, who gives a basket of homemade Easter candy to each of her children and grandchildren.We look forward to these tempting chocolate-dipped eggs all year long...and they disappear in a hurry.
—*Robin Perry, Seneca, Pennsylvania*

  6 **tablespoons butter, softened**
 1/4 **cup creamy peanut butter**
 1/4 **cup marshmallow creme**
1-3/4 **cups confectioners' sugar**
 3/4 **pound milk chocolate candy coating, chopped**
  2 **teaspoons shortening**
Colored sprinkles, optional

In a small mixing bowl, cream the butter, peanut butter and marshmallow creme until smooth. Gradually beat in confectioners' sugar. Drop by level tablespoonfuls onto a waxed paper-lined baking sheet; form into egg shapes. Freeze for 10 minutes.

In a microwave, melt candy coating and shortening; stir until smooth. Dip eggs into candy coating; allow excess to drip off. Return to baking sheet; immediately decorate with sprinkles if desired. Let stand until set. Store in an airtight container. **Yield:** about 1-1/2 dozen.

Dip Candy Eggs with Ease

IT'S EASY to avoid messy fingers when dipping the Peanut Butter Eggs into the melted chocolate candy coating. Simply place an egg on a fork and lower it into the coating. Let the egg sit on the fork momentarily to allow the excess coating to drip off, then place it back on the waxed paper-lined baking sheet to set. If you're decorating with sprinkles, add them immediately after placing the egg on the waxed paper.

Lemon Angel Cake
Creamy Strawberry Pie
Peanut Butter Eggs

Halloween Goodies Scare Up Fun

BOO! At Halloween time, do special occasions sneak up on you? From kids' parties to office functions and family celebrations, it seems sweet treats are needed at every turn this time of year.

Don't be afraid…the yummy desserts on these two pages are not only goof-proof, they're sure to be the talk of the buffet table.

Cranberry Nut Cupcakes

Prep: 25 min. **Bake:** 15 min. + cooling

 *I convinced my son to eat cranberries with these quick-to-fix cupcakes. With cranberries, walnuts and a hint of lemon, these treats are ideal at breakfast or as after-school snacks, yet they're special enough to serve to company.* —Anna Minegar *Zolfo Springs, Florida*

1-1/2 cups fresh *or* frozen cranberries, coarsely chopped
1-1/4 cups sugar, *divided*
  1/2 cup butter, softened
    2 eggs
    2 teaspoons vanilla extract
    3 cups all-purpose flour
    4 teaspoons baking powder
    1 teaspoon sweetened lemonade drink mix
  1/2 teaspoon salt
    1 cup milk
    1 cup chopped walnuts
    1 can (16 ounces) cream cheese frosting

In a small bowl, combine cranberries and 1/4 cup sugar; set aside. In a large mixing bowl, cream butter and remaining sugar. Add eggs, one at a time, beating well after each addition. Beat in vanilla. Combine the flour, baking powder, drink mix and salt; add to creamed mixture alternately with milk. Fold in walnuts and reserved cranberries.

Fill greased or paper-lined muffin cups two-thirds full. Bake at 400° for 12-17 minutes or until a toothpick comes out clean. Cool for 5 minutes before removing from pans to wire racks to cool completely. Frost with cream cheese frosting. Store in the refrigerator. **Yield:** 2 dozen.

Marshmallow Witches

(Pictured above right and on page 22)

Prep/Total Time: 30 min.

Get ready for an assembly line, because kids will want to help create these no-bake witches from our Test Kitchen staff. They're easy to prepare with store-bought items, including marshmallows, cookies and candy. Best of all, you can make a dozen in just half an hour. Whip up an extra batch, wrap each one individually in plastic wrap, and tie with ribbon for festive party favors.

  1/2 cup vanilla frosting, *divided*
   36 miniature semisweet chocolate chips
   12 large marshmallows
    1 drop *each* green, red and yellow food coloring
  1/4 cup flaked coconut
   12 chocolate wafers
   12 miniature peanut butter cups
   12 milk chocolate kisses

For the face of each witch, place a dab of frosting on the bottom of three chocolate chips; press two for eyes and one for nose onto each marshmallow.

For hair, combine green food coloring and a drop of water in a small resealable plastic bag; add coconut and shake well. Spread a small amount of frosting on top and sides of marshmallows; press coconut hair into frosting. Place 3 tablespoons of frosting in a small heavy-duty resealable plastic bag; tint orange with red and yellow food coloring. Set aside.

For hats, spread some of the remaining frosting in the center of chocolate wafers; press peanut butter cups upside down into frosting. Lightly spread bottoms of chocolate kisses with frosting; place on peanut butter cups. Cut a small hole in the corner of pastry or plastic bag; insert a small star tip. Fill the bag with the orange frosting and pipe stars around the base of each peanut butter cup. Place a hat on each witch. **Yield:** 1 dozen.

Two-Layer Silk Pie

(Pictured above right and on page 23)

Prep: 30 min. + chilling

This recipe eases event preparations because it makes two scrumptious pies that chill overnight. My family just loves the smooth texture of these silky pies. The combination of chocolate and peanut butter satisfies even the strongest sweet-tooth craving. —Maryann Thomas *Clay City, Kentucky*

    2 unbaked pastry shells (9 inches)
2-1/2 cups cold milk
    1 package (5.9 ounces) instant chocolate pudding mix
    1 can (14 ounces) sweetened condensed milk
  1/2 cup creamy peanut butter
    1 carton (12 ounces) frozen whipped topping, thawed
Chocolate curls, optional

Halloween Poke Cake
Marshmallow Witches
Two-Layer Silk Pie

Line unpricked pastry shells with a double thickness of heavy-duty foil. Bake at 450° for 8 minutes. Remove foil; bake 5 minutes longer. Cool on wire racks.

In a bowl, whisk milk and pudding mix for 2 minutes. Spread into crusts. In a large mixing bowl, beat condensed milk and peanut butter until smooth.

Set aside 2 cups whipped topping for garnish; cover and refrigerate. Fold remaining whipped topping into peanut butter mixture. Spread over pudding layer. Refrigerate for 6 hours or until set. Garnish with reserved whipped topping; top with chocolate curls if desired. **Yield:** 2 pies (6-8 servings each).

Halloween Poke Cake

(Pictured above and on page 23)

Prep: 20 min. **Bake:** 35 min. + chilling

This delicious treat created by our Test Kitchen staff will make guests smile with delight when you serve it on Halloween. The moist marble cake features a buttery frosting and cute candy pumpkins on top. Out of pumpkin candies? Decorate with candy corn instead.

1 package (18-1/4 ounces) fudge marble cake mix
2 packages (3 ounces *each*) orange gelatin
1 cup boiling water
1/2 cup cold water
1/2 cup butter, softened
3-1/2 cups confectioners' sugar
1/3 cup baking cocoa
1/4 cup milk
1 teaspoon vanilla extract
12 to 15 candy pumpkins

Prepare and bake cake according to package directions, using a greased 13-in. x 9-in. x 2-in. baking pan. Cool on a wire rack for 1 hour. In a small bowl, dissolve gelatin in boiling water; stir in cold water. With a meat fork or wooden skewer, poke holes in cake about 2 in. apart. Slowly pour gelatin over cake. Refrigerate for 2-3 hours.

For frosting, in a small mixing bowl, cream butter until fluffy. Beat in confectioners' sugar, cocoa, milk and vanilla until smooth. Spread over cake; top with candy pumpkins. Cover and refrigerate until serving. **Yield:** 12-15 servings.

Pack a Quick Summertime Picnic

WHEN the weather warms up, eating meals outdoors can be a fun change of pace. Whether it's a backyard barbecue with friends or a large family reunion, picnics are a great way to entertain. And with the fuss-free recipes you'll find here, planning a pleasing summer menu is a snap.

All of these delicious dishes can easily be assembled in advance, so you'll have fewer preparations to worry about on the day of your party. Just pick a sunny spot and invite some guests, and your recipe for a perfect picnic is complete!

Italian Submarine

(Pictured at right)

Prep/Total Time: 15 min.

My Italian husband grew up eating this flavorful sandwich his mother used to make after Saturday chores were finished. This sub can easily be made a few hours ahead and refrigerated until serving.
—Christine Lupella
Fifty Lakes, Minnesota

    1 loaf (1 pound) unsliced Italian bread
    2 to 3 tablespoons olive oil
    2 to 4 tablespoons shredded Parmesan cheese
    1 to 1-1/2 teaspoons dried oregano
    1 medium tomato, thinly sliced
1/2 pound thinly sliced deli ham
1/4 pound sliced provolone cheese
1/4 pound thinly sliced hard salami

Cut loaf of bread in half lengthwise. Hollow out the bottom half, leaving a 1/4-in. shell (discard removed the bread or save for another use). Brush olive oil over the cut sides of bread.

Combine the Parmesan cheese and oregano; sprinkle over bread. On the bottom half, layer the tomato, ham, provolone and salami. Replace bread top. Slice before serving. **Yield:** 4 servings.

Lime Fruit Slushies

(Pictured at right)

Prep: 15 min. + freezing

These frosty drinks have refreshing flavor. If you divide the mixture between two plastic containers before freezing, you can use the frozen container to help keep the items in your cooler chilled. They'll thaw to a slushy consistency. —Linda Horst
Newville, Pennsylvania

☑ Uses less fat, sugar or salt. Includes Nutritional Analysis and Diabetic Exchanges.

3/4 cup sugar
    1 package (3 ounces) lime gelatin
    1 cup boiling water
    3 cups cold water
    3 cups unsweetened pineapple juice
    1 can (6 ounces) frozen orange juice concentrate, thawed
    1 liter ginger ale, chilled

In a large container, dissolve sugar and gelatin in boiling water. Stir in the cold water, pineapple juice and orange juice concentrate. Freeze. Remove from the freezer 1-2 hours before serving. Stir in the ginger ale just before serving. **Yield:** 12 servings.

Nutritional Analysis: 1 cup (prepared with sugar substitute and sugar-free gelatin) equals 67 calories, trace fat (trace saturated fat), 0 cholesterol, 26 mg sodium, 16 g carbohydrate, trace fiber, 1 g protein. **Diabetic Exchange:** 1 fruit.

Grape Melon Medley

(Pictured at right)

Prep/Total Time: 15 min.

When preparing this simple fruit salad, I deliberately pick out both tart and sweet grapes for a little extra punch of taste. You can also substitute or add fruits that are in season. —Doris Russell, Fallston, Maryland

    2 cups cubed cantaloupe
1-1/2 cups green grapes, halved
1-1/2 cups seedless red grapes, halved
    1 can (11 ounces) mandarin oranges, drained
1/2 cup pineapple preserves

In a large bowl, combine the cantaloupe, grapes and oranges. Whisk the preserves; pour over fruit and toss to coat. Chill until serving. **Yield:** 8 servings.

Tame an Outdoor Tablecloth

A LIGHT BREEZE can be a welcome addition to an outdoor meal. But it can also set the tablecloth on a picnic table to flapping.

To prevent those loose corners from fluttering in the wind, tie a simple knot at each corner of the cloth. Or, bunch the fabric at each corner and tie the bunches with short lengths of complementary colored ribbon.

For a fun touch at a garden party, tuck a few fresh flowers (or even a few sprigs of herbs) into the bunched fabric as you tie the ribbon.

Lime Fruit Slushies
Italian Submarine
Grape Melon Medley

Christmas Desserts Deck the Table

WHEN Christmas is approaching and visions of sugarplums are dancing in your head, it's the perfect time to nibble all kinds of sensational sweets. And from platters of decorated cookies and candies to gorgeous cakes, pies and more, there are so many delightful December treats to try!

But between shopping, decorating and meal planning, it can be a challenge to find time to prepare holiday goodies. Here, fellow busy cooks share the fast and festive recipes they count on during the hustle and bustle of the Christmas season.

Need confections for your cookie tray? Try strawberry-flavored cookies and candy bark dotted with walnuts and cranberries. And for your holiday dinner, present a chocolatey trifle, frosty pumpkin pie and drizzled raspberry bars.

Each luscious treat is the kind you can whip up in a jiffy. With just a little time in the kitchen, you'll have plenty of seasonally pleasing sweets to serve your loved ones...and to leave for Santa, too!

Butter Pecan Pumpkin Pie

Prep: 20 min. + freezing

This pie was always a family favorite at holidays. Everyone thought that I worked all day to make it, but it's really easy to assemble. It's handy to have in the freezer when unexpected company stops in for coffee and dessert.
—Arletta Slocum, Venice, Florida

    1 quart butter pecan ice cream, softened
    1 pastry shell (9 inches), baked
    1 cup canned pumpkin
 1/2 cup sugar
 1/4 teaspoon *each* ground cinnamon, ginger and nutmeg
    1 cup heavy whipping cream, whipped
 1/2 cup caramel ice cream topping
Additional whipped cream

Spread ice cream into the crust; freeze for 2 hours or until firm. In a small mixing bowl, combine the pumpkin, sugar, cinnamon, ginger and nutmeg; fold in whipped cream. Spread over ice cream. Cover and freeze for 2 hours or until firm. The pie may be frozen for up to 2 months.

Remove from the freezer 15 minutes before slicing. Drizzle with ice cream topping; dollop with whipped cream. **Yield:** 6-8 servings.

Noel Cookie Gems

Prep: 35 min. **Bake:** 10 min. per batch

I found this cookie recipe when my husband and I were dating. Since our last name is Noel, I whip up a batch every Christmas. They're a cinch to assemble ahead and freeze, saving time during the holiday rush. If you like, fill them with preserves of a different flavor.
—Patsy Noel, Exeter, California

 1/4 cup butter, softened
 1/4 cup shortening
 3/4 cup sugar
    1 egg
    1 teaspoon vanilla extract
2-2/3 cups all-purpose flour
 1/2 teaspoon salt
 1/4 teaspoon baking powder
 1/4 teaspoon baking soda
 1/2 cup sour cream
 3/4 cup finely chopped nuts
 1/3 cup seedless strawberry jam

In a large mixing bowl, cream the butter, shortening and sugar. Beat in egg and vanilla. Combine the flour, salt, baking powder and baking soda; gradually add to creamed mixture alternately with sour cream. Mix well. Shape into 1-1/4-in. balls; roll in nuts.

Place 2 in. apart on greased baking sheets. Using the end of a wooden spoon handle, make a 3/8- to 1/2-in.-deep indentation in the center of each ball. Fill the indentations with strawberry jam. Bake at 350° for 10-12 minutes or until lightly browned. Remove to wire racks. **Yield:** 3 dozen.

White Candy Bark

Prep: 20 min. + chilling

Here is a speedy candy recipe that can be varied depending on the type of dried fruit or nuts you have on hand. Since we have a walnut tree, I use walnuts, but pecans could also be substituted. I'm sure dried cherries could take the place of the cranberries.
—Marcia Snyder
Grand Junction, Colorado

    1 tablespoon butter, melted
    2 packages (10 to 12 ounces *each*) vanilla *or* white chips
1-1/2 cups walnut halves
    1 cup dried cranberries
 1/4 teaspoon ground nutmeg

Line a 15-in. x 10-in. x 1-in. pan with foil. Brush with butter; set aside. Place the chips in a microwave-safe bowl. Microwave, uncovered, at 70% power for 3-4 minutes; stir until smooth.

Stir in the walnuts, dried cranberries and nutmeg. Spread into the prepared pan. Chill until firm. Break into pieces. **Yield:** 2 pounds.

Editor's Note: This recipe was tested in a 1,100-watt microwave.

Raspberry Coconut Bars

(Pictured above)

Prep: 20 min. **Bake:** 20 min. + chilling

I've been whipping up these delicious bars for more than 10 years, most recently with help from my 5-year-old daughter. I bake them every Christmas and have received many compliments and recipe requests. —Barb Bovberg
Fort Collins, Colorado

1-2/3 cups graham cracker crumbs
1/2 cup butter, melted
2-2/3 cups flaked coconut
1 can (14 ounces) sweetened condensed milk
1 cup seedless raspberry preserves
1/3 cup chopped walnuts, toasted
1/2 cup semisweet chocolate chips
1/4 cup vanilla *or* white chips

In a small bowl, combine graham cracker crumbs and butter. Press into a greased 13-in. x 9-in. x 2-in. baking dish. Sprinkle with coconut; drizzle with milk. Bake at 350° for 20-25 minutes or until lightly browned. Cool completely on a wire rack.

Spread preserves over the crust. Sprinkle with walnuts. In a microwave-safe bowl, melt chocolate chips; stir until smooth. Drizzle over walnuts. Repeat with vanilla chips. Cut into bars. Refrigerate for 30 minutes or until chocolate-vanilla drizzle is set. **Yield:** 3 dozen.

Irish Creme Chocolate Trifle

(Pictured above)

Prep: 20 min. **Bake:** 30 min. + chilling

When making this rich trifle for adults, I use Irish cream liqueur in place of the coffee creamer. —Margaret Wilson
Hemet, California

1 package (18-1/4 ounces) devil's food cake mix
1 cup refrigerated Irish creme nondairy creamer
3-1/2 cups cold milk
2 packages (3.9 ounces *each*) instant chocolate pudding mix
3 cups whipped topping
12 spearmint candies, crushed

Prepare and bake cake according to package directions, using a greased 13-in. x 9-in. x 2-in. baking pan. Cool on a wire rack for 1 hour. With a meat fork or wooden skewer, poke holes in cake about 2 in. apart. Slowly pour creamer over cake; refrigerate for 1 hour.

In a large bowl, whisk the milk and pudding mixes for 2 minutes. Let stand for 2 minutes or until soft-set. Cut cake into 1-1/2-in. cubes; place a third of the cubes in a 3-qt. glass bowl. Top with a third of the pudding, whipped topping and candies; repeat layers twice. Store in the refrigerator. **Yield:** 14-16 servings.

Holiday and Seasonal Pleasers **35**

Chapter 3

⏱ 30 Minutes to Mealtime

YOU GLANCE at the clock after returning home on a particularly hectic day—and discover that dinnertime is less than 1 hour away. You'll soon have a hungry family clamoring for a satisfying supper. What's a cook to do?

Don't panic! You'll have dinner under control on even the busiest weekdays when you turn to the simple supper solutions featured here.

Our Test Kitchen home economists paired reader recipes with some of their own quick creations to produce 18 terrific menus. From start to finish, preparing each delicious dish will take you a mere 30 minutes...or less.

So rest assured—for a family-pleasing homemade meal, half an hour is all you need.

DINNER IN A DASH. Colorful Spinach Salad, Creamy Onion Garlic Bread and Pasta Sausage Supper (all recipes on p. 53).

Surprise Cookie Pops
Tangy French Beans
Mozzarella Beef Roll-Ups

Fare for the Whole Family

MAKING a quick meal that the entire family will like can be a challenge if your household includes a fussy eater or two. But that's not a concern when you serve a delicious dinner like this one compiled by our Test Kitchen home economists. It's guaranteed to please even the pickiest of palates.

Plus, since each dish takes no more than 30 minutes to prepare, the whole family will be enjoying a hot home-cooked meal in record time.

For the entree, pizza-flavored Mozzarella Beef Roll-Ups are sure to be popular with everyone at your table. The sandwiches are easy to assemble because each tortilla is simply wrapped around a portion of hearty meat filling and a piece of string cheese.

As a side dish, Tangy French Beans will round out your speedy supper wonderfully. A sweet-and-sour bacon sauce gives fantastic flavor to frozen French-style green beans.

You'll need just two ingredients—and some Popsicle sticks—to make fun Surprise Cookie Pops for dessert. Store-bought dough and candy bars combine for a dozen sweet treats that will have your kids reaching for more.

Because these lollipop-like cookies are so quick and easy to make, you'll want to keep them in mind when you need goodies for bake sales, school events and children's parties, too.

Mozzarella Beef Roll-Ups

Prep/Total Time: 30 min.

    1 pound ground beef
    1 medium green pepper, chopped
  1/3 cup chopped onion
    1 can (8 ounces) pizza sauce
   28 slices pepperoni
  1/2 teaspoon dried oregano
    6 flour tortillas (10 inches), warmed
    6 pieces (1 ounce *each*) string cheese

In a large skillet, cook the beef, green pepper and onion over medium heat until the meat is no longer pink; drain. Stir in the pizza sauce, pepperoni and oregano.

Spoon about 1/2 cup beef mixture off-center on each tortilla; top with a piece of string cheese. Fold one side of each tortilla over filling and roll up from the opposite side. Place seam side down on an ungreased baking sheet.

Bake at 350° for 10 minutes or until heated through and cheese is melted. **Yield:** 6 servings.

Tangy French Beans

Prep/Total Time: 15 min.

  3 bacon strips, diced
  2 tablespoons sugar
  2 teaspoons cornstarch
  2 tablespoons cider vinegar
  4 tablespoons cold water, *divided*
  1 package (16 ounces) frozen French-style
    green beans

In a skillet, cook bacon over medium heat until crisp. In a small bowl, combine sugar and cornstarch; stir in vinegar and 2 tablespoons water until smooth. Stir into skillet. Bring to a boil; cook and stir for 1 minute or until thickened.

In a large microwave-safe bowl, combine the green beans and remaining water. Cover and microwave on high for 6-8 minutes or until heated through; drain. Add the cooked bacon mixture and toss to coat. **Yield:** 6 servings.

Editor's Note: This recipe was tested in a 1,100-watt microwave.

Surprise Cookie Pops

Prep/Total Time: 25 min.

   2 Milky Way candy bars (2.05 ounces *each*)
  12 Popsicle sticks
   1 tube (18 ounces) chocolate chip cookie
     dough

Cut each candy bar widthwise into six pieces; insert a Popsicle stick into each. Cut cookie dough into 12 pieces. Flatten dough; wrap each piece around each candy bar piece, forming a ball.

Place 3 in. apart on ungreased baking sheets. Bake at 350° for 13-15 minutes or until lightly browned. Cool for 3 minutes before removing to wire racks. **Yield:** 1 dozen.

Here's the Plan

TO PUT this meal on the table quickly, our Test Kitchen home economists suggest this step-by-step plan for preparing all three recipes:

1. For the roll-ups, cook the ground beef, green pepper and onion in a skillet.
2. While the meat is browning, assemble the cookie pops. Bake them in a 350° oven for 13-15 minutes.
3. While the cookies bake, cook the bacon for the side dish in another skillet.
4. Assemble the roll-ups and place them in the oven for 10 minutes.
5. Cook the beans in the microwave on high for 6-8 minutes. Finish making the sweet-and-sour bacon sauce; toss it with the beans.
6. Remove the cookie pops from the oven to cool.

**Cajun Vegetables
Chicken Milan**

delicious as well," she relates.

"I always keep the ingredients on hand. Choose whatever frozen vegetables your family prefers. I use broccoli, cauliflower and carrots," Chrissy notes. "I also like to substitute a can of whole baby corn for regular corn."

Chicken Milan

Prep/Total Time: 20 min.

✓ Uses less fat, sugar or salt. Includes Nutritional Analysis and Diabetic Exchanges.

   8 ounces uncooked linguine
   1 tablespoon minced garlic
   3 tablespoons olive oil, *divided*
 1/2 teaspoon dried parsley flakes
 1/2 teaspoon pepper, *divided*
 1/4 cup all-purpose flour
   1 teaspoon dried basil
 1/2 teaspoon salt
   2 eggs
1-1/2 pounds boneless skinless chicken breasts, cut into strips

Cook linguine according to package directions. In a large skillet, saute garlic in 1 tablespoon oil for 2-3 minutes or until golden; stir in parsley and 1/4 teaspoon pepper. Remove to a small bowl and set aside.

In a shallow bowl, combine the flour, basil, salt and remaining pepper. In another shallow bowl, beat the eggs. Dredge chicken strips in flour mixture, then dip in eggs.

In the same skillet, cook chicken in remaining oil over medium-high heat for 8-10 minutes or until juices run clear. Drain linguine and place on a serving platter. Pour reserved garlic mixture over linguine and toss to coat; top with chicken. **Yield:** 6 servings.

Nutritional Analysis: 3 ounces cooked chicken with 1/2 cup linguine (prepared with egg substitute) equals 349 calories, 10 g fat (2 g saturated fat), 63 mg cholesterol, 295 mg sodium, 32 g carbohydrate, 2 g fiber, 31 g protein. **Diabetic Exchanges:** 3 lean meat, 2 starch, 1/2 fat.

Cajun Vegetables

Prep/Total Time: 20 min.

1 package (16 ounces) frozen vegetable blend
1 cup frozen cut green beans
1 cup sliced fresh mushrooms
2 tablespoons butter
1 tablespoon olive oil
1 can (15-1/4 ounces) whole kernel corn, drained
2 to 3 teaspoons Cajun seasoning

Cook the vegetable blend and green beans according to package directions. Meanwhile, in a large skillet, saute mushrooms in butter and oil for 1 minute. Add corn; saute for 1 minute. Drain vegetable blend and beans; add to skillet. Stir in Cajun seasoning. **Yield:** 6 servings.

Count on This Quick Menu

YOU DON'T need dozens of recipes to serve a satisfying meal to guests. Our Test Kitchen proves that by pairing two reader recipes into a menu for six that's a snap to prepare on the stovetop.

"I'm a busy mother of a toddler, and my husband has unpredictable hours at work, so quick and delicious meals are my mainstay," writes Lara Priest of Gansevoort, New York.

"A dear friend shared the recipe for Chicken Milan a few years ago," she recalls. "Since then, I've prepared this memorable main dish for both family meals and get-togethers."

The lightly breaded chicken strips are served on a bed of linguine that's tossed with garlic sauce. "This cooks up quickly and tastes like you're dining out at a fine Italian restaurant," she says.

For an easy accompaniment, fix Cajun Vegetables from Chrissy Fessler of Hazleton, Pennsylvania. "This snappy side dish is not only fast and nutritious, but

Easy Fare Ideal For Company

IF YOU'D LIKE to invite guests over for dinner but can't spend hours in the kitchen, this meal is for you. This special menu serves eight people, yet can be prepared in only half an hour.

To start, make Crab Alfredo shared by Susan Anstine of York, Pennsylvania. She uses canned soup and sour cream to hurry along a rich sauce that coats imitation crab. When spooned over penne pasta and garnished with grated Parmesan cheese and minced fresh parsley, it's an easy entree that looks and tastes elegant.

For a pleasing side dish, keep it simple by serving a green vegetable that nicely complements your main course. Just microwave frozen peas and toss them with butter as shown in the photo below right.

Cap off the meal with Gingersnap Pears from Dodi Mahan. "We had unexpected company late one afternoon, and they stayed for dinner," writes the Lexington, Kentucky cook.

"While we had enough food, I didn't have a dessert made," she explains. "This recipe looked like an easy fruit crisp, and I happened to have all the ingredients on hand."

It's a breeze to assemble because it calls for only six ingredients, including canned pears. "It was a huge hit," Dodi recalls. "I'm sure it would be just as delicious with fresh pears."

Crab Alfredo

Prep/Total Time: 25 min.

- 1 package (16 ounces) penne *or* medium tube pasta
- 1/2 cup chopped onion
- 1/4 cup butter
- 2 cups (16 ounces) sour cream
- 1 can (10-3/4 ounces) condensed cream of mushroom soup, undiluted
- 1/2 cup milk
- 1/2 teaspoon salt
- 1/2 teaspoon garlic powder
- 1/2 teaspoon Italian seasoning
- 1/4 teaspoon pepper
- 2 packages (8 ounces *each*) imitation crabmeat, flaked
- 1/4 cup grated Parmesan cheese
- 2 tablespoons minced fresh parsley

Cook the pasta according to the package directions. Meanwhile, in a large skillet, saute the onion in butter until tender. Whisk in the sour cream, mushroom soup, milk, salt, garlic powder, Italian seasoning and pepper until blended. Cook and stir until heated through (do not boil). Stir in the crabmeat; heat through.

Drain pasta; top with crab sauce. Sprinkle with Parmesan cheese and parsley. **Yield:** 8 servings.

Gingersnap Pears

Prep/Total Time: 30 min.

- 4 cans (15-1/4 ounces *each*) sliced pears, drained
- 1 tablespoon all-purpose flour
- 1-1/2 cups finely crushed gingersnaps (about 32 cookies)
- 1/3 cup finely chopped walnuts
- 1/4 cup butter, melted

Vanilla ice cream *or* whipped topping

Place the pears in a large bowl; sprinkle with flour and toss gently to combine. Divide among eight ungreased 8-oz. custard cups. Combine the gingersnaps, walnuts and butter; sprinkle over pears.

Place custard cups on a baking sheet. Bake at 350° for 15-20 minutes or until heated through. Serve warm with ice cream. **Yield:** 8 servings.

Gingersnap Pears
Crab Alfredo

Standout Meal Is Simple

THERE'S no reason why meals made in minutes can't shine. In fact, this stunning trout and simple salad are nice for suppers where you want to impress but don't have a lot of time to fuss.

To start, toss together Mushroom Romaine Salad from Kathy Green of Mahomet, Illinois. "Any time I see a new salad recipe, I snatch it up for my collection," she writes. "As far as I'm concerned, you can never have enough salad recipes."

This medley features romaine hearts, onions and fresh mushrooms drizzled with a creamy homemade dressing that's seasoned with dried tarragon and a dash of cayenne pepper.

"Tossed green salads are always a great way to complete a nice meal, and this recipe goes well with just about any main course for an elegant presentation," Kathy says.

Trout Meuniere, shared by Nancy Kelley of Nashville, Tennessee, is a delicious main course. "Don't let the name intimidate you," she writes. "Though it looks and tastes special, it's actually quick and easy to make."

The trout fillets are covered in a crispy cracker coating. "There's no need to purchase the crumbs," Nancy relates. "Just put the saltine crackers in a sealed bag and crush them with a rolling pin until they're fairly fine."

After it's heated in a skillet, the fish is topped with lemon juice and toasted almonds. "I prefer to use fresh lemon juice instead of the bottled kind," recommends Nancy.

"It's so attractive, I've often prepared it for anniversaries or other romantic celebrations with my husband. I round out the meal with steamed asparagus, crusty French bread and chocolate croissants for dessert," she adds.

Or for a lighter ending to this lovely dinner, serve sliced watermelon as shown in the photo below left.

Mushroom Romaine Salad
Trout Meuniere

Mushroom Romaine Salad

Prep/Total Time: 15 min.

2 bunches romaine hearts, torn
1/4 pound sliced fresh mushrooms
2 green onions, thinly sliced
3 tablespoons olive oil
3 tablespoons cider vinegar
3 tablespoons heavy whipping cream
4-1/2 teaspoons sugar
1-1/2 to 2 teaspoons dried tarragon
1/4 to 1/2 teaspoon salt
Dash cayenne pepper

In a large salad bowl, combine romaine, mushrooms and onions. In a small bowl, whisk the oil, vinegar, cream, sugar, tarragon, salt and cayenne. Pour over the salad and toss to coat. **Yield:** 4-6 servings.

Trout Meuniere

Prep/Total Time: 15 min.

4 trout fillets (6 ounces *each*)
1-1/3 cups crushed saltines
4 tablespoons butter, *divided*
1 package (2-1/4 ounces) sliced almonds
2 tablespoons lemon juice

Coat both sides of fillets with crushed saltines. In a large skillet, melt 3 tablespoons butter over medium-high heat. Cook fillets for 3-5 minutes on each side or until fish flakes easily with a fork. Remove and keep warm.

In the same skillet, cook and stir the almonds in remaining butter until lightly toasted. Stir in the lemon juice. Serve over trout. **Yield:** 4 servings.

Serve Supper Italian-Style

Turkey Florentine
Lemon Angel Hair

WHEN dinnertime nears, do you have a need for speed? Then you'll want to consider this flavorful supper for a family of four that starts with elegant Turkey Florentine.

"I like to experiment with different ingredients and come up with not only tasty but healthy dishes," writes Lillian Butler of Stratford, Connecticut.

For this main course, Lillian tucks Swiss cheese and spinach into browned turkey slices, then tops them with store-bought spaghetti sauce before baking until they're heated through. "I usually serve these roll-ups with pasta, a green salad and rolls," she says.

Rather than plain pasta, serve the turkey with delightful Lemon Angel Hair from Meg Mongell of Plainfield, Indiana.

Her time-saving treatment for angel hair pasta gets loads of flavor from lemon and Parmesan cheese. A hint of garlic and flecks of fresh parsley add interest, too.

The simple side dish is so versatile, it also could accompany chicken, fish, seafood or pork.

For dessert in a dash, stir up a package of instant chocolate pudding and spoon it into individual dishes as shown in the photo above right.

Turkey Florentine

Prep/Total Time: 30 min.

- 1 cup seasoned bread crumbs
- 8 slices uncooked turkey breast
- 2 tablespoons vegetable oil
- 4 slices Swiss cheese, cut in half
- 1 package (10 ounces) frozen chopped spinach, thawed and squeezed dry
- 3 cups meatless spaghetti sauce

Place the bread crumbs in a large resealable plastic bag; add the turkey in batches and shake to coat. In a large skillet over medium heat, brown turkey in oil. Remove from the skillet.

Place half of a cheese slice and 2 tablespoons of spinach down the center of each turkey slice. Fold turkey over filling; secure with toothpicks. Place in a greased 9-in. square baking dish. Top with spaghetti sauce. Bake, uncovered, at 400° for 12-15 minutes or until heated through. Discard toothpicks. **Yield:** 4 servings.

Lemon Angel Hair

Prep/Total Time: 15 min.

- 8 ounces uncooked angel hair pasta
- 1/4 cup minced fresh parsley
- 3 teaspoons grated lemon peel
- 2 teaspoons minced garlic
- 6 tablespoons olive oil
- 3 tablespoons lemon juice
- 1/2 teaspoon salt
- 1/4 teaspoon pepper
- 1/3 cup grated Parmesan cheese

Cook pasta according to package directions. Meanwhile, in a large skillet, saute the parsley, lemon peel and garlic in oil until garlic is tender. Drain pasta; add to the skillet. Sprinkle with lemon juice, salt and pepper; toss to coat. Top with Parmesan cheese. **Yield:** 4 servings.

Easy Dessert Option

IF YOU rarely have time to spend preparing dessert, try this idea. When you do have a few spare moments, make some cookie dough. Most cookie doughs, including chocolate chip and peanut butter, may be refrigerated or frozen and then baked later. When placed in airtight wrapping, unbaked cookie dough can be refrigerated for a week or frozen for up to a year.

To freeze cookie dough, drop tablespoonsful onto baking sheets and freeze until solid. Then transfer it to freezer bags or freezer containers. To thaw, place the frozen dough on baking sheets. Cover it lightly with waxed paper and allow it to stand at room temperature for 30-45 minutes before baking. Then, just pop it in the oven for homemade cookies!

**Chili Con Queso
Chicken Quesadillas**

makes it completely worry-free when entertaining.

"I use hot salsa when fixing it for us, but I usually use mild or medium salsa for guests," she notes. "It's a great way to share a part of our home-state cuisine with other servicemen from around the U.S. and around the globe.

"On the rare occasion that I have leftovers, I like to pour the dip over burritos or use it in a pan of enchiladas," she adds.

While munching on the chips and warm cheese dip, turn to Sacha Roach's speedy recipe for Chicken Quesadillas.

For this effortless entree, the Warsaw, Ohio cook sandwiches cooked chicken, tomato, onion and cheese inside tortillas, then warms them on a griddle until the cheese is gooey.

"Garnish them with sour cream, your favorite salsa and refried beans," Sacha suggests. "I often complete the meal with steamed broccoli topped with cheese. Then I pour ginger ale and orange juice over ice for a refreshing beverage."

Or serve wedges of fresh honeydew melon from your supermarket's produce section (as pictured at left) for a cool accompaniment.

Chili Con Queso

Prep/Total Time: 15 min.

  1 **pound process cheese (Velveeta), cubed**
1/2 **cup chunky-style salsa**
  1 **can (4 ounces) chopped green chilies**
  1 **jar (4 ounces) diced pimientos, drained**
1/2 **teaspoon garlic powder**
1/4 **teaspoon cayenne pepper**
1/8 **teaspoon ground cumin**
1/8 **teaspoon crushed red pepper flakes**
Tortilla chips

In a microwave-safe bowl, combine the first eight ingredients. Cover and microwave on high for 6-7 minutes or until cheese is melted, stirring occasionally. Serve with tortilla chips. **Yield:** 2-3/4 cups.

Editor's Note: This recipe was tested in a 1,100-watt microwave.

Chicken Quesadillas

Prep/Total Time: 15 min.

  4 **flour tortillas (8 inches)**
  2 **teaspoons butter, melted**
  1 **cup (4 ounces) shredded cheddar cheese**
1/3 **cup finely chopped onion**
  1 **medium tomato, diced**
  1 **package (9 ounces) frozen diced cooked chicken, thawed and chopped**

Brush one side of each tortilla with butter. Place two tortillas, buttered side down, on a griddle; sprinkle with cheese, onion, tomato and chicken. Top with remaining tortillas, buttered side up. Cook over medium heat for 3-4 minutes on each side or until lightly browned. Cut into wedges. **Yield:** 2 servings.

Mexican Meal In Minutes

YOU DON'T NEED to travel south of the border to enjoy the fantastic flavors of Mexico...just fix these fast dishes shared by fellow readers.

Start with quick Chili Con Queso sent in by Marie Stout from Yokota Air Force Base, Japan.

"Both my husband and I are from New Mexico, but while we're here in Japan, it's hard to get a taste of home," she writes. "So we make this irresistible, spicy appetizer often. It's the perfect start to any Southwestern-style dinner.

"I love to make this dip for parties, because it is so easy and I usually have all the ingredients on hand," Marie explains. "I double the recipe and prepare it in my slow cooker, because it will not scorch. This

Half-Hour Ham Dinner

WHEN you're having guests over for dinner but you don't have a lot of time to spend in the kitchen, try this quick stovetop menu that offers lots of flavor with only a little effort.

For an appealing entree, serve Ham with Mixed Fruit from Mrs. Raymond Holtmann of Germantown, Illinois.

Apple pie filling and fruit cocktail are combined with a little brown sugar to create a sweet, chunky sauce that nicely complements ham steaks.

"I make this often for birthdays, and it's delicious," she assures. "It can be reheated, but I never have leftovers.

"For easy cleanup, I sometimes place the ham on a large piece of heavy-duty foil, put the fruit mixture on top, then pull up the corners of the foil and twist them to form a bundle," she explains. "I pop it in the oven to bake, and when it's done, there's no pan to wash."

For a speedy side dish, prepare Garlic Parmesan Orzo from Stephanie Moon of Nampa, Idaho. The buttery pasta side dish calls for orzo, which cooks quickly and is a nice change from ordinary pasta shapes.

"This fantastic recipe was inspired by a similar dish I once tried," Stephanie says. "It makes a superb side dish anytime. The garlic and Parmesan cheese really stand out."

For a refreshing dessert, serve scoops of lime sherbet as shown in the photo at right.

Ham with Mixed Fruit

Prep/Total Time: 10 min.

2 pounds bone-in fully cooked ham steaks, cut into serving-size portions
1 tablespoon vegetable oil
1 can (21 ounces) apple pie filling
1 can (15-1/4 ounces) fruit cocktail, drained
1/4 cup packed brown sugar
1/4 cup butter, melted

In two large skillets, cook ham in oil over medium-high heat for 3-4 minutes on each side or until lightly browned. Meanwhile, in a large microwave-safe bowl, combine the pie filling, fruit cocktail, brown sugar and butter. Microwave, uncovered, on high for 1-2 minutes or until heated through, stirring twice. Serve with ham. **Yield:** 8 servings.

Editor's Note: This recipe was tested in a 1,100-watt microwave.

Garlic Parmesan Orzo

Prep/Total Time: 20 min.

2 cups uncooked orzo pasta
3 teaspoons minced garlic
1/2 cup butter, cubed
1/2 cup grated Parmesan cheese
1/4 cup milk
2 tablespoons minced fresh parsley
1 teaspoon salt
1/4 teaspoon pepper

Cook orzo according to package directions; drain. In a large skillet, saute garlic in butter until tender. Add the orzo, Parmesan cheese, milk, parsley, salt and pepper. Cook and stir until heated through. **Yield:** 8 servings.

No Brown Sugar Blues

To prevent my brown sugar from becoming hard, I don't keep it on the kitchen counter or in the pantry. I store it in the freezer. I do the same thing with my marshmallows so they stay nice and soft.
—*Twila Odegaard, McFarland, Wisconsin*

Garlic Parmesan Orzo
Ham with Mixed Fruit

Meal Boasts Fresh Flavors

WHEN you want to serve refreshing food that's fast yet looks like you fussed, turn to this three-course meal from our Test Kitchen home economists. Each delicious dish is easy to assemble, eye-appealing and palate-pleasing as well.

To begin, you'll need just three ingredients to make Broccoli Roll-Ups. Broccoli spears and American cheese are wrapped in convenient crescent roll dough to create the savory baked bites.

The tender crescents are a tasty complement to Tuna-Stuffed Tomatoes. Fresh tomatoes are hollowed out, then filled with a flavorful tuna salad mixture that gets crunch from celery and cashews.

If you like, round out each plate with a simple salad of mixed greens with julienned yellow pepper, sliced fresh mushrooms and croutons as shown in the photo at right.

For dessert, serve slices of Mousse-Topped Pound Cake. A smooth creamy filling with a mild cocoa flavor is spread on layers of pound cake, then topped with sliced kiwifruit for a pretty presentation.

Broccoli Roll-Ups

Prep/Total Time: 20 min.

     1 tube (4 ounces) refrigerated crescent rolls
     1 slice process American cheese, quartered
     4 frozen broccoli spears, thawed and patted dry

Separate the crescent dough into four triangles. Place a piece of cheese and a broccoli spear along the wide edge of each triangle; roll up the dough. Place point side down on an ungreased baking sheet. Bake at 375° for 12-15 minutes or until golden brown. **Yield:** 4 servings.

Tuna-Stuffed Tomatoes

Prep/Total Time: 10 min.

✓ Uses less fat, sugar or salt. Includes Nutritional Analysis and Diabetic Exchanges.

     4 large tomatoes
 1/2 cup mayonnaise
 1/2 teaspoon celery salt
 1/2 teaspoon dill weed
 1/4 teaspoon pepper
     2 cans (6 ounces *each*) tuna, drained and flaked
     2 celery ribs, chopped
 1/2 cup chopped cashews, optional

Cut a thin slice off the top of each tomato. Scoop out pulp, leaving a 1/2-in. shell for each. Invert tomatoes onto paper towels to drain. In a bowl, combine mayonnaise, celery salt, dill and pepper. Stir in tuna, celery and cashews if desired. Spoon into tomato shells. **Yield:** 4 servings.

Nutritional Analysis: 1 stuffed tomato (prepared with reduced-fat mayonnaise and water-packed tuna; calculated without cashews) equals 241 calories, 11 g fat (2 g saturated fat), 36 mg cholesterol, 746 mg sodium, 12 g carbohydrate, 2 g fiber, 24 g protein. **Diabetic Exchanges:** 3 lean meat, 2 vegetable, 1 fat.

Mousse-Topped Pound Cake

Prep/Total Time: 10 min.

     1 cup heavy whipping cream
 1/4 cup confectioners' sugar
     2 teaspoons baking cocoa
 1/2 teaspoon vanilla extract
     1 frozen pound cake (10-3/4 ounces), thawed
     1 medium kiwifruit, peeled, halved and sliced, optional

In a small mixing bowl, beat cream until it begins to thicken. Add the confectioners' sugar, cocoa and vanilla; beat until stiff peaks form. Split cake into three horizontal layers. Spread about 1/2 cup mousse on bottom layer; repeat layers twice. Garnish with kiwi if desired. Refrigerate leftovers. **Yield:** 6-8 servings.

Savvy Shopping

WANT to pick up the fixings for this delicious dinner on your way home from work? First, check that you already have the following staples: mayonnaise, celery salt, dill weed, ground black pepper, confectioners' sugar, baking cocoa and vanilla extract.

Then put the items below on your shopping list to get the remaining ingredients needed to prepare the three recipes on this page.

     4 large tomatoes
     1 bunch celery
     1 medium kiwifruit
     2 cans (6 ounces *each*) tuna
     1 can (9.25 ounces) cashew halves and pieces
     1 half-pint heavy whipping cream
     1 tube (4 ounces) refrigerated crescent rolls
     1 package (8 ounces) sliced process American cheese
     1 package (16 ounces) frozen broccoli spears
     1 frozen pound cake (10-3/4 ounces)

If you'd like to round out your meal with the salad shown in the photo at right, just add the following items to your list: 1 package (5 ounces) mixed greens, 1 package (8 ounces) sliced fresh mushrooms, 1 yellow pepper, 1 box (6 ounces) croutons and 1 bottle (8 ounces) salad dressing.

Mousse-Topped Pound Cake
Tuna-Stuffed Tomatoes
Broccoli Roll-Ups

Take Shortcuts At Mealtime

SITTING DOWN to a homemade meal is quick and easy when you shave time off preparation by using convenience products from the supermarket. That's the strategy for this simple menu you can assemble in just 20 minutes.

For a fast take on a classic main dish salad, turn to Martha Crise's recipe for Chicken Nugget Caesar Salad.

"I was getting ready to prepare a Caesar salad with chicken strips when I discovered I didn't have enough chicken breasts in the freezer," explains the Lake Zurich, Illinois cook. "All I had was a package of frozen chicken nuggets, so I decided to try those as a substitute.

"My family was delighted with the results," Martha notes. "In fact, my husband enjoyed three generous helpings!"

To complement the salad, bake a batch of Onion Crescent Rolls. Barbara Nowakowski of North Tonawanda, New York dresses up a tube of crescent roll dough to create the golden bites.

"This is one of our favorites," she writes. "They're a nice addition to any buffet. We like them so much that I usually triple the recipe."

For a sweet ending to this swift supper, serve frosted brownies available in the bakery section of most grocery stores. A handful of sprinkles gives them a festive touch.

Chicken Nugget Caesar Salad
Prep/Total Time: 20 min.

8 to 10 frozen breaded chicken breast nuggets
6 cups torn romaine
1/2 cup sliced fresh mushrooms
3/4 cup Caesar salad dressing
3/4 cup Caesar salad croutons
1/4 cup shredded Parmesan cheese

Bake chicken nuggets according to package directions; cut into fourths. In a large bowl, combine the romaine, mushrooms and chicken. Drizzle with dressing and toss to coat. Sprinkle with croutons and Parmesan cheese. **Yield:** 4-6 servings.

Onion Crescent Rolls
Prep/Total Time: 20 min.

1 tube (8 ounces) refrigerated crescent rolls
1-1/3 cups french-fried onions, *divided*
1 egg
1 tablespoon water

Unroll crescent dough and separate into triangles. Sprinkle each with about 2 tablespoons onions. Roll up each from the wide end; place on an ungreased foil-lined baking sheet. Curve ends down to form crescents.

Beat the egg and water; brush over dough. Sprinkle with remaining onions. Bake at 400° for 10-12 minutes or until golden brown. Serve warm. **Yield:** 8 rolls.

Onion Crescent Rolls
Chicken Nugget Caesar Salad

Salads Make Supper Simple

- Here's a fast fruit salad that's especially good with a meat-and-potatoes meal. Simply drain an 11-ounce can of mandarin oranges and stir it gently into a drained 20-ounce can of crushed pineapple.
  —*Madeline Fisk, Queensbury, New York*
- When I have extra corn bread, I crumble it into a bowl and top it with pinto beans, chopped onions, green peppers, sweet pickles and tomatoes. Then I toss it with mayonnaise and pickle juice and refrigerate it so the flavors mingle. To finish, I add bits of bacon. —*Linda Rich, Bean Station, Tennessee*

Microwave Makes Main Dish Easy

Sesame Carrot Slices
Crumb-Coated Chicken

WHEN time is at a premium, many busy cooks rely on simple recipes that call for quick cooking methods, like the microwave and stovetop. And that's just what you'll need to make the mouth-watering meal featured here.

The microwave makes it a snap to get Crumb-Coated Chicken on the table in minutes. "This recipe is easy enough for kids to do, and our family loves it!" writes Ginny Watson of Broken Arrow, Oklahoma. A crumb coating adds savory flavor to the chicken and keeps it moist while it cooks.

To accompany the main dish, serve Sesame Carrot Slices shared by Jacqueline Thompson Graves of Cumming, Georgia.

The sweet carrot coins are cooked in butter on the stovetop until crisp-tender. Then Jacqueline dresses them up with a mixture featuring mustard, brown sugar and sesame seeds.

"This carrot dish is a welcome change of pace," Jacqueline assures. "It can be made more or less spicy, whichever your taste dictates, by altering the amount of hot pepper sauce," she adds.

Serve this delicious dinner with slices of marble rye bread (as shown in the photo at right), and you'll have a complete meal that's tasty and time-saving.

Crumb-Coated Chicken

Prep/Total Time: 15 min.

- 1/2 cup seasoned bread crumbs
- 1/4 cup grated Parmesan cheese
- 1/2 teaspoon garlic powder
- 1/4 teaspoon paprika
- 4 boneless skinless chicken breast halves (about 6 ounces *each*)
- 2 tablespoons butter, melted

In a shallow bowl, combine the bread crumbs, Parmesan cheese, garlic powder and paprika. Coat chicken with crumb mixture. Place on a microwave-safe plate. Drizzle with butter. Cover loosely with waxed paper. Microwave on high for 4-6 minutes or until juices run clear, turning once. **Yield:** 4 servings.

Editor's Note: This recipe was tested in a 1,100-watt microwave.

Sesame Carrot Slices

Prep/Total Time: 20 min.

- 3 cups sliced carrots
- 2 tablespoons butter
- 2 tablespoons brown sugar
- 1 teaspoon ground mustard
- 1/4 teaspoon salt
- Dash to 1/8 teaspoon hot pepper sauce
- Dash coarsely ground pepper
- 1-1/2 teaspoons minced fresh parsley
- 1 teaspoon sesame seeds, toasted

In a large skillet, cook and stir the carrots in butter over medium heat for 5 minutes. Stir in the brown sugar, mustard, salt, hot pepper sauce and pepper. Cook and stir 4 minutes longer or until carrots are crisp-tender and evenly coated. Sprinkle with parsley and sesame seeds. **Yield:** 4 servings.

Grill Up This Patriotic Meal

CELEBRATE Independence Day—or most any back-yard occasion—with this three-course menu shared by our Test Kitchen home economists. The fun casual meal is a breeze to prepare, so it's perfect for the lazy days of summer. And since both the main course and side dish cook on the grill, you don't need to spend hours over a hot stove.

To begin, fire up the grill for Teriyaki Turkey Burgers. Basted with a mouth-watering teriyaki sauce, the pineapple-topped burgers are moist, tender and ready in minutes.

At the same time, you can cook Grilled Honey-Ginger Corn, too. The perfect accompaniment to the tasty burgers, the corn has a sweet honey flavor that's jazzed up with zippy cayenne pepper.

End the meal with a bang when you bring out cute and oh-so-easy Dipped Ice Cream Sandwiches. With just a few ingredients, including red, white and blue sprinkles, these sweet frozen treats are sure to make your family ooh and aah!

Teriyaki Turkey Burgers

Prep/Total Time: 30 min.

1 egg
1/2 cup dry bread crumbs
3 green onions, chopped
4 tablespoons teriyaki sauce, *divided*
1/4 teaspoon onion powder
1 pound ground turkey
1 can (8 ounces) sliced pineapple, drained
4 hamburger buns, split and toasted

In a large bowl, combine the egg, bread crumbs, onions, 2 tablespoons teriyaki sauce and onion powder. Crumble turkey over mixture and mix well. Shape into four 3/4-in.-thick patties.

Coat grill rack with nonstick cooking spray before starting the grill. Grill patties, covered, over medium heat for 6-8 minutes on each side or until a meat thermometer reads 165°; brush with remaining teriyaki sauce during the last 5 minutes.

Grill pineapple slices for 3-4 minutes on each side or until heated through. Serve burgers and pineapple on buns. **Yield:** 4 servings.

Grilled Honey-Ginger Corn

Prep/Total Time: 25 min.

1/3 cup butter, softened
1 tablespoon minced chives
1 tablespoon honey
1/4 to 1/2 teaspoon ground ginger
1/8 teaspoon cayenne pepper
4 medium ears sweet corn

In a small bowl, combine the first five ingredients; spread over corn. Place each ear of corn on a double thickness of heavy-duty foil. Fold foil around corn and seal tightly. Grill, covered, over medium heat for 15-20 minutes or until tender, turning every 5 minutes. **Yield:** 4 servings.

Dipped Ice Cream Sandwiches

Prep/Total Time: 20 min. + freezing

6 squares (1 ounce *each*) semisweet chocolate, chopped
1 tablespoon shortening
4 ice cream sandwiches
Red, white and blue sprinkles

Line a baking sheet with waxed paper; set aside. In a microwave or heavy saucepan, melt chocolate and shortening; stir until smooth. Quickly dip ice cream sandwiches partway in melted chocolate; coat chocolate with sprinkles. Place on prepared baking sheet and freeze. **Yield:** 4 servings.

Dipped Ice Cream Sandwiches
Teriyaki Turkey Burgers
Grilled Honey-Ginger Corn

Serve Them Meat 'n' Potatoes

WANT to make your next dinner an outdoor feast? Then heat up the grill for this fast family-pleasing menu created by our Test Kitchen staff. It's hearty enough to satisfy big appetites yet is table-ready in less than a half hour.

For a stick-to-your-ribs entree, start with Meat 'n' Potato Kabobs. Your family is sure to enjoy these mildly seasoned skewers featuring tender steak and a bright mix of vegetables.

And you'll love that this recipe comes together quickly. The potatoes are cooked in the microwave first, so grilling is speedy. Plus, there's virtually no cleanup!

To accompany the hearty main course, whip up Parmesan Couscous on the stovetop in just 10 minutes. It has a hint of garlic and pretty color from green onion and pimientos.

For dessert, slice fresh peaches and serve with a small pitcher of rich cream as shown in the photo at right. It makes a fast-and-easy finish to this fabulous summer meal.

Meat 'n' Potato Kabobs
Parmesan Couscous

Meat 'n' Potato Kabobs

Prep/Total Time: 30 min.

✓ Uses less fat, sugar or salt. Includes Nutritional Analysis and Diabetic Exchanges.

    1 pound boneless beef sirloin steak, cut
      into 1-inch cubes
1-1/2 teaspoons steak seasoning, *divided*
    1 teaspoon minced garlic
    1 cup cola
    3 small red potatoes, cubed
    1 tablespoon water
    1 cup cherry tomatoes
    1 medium sweet orange pepper, cut
      into 1-inch pieces
    1 teaspoon canola oil
    1 cup pineapple chunks

Sprinkle beef cubes with 1 teaspoon steak seasoning and garlic; place in a large resealable plastic bag. Add cola. Seal bag and turn to coat; set aside.

Place the potatoes and water in a microwave-safe dish; cover and microwave on high for 4 minutes or until tender. Drain. Add the tomatoes, orange pepper, oil and remaining steak seasoning; toss gently to coat.

Drain and discard marinade. Alternately thread the beef, vegetables and pineapple onto eight metal or soaked wooden skewers. Grill, covered, over medium-hot heat or broil 4-6 in. from the heat for 4 minutes.

Turn; cook 4-6 minutes longer or until meat reaches desired doneness. **Yield:** 4 servings.

Nutritional Analysis: 1 kabob (prepared with diet cola) equals 251 calories, 7 g fat (2 g saturated fat), 63 mg cholesterol, 311 mg sodium, 23 g carbohydrate, 3 g fiber, 24 g protein. **Diabetic Exchanges:** 3 lean meat, 1 starch, 1/2 fruit.

Editor's Note: This recipe was tested in a 1,100-watt microwave.

Parmesan Couscous

Prep/Total Time: 10 min.

    1 cup water
    1 tablespoon butter
  3/4 cup uncooked couscous
  1/4 cup grated Parmesan cheese
    2 tablespoons chopped green onion
    1 tablespoon diced pimientos
    1 teaspoon minced garlic
  1/4 teaspoon coarsely ground pepper
  1/8 teaspoon salt

In a small saucepan, bring water and butter to a boil. Stir in couscous. Cover and remove from the heat; let stand for 5 minutes. Fluff with a fork. Stir in the remaining ingredients. **Yield:** 4 servings.

Colorful Spinach Salad
Creamy Onion Garlic Bread
Pasta Sausage Supper

Tasty Trio Is Time-Saving

SOMETIMES coming up with ideas for dinner is more difficult than actually preparing it. That's why the home economists in our Test Kitchen put together this meal that takes the work out of menu planning.

It starts with hearty helpings of Pasta Sausage Supper, a swift stovetop entree featuring sliced kielbasa and bright bell pepper strips served over tender penne pasta.

While the pasta is cooking, it's a breeze to saute the meat and veggies. At the same time, you can warm the jarred spaghetti sauce in the microwave or in a saucepan.

Slices of Creamy Onion Garlic Bread are a delightful accompaniment to the main dish. A cheesy mixture seasoned with green onions and garlic powder adds rich flavor to Italian bread.

It's simple to spread it on the loaf, or you can even use it to dress up leftover hamburger or hot dog buns. The aroma as the bread broils in the oven is sure to whet your family's appetites.

Complete the meal with Colorful Spinach Salad, a refreshing medley that says "springtime" with each bite.

Bagged spinach from the produce section hurries along the preparation of the salad that's topped with crunchy radishes, pretty slices of yellow summer squash and sweet chewy raisins.

Dress it with a simple homemade balsamic vinaigrette or choose your favorite bottled dressing for even quicker results.

Pasta Sausage Supper

Prep/Total Time: 25 min.

1 package (16 ounces) penne *or* medium tube pasta
1 pound fully cooked kielbasa *or* Polish sausage, cut into 1/4-inch slices
1 medium green pepper, julienned
1 medium sweet red pepper, julienned
1 medium onion, halved and sliced
1 tablespoon vegetable oil
1 jar (26 ounces) meatless spaghetti sauce, warmed

Cook pasta according to package directions. Meanwhile, in a large skillet, saute the sausage, peppers and onion in oil until vegetables are crisp-tender. Drain pasta; divide among six serving plates. Top with spaghetti sauce. Using a slotted spoon, top with sausage mixture. **Yield:** 6 servings.

Creamy Onion Garlic Bread

Prep/Total Time: 15 min.

2 packages (3 ounces *each*) cream cheese, softened
1/4 cup butter, softened
1/4 cup grated Parmesan cheese
1/2 teaspoon garlic powder
8 green onions, chopped
1 loaf (1 pound) unsliced Italian bread, halved lengthwise

In a small mixing bowl, beat the cream cheese, butter, Parmesan cheese and garlic powder until smooth. Beat in onions. Spread over cut sides of bread. Place on an ungreased baking sheet.

Broil 4 in. from the heat for 3-4 minutes or until lightly browned. Let stand for 5 minutes before cutting. **Yield:** 6-8 servings.

Colorful Spinach Salad

Prep/Total Time: 10 min.

4 cups fresh baby spinach
3/4 cup sliced radishes
1/2 cup sliced yellow summer squash
1/2 cup raisins
1 tablespoon balsamic vinegar
1 teaspoon Dijon mustard
1/8 teaspoon salt
1/8 teaspoon pepper
3 tablespoons olive oil

In a large bowl, toss the spinach, radishes, yellow squash and raisins. In a small bowl, whisk the vinegar, mustard, salt and pepper. Gradually whisk in oil. Serve with salad. **Yield:** 6 servings.

Fruit Desserts in a Dash

WANT to top off the delicious dinner on this page with a sweet treat? You don't need to spend a lot of extra time in the kitchen preparing one. Simply whip up any of these cool fruit creations that are sure to delight the whole family.

- Tuck fresh raspberries into store-bought crepes, then dollop them with sweetened sour cream.
- Serve ice cream in wide-mouth sundae cups that have lots of room for your favorite fruit toppings.
- For a pretty parfait, layer blueberries or peach slices with instant white chocolate or cheesecake pudding and vanilla wafers.
- Twirl strawberries, sliced kiwifruit and mandarin orange segments in microwavable dipping chocolate, found in both the baking aisle and near the ice cream toppings in grocery stores.
- Dress up purchased individual shortcakes or sliced pound cake with fresh strawberries and dollops of whipped topping.
- Offer store-bought caramel or cream cheese dip with apple slices, melon wedges or berries.

Weeknight Meal Made Easy

FROM Thanksgiving through Yuletide, busy holiday agendas and drop-in visitors keep many folks on the lookout for dishes that look and taste impressive but go together in minutes.

For a speedy but simply scrumptious meal, start with Weeknight Pork Chops shared by Cheryl Maher from Oceanside, California.

While the chops sizzle on the stovetop, Cheryl mixes mustard, vinegar and strawberry jam into a colorful sauce that she warms and drizzles over the chops for a sweet and tangy entree.

Kay Krause's Seasoned Potato Cubes are a flavorful accompaniment. "These wonderful potatoes are great with steak, pork chops or even burgers," writes the Sioux Falls, South Dakota cook.

"I found the recipe in a magazine years ago and added a few things to make it even more tasty," she explains.

Cap off this swift skillet supper with bowls of store-bought chocolate ice cream as shown in the photo below left. Your family is sure to request this delicious meal time and again.

Weeknight Pork Chops

Prep/Total Time: 20 min.

- **4 bone-in pork loin chops**
- **1 tablespoon vegetable oil**
- **1/4 cup seedless strawberry jam**
- **2 tablespoons cider vinegar**
- **1 tablespoon prepared mustard**

In a large skillet, brown pork chops in oil over medium-high heat for 2-3 minutes on each side. Reduce heat; cook, uncovered, for 10-15 minutes or until juices run clear.

In a small microwave-safe bowl, combine the jam, vinegar and mustard. Cover and microwave on high for 20-25 seconds or until heated through. Serve over the pork chops. **Yield: 4 servings.**

Seasoned Potato Cubes

Prep/Total Time: 25 min.

✓ Uses less fat, sugar or salt. Includes Nutritional Analysis and Diabetic Exchanges.

- **4 medium red potatoes, cut into 1/2-inch cubes**
- **1/4 cup butter, cubed**
- **1/2 teaspoon seasoned salt**
- **1/4 teaspoon garlic powder**
- **1/4 teaspoon pepper**
- **1 small sweet red pepper, chopped**
- **1 small onion, chopped**
- **1 small green pepper, chopped, optional**
- **1/4 cup chicken broth**
- **1/4 cup beer *or* additional chicken broth**
- **1 tablespoon brown sugar, optional**

In a large skillet, cook and stir the potatoes in butter over medium-high heat until lightly browned. Sprinkle with seasoned salt, garlic powder and pepper. Add red pepper, onion and green pepper if desired. Cook and stir for 5 minutes.

Combine the broth, beer or additional broth and brown sugar if desired; pour over vegetables. Bring to a boil. Reduce heat; simmer, uncovered, for 3-5 minutes or until tender. **Yield: 4 servings.**

Nutritional Analysis: 3/4 cup (prepared with reduced-fat butter; calculated without brown sugar) equals 151 calories, 6 g fat (4 g saturated fat), 20 mg cholesterol, 326 mg sodium, 21 g carbohydrate, 3 g fiber, 4 g protein. **Diabetic Exchanges:** 1 starch, 1 vegetable, 1 fat.

Seasoned Potato Cubes
Weeknight Pork Chops

Stir Up Supper In a Skillet

WELCOMING friends, kids at college and far-flung family members home for the holidays doesn't have to add up to stress and several hours spent in the kitchen.

Instead, turn to these two time-saving recipes that combine to make one mouth-watering meal you can have on the table in only 30 minutes. It's so delicious that no one will ever believe you didn't go to a lot of fuss just to make them feel special!

Start with moist and juicy Chicken Piccata shared by Cynthia Heil of Augusta, Georgia. Laced with lemon and simmered in white wine, this easy stove-top entree couldn't be more elegant. An added bonus is that it fills the house with a wonderful aroma.

Team it up with colorful Mushroom Bean Medley from our Test Kitchen home economists. Fresh mushrooms, onion and a splash of white wine flavor a savory sauce that really dresses up convenient frozen vegetables. The versatile side dish would complement just about any entree.

Served with a loaf of crusty French bread as shown in the photo at right, this dinner is likely to become a favorite in your household.

Mushroom Bean Medley
Chicken Piccata

Chicken Piccata

Prep/Total Time: 25 min.

1/4 cup all-purpose flour
1/2 teaspoon salt
1/2 teaspoon pepper
   4 boneless skinless chicken breast halves
      (4 ounces *each*)
1/4 cup butter, cubed
1/4 cup white wine *or* chicken broth
   1 tablespoon lemon juice

In a large resealable plastic bag, combine the flour, salt and pepper. Flatten chicken to 1/2-in. thickness; place in bag, one piece at a time, and shake to coat.

In a large skillet over medium heat, brown chicken in butter. Stir in wine or broth. Bring to a boil. Reduce heat; simmer, uncovered, for 12-15 minutes or until chicken juices run clear. Drizzle with lemon juice. **Yield:** 4 servings.

Mushroom Bean Medley

Prep/Total Time: 15 min.

 Uses less fat, sugar or salt. Includes Nutritional Analysis and Diabetic Exchanges.

1/2 pound sliced fresh mushrooms
   1 small onion, halved and sliced
   2 tablespoons butter
   1 package (16 ounces) frozen wax beans,
      green beans and carrots
1/2 cup white wine *or* chicken broth
1/4 teaspoon salt
1/4 teaspoon pepper

In a large skillet, saute mushrooms and onion in butter until tender. Add vegetables and wine or broth. Bring to a boil. Reduce heat; cover and simmer for 5 minutes or until vegetables are tender. Drain; sprinkle with salt and pepper. **Yield:** 4 servings.

Nutritional Analysis: 1 cup (prepared with reduced-fat butter) equals 104 calories, 3 g fat (2 g saturated fat), 10 mg cholesterol, 190 mg sodium, 13 g carbohydrate, 4 g fiber, 4 g protein. **Diabetic Exchanges:** 2 vegetable, 1 fat.

Special Supper Will Impress

FOLKS will think you fussed when you fix this tasty trio of rapid recipes to celebrate Valentine's Day.

The home economists in our Test Kitchen kept time in mind when they created the special meal. They streamlined preparation so all three courses could be completed in 30 minutes.

The recipes feed four people, so it's a snap to serve this taste-tempting menu to your family...or invite another couple over for a delicious double date.

Start the meal with a surf and turf entree that's elegant enough for any occasion. A creamy crab sauce drapes nicely over New York strip steaks.

Complement the saucy steaks with a vibrant side dish that cooks in the microwave in mere minutes. Fresh peas get extra color from a jar of pimientos, which eliminates the need to chop red pepper.

For dessert, present a sweet-tart combination of cherry pie filling and fresh cranberries. Individual servings of the warm fruit mixture are garnished with pretty pastry-crust hearts spiced with cinnamon.

Steaks with Crab Sauce

Prep/Total Time: 25 min.

  1 teaspoon dried rosemary, crushed
1/2 teaspoon salt
1/2 teaspoon pepper
  4 beef strip steaks (about 8 ounces *each*)
  1 tablespoon vegetable oil
SAUCE:
  2 teaspoons cornstarch
1/4 cup white wine *or* chicken broth
3/4 cup heavy whipping cream
  1 tablespoon Dijon mustard
1/2 teaspoon prepared horseradish
1/8 teaspoon salt
1/8 teaspoon pepper
  1 package (8 ounces) imitation crabmeat, coarsely chopped

Combine the rosemary, salt and pepper; rub over steaks. In a large skillet over medium-high heat, cook steaks in oil for 5-8 minutes on each side or until meat reaches desired doneness (for medium-rare, a meat thermometer should read 145°; medium, 160°; well-done, 170°).

Meanwhile, in a small saucepan, combine the cornstarch and wine or broth until smooth. Stir in the cream, mustard, horseradish, salt and pepper. Bring to a boil; cook and stir for 2 minutes or until thickened. Stir in crab; heat through. Serve over steaks. **Yield:** 4 servings.

Editor's Note: Steak may be known as strip steak, Kansas City steak, New York strip steak, Ambassador steak or boneless Club Steak in your region.

Basil Sugar Snap Peas

Prep/Total Time: 10 min.

✓ Uses less fat, sugar or salt. Includes Nutritional Analysis and Diabetic Exchanges.

  1 pound fresh sugar snap peas
  2 tablespoons water
  1 jar (2 ounces) sliced pimientos, drained
  2 tablespoons butter, melted
  1 teaspoon dried basil
1/4 teaspoon salt
1/8 teaspoon pepper

In a large microwave-safe bowl, combine the peas and water. Cover and cook on high for 3-5 minutes or until crisp-tender; drain. Stir in the remaining ingredients. **Yield:** 4 servings.

Nutritional Analysis: 3/4 cup (prepared with reduced-fat butter) equals 77 calories, 3 g fat (2 g saturated fat), 10 mg cholesterol, 189 mg sodium, 9 g carbohydrate, 4 g fiber, 4 g protein. **Diabetic Exchanges:** 2 vegetable, 1/2 fat.

Editor's Note: This recipe was tested in a 1,100-watt microwave.

Sweetheart Dessert

Prep/Total Time: 25 min.

1/2 cup plus 1 tablespoon sugar, *divided*
  1 tablespoon cornstarch
  1 can (21 ounces) cherry pie filling
  1 cup fresh *or* frozen cranberries, coarsely chopped
  1 sheet refrigerated pie pastry
1/4 teaspoon ground cinnamon

In a large bowl, combine 1/2 cup sugar and cornstarch. Stir in the pie filling and cranberries. Spoon into four ungreased 6-oz. baking dishes. Bake at 425° for 15-20 minutes or until thickened and bubbly.

Meanwhile, cut eight hearts from pastry with a 2-1/2-in. heart-shaped cookie cutter. Place on an ungreased baking sheet. Combine cinnamon and remaining sugar; sprinkle over hearts. Bake for 8-11 minutes or until edges are lightly browned. Place two hearts on each dessert. Serve warm. **Yield:** 4 servings.

Sweet Holiday Treat

WITH the gorgeous ruby-red color of cherries and cranberries, Sweetheart Dessert could make a wonderful treat for your family and friends at Christmastime, too. Instead of using a cookie cutter shaped like a heart, choose a 2-1/2-inch bell, star, candy cane, Christmas tree or other Yuletide motif.

Living on one can of tuna in the real world

Mary Hunt

EVERYDAY *Cheapskate*

Are the "reality" television shows anything close to what you consider reality? To me, "Survivor" seems more like fantasy than reality. Honestly, I can't remember the last time I had to survive on approximately 14 grams of rice per day, or think of multi-legged creatures in terms of grams of protein. Still, I think that borrowing a few basic "survivor" attitudes and skills could help us see the contents of our freezers, refrigerators and pantries a bit differently.

Let's say that a 6-ounce can of water-packed tuna in your pantry is the only scrap of protein in the house — and you've got four hungry people to feed. A trip to the store is completely out of the question (did I mention you're marooned on a deserted island? ... wink, wink). What will you do? What WILL you do?!

That's the question I posed to three of my favorite frugal food experts. Their responses, while varied, prompted me to put tuna on my shopping list just as soon as I get back to civilization.

Pat Varetto, our friendly neighborhood guide to frugal living at About.com, says, "I would probably make a tuna pie (my personal favorite), using leftover vegetables from the freezer, which I always seem to have in abundance."

Make a simple piecrust and line a baking dish with it. Drain 2 to 3 cups of vegetables (mixed vegetables, beans, corn, peas and carrots ... just about any combination will do) and set aside the liquid. Add tuna to the vegetables (don't drain the tuna). Add a generous tablespoon or so of cornstarch in a half cup of the vegetable liquid, mix well, then add to the vegetable/tuna mix. Pour into the piecrust and top with more crust and prick in several places. Bake at about 350 degrees until the crust is slightly browned, about 30 minutes.

Brenda Ponichtera, registered dietitian and author of "Quick & Healthy Low-Fat, Carb Conscious Cooking" (ScaleDown Publishing, 2005), says of her Tuna Macaroni Salad, "Try this on a bed of lettuce accompanied by sliced tomatoes. A whole-wheat roll completes this meal."

4 ounces medium-size shell pasta (about 2 cups dry)
1 cup chopped celery
1 cup chopped red bell pepper
1/2 cup sliced green onion
1 or 2 cans (6 ounces each) water-packed tuna, drained
1/2 cup nonfat ranch-style dressing

Cook macaroni according to package directions, omitting salt and oil. Drain. Add remaining ingredients and toss with dressing. Refrigerate until serving.

Here's what Rhonda Barfield, home-schooling mother to four and author of "15-Minute Cooking" (Lilac Publishing, 1996), would do with a can of tuna:

In a 2-quart bowl, add a 6-ounce can of chunk-light water-packed tuna, drained. Add 1 cup diced (canned and drained) water chestnuts, 1 cup seedless red grapes (halved) and 1/2 cup diced celery. Set aside.

In a 1-quart mixing bowl, combine 1 cup Miracle Whip Light, 2 tablespoons soy sauce and 2 tablespoons lemon juice. Mix well. Pour sauce over tuna and other ingredients. Toss together. Chill. Serve in warmed pita pockets. She calls it her Exotic Tuna Salad.

Now before you fill my mailbox with "Uh, Mary ... I do believe those recipes contain just a few more ingredients than a can of tuna!" keep in mind I didn't say that all you had in your pantry was that lonely can of tuna!

figure out ways to
prices. Just three
nois Department of
o cut back mowing
o conserve fuel. Now
ming in oil.
me us motorists for
and concocting con-
prices seem to peak
whims of the wind. As
o, is there another liq-
Never seen a gallon of
cents overnight. Gas
uch, we don't know

clear our confusion. If anything, they feed conspiracy theories. All of the following have been cited by the experts over the last 18 months for why Americans should prepare themselves for rising gas prices: hurricanes, Middle East tensions, refinery capacity, holiday demand, geopolitical uncertainties, tight global supplies, and corroded pipelines up in Alaska. Did all of those suddenly vanish? How could Grandma's head cold not have made the list?

**(Peoria) Journal Star
Sept. 27.**

on security:
Democratic weakness

Bush administration came up with a pre-election Congressional strategy to legalize the detainee program — as well as the National Security Agency's terrorist wiretapping program — that set a new trap for Democrats to show voters that they are "weak" on terrorism.

It was a reprise of the GOP's 2002 sudden support of a Department of Homeland Security and its fashioning of a fight over civil service rules into a test of strength against terrorism.

Again, this year, the Democrats walked right into it. In the debate, Democrats (and a few Republicans) basically argued that noncitizen terrorist captives deserve the same constitutional protections as domestic criminal defendants, fulfilling GOP caricatures that they don't really regard the war on terror as a war.

During the debate on NSA spying, Rep. Maurice Hinchey, D-N.Y., declared that "this bill is contrary to every basic principle of our country. If we pass (it), we are opening up new opportunities for an increasingly despotic administration to continue to erode the basic freedoms and liberties of the American people."

On final passage, 177 House Democrats (and 13 Republicans) voted against the NSA program — which is designed to intercept international, not

Rumsfeld and called for his replacement.

But on the issue of what to do in Iraq, the officers did not hew to the Democratic line — or the Bush line. Maj. Gen. John Batiste declared: "There is no substitute for victory and I believe we must complete what we started in Iraq and Afghanistan."

Maj. Gen. Paul Eaton said, "We need a Manhattan Project" to equip Iraqi forces with better armor and weapons and triple the U.S. training force. The U.S. Army also needs 60,000 more personnel, he said.

Col. Thomas Hammes said the United Sates actually has a good military strategy — "clear, hold and build" — but it lacks the troops and resources to accomplish it. He called for "putting the U.S. government on a war footing," with tax increases to pay for it. And, he said, success might take 10 years.

"If we fail in Iraq," he warned, "I am convinced that our children will pay for the mistake." Sectarian civil war will spread to other countries, he said, and they will send forces into Iraq to protect their interests. Sunni areas will become "Afghanistan on steroids" for terrorists. And Iran will dominate the Gulf.

Neither the Bush administration nor Congressional Democrats have the will to do what's necessary to salvage the situa-

Sweetheart Dessert
Basil Sugar Snap Peas
Steaks with Crab Sauce

Swift Skillet Fare Satisfies

DO YOU NEED to get dinner on the table fast? Don't preheat the oven so you can throw in a frozen pizza. Turn to your stovetop instead to cook this easy skillet entree that's great for busy weeknights.

"I've been making Pork Chops Italiano for more than 30 years," says Janene Christensen of Eureka, Missouri. "Children as well as adults love them."

The juicy chops are covered with a basil-seasoned tomato sauce and melted cheese. "You'll be surprised how great they taste," Janene notes. "They're so easy and so fast, too. Any cut of chop can be used...I like to use boneless."

For a speedy side dish that also cooks on the stovetop, try Noodles with Broccoli from Lesley Robeson of Warren, Pennsylvania.

"I found a recipe for a noodle and broccoli side dish, then changed it to use what I had on hand and to make it faster," she explains. "Wow, it is good!

"My husband and I have two sons, so quick kidfriendly dishes like this one are popular in our house," she says.

Warm up slices of store-bought apple pie for a comforting finish to this delicious dinner.

Pork Chops Italiano

Prep/Total Time: 25 min.

    4 bone-in pork loin chops (3/4 inch thick)
1/4 teaspoon pepper
    2 tablespoons butter
    1 can (8 ounces) tomato sauce
1/4 cup water
    1 teaspoon Italian seasoning
1/2 teaspoon dried basil
    4 slices mozzarella cheese
    1 medium green pepper, cut into rings

Sprinkle the pork chops with pepper. In a large skillet, brown the pork chops in butter on both sides; drain. Combine the tomato sauce, water, Italian seasoning and basil; pour over chops. Bring to a boil. Reduce heat; cover and simmer for 6-8 minutes or until the meat juices run clear.

Top each pork chop with cheese and green pepper. Cover and cook 3-5 minutes longer or until cheese is melted. **Yield:** 4 servings.

Noodles with Broccoli

Prep/Total Time: 20 min.

    5 cups chicken broth
    4 cups uncooked spiral pasta *or* egg noodles
    1 package (10 ounces) frozen broccoli florets
1/2 cup shredded Asiago cheese, *divided*
1/4 teaspoon salt
1/4 teaspoon garlic powder
1/2 cup butter, cubed
    2 tablespoons vegetable oil

In a large saucepan, bring broth to a boil; add pasta and broccoli. Cook, uncovered, for 5-6 minutes or until tender; drain.

In a large skillet, saute the pasta, broccoli, 1/4 cup cheese, salt and garlic powder in butter and oil. Toss until well coated. Sprinkle with remaining cheese. **Yield:** 4 servings.

Noodles with Broccoli
Pork Chops Italiano

More Pasta Pleasers

- Whenever I have leftover lasagna, I make Lasagna Soup. I just cut the leftovers into small pieces and stir them into a can of tomato soup and the same amount of milk. After heating the soup, I serve it with leftover garlic bread or garlic croutons for a complete dinner. My kids enjoy the soup more than the original lasagna! —*Bonnie Knight*
Pewaukee, Wisconsin

- After preparing a package of macaroni and cheese dinner, I like to mix in 1/2 cup chopped green pepper, 1/2 cup chopped fresh tomato and three slices of cooked and crumbled bacon. Those simple but flavorful additions really dress up the pasta and create a delicious dish. —*Millie Glick*
Montesano, Washington

Cold-Weather Comfort Food

Pecan Baked Apples
Swirled Dill Rolls
Ham with Creamed Vegetables

NOTHING SOOTHES the spirit on blustery winter days like a hot home-cooked meal. Our Test Kitchen staff put together this mouth-watering menu that you can have on the table in only minutes.

Start with a hearty skillet entree of Ham with Creamed Vegetables. It's easy to fix and chock-full of garden flavor and nutrition. Plus, it's sure to warm your family right down to their toes.

You'll need just four ingredients to bake a pan of golden-brown Swirled Dill Rolls. With their fresh-from-the-oven aroma and mild dill flavor, they complement the ham dish nicely. Or serve the rolls with most any entree.

Cooked in the microwave, Pecan Baked Apples offer a time-saving twist on tradition. They're stuffed with dried cherries, nuts and brown sugar, drizzled with their own juices and served warm for a homey, comforting dessert.

Ham with Creamed Vegetables

Prep/Total Time: 30 min.

✓ Uses less fat, sugar or salt. Includes Nutritional Analysis and Diabetic Exchanges.

- 1/4 cup *each* julienned sweet red and yellow pepper
- 1/4 cup chopped onion
- 2 tablespoons sliced celery
- 2 tablespoons chopped carrot
- 2 tablespoons butter
- 1 tablespoon all-purpose flour
- 1/8 teaspoon pepper
- 1 cup milk
- 1-1/2 teaspoons chicken bouillon granules
- 1 boneless fully cooked ham steak (1 pound)

In a large skillet, saute the peppers, onion, celery and carrot in butter for 3-4 minutes or until crisp-tender. Sprinkle with flour and pepper. Gradually whisk in milk and bouillon until smooth. Bring to a boil; cook and stir for 2 minutes or until thickened.

Cut ham steak into four pieces. Cook in a large skillet coated with nonstick cooking spray over medium heat for 2-4 minutes or until browned on both sides. Serve with vegetable mixture. **Yield:** 4 servings.

Nutritional Analysis: 1 serving (prepared with reduced-fat butter, reduced-sodium bouillon and fat-free milk) equals 251 calories, 13 g fat (5 g saturated fat), 71 mg cholesterol, 1,638 mg sodium, 10 g carbohydrate, 1 g fiber, 24 g protein. **Diabetic Exchanges:** 3 lean meat, 2 vegetable, 1 fat.

Swirled Dill Rolls

Prep/Total Time: 20 min.

- 1 tube (8 ounces) refrigerated crescent rolls
- 2 tablespoons butter, softened
- 1/4 teaspoon onion powder
- 1/4 teaspoon snipped fresh dill

Do not unroll crescent dough; cut into eight equal slices. Place the cut side down on an ungreased baking sheet. Bake at 375° for 11-13 minutes or until golden brown. Meanwhile, in a small bowl, combine the butter, onion powder and dill. Spread over warm rolls. **Yield:** 8 rolls.

Pecan Baked Apples

Prep/Total Time: 20 min.

- 1/4 cup butter, softened
- 1/4 cup chopped pecans
- 1/4 cup packed brown sugar
- 1/4 cup dried cherries
- 1/2 teaspoon ground cinnamon
- 1/8 teaspoon ground nutmeg
- 4 medium tart apples

In a small bowl, combine the first six ingredients. Core apples; fill with pecan mixture. Place in a greased 8-in. square microwave-safe dish. Microwave, uncovered, on high for 8-12 minutes or until apples are tender. Drizzle with pan juices. **Yield:** 4 servings.

Editor's Note: This recipe was tested in a 1,100-watt microwave.

Chapter 4

THINK that wholesome, delicious, home-cooked food for your family requires an endless shopping list of ingredients? Think again!

Just take a look at the rapid recipes here. Only five ingredients (not including everyday basics like salt, pepper and water) are necessary to prepare each terrific dish.

You'll be amazed at how just a handful of ingredients can yield such flavorful, satisfying fare. And your loved ones will never suspect that these tasty creations took so little time and effort to fix.

These fast foods are proof—you don't need long, complicated recipes in order to prepare family-pleasing food.

SIMPLE SENSATIONS. Frozen Orange Cream Pie, European Tossed Salad and Chicken in Baskets (all recipes on pp. 66 and 67).

Chocolate Chip Mallow Pie

Prep: 10 min. + freezing

I combine the yummy flavors of s'mores in this sweet kid-pleasing pie. I like to top each piece with mini marshmallows.　　—Jenny Bull, Highlands Ranch, Colorado

　　2 pints chocolate chip ice cream, softened
　　1 graham cracker crust (9 inches)
　　1 cup marshmallow creme
　1/3 cup hot fudge ice cream topping, warmed

Spoon ice cream into crust. Cover and freeze for at least 3 hours or until set. Remove from the freezer; spread with marshmallow creme. Let stand for 15 minutes before cutting. Drizzle with fudge topping. **Yield:** 8 servings.

Creamy Ham Fettuccine

(Pictured at right)

Prep/Total Time: 25 min.

When my husband was stationed with the Navy in Italy, we enjoyed the local cuisine. I loved the pasta and learned to make this rich dish from frequent restaurant visits. Prepare it with spinach fettuccine if it's available at your supermarket.　　—Valerie Holter, Waveland, Mississippi

　1 package (12 ounces) fettuccine
　3 cups cubed fully cooked ham
　2 cups frozen peas, thawed
　2 cups grated Parmesan cheese
　1 cup heavy whipping cream

In a large saucepan or Dutch oven, cook fettuccine according to package directions; drain. In the same pan, heat the ham; add the peas, Parmesan cheese, cream and fettuccine. Cook and stir until heated through. **Yield:** 6-8 servings.

Sour Cream Salad Dressing

(Pictured at right)

Prep/Total Time: 5 min.

This tangy dressing is easy to prepare ahead of time...or at the last minute. You can even eliminate the milk and serve the mixture as a sauce over almost any vegetable.　　—Phyllis Groves, Ukiah, California

 Uses less fat, sugar or salt. Includes Nutritional Analysis and Diabetic Exchanges.

　　1 cup (8 ounces) sour cream
　　2 tablespoons milk
　　1 tablespoon brown sugar
　　1 tablespoon cider vinegar
　1/2 teaspoon ground mustard
　1/4 to 1/2 teaspoon salt

In a bowl, combine the sour cream, milk, brown sugar, vinegar, mustard and salt. Serve immediately; refrigerate leftovers. **Yield:** about 1 cup.

Nutritional Analysis: 2 tablespoons (prepared with

Orange-Glazed Chicken Wings

Orange-Glazed Chicken Wings

(Pictured above)

Prep: 15 min. + marinating **Bake:** 1 hour

I normally don't care for wings, but after I tried this recipe that was shared by a co-worker, it changed my mind. A simple overnight marinade coats the wings to create a lovely glaze when baked. They always get compliments.　　—Holly Mann Temple, New Hampshire

　　3 pounds chicken wings
　1-1/2 cups soy sauce
　　1 cup orange juice
　　1 teaspoon garlic powder

Cut chicken wings into three sections; discard wing tips. In a large resealable plastic bag, combine the soy sauce, orange juice and garlic powder; add wings. Seal bag and turn to coat. Refrigerate overnight.

　　Drain and discard marinade. Place chicken wings in a greased foil-lined 15-in. x 10-in. x 1-in. baking pan. Bake at 350° for 1 hour or until juices run clear and glaze is set, turning twice. **Yield:** 2-1/2 dozen.

　　Editor's Note: Three pounds of uncooked chicken wing sections (wingettes) may be substituted for the whole chicken wings. Omit the first step.

reduced-fat sour cream) equals 46 calories, 2 g fat (2 g saturated fat), 9 mg cholesterol, 95 mg sodium, 4 g carbohydrate, trace fiber, 2 g protein. **Diabetic Exchange:** 1/2 fat-free milk.

Frozen Sandwich Cookies

(Pictured below)

Prep/Total Time: 30 min.

These creamy treats are a snap to make! Calling for just three ingredients, the simple but yummy cookies delight young and old alike. I always keep a batch handy in the freezer. —Mary Ann Gómez, Lombard, Illinois

1/2 cup spreadable strawberry cream cheese
1/4 cup strawberry yogurt
16 chocolate wafers

In a small mixing bowl, beat the cream cheese and yogurt until smooth. Spread on the bottoms of half of the chocolate wafers; top with remaining wafers. Place on a baking sheet. Cover and freeze for 25 minutes. Serve or wrap in plastic wrap and store in the freezer. **Yield:** 8 cookies.

Sour Cream Salad Dressing
Creamy Ham Fettuccine
Frozen Sandwich Cookies

Spinach Cheese Pinwheels
Maple Raisin Carrots
Dijon-Peach Pork Chops

Dijon-Peach Pork Chops

(Pictured above)

Prep/Total Time: 25 min.

This is a dish I invented one night when I was missing half the ingredients for the pork chop recipe I planned to make. The moist chops are swiftly simmered on the stove along with canned peaches, mustard and cloves.
—Debbie Liberton
Boerne, Texas

4 bone-in pork loin chops (1/2 inch thick)
1 can (15-1/4 ounces) sliced peaches, undrained
1/4 cup packed brown sugar
1/4 cup Dijon mustard
1/4 teaspoon ground cloves

In a large skillet coated with nonstick cooking spray, brown the pork chops over medium-high heat for 4-5 minutes on each side. Stir in the remaining ingredients. Bring to a boil. Reduce heat; cover and simmer for 10 minutes or until meat is tender. **Yield:** 4 servings.

Maple Raisin Carrots

(Pictured at left)

Prep/Total Time: 10 min.

Golden raisins are a sweet addition to this time-saving treatment for carrots. This side dish is mildly flavored with maple syrup. —Gay Duhon, Paulina, Louisiana

  2 tablespoons butter
  2 tablespoons brown sugar
  2 tablespoons maple syrup
  3 cups frozen sliced carrots
1/4 cup golden raisins
1/4 teaspoon salt
1/4 teaspoon pepper

In a large saucepan, melt the butter. Stir in the brown sugar and syrup. Cook, uncovered, over medium heat for 3-5 minutes or until thickened. Stir in the carrots and raisins. Sprinkle with salt and pepper. Cook 3-5 minutes longer or until the carrots are tender. **Yield:** 4-6 servings.

Spinach Cheese Pinwheels

(Pictured at left)

Prep/Total Time: 30 min.

Crescent roll dough hurries along these pretty pinwheels. You can prepare a plate of them in about half an hour, then serve them as appetizers or to round out a meal. —Diane Robbins, McCleary, Washington

  1 tube (8 ounces) refrigerated crescent rolls
1/3 cup spreadable garlic and herb cream cheese
  4 slices thinly sliced deli ham
1/2 cup packed fresh baby spinach

Separate crescent dough into four rectangles; seal perforations. Spread cream cheese over each rectangle to within 1/4 in. of edges; top with ham and spinach. Roll up each jelly-roll style, starting with a short side; pinch seams to seal. Cut each into six slices.

Place the slices cut side down on greased baking sheets. Bake at 400° for 8-10 minutes or until golden brown. Serve warm. Refrigerate leftovers. **Yield:** 2 dozen.

Almond Cherry Fudge

Prep: 20 min. + chilling

Cooked in the microwave, this fast fudge is a sweet addition to any holiday gathering. I make this when I need a quick treat for a school party or to take to a neighbor. —Shellie Tucker, Hendersonville, Tennessee

  2 cups (12 ounces) semisweet chocolate chips
  1 can (14 ounces) sweetened condensed milk
1/2 cup chopped almonds
1/2 cup red candied cherries, chopped
  1 teaspoon almond extract

Line an 8-in. square pan with foil and grease the foil; set aside. In a microwave-safe bowl, combine chocolate

chips and milk. Cover and microwave on high for 1 to 1-1/2 minutes or until chocolate chips are melted; stir until smooth. Stir in the almonds, candied cherries and extract. Spread into prepared pan. Cover; chill for 2 hours or until set.

Using foil, lift fudge out of pan. Discard foil; cut fudge into 1-in. squares. Store in the refrigerator. **Yield:** about 1 pound.

Editor's Note: This recipe was tested in a 1,100-watt microwave.

Ranch Potato Salad

(Pictured below)

Prep: 30 min. + chilling

I jazz up creamy potato salad with cheddar cheese, bacon and ranch salad dressing. —Lynn Breunig, Wind Lake, Wisconsin

  2 pounds red potatoes
  1 bottle (8 ounces) ranch salad dressing
  1 cup (4 ounces) shredded cheddar cheese
  1 package (2.8 ounces) real bacon bits
1/4 teaspoon pepper
Dash garlic powder

Place potatoes in a large saucepan and cover with water. Bring to a boil. Reduce heat; cover and simmer for 20-25 minutes or until tender.

In a large bowl, combine the remaining ingredients (dressing will be thick). Drain potatoes and cut into cubes; add to the dressing and gently toss to coat. Cover and refrigerate for 2 hours or until chilled. Refrigerate leftovers. **Yield:** 6-8 servings.

Ranch Potato Salad

Fiesta Ravioli

have lots of blueberries on hand, and it became an instant favorite. —*Reneé Endress, Galva, Illinois*

✓ Uses less fat, sugar or salt. Includes Nutritional Analysis and Diabetic Exchanges.

  3 cups water
  2 cups quick-cooking oats
2/3 cup sugar
1/8 teaspoon salt
  1 cup fresh *or* frozen blueberries
  2 tablespoons plus 1-1/2 teaspoons refrigerated French vanilla nondairy creamer

In a large saucepan, bring water to a boil. Stir in the oats, sugar and salt. Remove from the heat; stir in the blueberries and creamer. **Yield:** 4 servings.

Nutritional Analysis: 1 cup (prepared with sugar substitute) equals 216 calories, 4 g fat (trace saturated fat), 0 cholesterol, 80 mg sodium, 38 g carbohydrate, 5 g fiber, 6 g protein. **Diabetic Exchanges:** 2 starch, 1/2 fruit.

Chicken in Baskets

(Pictured at right and on page 60)

Prep/Total Time: 25 min.

My family loves this quick delicious meal that looks fancy. No one has to know the impressive entree starts with packaged pastry shells, canned soup and frozen chicken and vegetables. After popping the pastry shells in the oven, I prepare the quick sauce in the microwave.
  —*Cheryl Miller, Robesonia, Pennsylvania*

  1 package (10 ounces) frozen pastry shells
  1 can (10-3/4 ounces) condensed cream of chicken soup, undiluted
  1 package (9 ounces) frozen diced cooked chicken, thawed
  1 cup frozen mixed vegetables, thawed
3/4 cup milk

Bake pastry shells according to package directions. Meanwhile, in a microwave-safe bowl, combine the soup, chicken, vegetables and milk. Cover and microwave on high for 4-5 minutes or until bubbly. Cut the top off each pastry shell; fill with chicken mixture. Replace tops. **Yield:** 3 servings.

Editor's Note: This recipe was tested in a 1,100-watt microwave.

Fiesta Ravioli

(Pictured above)

Prep/Total Time: 20 min.

I adapted this recipe to suit our taste for spicy food. The ravioli taste like mini enchiladas. I serve them with a Mexican-inspired salad and pineapple sherbet for dessert.
  —*Debbie Purdue, Freeland, Michigan*

  1 package (25 ounces) frozen beef ravioli
  1 can (10 ounces) enchilada sauce
  1 jar (8 ounces) salsa
  2 cups (8 ounces) shredded Monterey Jack cheese
  1 can (2-1/4 ounces) sliced ripe olives, drained

Cook ravioli according to package directions. Meanwhile, in a large skillet, combine enchilada sauce and salsa. Cook and stir over medium heat until heated through. Drain ravioli; add to sauce. Top with cheese and olives. Cover and cook over low heat for 3-4 minutes or until cheese is melted. **Yield:** 4-6 servings.

Vanilla Blueberry Oatmeal

Prep/Total Time: 10 min.

My family loves fruity flavored oatmeals like this one for breakfast. I came up with this recipe when I happened to

European Tossed Salad

(Pictured at right and on page 61)

Prep/Total Time: 10 min.

Here's a swift salad I turn to when time is tight. The sweet dressing easily tops off packaged salad greens and grape tomatoes.   —*Rachel Rosenbaum, Brooklyn, New York*

  1 package (10 ounces) ready-to-serve European blend salad greens
1/2 cup grape tomatoes
1/2 cup mayonnaise

1 to 2 tablespoons sugar
1 to 2 tablespoons lemon juice

In a salad bowl, combine the greens and tomatoes. In a small bowl, whisk the mayonnaise, sugar and lemon juice. Pour over salad and toss to coat. **Yield:** 6-8 servings.

Frozen Orange Cream Pie

(Pictured below and on page 60)

Prep: 5 min. + freezing

Dessert doesn't get much easier than this frosty five-ingredient favorite, which offers make-ahead convenience. After a hearty diner, a slice of this citrusy pie is cool and refreshing. Both children and adults say they like it because it reminds them of a popular ice cream treat.
—*Nancy Horsburgh, Everett, Ontario*

2-1/2 cups vanilla ice cream, softened
    1 cup orange juice concentrate
    3 drops red food coloring, optional
    1 drop yellow food coloring, optional
    1 graham cracker crust (9 inches)

In a bowl, combine the ice cream and orange juice concentrate. Stir in food coloring if desired. Spoon into crust. Cover and freeze for 8 hours or overnight. Remove from the freezer 10 minutes before serving. **Yield:** 6-8 servings.

Frozen Orange Cream Pie
European Tossed Salad
Chicken in Baskets

Cream Cheese Cookie Cups
Tomato Asparagus Salad
Parmesan Orange Roughy

Parmesan Orange Roughy

(Pictured above)

Prep/Total Time: 25 min.

I've always enjoyed orange roughy. This moist, delicious dish has been a regular entree at our house.
—Laura Freeman, Ruffin, North Carolina

✓ Uses less fat, sugar or salt. Includes Nutritional Analysis and Diabetic Exchanges.

    1 egg
1/4 cup milk
    1 cup dried bread crumbs
1/3 cup grated Parmesan cheese
    4 orange roughy fillets (4 ounces *each*)

In a shallow bowl, beat the egg and milk. In another shallow bowl, combine bread crumbs and Parmesan cheese. Dip the fillets in egg mixture, then coat with crumb mixture. Place in a greased 13-in. x 9-in. x 2-in. baking dish. Bake, uncovered, at 425° for 15-20 minutes or until fish flakes easily with a fork. **Yield:** 4 servings.

    Nutritional Analysis: 1 serving (prepared with fat-free milk) equals 239 calories, 6 g fat (2 g saturated fat), 81 mg cholesterol, 451 mg sodium, 21 g carbohydrate, 1 g fiber, 25 g protein. **Diabetic Exchanges:** 3 lean meat, 1 starch.

Tomato Asparagus Salad

(Pictured above)

Prep/Total Time: 15 min.

This refreshing salad is one of the first requests from my family as soon as the spring asparagus is on the market.

With plum tomatoes and red onion, it always pleases company, too. —Lois Crissman, Mansfield, Ohio

- 3/4 **pound fresh asparagus, trimmed and cut into 1-1/2-inch pieces**
- 3 **plum tomatoes, halved and sliced**
- 3/4 **cup chopped red onion**
- 1/2 **cup balsamic vinaigrette**

Place asparagus in a steamer basket; place in a saucepan over 1 in. of water. Bring to a boil; cover and steam for 5-7 minutes or until crisp-tender. Drain and immediately place asparagus in ice water. Drain and pat dry.

In a large bowl, combine the asparagus, tomatoes and onion. Drizzle with vinaigrette and gently toss to coat. Serve with a slotted spoon. **Yield:** 4 servings.

Cream Cheese Cookie Cups

(Pictured at left)

Prep: 15 min. **Bake:** 10 min. + cooling

Need a quick dessert or party treat? Try these yummy cookie bites that start with convenient refrigerated dough. For an extra-special presentation, use an icing bag to pipe the filling into the cups. Then top each one with mini M&M candies, nuts or chocolate chips.
—Rachel Blackston, Mauk, Georgia

- 1 **tube (18 ounces) refrigerated chocolate chip cookie dough**
- 4 **ounces cream cheese, softened**
- 2 **tablespoons butter, softened**
- 1/2 **teaspoon vanilla extract**
- 1-1/4 **cups confectioners' sugar**

Cut cookie dough in half (save one portion for another use). With floured hands, press about 1 tablespoon of dough onto the bottom and up the sides of each of 12 ungreased miniature muffin cups. Bake at 350° for 8-10 minutes or until lightly browned.

Using the end of a wooden spoon handle, reshape the puffed cookie cups. Cool for 5 minutes before removing from pan to a wire rack to cool completely.

In a small mixing bowl, beat the cream cheese, butter and vanilla until blended. Gradually beat in confectioners' sugar. Spoon into cookie cups. Store in the refrigerator. **Yield:** 1 dozen.

Macadamia Coconut Bars

Prep: 10 min. **Bake:** 15 min. + cooling

These are absolutely divine. No one will believe that a packaged cookie mix is the main ingredient. Not fond of macadamia nuts? Try pecans, walnuts, almonds or cashews. —Sarah Wilkinson, Bellevue, Nebraska

- 1 **package (17-1/2 ounces) sugar cookie mix**
- 1 **cup vanilla** *or* **white chips**
- 1/2 **cup chopped macadamia nuts**
- 1/4 **cup flaked coconut**

Prepare cookie mix according to package directions. Stir in chips, nuts and coconut. Spread into a greased 13-in. x 9-in. x 2-in. baking pan. Bake at 375° for 12-15 minutes or until lightly browned around edges. Cool on a wire rack for 25 minutes before cutting. **Yield:** 3 dozen.

Finger-Lickin'-Good Shrimp

(Pictured below)

Prep: 10 min. + marinating **Grill:** 10 min.

My husband and I were vacationing in Cabo San Lucas, Mexico when we happened upon a terrific restaurant that served shrimp wrapped in bacon. Though I've changed them slightly, these delicious appetizers are enjoyed by everyone who tries them. —Sandi Solari, Manteca, California

- 12 **uncooked jumbo shrimp, peeled and deveined**
- 1/4 **cup Italian salad dressing**
- 1/4 **cup orange juice**
- 6 **bacon strips, cut in half**
- 1 **ounce pepper Jack** *or* **cheddar cheese, julienned**

Cut a small slit on the back of each shrimp, not cutting all the way through. In a large resealable plastic bag, combine the salad dressing and orange juice; add shrimp. Seal bag and turn to coat; refrigerate for 30 minutes. Meanwhile, in a skillet or microwave, cook bacon over medium heat until cooked but not crisp. Drain on paper towels.

If grilling the shrimp, coat grill rack with nonstick cooking spray. Prepare grill for indirect heat. Drain and discard marinade; place a piece of cheese in the slit of each shrimp. Wrap bacon around shrimp; secure ends with wooden toothpicks. Grill over indirect medium heat or broil 4 in. from the heat for 3 minutes on each side or until the shrimp turn pink. **Yield:** 6 servings.

Finger-Lickin'-Good Shrimp

1 can (15-1/4 ounces) sliced peaches, drained
1 package (9 ounces) yellow cake mix
1/4 cup butter, cut into 1/8-inch pieces

In a large bowl, combine the pie filling, pears and peaches; spoon into a greased 8-in. square baking dish. Sprinkle with cake mix; dot with butter. Bake at 350° for 45-50 minutes or until golden brown. Serve warm. **Yield:** 6-8 servings.

Sour Cream Oven Omelet

(Pictured below right)

Prep/Total Time: 30 min.

Prepared with flavorful ham and sour cream, this egg mixture bakes up to a fluffy finish. The recipe was handed down to me from my grandmother, who got it from her mother. After baking, serve the omelet on a warm plate alone or with applesauce. —Jennifer Holub
Clarendon Hills, Illinois

  6 eggs, *separated*
  1 cup (8 ounces) sour cream, *divided*
1/8 teaspoon pepper
1-1/4 cups chopped fully cooked ham
  2 tablespoons butter

In a mixing bowl, beat egg yolks on high speed for 3 minutes or until light and fluffy. Beat in 1/2 cup sour cream and pepper. In another mixing bowl, beat egg whites until stiff peaks form; fold into yolk mixture. Fold in ham.

In a deep ovenproof 10-in. skillet, melt the butter. Add egg mixture. Cook, uncovered, over medium-low heat for 6-8 minutes or until bottom is set (do not stir). Bake, uncovered, at 325° for 6-8 minutes or until a knife inserted near the center comes out clean. Cut omelet into wedges. Serve with the remaining sour cream. **Yield:** 4 servings.

Berry-Filled Doughnuts

Berry-Filled Doughnuts

(Pictured above)

Prep/Total Time: 25 min.

Four ingredients are all you'll need for this sure-to-be-popular treat. Friends and family will never guess that these golden jam-filled doughnuts start with a tube of refrigerated buttermilk biscuits. Vary the flavor by using different jams. —Ginny Watson, Broken Arrow, Oklahoma

4 cups vegetable oil
1 tube (7-1/2 ounces) refrigerated buttermilk biscuits, separated into 10 biscuits
3/4 cup seedless strawberry jam
1 cup confectioners' sugar

In an electric skillet or deep-fat fryer, heat oil to 375°. Fry biscuits, a few at a time, for 1-2 minutes on each side or until golden brown. Drain on paper towels.

Cut a small hole in the corner of a pastry or plastic bag; insert a very small tip. Fill bag with jam. Push the tip through the side of each doughnut to fill with jam. Dust with confectioners' sugar while warm. Serve doughnuts immediately. **Yield:** 10 servings.

Three-Fruit Dump Cake

Prep: 5 min. **Bake:** 45 min.

This down-home dessert is perfect served warm with vanilla ice cream. Just "dump" the peaches, pears and apple pie filling into a dish, top with cake mix and bake until golden. —Wendy Crochet, Houma, Louisiana

1 can (21 ounces) apple pie filling
1 can (15-1/4 ounces) sliced pears, drained

Five-Fruit Salad

(Pictured at right)

Prep/Total Time: 5 min.

I attended a brunch one summer, and when I tried this fruit salad, I had to have the recipe. I later made it for a class reunion, and everyone loved it. The colorful medley looks most impressive when served in a clear glass bowl. —Sharron Botts
Huntsville, Ohio

1-1/3 cups frozen unsweetened strawberries, thawed and halved
  1 cup fresh blueberries
  1 medium banana, sliced
3/4 cup green grapes
  1 can (21 ounces) peach pie filling

In a large bowl, combine all ingredients. Refrigerate salad until serving. **Yield:** 6 servings.

Surprise Banana Muffins

(Pictured below)

Prep/Total Time: 30 min.

I created these easy muffins after I had stocked up on too much candy and banana bread mix. My family loves the peanut butter surprise in the middle. I took these muffins to a church potluck, and they were a huge hit. If you're not a fan of banana bread, try a different quick bread mix instead. —Teresa Heavilin, Kokomo, Indiana

1 package (14 ounces) banana quick bread and muffin mix

1 cup milk
1/2 cup vegetable oil
2 eggs
12 miniature peanut butter cups

Prepare banana bread batter according to package directions, using milk, oil and eggs. Fill greased muffin cups two-thirds full. Place a peanut butter cup in the center of each; spoon remaining batter over top.

Bake at 400° for 15-20 minutes or until a toothpick inserted into muffin comes out clean. Cool 5 minutes before removing to a wire rack. **Yield:** 1 dozen.

Editor's Note: This recipe was prepared with Pillsbury banana quick bread and muffin mix.

Sour Cream Oven Omelet
Five-Fruit Salad
Surprise Banana Muffins

Cranberry Pear Tart

Cranberry Pear Tart

(Pictured above)

Prep: 15 min. **Bake:** 30 min. + cooling

Our Test Kitchen home economists came up with this yummy pear tart accented with cranberries. While it's lovely as is, it's also good served warm with ice cream.

> 1 sheet refrigerated pie pastry
> 4 cups sliced peeled fresh pears (about 4 medium)
> 1/3 cup dried cranberries
> 1/3 cup apple juice concentrate
> 1 teaspoon apple pie spice

Press pastry onto the bottom and up the sides of an ungreased 9-in. tart pan with removable bottom; trim edges. Generously prick the bottom with a fork; set aside.

In a large skillet, cook the pears, cranberries, apple juice concentrate and apple pie spice over medium heat until pears are tender. Pour into crust. Bake at 375° for 30-35 minutes or until crust is golden brown. Cool on a wire rack. **Yield:** 8-10 servings.

Warm Sweet Onion Spread

Prep: 5 min. **Cook:** 30 min.

This is such a simple appetizer, but it's one of the most delicious I've ever tasted. The rich onion mixture is terrific served with crackers or tortilla chips. —Chris Greissinger Hollis, New Hampshire

> 2 small sweet onions, chopped
> 1-1/2 cups mayonnaise

1-1/2 cups (6 ounces) shredded Swiss cheese
Assorted crackers

In a large bowl, combine the onions, mayonnaise and cheese. Spoon into an ungreased 9-in. pie plate. Bake, uncovered, at 350° for 25-30 minutes. Broil 6 in. from the heat for 2-3 minutes or until bubbly. Serve with crackers. **Yield:** about 4 cups.

Blueberry Fluff Pie

Prep: 25 min. + chilling

This light dessert is a perfect ending to a meal. The original recipe from Mom called for sliced peaches, which are also good. I have used fresh raspberries, too.
—Shirley Dierolf, Stroudsburg, Pennsylvania

> 20 large marshmallows
> 1/4 cup milk
> 4 cups fresh blueberries, *divided*
> 1 carton (8 ounces) frozen whipped topping, thawed
> 1 pastry shell (9 inches), baked

In a heavy saucepan, combine marshmallows and milk. Cook and stir over medium-low heat until marshmallows are melted and mixture is smooth. Cool for 8-10 minutes, stirring several times.

Stir in 3-1/2 cups blueberries. Set aside 1/2 cup whipped topping; fold remaining topping into blueberry mixture. Pour into crust. Refrigerate for at least 2 hours. Garnish with remaining blueberries and reserved topping. **Yield:** 8 servings.

Feta Cheese Mashed Potatoes

Prep/Total Time: 30 min.

I dress up my mashed potatoes with feta cheese and garlic. I don't peel the potatoes because my family likes the texture better, but feel free to peel them if desired.
—Jan Stone, Cincinnati, Ohio

> 5 medium Yukon Gold potatoes (about 1-1/2 pounds), unpeeled and cubed
> 4 to 6 garlic cloves, peeled
> 1 package (4 ounces) crumbled feta cheese
> 1/2 cup heavy whipping cream
> 1/4 teaspoon salt
> 1/4 teaspoon pepper

Place the potatoes and garlic in a large saucepan; cover with water. Bring to a boil over medium-high heat. Reduce heat; cover and cook for 15-20 minutes or until tender. Drain and transfer to a mixing bowl; mash. Add the feta cheese, cream, salt and pepper; beat until fluffy. **Yield:** 6 servings.

Gelatin Fruit Salad

Prep: 10 min. + chilling

I combine cherry gelatin with three pantry staples to create this sweet sensation. The no-fuss salad can be as-

sembled in just 10 minutes. Then, let it firm up in the refrigerator. —Margaret McNeil, Memphis, Tennessee

1 cup applesauce
2 packages (3 ounces *each*) cherry gelatin
1 can (12 ounces) lemon-lime soda
1 can (8 ounces) crushed pineapple, undrained

In a saucepan, bring applesauce to a boil. Remove from the heat; stir in gelatin until dissolved. Slowly add soda and pineapple. Pour into a 1-1/2-qt. serving bowl. Refrigerate until firm. **Yield:** 8 servings.

Chicken Spiral Salad

(Pictured below)

Prep/Total Time: 20 min.

My family loves this zesty salad, and they eat it so fast that it barely has time to chill in the fridge. Try serving the savory main dish over a bed of fresh torn greens.
—Cynthia Griffith, Danville, Virginia

✓ Uses less fat, sugar or salt. Includes Nutritional Analysis and Diabetic Exchanges.

1 package (7 ounces) spiral pasta
2 cans (15 ounces *each*) black beans, rinsed and drained
1 package (9 ounces) frozen diced cooked chicken breast, thawed

Butter Pecan Cookies

1 large tomato, seeded and chopped
1 cup Italian salad dressing

Cook pasta according to package directions; drain and rinse in cold water. In a large bowl, combine the beans, chicken and tomato. Add pasta. Drizzle with dressing and toss to coat. Cover and refrigerate until serving. **Yield:** 8 servings.

Nutritional Analysis: 1 cup (prepared with fat-free dressing) equals 262 calories, 3 g fat (1 g saturated fat), 29 mg cholesterol, 662 mg sodium, 38 g carbohydrate, 5 g fiber, 18 g protein. **Diabetic Exchanges:** 2-1/2 starch, 1 lean meat.

Butter Pecan Cookies

(Pictured above)

Prep/Total Time: 30 min.

These crisp shortbread-like cookies are wonderful with a cup of coffee. They're delicious and so easy to make.
—Sharon Crider, Lebanon, Missouri

3/4 cup butter, softened
1 package (3.4 ounces) instant butterscotch pudding mix
1-1/4 cups all-purpose flour
1/2 cup chopped pecans

In a small mixing bowl, cream butter and pudding mix. Gradually beat in flour. Fold in pecans. Roll into 1-1/2-in. balls. Place 2 in. apart on greased baking sheets; flatten to 1/2 in. with a greased glass. Bake at 375° for 10-13 minutes or until light golden brown. Remove to wire racks. **Yield:** about 2 dozen.

Chicken Spiral Salad

Cider Cheese Fondue

(Pictured below)

Prep/Total Time: 15 min.

Cheese lovers are sure to enjoy dipping into this creamy quick-to-fix fondue that has just a hint of apple. You can also serve this appetizer with apple or pear wedges.
—Kim Marie Van Rheenen, Mendota, Illinois

    3/4 cup apple cider *or* juice
    2 cups (8 ounces) shredded cheddar cheese
    1 cup (4 ounces) shredded Swiss cheese
    1 tablespoon cornstarch
    1/8 teaspoon pepper
    1 loaf (1 pound) French bread, cut into cubes

In a large saucepan, bring cider to a boil. Reduce heat to medium-low. Toss the cheeses with cornstarch and pepper; stir into cider. Cook and stir for 3-4 minutes or until cheese is melted. Transfer to a small ceramic fondue pot or slow cooker; keep warm. Serve with bread cubes. **Yield:** 2-2/3 cups.

Honey-Mustard Turkey Breast

(Pictured at right)

Prep: 10 min. **Bake:** 1-3/4 hours

Honey mustard adds subtle flavor to this moist roasted turkey breast from our Test Kitchen. Don't have honey mustard? Use 1/4 cup each honey and brown mustard.

Cider Cheese Fondue

    1 bone-in turkey breast (6 to 7 pounds)
    1/2 cup honey mustard
    3/4 teaspoon dried rosemary, crushed
    1/2 teaspoon onion powder
    1/4 teaspoon salt
    1/8 teaspoon garlic powder
    1/8 teaspoon pepper

Place the turkey breast in a shallow roasting pan. In a small bowl, combine the remaining ingredients. Spoon over turkey. Bake, uncovered, at 325° for 1-3/4 to 2-1/2 hours or until a meat thermometer reads 170°, basting every 30 minutes. **Yield:** 10-12 servings.

Herbed Biscuit Knots

(Pictured at right)

Prep/Total Time: 20 min.

Shape these simply seasoned biscuits into knots or twists. After baking, they can be frozen for up to 2 months. Reheat in a 350° oven for 6 to 8 minutes. —Mary Smith
Columbia, Missouri

    1 tube (12 ounces) refrigerated buttermilk
      biscuits
    1/4 cup vegetable oil
    1/2 teaspoon salt
    1/2 teaspoon garlic powder
    1/2 teaspoon Italian seasoning

Cut each biscuit in half. Roll each portion into a 6-in. rope; tie in a loose knot. Place on a greased baking sheet. Bake at 400° for 9-11 minutes or until golden brown. In a small bowl, combine the oil and seasonings; immediately brush over warm biscuits, then brush again. **Yield:** 20 rolls.

Red-Hot Gelatin Salad

(Pictured above right)

Prep: 15 min. + chilling

This is my grandma's recipe. My mother makes this salad just about every year during the holidays. It has a spicy cinnamon taste that is really good. Even my daughter, who is a picky eater, likes it.
—Paula Ptomey
Porterville, California

       1 package (3 ounces) cherry gelatin
    1-1/2 cups boiling water, *divided*
       1/4 cup red-hot candies
       1/4 cup plus 1-1/2 teaspoons cold water
         1 cup chopped green apple
         1 cup chopped celery
       1/2 cup chopped walnuts

In a small bowl, dissolve gelatin in 1 cup boiling water. In another bowl, dissolve red-hots in remaining water; stir into gelatin. Stir in cold water. Refrigerate until slightly thickened, about 1 hour.
   Fold in the apple, celery and walnuts. Pour into a 4-cup mold coated with nonstick cooking spray. Refrigerate for 2 hours or until firm. **Yield:** 6 servings.

**Red-Hot Gelatin Salad
Broccoli Casserole
Honey-Mustard Turkey Breast
Herbed Biscuit Knots**

Broccoli Casserole

(Pictured above)

Prep: 20 min. **Bake:** 35 min.

Everybody who has tried this side dish absolutely raves about it. People who don't even like broccoli ask me to make it. —Elaine Hubbard, Blakeslee, Pennsylvania

  2 **packages (16 ounces** *each***) frozen broccoli
     florets**
  1 **can (10-3/4 ounces) condensed cream of
     mushroom soup, undiluted**
  1 **cup (8 ounces) sour cream**
1-1/2 **cups (6 ounces) shredded sharp cheddar
     cheese,** *divided*
  1 **can (6 ounces) french-fried onions,** *divided*

Cook broccoli according to package directions; drain well. In a large saucepan, combine the soup, sour cream, 1 cup cheese and 1-1/4 cups onions. Cook over medi-um heat for 4-5 minutes or until heated through. Stir in the broccoli.

Pour into a greased 2-qt. baking dish. Bake, uncov-ered, at 325° for 25-30 minutes or until bubbly. Sprinkle with the remaining cheese and onions. Bake 10-15 min-utes longer or until cheese is melted. **Yield:** 6-8 servings.

Two-Ingredient Treat

Need to satisfy a chocolate craving in a hurry? Com-bine a cup of chocolate chips and 3/4 cup of chunky peanut butter. Melt the mixture in the microwave, then drop it into small circles on waxed paper. Chill them in the freezer until firm.

Eat these immediately (they'll melt if held in your hand too long), or store them in the freezer for anoth-er "emergency." —*Jane Craig, Big Bend, Wisconsin*

Cheesy Sausage Potatoes

Pineapple Carrot Salad

Prep/Total Time: 10 min.

With carrots, celery and pineapple, this medley has a crunchy texture and tangy taste, but I believe one ingredient makes the salad extra special. Dates add just the right amount of sweetness. —Ruth Noland
San Jose, California

  1 can (20 ounces) pineapple tidbits, drained
  1 package (10 ounces) julienned carrots
  1 cup sliced celery
  1 cup chopped dates
1/2 cup sour cream

In a large bowl, combine the pineapple, carrots, celery and dates. Stir in sour cream until coated. Serve immediately. Refrigerate leftovers. **Yield:** 6-7 servings.

Poached Orange Pears

Prep/Total Time: 30 min.

This dessert is very simple to prepare, but so elegant. These pears make a beautiful presentation for special occasions and are always well liked by both young and old. When I use home-canned pear halves, I cook them for only a few minutes. —Edna Lee, Greeley, Colorado

1-1/2 cups orange juice
  1/2 cup packed brown sugar
    1 cinnamon stick (3 inches)
    4 large pears, peeled, halved and cored
  1/2 cup fresh raspberries

In a large saucepan, bring the orange juice, brown sugar and cinnamon stick to a boil. Reduce heat; cook and stir over medium heat until sugar is dissolved. Add pears; cover and simmer for 15-20 minutes or until tender but firm.

Using a slotted spoon, place each pear half in a dessert dish. Garnish with raspberries. Drizzle with poaching liquid. **Yield:** 8 servings.

Cheesy Sausage Potatoes

(Pictured above)

Prep/Total Time: 25 min.

For a satisfying brunch, try these tender potato slices that are loaded with sausage and cheese. I never have to worry about leftovers with these tasty potatoes. Everyone loves them and the pan is always empty. You can also serve this as a side dish at Sunday supper or potlucks.
—Linda Hill, Marseilles, Illinois

  3 pounds potatoes, peeled and cut
    into 1/4-inch slices
  1 pound bulk pork sausage
  1 medium onion, chopped
1/4 cup butter, melted
  2 cups (8 ounces) shredded cheddar cheese

Place potatoes in a large saucepan and cover with water. Bring to a boil. Reduce heat; simmer, uncovered, for 8-10 minutes or until tender. Meanwhile, crumble sausage into a large skillet; add onion. Cook over medium heat until meat is no longer pink; drain if necessary.

Drain potatoes; arrange in an ungreased 13-in. x 9-in. x 2-in. baking dish. Drizzle with butter. Add sausage mixture and stir gently. Sprinkle with cheese. Bake, uncovered, at 350° for 5-7 minutes or until the cheese is melted. **Yield:** 6-8 servings.

Cheesy Artichoke Squares

Prep/Total Time: 25 min.

This is a wonderful appetizer that suits just about any get-together. Guests love the taste-tempting topping of cheese, artichokes and garlic on the warm squares... and you'll love how easy they are to make with convenient crescent roll dough.
—Katy Joosten, Suamico, Wisconsin

  2 cups (8 ounces) shredded mozzarella cheese
  1 carton (8 ounces) spreadable chive and
    onion cream cheese
  2 cans (14 ounces *each*) water-packed
    artichoke hearts, rinsed, drained and
    chopped
1/2 teaspoon minced garlic
  2 tubes (8 ounces *each*) refrigerated crescent
    rolls

In a small mixing bowl, beat the mozzarella cheese, cream cheese, artichokes and garlic until blended.

Unroll both tubes of crescent dough into rectangles. Place dough in an ungreased 15-in. x 10-in. x 1-in. baking pan; press onto the bottom of pan, sealing seams and perforations. Spread with artichoke mixture. Bake at 375° for 18-20 minutes or until the crust is golden brown. Cut into squares and serve warm. **Yield:** 2-1/2 dozen.

Cappuccino Chip Cupcakes

Caesar New York Strips

(Pictured below)

Prep/Total Time: 20 min.

I season New York strip steaks with a Caesar dressing mixture, then grill them for a tasty entree that's ready in minutes. As a side dish, I serve baked potatoes topped with chunky salsa and sour cream. —Melissa Morton
Philadelphia, Pennsylvania

4 tablespoons Caesar salad dressing, *divided*
2 teaspoons garlic powder
1 teaspoon salt
1 teaspoon coarsely ground pepper
2 New York strip steaks (12 ounces *each*)

In a small bowl, combine 2 tablespoons salad dressing, garlic powder, salt and pepper. Spoon over both sides of steaks. Grill, covered, over medium heat or broil 4 in. from the heat for 7-9 minutes on each side or until meat

Caesar New York Strips

reaches desired doneness (for medium-rare, a meat thermometer should read 145°; medium, 160°; well-done, 170°), basting occasionally with remaining salad dressing. Cut steaks in half to serve. **Yield:** 4 servings.

Cappuccino Chip Cupcakes

(Pictured above)

Prep/Total Time: 30 min.

With a muffin mix, vanilla chips and instant coffee granules, I can have a batch of these moist morsels ready in half an hour. Their big chocolate flavor gets a smile from everyone who tries them. —Kris Presley
Summerville, South Carolina

1 package (18-1/4 ounces) double chocolate muffin mix
1 cup water
1 egg
2 tablespoons instant coffee granules
1 teaspoon ground cinnamon
1/2 cup vanilla *or* white chips

In a large bowl, combine the muffin mix, water, egg, coffee granules and cinnamon just until moistened. Fold in chips. Fill greased muffin cups three-fourths full. Bake at 425° for 18-21 minutes or until a toothpick comes out clean. Cool for 5 minutes before removing from pan to a wire rack. **Yield:** 1 dozen.

Chapter 5

WHEN you can spare just 10 minutes to cook, it may seem that stopping at a fast food restaurant is your only option. But it's not! Serving your family homemade food is still possible thanks to the fast-as-can-be fare featured here.

You'll find everything from mouth-watering main courses and side dishes to delicious desserts and appetizers. Each rapid recipe takes only 10 minutes—or less—to prepare from start to finish.

Whether you need a lickety-split supper for your family, an after-school snack or effortless hors d'oeuvres for a dinner party, you'll have home-cooked dishes that take mere moments of your time in the kitchen but taste like you fussed.

MADE IN MOMENTS. Tilapia with Corn Salsa (p. 87), Creamy Prosciutto Pasta (p. 85), Fiery Chicken Spinach Salad (p. 83) and Mousse Tarts (p. 85).

Easy Meatballs
Pumpkin Pie Dip

Easy Meatballs

(Pictured above)

Prep/Total Time: 10 min.

Just three ingredients are needed for this speedy appetizer. These meatballs are so different from all the others... you will never carry any leftovers home. I prepared a big batch when I catered my daughter's wedding. You can also serve them over rice for a main dish.

—Christine Smoot, Childress, Texas

  24 frozen cooked Italian meatballs (1 ounce each), thawed
    1 cup barbecue sauce
 1/2 cup sweet-and-sour sauce

Place the meatballs in a 3-qt. microwave-safe dish; cover and microwave on high for 3-4 minutes or until heated through. In a small microwave-safe bowl, combine the sauces; cover and heat on high for 2-3 minutes or until heated through. Pour over the meatballs; cover and microwave on high for 1-2 minutes, stirring occasionally. **Yield:** 8 servings.

    Editor's Note: This recipe was tested in a 1,100-watt microwave.

Pumpkin Pie Dip

(Pictured above)

Prep/Total Time: 10 min.

I came up with this rich creamy dip when I had a small amount of canned pumpkin left in the refrigerator after I finished all of my holiday baking. The dip is also great with sliced pears and apples or spread on zucchini bread or any nut bread.

—Laurie LaClair
North Richland Hills, Texas

    1 package (8 ounces) cream cheese, softened
    2 cups confectioners' sugar
    1 cup canned pumpkin
 1/2 cup sour cream
    1 teaspoon ground cinnamon
    1 teaspoon pumpkin pie spice
 1/2 teaspoon ground ginger
Gingersnap cookies

In a large mixing bowl, beat the cream cheese and confectioners' sugar until smooth. Gradually add the pumpkin, sour cream, cinnamon, pumpkin pie spice and ginger; beat until smooth. Serve with gingersnaps. Refrigerate leftovers. **Yield:** 4 cups.

Chicken Salad Melts

Prep/Total Time: 10 min.

I use up leftover chicken to create a creamy spread for open-faced sandwiches. They're delicious, satisfying and inexpensive. You can also tuck the filling into buns, wrap them in foil and heat them in the oven for a few minutes. —Ruth Peterson, Jenison, Michigan

1-1/2 cups finely chopped cooked chicken
1/2 cup mayonnaise
4 ounces process cheese (Velveeta), cubed
2 tablespoons *each* chopped green pepper, onion and ripe olives
2 tablespoons sweet pickle relish
4 sandwich rolls

In a bowl, combine the chicken, mayonnaise, cheese, green pepper, onion, olives and relish. Split rolls in half; place cut side up on a greased baking sheet. Spoon about 1/4 cup chicken salad on each roll half. Broil 4 in. from the heat for 5-6 minutes or until cheese is melted. **Yield:** 4 servings.

Roast Beef Barbecue

Fast Vegetable Soup

(Pictured below)

Prep/Total Time: 10 min.

I dress up canned minestrone to make this shortcut soup that's loaded with colorful vegetables. Serve bowls with a sandwich or salad for a satisfying yet super-fast meal. —Jennifer Shields, Chesnee, South Carolina

1 can (19 ounces) ready-to-serve minestrone soup
1 package (16 ounces) frozen mixed vegetables
1 can (15-1/4 ounces) whole kernel corn, drained

Fast Vegetable Soup

1 can (15 ounces) black beans, rinsed and drained
1 can (14-1/2 ounces) Italian diced tomatoes, undrained

Combine all ingredients in a 2-1/2-qt. microwave-safe bowl. Cover; microwave on high for 8-10 minutes, stirring twice. **Yield:** 9 servings.

Editor's Note: This recipe was tested in a 1,100-watt microwave.

Roast Beef Barbecue

(Pictured above)

Prep/Total Time: 10 min.

When I'm in a hurry and want something good, this sandwich fills the bill. It tastes great with a salad and pork and beans on the side. Instead of using ketchup, I occasionally use barbecue sauce with a little Tabasco for extra zip. —Agnes Ward, Stratford, Ontario

2/3 pound thinly sliced deli roast beef
1/2 cup water
1/4 cup ketchup
1 tablespoon brown sugar
1/2 teaspoon prepared mustard
1/4 teaspoon hot pepper sauce
1/8 teaspoon salt
1/8 teaspoon pepper
1/8 teaspoon chili powder
4 hamburger buns, split

In a small saucepan, combine the first nine ingredients. Cook over medium-high heat for 4-6 minutes or until heated through. Serve on buns, using a slotted spoon. **Yield:** 4 servings.

Pea Salad

Prep/Total Time: 10 min.

You'll need just five ingredients for this cool salad that's nicely sized for two people. I like trying new recipes, and when I found this salad, I loved it. It's really nice on those hot summer days.
—*Katie Anderson*
Cheney, Washington

1-1/2 cups frozen peas, thawed
1/2 cup shredded cheddar cheese
2 tablespoons finely chopped onion
1/4 cup mayonnaise
1-1/2 teaspoons prepared mustard

In a bowl, combine the peas, cheese and onion. Stir in the mayonnaise and mustard. Cover and refrigerate until serving. **Yield:** 2 servings.

Spicy Cashews

(Pictured below)

Prep/Total Time: 10 min.

These seasoned nuts are so good, it's hard to stop eating them. I made them for gift baskets and got many compliments. They are perfect for the holidays but delicious to munch anytime. Package them in a festive tin to give as a hostess gift.
—*Jean Voan, Shepherd, Texas*

2 cans (10 ounces *each*) salted cashews
3 tablespoons butter
1 tablespoon vegetable oil
1/2 teaspoon salt

1/2 teaspoon chili powder
1/4 to 1/2 teaspoon crushed red pepper flakes

In a large skillet, saute cashews in butter and oil for 4-5 minutes or until golden brown. Spread on a paper towel-lined baking sheet; let stand for 2-3 minutes. Transfer to a large bowl. Sprinkle with salt, chili powder and pepper flakes; toss to coat. Store in an airtight container. **Yield:** 2-2/3 cups.

Rocky Ford Chili

Prep/Total Time: 10 min.

When my brother and sister were in grade school in little Rocky Ford, Colorado, this comforting chili dish was served in the school cafeteria. My siblings described it to my mother so she could duplicate it at home. We all enjoy preparing it for our own families now.
—*Karen Golden, Phoenix, Arizona*

2 cans (14.3 ounces *each*) chili with beans
1 package (10 ounces) frozen corn
4 cups corn chips
1 cup shredded lettuce
1 cup (4 ounces) shredded Mexican cheese blend
1 can (2-1/4 ounces) sliced ripe olives, drained
1/4 cup sour cream
1/4 cup salsa

In a large microwave-safe bowl, heat chili and corn on high for 2-4 minutes or until heated through. Place corn chips in four large soup bowls; top with the chili mixture, lettuce, cheese, olives, sour cream and salsa. **Yield:** 4 servings.

Editor's Note: This recipe was tested in a 1,100-watt microwave.

Chicken Rice Bowl

Prep/Total Time: 10 min.

This is so easy to toss together on a busy weeknight, and I usually have the ingredients on hand. I start sauteing the onion and pepper first, then I prepare the instant rice.
—*Tammy Daniels, Batavia, Ohio*

1 cup uncooked instant rice
1 cup chicken broth
1/2 cup chopped frozen green pepper, thawed
1/4 cup chopped onion
2 teaspoons olive oil
1 package (9 ounces) ready-to-serve grilled chicken breast strips
1/2 cup frozen corn, thawed
1/2 cup frozen peas, thawed
1 teaspoon dried basil
1 teaspoon rubbed sage
1/8 teaspoon salt
1/8 teaspoon pepper

Cook rice according to package directions using broth instead of water. Meanwhile, in a large skillet, saute the green pepper and onion in oil for 2-3 minutes or until

Spicy Cashews

Loaded Tortillas

black beans, Mexicorn and packaged breaded chicken breast strips. No one can believe it takes just 10 minutes! I sometimes add a can of ripe olives and fresh-picked cherry tomatoes from our garden. —*Kati Spencer* *Taylorsville, Utah*

  6 frozen breaded spicy chicken breast strips
  1 package (6 ounces) fresh baby spinach
  1 medium tomato, cut into 12 wedges
1/2 cup chopped green pepper
1/2 cup fresh baby carrots
  1 can (15 ounces) black beans, rinsed and drained
  1 can (11 ounces) Mexicorn, drained
  3 tablespoons salsa
  3 tablespoons barbecue sauce
  3 tablespoons prepared ranch salad dressing
  2 tablespoons shredded Mexican cheese blend

Heat chicken strips in a microwave according to package directions. Meanwhile, arrange the spinach on individual plates; top with tomato, green pepper, carrots, beans and corn.

In a small bowl, combine the salsa, barbecue sauce and ranch dressing. Place chicken over salads. Drizzle with dressing; sprinkle with cheese. **Yield:** 6 servings.

Editor's Note: This recipe was tested in a 1,100-watt microwave.

crisp-tender. Stir in chicken, corn, peas, basil and sage.

Cook, uncovered, for 4-5 minutes over medium heat or until heated through. Stir in the rice, salt and pepper. **Yield:** 4 servings.

Loaded Tortillas

(Pictured above)

Prep/Total Time: 10 min.

My husband and daughter love these "broiler pizzas." The recipe serves two, but you can easily increase the ingredients to make more. —*Terri Keeney, Greeley, Colorado*

  2 flour tortillas (7 inches)
1/2 cup refried beans
1/2 cup salsa
1/2 cup shredded mozzarella cheese
1/2 cup shredded cheddar cheese
1/3 cup real bacon bits
1/4 cup chopped tomato
1/4 cup chopped green onions

Place tortillas on an ungreased baking sheet. Spread with beans and salsa. Top with cheeses, bacon and tomato. Broil 4 in. from the heat for 4-6 minutes or until cheese is melted and edges of tortillas are lightly browned. Sprinkle with onions. **Yield:** 2 servings.

Fiery Chicken Spinach Salad

(Pictured at right and on page 78)

Prep/Total Time: 10 min.

This hearty and colorful main-course salad is easy to make when I get home from work because it uses canned

Fiery Chicken Spinach Salad

BLT Salad
Split-Second Shrimp

Split-Second Shrimp

(Pictured above)

Prep/Total Time: 10 min.

I use my microwave to hurry along preparation of this super-fast shrimp scampi that's buttery and full of garlic flavor. Serve it as an elegant entree or special-occasion appetizer. —Jalayne Luckett, Marion, Illinois

✓ Uses less fat, sugar or salt. Includes Nutritional Analysis and Diabetic Exchanges.

        2 tablespoons butter
    1-1/2 teaspoons minced garlic
      1/8 to 1/4 teaspoon cayenne pepper
        2 tablespoons white wine *or* chicken broth
        5 teaspoons lemon Juice
        1 tablespoon minced fresh parsley
      1/2 teaspoon salt
        1 pound uncooked large shrimp, peeled and deveined

In a 9-in. microwave-safe pie plate, combine the butter, garlic and cayenne. Cover and cook on high for 1 minute or until butter is melted. Stir in the wine or broth, lemon juice, parsley and salt. Add shrimp; toss to coat. Cover and cook on high for 2-1/2 to 3-1/2 minutes or until shrimp turn pink, rotating once. Stir before serving. **Yield:** 6 servings.

   Nutritional Analysis: 1 serving (prepared with reduced-fat butter) equals 79 calories, 3 g fat (2 g saturated fat), 119 mg cholesterol, 349 mg sodium, 1 g carbohydrate, trace fiber, 12 g protein. **Diabetic Exchange:** 2 very lean meat.

   Editor's Note: This recipe was tested in a 1,100-watt microwave.

BLT Salad

(Pictured above)

Prep/Total Time: 10 min.

My husband and I love BLT sandwiches, especially in the summer when tomatoes are fresh and plentiful. This salad showcases the flavors of that classic sandwich easily and deliciously. —Deborah Heatwole
Waynesboro, Georgia

4 bacon strips, diced
4 cups spring mix salad greens
1 medium tomato, chopped
1/2 cup cubed cheddar cheese
1/3 cup mayonnaise
1 to 2 tablespoons sugar
2 teaspoons cider vinegar
Salt and pepper to taste
1/2 cup salad croutons

In a skillet or microwave, cook bacon until crisp. Drain on paper towels. In a salad bowl, combine the greens, tomato and cheese. In a small bowl, combine the mayonnaise, sugar, vinegar, salt and pepper. Pour over salad; toss to coat. Sprinkle with bacon and croutons. **Yield:** 4 servings.

Mousse Tarts

(Pictured below and on page 78)

Prep/Total Time: 10 min.

Rich white chocolate and whipped cream combine in these fast-to-fix berry-topped treats. Although the tarts originally called for dark chocolate, I prepare them with white chocolate. I double the recipe when I'm asked to bring a dessert to special events. —Angela Lively
Cookeville, Tennessee

3 squares (1 ounce *each*) white baking
   chocolate
1 cup heavy whipping cream
1/2 cup sweetened condensed milk
1/4 teaspoon vanilla extract
6 individual graham cracker tart shells
18 fresh raspberries
6 mint sprigs

Creamy Prosciutto Pasta

In a microwave-safe bowl, melt white chocolate at 30% power for 2-4 minutes, stirring every 30 seconds. Cool for 1 minute, stirring several times.

Meanwhile, in a small mixing bowl, beat cream until stiff peaks form; set aside.

In another mixing bowl, combine the milk, vanilla and melted chocolate. Add half of the whipped cream; beat on low speed just until combined. Fold in remaining whipped cream. Spoon into tart shells. Garnish with raspberries and mint. **Yield:** 6 servings.

Creamy Prosciutto Pasta

(Pictured above and on page 79)

Prep/Total Time: 10 min.

I'm always looking for dinners that I can put together quickly. I re-created a favorite pasta dish from an Italian restaurant by using grocery store convenience products. Add crusty bread and a salad for a complete meal.
—Christina Ward, Austin, Texas

1 package (9 ounces) refrigerated fettuccine *or*
   linguine
1/2 pound sliced fresh mushrooms
1 small onion, chopped
1 tablespoon butter
1 package (10 ounces) fresh baby spinach
1 jar (17 ounces) Alfredo sauce
1/3 pound thinly sliced prosciutto, chopped

Cook pasta according to package directions. Meanwhile, in a large saucepan, saute the mushrooms and onion in butter until tender. Add spinach. Bring to a boil. Reduce heat; cook just until the spinach is wilted.

Add Alfredo sauce and prosciutto; cook for 1-2 minutes or until heated through. Drain pasta; add to sauce and toss to coat. **Yield:** 4 servings.

Mousse Tarts

Mandarin-Nut Tossed Salad

Prep/Total Time: 10 min.

With my busy schedule, I have to cook fast dishes. Even picky eaters like this speedy salad. —Barbara Gibney
Lillian, Alabama

 Uses less fat, sugar or salt. Includes Nutritional Analysis and Diabetic Exchanges.

    1 package (16 ounces) ready-to-serve salad greens
    1 can (11 ounces) mandarin oranges, drained
3/4 cup chopped salted peanuts
1/2 to 2/3 cup Italian salad dressing
    1 tablespoon reduced-sodium soy sauce

In a bowl, combine the salad greens and oranges. Sprinkle with the peanuts. Combine the salad dressing and soy sauce; drizzle over salad and toss to coat. **Yield:** 12 servings.

    Nutritional Analysis: 3/4 cup (prepared with fat-free dressing) equals 78 calories, 5 g fat (1 g saturated fat), trace cholesterol, 242 mg sodium, 7 g carbohydrate, 2 g fiber, 3 g protein. **Diabetic Exchanges:** 1 fat, 1/2 fruit.

Granola Trail Mix

(Pictured below)

Prep/Total Time: 5 min.

*My family has always enjoyed this crunchy four-ingredient snack. When we go camping, each person includes one ad-*ditional ingredient like mini marshmallows, corn chips or cookie pieces. The taste is never the same, and we're often surprised by the combinations.* —Shelley Riddlespurger
Amarillo, Texas

    1 package (16 ounces) banana-nut granola
    1 package (15 ounces) raisins
    1 package (14 ounces) milk chocolate M&M's
    1 can (12 ounces) honey roasted peanuts

In a large bowl, combine all of the ingredients. Store in an airtight container. **Yield:** 11 cups.

Granola Trail Mix

Dried Beef Cheese Spread

Prep/Total Time: 10 min.

 *A friend shared this thick cracker spread with my sister a while ago, and we all agree it's delicious. People just can't stop munching when this appetizer is on the table. Be ready to hand out the recipe whenever you make it.* —Laura Martin
Indianapolis, Indiana

    3 packages (8 ounces *each*) cream cheese, softened
2-1/2 teaspoons lemon juice
1-1/2 teaspoons garlic powder
    1 jar (5 ounces) dried beef, finely chopped
    4 green onions, chopped
Assorted crackers

In a small mixing bowl, beat the cream cheese, lemon juice and garlic powder until smooth. Beat in the chopped beef and onions. Serve with assorted crackers. **Yield:** about 3-1/2 cups.

Toasty Egg Sandwiches

Prep/Total Time: 10 min.

When I'm running late, these five-ingredient sandwiches make dinner easy and tasty for everyone. Both my son and daughter often request them—even on lazy days when I have time to spare in the kitchen. I serve fresh fruit and potato chips alongside to create a satisfying meal.
—Denise Helms, Glenview, Illinois

    2 tablespoons butter, softened, *divided*
    2 eggs
    4 slices bread
    2 teaspoons mayonnaise
    2 slices American cheese

In a small skillet, heat 1 tablespoon butter until melted. Break each egg into skillet; reduce heat to low. Cook until white is completely set and yolk begins to thicken but is not hard.

    Meanwhile, toast the bread. Spread the remaining butter over one side of each slice of bread. Spread mayonnaise over buttered side of two bread slices; top with cheese slices, eggs and remaining bread. **Yield:** 2 servings.

Pecan Spinach Salad

Tilapia with Corn Salsa

(Pictured below and on page 79)

Prep/Total Time: 10 min.

My family loves fish, and this super-fast and delicious dish is very popular at my house. Though it tastes like it takes a long time, it cooks in minutes under the broiler. We like it garnished with lemon wedges with couscous on the side. —Brenda Coffey, Singer Island, Florida

    4 tilapia fillets (6 ounces *each*)
    1 tablespoon olive oil
    1/4 teaspoon salt
    1/4 teaspoon pepper
    1 can (15 ounces) black beans, rinsed and
      drained
    1 can (11 ounces) whole kernel corn, drained
    3/4 cup Italian salad dressing
    2 tablespoons chopped green onion
    2 tablespoons chopped sweet red pepper

Brush both sides of the fish fillets with oil; sprinkle with salt and pepper. Place on a broiler pan. Broil 4-6 in. from the heat for 5-7 minutes or until the fish is completely opaque and firm.

Meanwhile, in a bowl, combine the remaining ingredients. Serve with the fish. **Yield:** 4 servings.

Pecan Spinach Salad

(Pictured above)

Prep/Total Time: 10 min.

My family thinks this refreshing salad is sensational. Coated with a pleasant vinaigrette and topped with toasted pecans and blue cheese, it has an impressive look and taste. Though it can be prepared in 10 minutes or less, don't tell my family because they'd never believe it!
—Karen Robinson, Calgary, Alberta

    3 cups fresh baby spinach
    1/2 cup chopped pecans, toasted
    1/3 cup real bacon bits
    1/4 cup crumbled blue cheese
DRESSING:
    1/3 cup olive oil
    2 tablespoons cider vinegar
    2 teaspoons brown sugar
    1/2 teaspoon dried thyme
    1/2 teaspoon minced garlic
    1/4 teaspoon salt

In a large salad bowl, combine the spinach, pecans, bacon and blue cheese. In a jar with a tight-fitting lid, combine the dressing ingredients; shake well. Drizzle over salad and toss to coat. **Yield:** 4 servings.

Tilapia with Corn Salsa

Green Chili Tomato Soup
Two-Tone Grilled Cheese

Green Chili Tomato Soup

(Pictured at left)

Prep/Total Time: 10 min.

I found an easy way to jazz up canned tomato soup. I created this recipe after eating some tangy tomato soup in a restaurant. They wouldn't divulge the ingredients, so after a few tries, I came up with this version. With only four ingredients, it's so simple and very tasty.
—Chris Christopher, Albuquerque, New Mexico

  1 can (10-3/4 ounces) condensed tomato
    soup, undiluted
3/4 cup milk
  1 can (4 ounces) chopped green chilies
1/2 cup shredded cheddar cheese

In a small saucepan, combine the soup, milk and chilies until blended. Cook and stir over medium heat until heated through. Sprinkle with cheese. **Yield:** 2 servings.

Pizza Quesadillas

Prep/Total Time: 10 min.

When my husband and I needed a quick meal, I fixed this using leftover ingredients. Unlike traditional Mexican quesadillas, it calls for Italian meats, cheeses and seasonings. Serve it with a green salad topped with Italian dressing for a simple dinner for two.
—Barbara Rupert
Edgefield, South Carolina

  1 cup meatless spaghetti sauce
  2 teaspoons butter, softened
  4 flour tortillas (10 inches)
  1 cup (4 ounces) shredded mozzarella cheese
  8 thin slices hard salami
  4 slices pepperoni
1/4 cup shredded Parmesan cheese
1/2 teaspoon dried oregano

In a small saucepan, cook the spaghetti sauce over medium-low heat for 3-4 minutes or until heated through.

Meanwhile, spread butter over one side of each tortilla. Sprinkle unbuttered side of two tortillas with mozzarella cheese; top with salami and pepperoni. Sprinkle with Parmesan cheese and oregano. Top with remaining tortillas, buttered side up.

Cook on a griddle over medium heat for 2-3 minutes on each side or until cheese is melted. Cut into wedges and serve with warmed spaghetti sauce. **Yield:** 2 servings.

Two-Tone Grilled Cheese

(Pictured above)

Prep/Total Time: 10 min.

My family loves these fast-to-fix sandwiches that I make with two kinds of bread and two kinds of cheese. I serve them with tomato-vegetable soup and milk for a wholesome nutritious meal.
—Rhonda Beckett
Independence, Missouri

2 to 4 tablespoons butter, softened
4 slices whole wheat bread
2 to 4 tablespoons mayonnaise
4 slices white bread
4 slices process American cheese
4 slices Swiss cheese

Spread desired amount of butter over one side of each slice of whole wheat bread. Spread mayonnaise over one side of each slice of white bread. Place whole wheat bread, buttered side down, on a hot griddle. Layer with American and Swiss cheese; top with white bread, mayonnaise side up. Cook until golden brown on both sides. **Yield:** 4 servings.

Buffalo Chicken Sandwiches

(Pictured at right)

Prep/Total Time: 10 min.

This is a simple way to dress up breaded chicken patties. We like these sandwiches with additional blue cheese dressing for dipping. Or try them with Monterey Jack cheese and ranch dressing instead.
—Dawn Onuffer
Crestview, Florida

2 refrigerated breaded chicken patties
1/4 cup Louisiana-style hot sauce
2 teaspoons vegetable oil
2 tablespoons butter, softened
2 sandwich buns, split
2 slices provolone cheese
2 tablespoons blue cheese salad dressing
Lettuce, tomato and red onion slices
Additional hot sauce

Place chicken patties in a large resealable plastic bag; add hot sauce. Seal bag and turn to coat. In a large skillet, brown patties in oil over medium heat for 1-2 minutes on each side or until heated through. Remove and keep warm.

Spread butter over cut sides of buns. In the same skillet, toast buns, buttered side down, over medium heat for 1-2 minutes or until lightly browned. Top each with a chicken patty, provolone cheese, salad dressing, lettuce, tomato and onion. Serve with additional hot sauce. **Yield:** 2 servings.

Editor's Note: This recipe was prepared with Frank's Hot Pepper Sauce.

Garbanzo Bean Medley

Garbanzo Bean Medley

(Pictured above right)

Prep/Total Time: 10 min.

I'm a vegetarian looking for tasty dishes without meat. This Italian bean recipe is fast, flavorful and filling. I serve it as a side dish, but it's good as a main course as well. Sprinkle feta cheese on top for a change of pace.
—Denise Neal, Yorba Linda, California

✓ Uses less fat, sugar or salt. Includes Nutritional Analysis and Diabetic Exchanges.

1 small zucchini, cubed
1 teaspoon olive oil
2 teaspoons minced garlic
1 can (15 ounces) garbanzo beans or chickpeas, rinsed and drained
1 can (14-1/2 ounces) diced tomatoes, undrained
1 teaspoon Italian seasoning
1/4 teaspoon crushed red pepper flakes, optional
1/4 cup shredded Parmesan cheese

In a small skillet, saute zucchini in oil until tender. Add garlic; saute 1 minute longer. Stir in the garbanzo beans, tomatoes, Italian seasoning and pepper flakes if desired; heat through. Sprinkle with Parmesan cheese. **Yield:** 4 servings.

Nutritional Analysis: 3/4 cup equals 157 calories, 5 g fat (1 g saturated fat), 4 mg cholesterol, 354 mg sodium, 23 g carbohydrate, 6 g fiber, 7 g protein. **Diabetic Exchanges:** 1 starch, 1 lean meat, 1 vegetable.

Buffalo Chicken Sandwiches

Finding Red Pepper Flakes

WITH so many types of red pepper and differing product labels, it can be difficult to know if you're using the right ingredient when a recipe calls for red pepper flakes. When *Quick Cooking* recipes call for crushed red pepper flakes, we're referring to crushed red pepper.

Proceed with caution when using a new jar of crushed red pepper flakes, because the heat level can vary depending on the brand you purchase.

Chapter 6

⏱ *What's in Store?*

TOO RUSHED to cook? Let the convenience products found in your local grocery store do most of the work for you!

Today's supermarkets carry a wide variety of handy packaged mixes, canned goods, frozen foods, cooked meats and other helpful items. When you use them in recipes, you have a built-in "shortcut."

The delicious dishes here take advantage of those products to speed up preparation...without sacrificing all the made-from-scratch flavor that your loved ones crave.

With some savvy shopping at the market, you'll be well on your way to quickly preparing main dishes, treats and more.

MARKET MAINSTAYS. Rustic Vegetarian Pizza (p. 96) and Creamy Peach Pudding (p. 92).

Open-Faced Beef Sandwiches

Prep/Total Time: 15 min.

As a working mom, I'm always looking for a quick meal. I make these sandwiches when I'm in a particular hurry.
—Christine Weimar, New Britain, Pennsylvania

1/2 cup chopped onion
1/2 teaspoon minced garlic
1 tablespoon butter
1 pound thinly sliced deli roast beef
1 jar (12 ounces) beef gravy
6 slices Italian bread (1 inch thick), toasted
1 tablespoon prepared horseradish
6 slices provolone cheese

In a large skillet, saute the onion and garlic in butter until tender. Add the beef and gravy; cook and stir until heated through.

Place bread on an ungreased baking sheet. Spread each with horseradish and top with beef mixture and cheese. Broil 4 in. from the heat for 1-2 minutes or until cheese is melted. **Yield:** 6 servings.

Creamy Peach Pudding

(Pictured on page 90)

Prep/Total Time: 20 min.

Instant pudding hurries along preparation of this fruity pudding. Pretty and refreshing, it's a great dish to take to wedding showers, baby showers or graduation parties. I like to make it ahead of time and chill it for several hours before serving. —Tori Krick, Tilden, Nebraska

1 cup uncooked acini de pepe *or* orzo pasta
1 can (29 ounces) sliced peaches
1-3/4 cups cold milk
1 package (3.4 ounces) instant vanilla pudding mix
1/4 cup sugar
3 cups miniature marshmallows
2 cups whipped topping

Cook pasta according to package directions; drain and rinse in cold water. Drain peaches, reserving 1/4 cup syrup; set peaches aside. In a bowl, whisk the milk, pudding mix, sugar and reserved syrup for 2 minutes. Stir in peaches and pasta. Fold in the marshmallows and whipped topping. Cover and refrigerate until serving. **Yield:** 9 servings.

Shrimp and Ham Alfredo

Shrimp and Ham Alfredo

(Pictured above)

Prep/Total Time: 20 min.

This fast dinner for two is one of my favorites and is a simple way to dress up a boxed pasta mix. While it's cooking, I toast garlic bread and warm up some green beans. It's a great meal that always satisfies. —Cindy Preston Benkelman, Nebraska

1 package (4.7 ounces) fettuccine noodles and Alfredo sauce mix
10 frozen peeled cooked medium shrimp, thawed
1/2 cup cubed fully cooked ham (1/2-inch pieces)
1/4 teaspoon garlic powder
Dash cayenne pepper
1 green onion, chopped

In a large saucepan, prepare noodles and sauce mix according to package directions. Stir in the shrimp, ham, garlic powder and cayenne; heat through. Sprinkle with onion. **Yield:** 2 servings.

Italian Dipping Sticks

Prep/Total Time: 25 min.

This is a favorite snack in our house during the Super Bowl and for munching the rest of the year, too.
—Michelle Revelle, Guyton, Georgia

1 tube (11 ounces) refrigerated breadsticks
1/4 cup grated Parmesan cheese
1/2 teaspoon Italian seasoning

1 cup pizza sauce
1/4 cup shredded mozzarella cheese

Unroll breadstick dough; cut each piece in half width-wise and separate. In a large resealable plastic bag, combine Parmesan cheese and Italian seasoning. Add dough pieces, a few at a time, and shake to coat. Place on an ungreased baking sheet. Bake at 375° for 10-13 minutes or until golden brown.

Meanwhile, place the pizza sauce in a microwave-safe bowl. Cover; microwave on high for 1-2 minutes or until bubbly. Sprinkle with the mozzarella cheese. Microwave 1 minute longer or until cheese is melted. Serve with breadsticks. **Yield:** 2 dozen.

Editor's Note: This recipe was tested in a 1,100-watt microwave.

Snowman Sugar Cookies

(Pictured below)

Prep: 30 min. **Bake:** 10 min. + cooling

Store-bought dough speeds up the preparation time of these cute cookies. They're so easy that the whole family—even young children—can help decorate them with candy.
—*Jean Wardrip Burr, Hope Mills, North Carolina*

1 tube (18 ounces) refrigerated sugar cookie dough
1/2 cup shortening
1/2 cup butter, softened
4 cups confectioners' sugar
1 tablespoon milk
1 teaspoon vanilla extract
48 miniature semisweet chocolate chips
24 candy corn candies
1/2 cup red-hot candies

Cut the sugar cookie dough into 1/4-in. slices. Place the slices 2 in. apart on ungreased baking sheets. Bake at 350° for 8-12 minutes or until the edges are lightly browned. Cool for 2 minutes before removing to wire racks to cool completely.

For the frosting, in a small mixing bowl, cream the shortening and butter. Gradually beat in the confectioners' sugar. Beat in the milk and vanilla until smooth. Spread the frosting over cookies. Decorate the cookies with the chocolate chips, candy corn and red-hot candies. **Yield:** 2 dozen.

Snowman Sugar Cookies

Meat Loaf Pie

(Pictured below)

Prep: 25 min. **Bake:** 40 min.

I easily whip up this meaty pie with instant mashed potatoes, which cuts down the prep time but not the taste. The recipe is very fast and easy to put together. It's been a family favorite since 1969 and remains my children's most-asked-for meat loaf.
—Juanita Rocha
San Angelo, Texas

    2 eggs
    1 cup milk
1-3/4 cups soft bread crumbs
  1/4 cup chopped onion
    1 teaspoon salt
  1/2 teaspoon rubbed sage
  1/4 teaspoon pepper
1-1/2 pounds ground beef
    1 envelope butter and herb instant mashed
      potatoes
    1 teaspoon prepared mustard
  1/2 cup shredded cheddar cheese

In a large bowl, combine the first seven ingredients. Crumble beef over mixture and mix well. Press onto the bottom and up the sides of an ungreased deep-dish 9-in. pie plate. Bake at 350° for 35-40 minutes or until meat is no longer pink.

Meanwhile, prepare mashed potatoes according to package directions; stir in mustard. Drain meat loaf; spread potatoes over top. Sprinkle with cheese. Bake 3-5 minutes longer or until cheese is melted. Let stand for 5 minutes before cutting. **Yield:** 6 servings.

Editor's Note: This recipe was tested with Betty Crocker Butter and Herb instant mashed potatoes. You may substitute 4-1/2 cups hot mashed potatoes, prepared with milk and butter.

Seafood Pitas

Prep/Total Time: 15 min.

I first prepared these sandwiches when I had to put together a quick lunch for guests and was busy until the last minute. I served them with bowls of nicely seasoned tomato soup and received warm compliments.
—Judy Mynsberge
Flushing, Michigan

1 can (7-1/2 ounces) salmon, drained, bones
  and skin removed
1 can (6 ounces) crabmeat, drained, flaked
  and cartilage removed
1 can (4 ounces) shrimp, rinsed and drained *or*
  1 cup frozen cooked small shrimp
3/4 cup mayonnaise
1/4 cup finely chopped celery
1/4 cup finely chopped onion

Meat Loaf Pie

Pastel Gelatin Salad

1 teaspoon dill weed
3 pita breads (6 inches), halved
3 lettuce leaves

In a bowl, combine the salmon, crab, shrimp, mayonnaise, celery, onion and dill. Line each pita half with lettuce; fill with seafood mixture. **Yield:** 3 servings.

Vermicelli Chicken Salad

Prep: 25 min. + chilling

This recipe was given to me by a friend, and it's wonderful! Marinated artichokes and ripe olives lend flavor to this chilled rice salad that starts with a packaged rice mix.
—Liz Hughes, Burnsville, Minnesota

1 package (6.9 ounces) chicken-flavored rice and vermicelli mix
2 cups cubed cooked chicken breast
1-1/2 cups mayonnaise
1 jar (6-1/2 ounces) marinated artichoke hearts, drained and chopped
1/2 cup finely chopped onion
1 can (2-1/4 ounces) sliced ripe olives, drained
1/2 teaspoon lemon-pepper seasoning

Cook rice mix according to package directions. Stir in chicken, mayonnaise, artichokes, onion, olives and lemon-pepper. Cover and refrigerate until chilled. **Yield:** 8 servings.

Pastel Gelatin Salad

(Pictured above)

Prep: 25 min. + chilling

I top this gelatin salad with pretty pastel mini marshmallows to add color to holiday menus. With its creamy lemon-lime base and tangy pineapple flavor, it's a tasty accompaniment to any meal.
—Teresa Ries
Santee, California

1 package (3 ounces) lemon gelatin
1 package (3 ounces) lime gelatin
2 cups boiling water
1 package (8 ounces) cream cheese, cubed
1/2 cup evaporated milk
1/2 cup mayonnaise
1 can (8 ounces) unsweetened crushed pineapple, undrained
1/2 cup chopped walnuts
1 package (10-1/2 ounces) pastel miniature marshmallows

In a large mixing bowl, combine lemon and lime gelatin with boiling water; stir until dissolved. Add cream cheese; let stand for 10 minutes. Beat on high speed until smooth. Stir in milk and mayonnaise. Fold in the pineapple.

Pour into an ungreased 13-in. x 9-in. x 2-in. dish. Sprinkle with the nuts and marshmallows. Cover and refrigerate until set. **Yield:** 12-15 servings.

Rustic Vegetarian Pizza

Rustic Vegetarian Pizza

(Pictured above and on page 90)

Prep: 20 min. **Bake:** 30 min. + standing

While my husband was stationed in the service in Naples, Italy, we tried all kinds of pizzas with fresh ingredients. This veggie pizza is delicious, but not complicated to assemble. It's great when you want a meatless dish. —Priscilla Gilbert
Indian Harbour Beach, Florida

  1 tablespoon cornmeal
  1 tube (13.8 ounces) refrigerated pizza crust
1-1/2 teaspoons olive oil, *divided*
 11 slices mozzarella cheese, *divided*
  1 small zucchini, cut into 1/8-inch slices, patted dry, *divided*
  1 small onion, sliced
  4 plum tomatoes, cut into 1/4-inch slices
1/4 teaspoon salt
1/4 teaspoon pepper
1/4 cup torn fresh basil

Sprinkle cornmeal over a greased baking sheet. Unroll pizza crust; shape into a 12-in. square. Place on the baking sheet. Brush with 1 teaspoon oil. Arrange nine slices cheese over dough to within 1 in. of edges. Cut each remaining cheese slice into four pieces; set aside.

Place half of the zucchini, about 2 in. apart, around edges of cheese. Fold edges of dough about 1 in. over

zucchini. Bake at 400° for 6 minutes. Layer with onion and remaining zucchini; top with tomatoes. Sprinkle with salt and pepper. Bake for 16 minutes or until crust is golden brown.

Arrange reserved cheese over the tomatoes; bake 4 minutes longer or until cheese is melted. Drizzle with remaining oil. Sprinkle with basil. Let stand for 10 minutes before slicing. **Yield:** 4-6 servings.

Texas Tamale Pie

Prep/Total Time: 25 min.

My aunt shared this great South Texas dish with me. With just four ingredients, the spicy southwestern casserole can be served swiftly...and will undoubtedly disappear quickly. When I take it to church dinners, there are no leftovers. —Billy Boyd, Houston, Texas

1 package (6.8 ounces) Spanish rice and vermicelli mix
1 can (15 ounces) chili with beans
1 can (15 ounces) beef tamales, drained and cut into 1-inch pieces
1 cup (4 ounces) shredded cheddar cheese

Prepare rice mix according to package directions. Meanwhile, spoon chili into a greased 8-in. square baking dish. Top with tamales. Bake, uncovered, at 350° for 10 minutes. Top with cooked rice; sprinkle with cheese. Bake 5 minutes longer or until cheese is melted. **Yield:** 6 servings.

Deviled Ham Muffins

Prep/Total Time: 30 min.

I'm always happy to reveal the secret filling for these savory muffins. It's a surprising mixture of deviled ham and chopped carrot, celery and onion that makes them hearty and moist. —Roberta Morgan, Yakima, Washington

 2 tablespoons finely chopped carrot
 2 tablespoons finely chopped celery
 2 tablespoons finely chopped onion
 1 tablespoon butter
 1 can (4-1/4 ounces) deviled ham spread
 2 cups biscuit/baking mix
 1 tablespoon sugar
 1 egg
 2/3 cup milk
 1/2 cup shredded cheddar cheese

In a small skillet, saute the carrot, celery and onion in butter until tender. Remove from the heat; stir in ham and set aside. In a large bowl, combine the biscuit mix and sugar. Whisk the egg and milk; stir into dry ingredients just until moistened. Fold in cheese.

Fill greased or paper-lined muffin cups three-fourths full. Make an indentation in the center of each muffin; fill with 1 tablespoon ham mixture. Bake at 400° for 15-17 minutes or until a toothpick inserted in muffin comes out clean. Cool 5 minutes before removing from pan. Serve warm. **Yield:** 10 muffins.

Corny Potato Chowder

Prep/Total Time: 15 min.

Nothing warms my body and brings back memories of home like a bowl of corn chowder. My mother's recipe was more time-consuming than mine, but I like this one just as well. —Lee Deneau, Lansing, Michigan

 4 bacon strips, diced
 1/2 cup chopped onion
 1 can (15 ounces) whole potatoes, drained
    and diced
 2 cups milk
 1 can (14-3/4 ounces) cream-style corn
 1/2 teaspoon garlic salt
 1/8 teaspoon pepper

In a large saucepan, cook the bacon and onion until bacon is almost crisp; drain. Add potatoes; saute for 2-3 minutes. Stir in the milk, corn, garlic salt and pepper. Simmer, uncovered, until heated through. **Yield:** 4-6 servings.

Spicy Bratwurst Supper

(Pictured at right)

Prep/Total Time: 25 min.

With a zesty sauce and shredded Gouda cheese that melts over the top, this bratwurst dish from our Test Kitchen is a delicious combination that's swiftly prepared in a skillet. Don't have Gouda? Try shredded provolone or mozzarella cheese instead.

 6 bacon strips, diced
 1/3 cup chopped onion
 5 fully cooked bratwurst, cut into 1/2-inch
    slices
 1/2 pound sliced fresh mushrooms
 1 tablespoon diced jalapeno pepper
 2 cups meatless spaghetti sauce
 2 ounces Gouda cheese, shredded
Hot cooked rice

In a large skillet, cook bacon and onion over medium heat until bacon is almost crisp. Remove to paper towels to drain. In the same skillet, saute the bratwurst, mushrooms and jalapeno for 3-4 minutes or until mushrooms are tender.

Stir in spaghetti sauce and bacon mixture. Cover and cook for 4-6 minutes or until heated through. Sprinkle with cheese. Serve with rice. **Yield:** 4 servings.

Editor's Note: When cutting or seeding hot peppers, use rubber or plastic gloves to protect your hands. Avoid touching your face.

Spicy Bratwurst Supper

Lemon Chicken and Peppers

(Pictured below)

Prep/Total Time: 20 min.

Store-bought packages of marinated chicken breasts speed assembly of this colorful main course. A friend of mine shared the recipe with me several years ago. I usually prepare this when I need a fast meal that tastes great.
—Gertrudis Miller, Evansville, Indiana

☑ Uses less fat, sugar or salt. Includes Nutritional Analysis and Diabetic Exchanges.

- 2 packages (10 ounces *each*) lemon-pepper marinated chicken breast fillets
- 1/2 teaspoon paprika
- 1/4 teaspoon dried thyme
- 1 tablespoon butter
- 1 medium green pepper, cut into 1/4-inch strips
- 1 medium sweet red pepper, cut into 1/4-inch strips

Sprinkle chicken with paprika and thyme. In a large non-stick skillet, cook chicken in butter for 4-6 minutes on each side or until no longer pink; drain and set aside. Saute the peppers for 3-4 minutes or until tender. Return chicken to the pan; heat through. **Yield:** 4 servings.

Nutritional Analysis: 1 serving equals 207 calories, 7 g fat (2 g saturated fat), 77 mg cholesterol, 1,157 mg sodium, 8 g carbohydrate, 1 g fiber, 28 g protein. **Diabetic Exchanges:** 3 lean meat, 1 vegetable.

Tangy Beef Stroganoff

Prep/Total Time: 20 min.

If you're looking for a main course that's simple and yummy, Stroganoff fills the bill. I spice up the creamy sauce for this satisfying beef dish with ketchup and Worcester-shire. —*Joan Roth, Jackson, New Jersey*

- 1 pound boneless beef sirloin steak, thinly sliced
- 1 tablespoon butter

Lemon Chicken and Peppers

1 medium onion, sliced
1/2 teaspoon minced garlic
1 can (10-3/4 ounces) condensed cream of
   mushroom soup, undiluted
1 cup (8 ounces) sour cream
1 jar (6 ounces) sliced mushrooms, drained
2 tablespoons ketchup
2 teaspoons Worcestershire sauce
Hot cooked noodles

In a large skillet, saute beef in butter until no longer pink; drain. Add onion and garlic; cook for 3-4 minutes or until onion is tender. Stir in the soup, sour cream, mushrooms, ketchup and Worcestershire sauce; heat through (do not boil). Serve over noodles. **Yield:** 5 servings.

Cranberry Peach Cobbler
Triple-Tier Brownies

Tuna-Stuffed Portobellos

Prep/Total Time: 15 min.

For a filling lunch or light supper, I like to stuff large portobello mushrooms with tasty tuna salad. You can buy it from the deli or make it yourself using your favorite recipe. Add a green salad, and you'll have a delightful meal.
—Barbara Wassler, Williamsport, Pennsylvania

8 large portobello mushrooms (3 to 3-1/2
   inches)
1 pound prepared tuna salad
8 slices Swiss cheese

Remove and discard stems from mushrooms. Place caps on a greased baking sheet. Broil 4-6 in. from the heat for 4-5 minutes or until tender. Stuff with tuna salad; top with cheese. Broil 2-3 minutes longer or until cheese is melted. **Yield:** 8 servings.

Cranberry Peach Cobbler

(Pictured above)

Prep: 15 min. **Bake:** 45 min.

This cobbler is a little non-traditional, but it will soon be at the top of your recipe list because it's an easy and tasty dessert. Serve it warm with a scoop of French vanilla ice cream, and you'll have a wonderful treat.
—Graciela Sandvigen Rochester, New York

1/2 cup butter, melted
  2 cans (29 ounces *each*) sliced peaches
  1 package (15.6 ounces) cranberry quick bread
     mix
  1 egg
  2 tablespoons grated orange peel, *divided*
1/3 cup dried cranberries
1/3 cup sugar

Triple-Tier Brownies

(Pictured above right)

Prep: 15 min. **Bake:** 30 min. + chilling

With a creamy frosting filling and a crunchy topping, these rich three-layer bars are a decadent treat. They're a snap to assemble and simply irresistible.
—Annmarie Savage, Skowhegan, Maine

1 package fudge brownie mix (13-inch
   x 9-inch pan size)
1 package (11-1/2 ounces) milk chocolate chips
1 cup peanut butter
3 cups crisp rice cereal
1 can (16 ounces) cream cheese frosting
1 cup salted peanuts, chopped

Prepare and bake brownie mix according to package directions, using a greased 13-in. x 9-in. x 2-in. baking pan. Cool on a wire rack. In a large saucepan, combine the chocolate chips and peanut butter. Cook over low heat for 4-5 minutes or until blended, stirring occasionally. Stir in cereal; set aside.

Spread frosting over brownies. Sprinkle with peanuts. Spread with peanut butter mixture. Chill for 30 minutes or until set before cutting. Store in the refrigerator. **Yield:** about 5 dozen.

Pour butter into a 13-in. x 9-in. x 2-in. baking dish. Drain peaches, reserving 1 cup juice. Pat peaches dry and set aside. In a large bowl, combine the quick bread mix, egg, 1 tablespoon orange peel and reserved peach juice.

Drop batter by tablespoonfuls over butter, spreading slightly. Arrange peaches over the top; sprinkle with cranberries. Combine sugar and remaining orange peel; sprinkle over peaches. Bake at 375° for 45-50 minutes or until golden brown. Serve warm. **Yield:** 12-15 servings.

Country-Style Chicken

Louisiana-Style Taco Soup

Prep: 5 min. **Cook:** 35 min.

This is one of my family's favorite quick-and-easy soups for a cold winter's day. With just a few ingredients, it comes together in no time. Serve it with shredded cheeses and tortilla chips for extra flair.
—Julie Whitlow
Alexandria, Indiana

    1 package (8 ounces) red beans and rice mix
    1 package (9 ounces) tortilla soup mix
    1 pound ground beef
    1 cup salsa
1/4 cup sour cream

Prepare mixes according to package directions. Meanwhile, in a Dutch oven or soup kettle, cook beef over medium heat until no longer pink; drain. Stir in salsa and the prepared rice and soup. Cook, uncovered, for 5 minutes or until heated through. Garnish with sour cream. **Yield:** 13 servings (3 quarts).

    Editor's Note: This recipe was prepared with Zatarain's New Orleans-Style Red Beans and Rice and Bear Creek Tortilla Soup mix.

Creamy Garlic Meatballs

Prep/Total Time: 30 min.

This main course from our Test Kitchen home economists relies on canned soup and frozen meatballs for swift preparation. The tender meatballs and rich cream sauce are served over mashed potatoes for a savory meal.

    3 tablespoons all-purpose flour
    1 can (10-3/4 ounces) condensed cream of
      mushroom soup, undiluted
    1 can (10-3/4 ounces) condensed cream of
      chicken soup, undiluted
3-1/2 cups water
    1 tablespoon Italian seasoning
    1 teaspoon garlic powder
1/2 teaspoon salt
1/4 teaspoon pepper
    1 package (32 ounces) frozen fully cooked
      meatballs, thawed
Hot mashed potatoes

In a large saucepan, combine the flour and soups. Stir in the water and seasonings until blended. Bring to a boil. Reduce heat; cook and stir for 2 minutes or until the sauce is thickened.

    Add the meatballs and return to a boil. Reduce heat; cover and simmer for 10-12 minutes or until heated through. Serve the meatballs and sauce over mashed potatoes. **Yield:** 8 servings.

Hot Diggity Dogs

Prep/Total Time: 20 min.

I like speedy recipes that use boxed pasta or rice. I stock up on hot dogs when they're on sale and freeze them so I can make this kid-pleasing dish anytime. Add a tossed

Country-Style Chicken

(Pictured above)

Prep: 15 min. **Bake:** 20 min.

Flavored with onion soup mix, these savory breaded chicken breasts make a delightful weeknight main dish that's sure to please every family member. The recipe's ready in no time and tastes wonderful with broccoli cheddar rice from a boxed mix.
—Clara Coulston
Washington Court House, Ohio

    6 boneless skinless chicken breast halves
      (6 ounces *each*)
    1 egg
    1 tablespoon water
3/4 cup dry bread crumbs
1/4 cup grated Parmesan cheese
    1 envelope onion soup mix
    1 tablespoon butter, melted
    1 package (4.7 ounces) broccoli cheddar rice
      and sauce mix

Flatten chicken to 1/2-in. thickness. In a shallow bowl, beat egg and water. In another shallow bowl, combine the bread crumbs, Parmesan cheese and soup mix. Dip chicken in egg mixture, then coat with crumb mixture. Place in a greased 15-in. x 10-in. x 1-in. baking pan; drizzle with butter.

    Bake, uncovered, at 350° for 20-25 minutes or until the cooking juices run clear. Meanwhile, prepare rice according to package directions. Serve with chicken. **Yield:** 6 servings.

green salad and warm-from-the-oven bread for a supper that's a snap to fix.
—Margaret Wilson
Hemet, California

    1 package (6 ounces) four-cheese corkscrew
      pasta
1-1/3 cups water
  3/4 cup milk
    2 tablespoons butter
    5 hot dogs, halved lengthwise and cut
      into 1/2-inch slices
    1 cup frozen peas
    2 teaspoons prepared mustard

Prepare pasta according to package directions, using the water, milk and butter. Stir in the hot dogs, peas and mustard. Remove from the heat; cover and let stand for 3-5 minutes. **Yield:** 4 servings.

  Editor's Note: This recipe was tested with Pasta Roni Home-Style Deluxe Corkscrew Pasta with Four Cheeses.

Chicken Salad Shells

(Pictured below)

Prep/Total Time: 30 min.

These stuffed shells are great for a summer meal. Calling for just four ingredients, including chicken salad from the deli, they are easy to assemble. The only thing you have to cook are the pasta shells, which take just minutes.
—Karen Lee, Waynesville, North Carolina

1-1/2 pounds prepared chicken salad
  1/2 cup seedless red grapes, halved
   18 jumbo pasta shells, cooked, drained and
      cooled
  2/3 cup ranch salad dressing

In a large bowl, combine the chicken salad and grapes. Spoon about 2 tablespoons into each pasta shell. Refrigerate until serving. Drizzle with salad dressing. **Yield:** 6 servings.

Chicken Salad Shells

Taquitos with Salsa

(Pictured below)

Prep/Total Time: 15 min.

Our Test Kitchen home economists jazzed up store-bought quesadilla rolls from the freezer section with a spicy salsa that's a breeze to stir up. Serve this southwestern combo as an appetizer, snack or quick dinner.

>   2 packages (9 ounces *each*) frozen steak
>   quesadilla rolls
>   1 jar (16 ounces) lime-garlic salsa
>   1 can (10 ounces) diced tomatoes and green
>   chilies, drained
>   2 green onions, thinly sliced
>   2 tablespoons minced fresh parsley
>   2 tablespoons minced fresh cilantro
>   2 teaspoons minced garlic
>   1/2 teaspoon onion salt
>   1/2 teaspoon pepper

Prepare quesadilla rolls according to package directions for microwave cooking. Meanwhile, for salsa, combine the remaining ingredients in a small bowl. Serve with quesadilla rolls. **Yield:** 1 dozen rolls and 2-1/2 cups salsa.

Raisin-Spice Snack Cake

Prep: 15 min. **Bake:** 30 min. + cooling

I turn a yellow cake mix into this nicely spiced dessert topped with crunchy pecans. My husband's aunt gave me the recipe several years ago. Each time I bring it to work or a get-together, everyone enthusiastically consumes every crumb.
—*Ruth Marie Lyons, Boulder, Colorado*

>   1 package (18-1/4 ounces) yellow cake mix
>   1 package (3.4 ounces) instant butterscotch
>   pudding mix
>   4 eggs
>   3/4 cup water
>   1/2 cup vegetable oil
>   1/4 cup honey

Taquitos with Salsa

3/4 teaspoon ground cinnamon
3/4 teaspoon ground nutmeg
1/2 teaspoon ground cloves
1/2 to 1 cup raisins
3/4 cup chopped pecans

In a large mixing bowl, combine the first nine ingredients. Beat on medium speed for 2 minutes. Stir in raisins. Pour into a greased 13-in. x 9-in. x 2-in. baking pan. Sprinkle with pecans. Bake at 350° for 30-35 minutes or until a toothpick inserted near the center comes out clean. Cool on a wire rack. **Yield:** 12-15 servings.

Pinto Bean Chicken Soup

Prep/Total Time: 20 min.

Mexican Velveeta and green chilies add a kick to this satisfying soup. The recipe calls for a number of canned goods, so it's simple to stir up, simmer and serve.
—Sybil Brown, Highland, California

1/3 cup all-purpose flour
2 cans (14-1/2 ounces *each*) chicken broth
1 can (15-1/4 ounces) whole kernel corn, drained
1 can (15 ounces) pinto beans, rinsed and drained
1 can (14-1/2 ounces) stewed tomatoes, cut up
1 can (4 ounces) chopped green chilies
1 can (10 ounces) chunk white chicken
8 ounces Mexican process cheese (Velveeta), cubed

In a large saucepan, combine flour and broth until smooth. Stir in the corn, beans, tomatoes and chilies. Bring to a boil; cook and stir for 2 minutes or until thickened. Reduce heat. Add the chicken and cheese; stir until cheese is melted. **Yield:** 8 servings.

Shortcut Shortcake

Prep: 20 min. + chilling

Fresh strawberries, instant pudding and Twinkies make this shortcake fast and flavorful. Even my son-in-law, who usually doesn't care for dessert, enjoys this one.
—Jo Smith, Camden, Arkansas

2 cups cold milk
1 package (5.1 ounces) instant vanilla pudding mix
1 package (15 ounces) cream-filled sponge cakes
4 cups sliced fresh strawberries
1 carton (8 ounces) frozen whipped topping, thawed
Additional strawberries, halved, optional

In a large bowl, whisk milk and pudding mix for 2 minutes. Let stand for 2 minutes or until soft-set; set aside. Slice sponge cakes in half lengthwise; place filling side up in an ungreased 13-in. x 9-in. x 2-in. dish. Spread pudding over the top.

Antipasto Potato Bake

Arrange sliced strawberries over pudding. Spread whipped topping over berries. Cover and refrigerate at least 1 hour before cutting. Garnish with strawberry halves if desired. Refrigerate leftovers. **Yield:** 12-15 servings.

Antipasto Potato Bake

(Pictured above)

Prep: 15 min. **Bake:** 20 min.

This hearty side dish has a great Mediterranean flavor. It serves a crowd and is a snap to assemble because it calls for several canned and jarred items. Pair it with a chicken, pork or beef entree.
—Kelley Butler-Ludington
East Haven, Connecticut

2 cans (14-1/2 ounces *each*) sliced potatoes, drained
2 cans (14 ounces *each*) water-packed artichoke hearts, rinsed and drained
2 jars (7 ounces *each*) roasted sweet red peppers, drained
1 can (3.8 ounces) sliced ripe olives, drained
1/4 cup grated Parmesan cheese
1-1/2 teaspoons minced garlic
1/3 cup olive oil
1/2 cup seasoned bread crumbs
1 tablespoon butter, melted

In a large bowl, combine potatoes, artichokes, peppers, olives, Parmesan cheese and garlic. Drizzle with oil; toss gently to coat. Transfer to a greased 3-qt. baking dish. Toss bread crumbs and butter; sprinkle over the top.

Bake, uncovered, at 375° for 20-25 minutes or until lightly browned. **Yield:** 10 servings.

Chapter 7

⏱ *Look Ahead for Lively Leftovers*

GET READY to hear cheers for leftovers! You're guaranteed to get that reaction when you serve these sensational main courses, soups, side dishes and more.

Every rave-winning recipe provides a mouth-watering way to use up yesterday's extras—from taco meat and turkey to mashed potatoes and macaroni. These dishes taste so good, your family members are bound to think they're eating all-new, made-from-scratch fare!

And since you'll be preparing these recipes using pre-cooked foods, you'll need less time in the kitchen to assemble an appealing meal.

So go ahead—make a big dinner today and enjoy deliciously different dishes tomorrow.

EXTRA SPECIAL. Taco Casserole (p. 110).

Turkey Bundles

(Pictured below)

Prep/Total Time: 30 min.

This recipe is definitely a must-try! Convenient crescent roll dough is wrapped around a creamy turkey filling to form cute golden bundles. My family loves them. I also have made them to share with friends, and everyone has asked for the recipe. I usually double it, so I have extra bundles for lunch the next day. —Lydia Garrod
Tacoma, Washington

      4 ounces cream cheese, softened
      2 tablespoons milk
  1/2 teaspoon dill weed
  1/4 teaspoon celery salt
  1/4 teaspoon pepper
      2 cups cubed cooked turkey
  1/4 cup chopped water chestnuts
      2 tablespoons chopped green onion
      2 tubes (one 8 ounces, one 4 ounces)
         refrigerated crescent rolls
      2 tablespoons butter, melted
      2 tablespoons seasoned bread crumbs

In a mixing bowl, beat the cream cheese, milk, dill, celery salt and pepper until smooth. Stir in the turkey, water chestnuts and onion.

Separate crescent dough into six rectangles; seal perforations. Spoon 1/3 cup turkey mixture onto the center of each rectangle; bring edges into center and pinch to seal.

Place on a baking sheet. Brush with butter; sprinkle with bread crumbs. Bake at 375° for 15-20 minutes or until golden brown. **Yield:** 6 servings.

Avocado Turkey Salad

(Pictured below left)

Prep/Total Time: 15 min.

Grape tomatoes and avocado chunks add pretty color and fresh flavor to this main-dish salad from our Test Kitchen home economists. In a pinch, substitute half-and-half or milk for the whipping cream, adding a teaspoon at a time until you get the desired consistency.

      3 cups torn mixed salad greens
      2 cups cubed cooked turkey breast
      1 medium ripe avocado, peeled and chopped
      1 cup grape tomatoes
DRESSING:
  1/4 cup vegetable oil
      2 tablespoons sour cream
      1 tablespoon heavy whipping cream
  1/4 teaspoon salt
  1/8 to 1/4 teaspoon minced garlic

In a large bowl, gently toss greens, turkey, avocado and tomatoes. In a small bowl, whisk dressing ingredients until smooth. Drizzle over salad and toss. Serve immediately. **Yield:** 6 servings.

Linguine Alfredo

Prep/Total Time: 20 min.

Use up leftover noodles by tossing them with this wonderful creamy garlic sauce. This is my version of several recipes I've tried through the years, and it's so simple to make. If you prefer, top this dish with broiled shrimp or scallops.
—Loretta Ruda, Kennesaw, Georgia

  1/4 teaspoon minced garlic
      2 tablespoons butter
  1/2 cup half-and-half cream
1-1/2 teaspoons minced fresh parsley, *divided*
      1 teaspoon cornstarch
      1 teaspoon cold water
  1/4 cup grated Parmesan cheese
      2 cups cooked linguine
Salt and pepper to taste

In a large saucepan, saute garlic in butter. Stir in the cream and 1 teaspoon parsley. Combine cornstarch and water until smooth; stir into cream mixture. Bring to a boil; cook and stir for 2 minutes or until thickened.

Remove from the heat; stir in Parmesan cheese until melted. Toss with linguine; sprinkle with salt, pepper and remaining parsley. **Yield:** 2 servings.

Avocado Turkey Salad
Turkey Bundles

Broccoli Ham Bake

(Pictured above)

Prep: 20 min. **Bake:** 25 min.

Looking for a family-pleasing way to use up extra ham? Try this quick casserole that will satisfy even folks not fond of broccoli. Our minister's wife served this and was kind enough to share the recipe. Feel free to replace the stuffing croutons with crushed stuffing mix. —Helen Phillips Greensburg, Indiana

> 1 package (10 ounces) frozen chopped broccoli
> 1/4 cup chopped onion
> 4 tablespoons butter, *divided*
> 2 tablespoons all-purpose flour
> 2-1/4 cups milk
> 1/2 cup shredded cheddar cheese
> 2 cups cubed fully cooked ham
> 1-1/2 cups seasoned stuffing croutons, *divided*

Cook broccoli according to package directions. Meanwhile, in a large saucepan, saute onion in 3 tablespoons butter until tender. Stir in flour until blended; gradually add milk. Bring to a boil; cook and stir for 2 minutes or until thickened. Reduce heat; stir in cheese until melted.

Drain broccoli. Add the broccoli, ham and 1 cup stuffing croutons to cheese sauce. Transfer to a greased 2-qt. baking dish. Melt remaining butter; toss with remaining croutons. Sprinkle around edge of casserole. Bake, uncovered, at 350° for 25-30 minutes or until golden brown. **Yield:** 4 servings.

Ground Beef Lo Mein

Prep/Total Time: 25 min.

I tried this when I was going to school full-time and wanted something quick, foolproof and delicious. My family loves it. For a change, use chicken breasts and chicken gravy instead of ground beef and beef gravy.
—Penny Auclair, Amesbury, Massachusetts

✓ Uses less fat, sugar or salt. Includes Nutritional Analysis.

> 8 ounces uncooked spaghetti
> 1/2 pound cooked ground beef
> 1 package (16 ounces) frozen stir-fry vegetable blend, thawed
> 1 jar (12 ounces) home-style beef gravy
> 1/4 teaspoon reduced-sodium soy sauce
> 1/4 teaspoon garlic powder
> 1/8 teaspoon pepper

Cook spaghetti according to package directions. Meanwhile, in a large skillet, cook beef over medium heat for 2-3 minutes or until heated through. Add the vegetables, gravy, soy sauce, garlic powder and pepper. Bring to a boil. Reduce heat; cover and simmer for 8-10 minutes or until vegetables are crisp-tender. Drain spaghetti; stir into beef mixture. **Yield:** 6 servings.

Nutritional Analysis: 1 cup (prepared with lean ground beef and fat-free gravy) equals 267 calories, 4 g fat (1 g saturated fat), 21 mg cholesterol, 425 mg sodium, 42 g carbohydrate, 4 g fiber, 16 g protein.

Italian Turkey Skillet

Italian Turkey Skillet

(Pictured above)

Prep/Total Time: 20 min.

I try to find imaginative ways to use leftovers—especially turkey. This pasta toss is lightly coated with tomato sauce and accented with fresh mushrooms. For make-ahead convenience, prepare the recipe as directed, then transfer it to a casserole dish. Refrigerate up to 24 hours or freeze 2-3 months, then bake until heated through. —*Patty Kile Elizabethtown, Pennsylvania*

✓ Uses less fat, sugar or salt. Includes Nutritional Analysis.

   1 package (1 pound) linguine
3/4 cup sliced fresh mushrooms
1/2 cup chopped onion
1/2 cup chopped celery
1/2 cup chopped green pepper
   2 tablespoons vegetable oil
   2 cups cubed cooked turkey
   1 can (14-1/2 ounces) diced tomatoes, drained
   1 can (10-3/4 ounces) condensed tomato soup, undiluted
   1 tablespoon Italian seasoning
   1 tablespoon minced fresh parsley
1/4 teaspoon pepper
1/8 teaspoon salt
   1 cup (4 ounces) shredded cheddar cheese, optional

Cook linguine according to package directions. Meanwhile, in a large skillet, saute the mushrooms, onion, celery and green pepper in oil over medium heat until tender. Stir in the turkey, tomatoes, soup, Italian seasoning, parsley, pepper and salt.

Drain linguine; stir into turkey mixture. If desired, sprinkle with cheese; cover and cook for 3-4 minutes or until mixture is heated through and cheese is melted. **Yield:** 8 servings.

Nutritional Analysis: 1 cup (calculated without cheese) equals 338 calories, 7 g fat (1 g saturated fat), 27 mg cholesterol, 362 mg sodium, 51 g carbohydrate, 4 g fiber, 19 g protein.

Brunch Pizza

Prep/Total Time: 20 min.

Since the country sausage gravy that my recipe called for isn't widely available, use leftover cooked pork sausage and cream gravy. This brunch recipe is unbelievably quick and easy, but also very delicious.
—*Angela Hart Cool Ridge, West Virginia*

   1 prebaked Italian bread shell crust (14 ounces)
   1 tablespoon butter
   5 eggs, beaten
   1 can (14-1/2 ounces) country-style cream gravy
   2 cups (8 ounces) shredded cheddar cheese
1/2 cup real bacon bits
1/4 cup cooked pork sausage

Place the crust on an ungreased pizza pan or baking sheet. Bake at 425° for 5 minutes. In a large skillet, melt butter over medium heat. Add eggs; cook until soft-set, stirring occasionally.

Spread the gravy over crust; top with scrambled eggs, cheese, bacon and sausage. Broil 4-6 in. from the heat for 6 minutes or until cheese is melted. **Yield:** 6 servings.

Twice-Baked Mashed Potatoes

Prep/Total Time: 30 min.

If you like the filling in twice-baked potatoes, you'll love the flavor of this savory side dish that complements most entrees. It's a wonderful way to finish up extra mashed potatoes.
—Margaret Mayhugh
Murphysboro, Illinois

- 1/2 cup chopped onion
- 1/2 cup chopped green pepper
- 1 tablespoon vegetable oil
- 4 cups mashed potatoes (prepared with milk and butter)
- 1 cup (4 ounces) shredded cheddar cheese, *divided*
- 1/4 cup crumbled cooked bacon
- 1 teaspoon salt
- 1/2 teaspoon pepper

In a small skillet, saute the onion and green pepper in oil until tender. In a large bowl, combine the onion mixture, mashed potatoes, 1/2 cup cheese, bacon, salt and pepper. Spoon into a greased 2-qt. baking dish. Sprinkle with remaining cheese. Bake, uncovered, at 350° for 20-25 minutes or until cheese is melted. **Yield:** 6 servings.

Wild Rice Chowder

(Pictured at right)

Prep/Total Time: 25 min.

I discovered this recipe years ago, and it has since become a family favorite. Cooked wild rice combines with cheese, bacon and seasonings to create a flavorful, satisfying chowder. It's especially good on a cool day.
—Amy Chop, Oak Grove, Louisiana

- 8 bacon strips, diced
- 1/3 cup chopped onion
- 1/3 cup all-purpose flour
- 1/2 to 1 teaspoon salt
- 4 cups water
- 1 can (14-1/2 ounces) chicken broth
- 1-1/2 cups cooked wild rice
- 1 can (12 ounces) evaporated milk
- 2 cups (8 ounces) cubed process American cheese
- 2 tablespoons minced fresh parsley

In a large saucepan, cook bacon until crisp. Remove with a slotted spoon to paper towels. Drain, reserving 1 tablespoon drippings. Saute onion in drippings until tender.

Stir in flour and salt. Gradually stir in water and broth. Bring to a boil; cook and stir for 2 minutes or until slightly thickened. Stir in rice.

Reduce heat; cover and simmer 5 minutes. Add milk, cheese, parsley and bacon; cook and stir until heated through and cheese is melted. **Yield:** 6-8 servings.

No Rice is No Problem

DON'T HAVE any leftover cooked wild rice to use for making delicious Wild Rice Chowder? If you have a little spare time to spend in the kitchen, it's worth making a batch of rice just so you and your family can enjoy this sensational soup.

Simply add 1 cup rinsed uncooked wild rice and 1 teaspoon salt to a saucepan containing 4 cups of boiling water. Cook, covered, for 40 minutes or until the rice is tender.

All that's left to do is use the cooked rice to prepare the chowder recipe as directed. Then, enjoy!

Wild Rice Chowder

Taco Casserole

(Pictured below and on page 104)

Prep: 15 min. **Bake:** 20 min.

Our family was pleasantly surprised by this delightful dish that calls for leftover taco fixings. Some of us enjoyed it even more than the original tacos! It's easy to put together and tasty enough to serve to company. —Bonnie King Lansing, Michigan

> 3 cups leftover taco-seasoned ground beef
> 1 can (16 ounces) kidney beans, rinsed and drained
> 1 cup (4 ounces) shredded Monterey Jack cheese
> 2 eggs, lightly beaten
> 1 cup milk
> 1-1/2 cups biscuit/baking mix
> 1 cup (8 ounces) sour cream
> 2 cups shredded lettuce
> 1 medium tomato, diced
> 1 can (2-1/4 ounces) sliced ripe olives, drained

In a large bowl, combine the taco meat and beans; spoon into a greased 8-in. square baking dish. Sprinkle with cheese. In another bowl, combine the eggs, milk and biscuit mix until moistened. Pour over cheese.

Bake, uncovered, at 400° for 20-25 minutes or until lightly browned and a knife inserted near the center comes out clean. Spread with sour cream. Top with lettuce, tomato and olives. **Yield:** 6 servings.

Taco Casserole

Chicken Stuffing Casserole

Prep: 15 min. **Bake:** 40 min.

As a busy mom of two small children, I try to find quick satisfying meals that my whole family will enjoy. This hearty chicken bake is simple to assemble and tastes delicious. It's a recipe I rely on all the time. —Susan VanHorn Greensboro, North Carolina

> 2 large potatoes, peeled and cubed
> 2 medium carrots, coarsely chopped
> 1 package (8 ounces) crushed corn bread stuffing
> 1/2 cup butter, melted
> 3 cups cubed cooked chicken
> 1 can (10-3/4 ounces) condensed cream of chicken soup, undiluted
> 1 can (10-3/4 ounces) condensed cream of celery soup, undiluted
> 1 cup chicken broth

Place 1 in. of water in a saucepan; add the potatoes and carrots. Bring to a boil. Reduce heat; cover and simmer for 5-7 minutes or until crisp-tender. Drain and set aside.

Toss the stuffing and butter; spread half in a greased 13-in. x 9-in. x 2-in. baking dish. Top with chicken. In a large bowl, combine the soups, broth, potatoes and carrots; spread evenly over chicken. Sprinkle with remaining stuffing mixture. Bake, uncovered, at 350° for 40-45 minutes or until heated through. **Yield:** 6-8 servings.

White Turkey Chili

Prep/Total Time: 30 min.

I combine white corn, great northern beans and leftover turkey to prepare this steaming chili. I appreciate how fast it is to make—and that my husband and our four children like it. I often bake a pan of corn bread to go with it. —Lauri Pobanz, Lincoln, Nebraska

> 1/3 cup chopped onion
> 1 celery rib, chopped
> 1-1/2 teaspoons vegetable oil
> 1-3/4 cups chicken *or* turkey broth
> 2 cups cubed cooked turkey
> 1 can (15-1/2 ounces) great northern beans, rinsed and drained
> 1 can (11 ounces) white *or* shoepeg corn, drained
> 2 tablespoons chopped green chilies
> 1 teaspoon ground cumin
> 1/2 teaspoon salt
> Shredded Monterey Jack cheese

In a large saucepan, saute onion and celery in oil until tender. Stir in the broth, turkey, beans, corn, chilies, cumin and salt. Bring to a boil. Reduce heat; cover and simmer for 15-20 minutes. Garnish with cheese. **Yield:** 5 servings.

Cheesy Ham Tortellini

Tex-Mex Macaroni

Prep: 10 min. **Bake:** 25 min.

My husband and I really like macaroni and cheese. When we had a lot left over on one occasion, I came up with this Tex-Mex treatment to use it up...and he didn't even realize we were eating leftovers! This quick casserole is excellent with a green salad.
—Arlene Lacell
Zillah, Washington

  1/2 **pound ground beef**
  1/2 **cup chopped onion**
    3 **cups prepared macaroni and cheese**
    1 **cup salsa**
  1/2 **cup shredded cheddar cheese**

In a large skillet, cook beef and onion over medium heat until meat is no longer pink; drain. Add the macaroni and cheese and salsa.

Transfer mixture to a greased 1-qt. baking dish and sprinkle with cheddar cheese. Bake, uncovered, at 350° for 25 minutes or until the casserole heated through. **Yield:** 4 servings.

Cheesy Ham Tortellini

(Pictured above)

Prep/Total Time: 30 min.

I came up with this creamy skillet supper when trying to finish up leftover ham. It's colorful as well as quick to make. —Margaret Wilson, Hemet, California

    1 **package (19 ounces) frozen cheese tortellini**
    1 **jar (17 ounces) Alfredo sauce**
    1 **package (16 ounces) frozen California-blend**
      vegetables, thawed
    2 **cups cubed fully cooked ham**
  1/3 **cup grated Parmesan cheese**
    1 **tablespoon minced fresh parsley**

Cook tortellini according to package directions. Meanwhile, in a large saucepan, combine the Alfredo sauce, vegetables and ham. Bring to a boil over medium heat. Reduce heat; cover and simmer for 15-20 minutes or until vegetables are crisp-tender. Drain tortellini; add to sauce. Stir in Parmesan cheese; heat through. Sprinkle with parsley. **Yield:** 6 servings.

Asian Noodle Toss

(Pictured above)

Prep/Total Time: 20 min.

I combine yesterday's chicken with mandarin oranges, crisp veggies and spaghetti to create a colorful medley. To vary the taste, use citrus-flavored stir-fry sauce.
—Clara Coulston, Washington Court House, Ohio

✓ Uses less fat, sugar or salt. Includes Nutritional Analysis.

    8 ounces uncooked thin spaghetti
    1 package (10 ounces) julienned carrots
    1 package (8 ounces) sugar snap peas
    2 cups cubed cooked chicken
    1 can (11 ounces) mandarin oranges,
      undrained
  1/2 cup stir-fry sauce

Cook spaghetti according to package directions. Stir in carrots and peas; cook 1 minute longer. Drain; place in a bowl. Add the chicken, oranges and stir-fry sauce; toss to coat. **Yield:** 5 servings.

Nutritional Analysis: 1-1/2 cups equals 346 calories, 5 g fat (1 g saturated fat), 50 mg cholesterol, 73 mg sodium, 49 g carbohydrate, 4 g fiber, 24 g protein.

Green Bean Turkey Bake

Prep/Total Time: 20 min.

For this hearty meal-in-one, I microwave extra turkey and mashed potatoes with convenient canned soup and frozen green beans. Don't have leftover potatoes? Try preparing instant mashed potatoes from a box. —Ann Wood
Battle Ground, Washington

    2 cups frozen cut green beans, thawed
1-1/2 cups cubed cooked turkey breast
    1 can (10-3/4 ounces) condensed cream of
      mushroom soup, undiluted
    1 cup (4 ounces) shredded cheddar cheese
  1/3 cup milk
    3 cups mashed potatoes
  1/2 cup cheese-flavored snack crackers, crushed

In a 2-qt. microwave-safe dish, combine green beans, turkey, soup, cheese and milk. Cover and microwave on high for 5-6 minutes or until bubbly, stirring once.

Carefully spread mashed potatoes over turkey mixture; sprinkle with cracker crumbs. Cover and cook on high for 2-4 minutes or until heated through. Let stand for 5 minutes before serving. **Yield:** 6 servings.

Editor's Note: This recipe was tested in a 1,100-watt microwave.

Cheeseburger Pitas

Prep/Total Time: 30 min.

Years ago, my mom converted a stuffed pepper recipe into this sandwich that calls for leftover rice. You can save time by using frozen diced vegetables. —Becky Floyd Riverside, California

    1 pound ground beef
    1/2 cup chopped onion
    1/2 cup chopped green pepper
    1 cup cold cooked rice
    1 can (8 ounces) tomato sauce
    2 teaspoons Worcestershire sauce
    1/2 teaspoon salt
    1/4 teaspoon pepper
    2 cups (8 ounces) shredded cheddar cheese
    4 pita breads (6 inches), halved

In a large skillet, cook the beef, onion and green pepper over medium heat until meat is no longer pink; drain. Add the rice, tomato sauce, Worcestershire sauce, salt and pepper. Bring to a boil. Reduce heat; cover and simmer for 10-15 minutes.

Stir in cheese, cover and cook 2-3 minutes longer or until cheese is melted. Spoon 1/2 cup into each pita half. **Yield:** 4 servings.

Barbecued Chicken Pizza

Prep: 25 min. **Bake:** 20 min.

A boxed crust mix and cooked chicken make this flavorful pizza a cinch to prepare. It's guaranteed to please pizza lovers. We like dark molasses-based barbecue sauce and sometimes use refrigerated dough instead of the boxed mix. —Autumn Ruhl, Montgomery, Michigan

    1 medium onion, halved and thinly sliced
    1 small green pepper, julienned
    1 small sweet red pepper, julienned
    2 tablespoons vegetable oil
    1 package (6-1/2 ounces) pizza crust mix
    1 cup barbecue sauce
    2 cups shredded cooked chicken
    2 cups (8 ounces) shredded cheddar cheese

In a large skillet, saute onion and peppers in oil until tender; set aside. Prepare pizza dough according to package directions. With floured hands, press onto a greased 12-in. pizza pan. Spread barbecue sauce to within 1 in. of edges.

Layer with chicken, onion mixture and cheese. Bake at 450° for 18-22 minutes or until cheese is melted and crust is golden brown. **Yield:** 4-6 servings.

Beer 'n' Brat Biscuits

(Pictured at right)

Prep/Total Time: 30 min.

My husband, our three daughters and I all love to cook and experiment in the kitchen, so we're always coming up with something new to try. These golden brown bites require just four ingredients, including leftover bratwurst. Baked in a muffin pan, the biscuits are terrific served with mustard and a big bowl of rice and beans. —Nancy Bourget, Round Rock, Texas

    2 fully cooked bratwurst, casings removed
    4 cups biscuit/baking mix
    2 to 3 teaspoons caraway seeds
    1 can (12 ounces) beer or nonalcoholic beer

Cut bratwurst into bite-size pieces. In a bowl, combine the biscuit mix, caraway seeds and bratwurst; stir in beer just until moistened. Fill greased muffin cups two-thirds full.

Bake at 400° for 18-20 minutes or until golden brown. Cool for 5 minutes before removing from pans to wire racks. Serve warm. Refrigerate leftovers. **Yield:** 16 biscuits.

Beer 'n' Brat Biscuits

Kielbasa Biscuit Pizza

(Pictured below)

Prep: 15 min. **Bake:** 35 min.

This is an extremely quick and very tasty pizza that my family loves. It's a bit different because you use buttermilk biscuits instead of pizza dough. It makes enough for a large family and is great for company.

—Jennifer Zukiwsky, Glendon, Alberta

  2 tubes (12 ounces *each*) refrigerated
    buttermilk biscuits
2-1/2 cups garden-style spaghetti sauce
  1/2 pound fully cooked kielbasa *or* Polish
    sausage, cubed
  1 can (8 ounces) mushroom stems and pieces,
    drained
  1/2 cup chopped green pepper
  1/2 cup chopped sweet red pepper
  1 cup (4 ounces) shredded mozzarella cheese
  1 cup (4 ounces) shredded cheddar cheese

Separate biscuits; cut each biscuit into fourths. Arrange in a greased 13-in. x 9-in. x 2-in. baking dish (do not flatten). Bake at 375° for 12-15 minutes or until biscuits begin to brown.

Spread spaghetti sauce over biscuit crust. Sprinkle with sausage, mushrooms, peppers and cheeses. Bake for 20-25 minutes or until bubbly and the cheese is melted. Let stand for 5 minutes before cutting. **Yield:** 8 servings.

Beefy Macaroni

Prep/Total Time: 30 min.

If you like to brown a few pounds of ground beef at one time to have it ready for all kinds of dishes, you'll enjoy this recipe. The pleasing pasta skillet combines beef and macaroni with cheese, olives, spaghetti sauce and seasonings.

—Edie Farm, Farmington, New Mexico

1-1/4 cups cooked ground beef
  1 cup uncooked elbow macaroni
  1 cup hot water
  1 cup meatless spaghetti sauce
  1/4 cup sliced ripe olives
  1/4 teaspoon dried oregano
  1/4 teaspoon minced garlic
  1/8 teaspoon salt
  1/8 teaspoon pepper
  1/3 cup shredded cheddar cheese

In a small skillet, combine the first nine ingredients. Bring to a boil. Reduce heat; cover and simmer for 10-12 minutes or until the macaroni is tender. Stir in the cheese. Remove from the heat; cover and let stand until cheese is melted. **Yield:** 2 servings.

Homemade Turkey Soup

Prep: 30 min. **Cook:** 2 hours 35 min.

You can make the most of even the smallest pieces of leftover meat on your holiday turkey. I simmer the bones to get the rich flavor, then easily remove any meat that remains. I add rice, vegetables and cream soup for a hearty soup that's tasty and economical. —June Sangrey
Manheim, Pennsylvania

  1 leftover turkey carcass (from a 10-
    to 12-pound turkey)
  2 quarts water
  1 medium onion, halved
  1/2 teaspoon salt
  2 bay leaves
  1 cup chopped carrots
  1 cup uncooked long grain rice
  1/3 cup chopped celery
  1/4 cup chopped onion
  1 can (10-3/4 ounces) condensed cream of
    chicken *or* cream of mushroom soup,
    undiluted

Place the turkey carcass, water, onion, salt and bay leaves in a soup kettle or Dutch oven; bring to a boil. Reduce

Kielbasa Biscuit Pizza

Ham Potato Puffs

heat; cover and simmer for 2 hours.

Remove the turkey carcass; cool. Strain the broth and skim off the fat; discard the onion and bay leaves. Return the broth to the pan. Add the carrots, rice, celery and chopped onion; cover and simmer until the rice and vegetables are tender.

Remove turkey from the bones; cut into bite-size pieces. Add turkey and cream soup to broth; heat through. **Yield:** 8-10 servings (about 2 quarts).

Ham Potato Puffs

(Pictured above)

Prep: 20 min. **Bake:** 20 min.

This is a deliciously different way to use up leftover mashed potatoes and was an instant hit with our teenagers. I most often serve the puffs with a side of steamed green beans, cauliflower or broccoli. —Brad Eichelberger York, Pennsylvania

1 tube (12 ounces) refrigerated buttermilk biscuits
1 cup cubed fully cooked ham
1 cup leftover mashed potatoes
1 cup (4 ounces) shredded cheddar cheese, *divided*
1/2 teaspoon dried parsley flakes
1/4 teaspoon garlic powder

Press each biscuit onto the bottom and up the sides of a greased muffin cup. In a bowl, combine the ham, potatoes, 1/2 cup cheese, parsley and garlic powder. Spoon 1/4 cup into each prepared cup. Sprinkle with remaining cheese. Bake at 350° for 20-25 minutes or until lightly browned. Serve warm. Refrigerate leftovers. **Yield:** 10 puffs.

More Second-Day Dishes

- Here's how I use up extra chili. I make a batch of corn bread batter, fill muffin cups two-thirds full, then put a heaping spoonful of chili in the middle of each. When the muffins are baked as directed, the batter rises up around the chili. These bites are great hot or cold. —*Judy Benevy Springfield, West Virginia*

- When I have chicken nuggets or french fries left over from dinner, I mix them into scrambled eggs the next morning. It's an effortless way to use them up, and it gives ordinary eggs a taste-tempting twist. —*Shea Morley, Seattle, Washington*

- There's rarely leftover roast in our house, but when there is, I cut it into bite-size pieces, add plenty of barbecue sauce and reheat it on the stove. I serve the meat on toasted buns with cheese and mustard on top. —*Lynn Dippon, Stafford, Texas*

Luncheon Chicken Salad

Luncheon Chicken Salad

(Pictured above)

Prep/Total Time: 15 min.

This refreshing medley of veggies, citrus fruit and chicken is just right for a special spring brunch or luncheon. Flavored with a tempting homemade dressing, the colorful combination is a welcome change of pace from the usual salad.
—Angie Dierikx, Andalusia, Illinois

  4 cups cubed cooked chicken breast
  1 can (20 ounces) pineapple tidbits, drained
  1 can (11 ounces) mandarin oranges, drained
  1 cup chopped celery
  6 green onions, chopped
1/2 cup chopped green pepper
2/3 cup mayonnaise
7-1/2 teaspoons brown mustard
  1 tablespoon brown sugar
1/2 teaspoon minced garlic

In a large bowl, gently combine the chicken, pineapple, oranges, celery, onions and green pepper. In a small bowl, combine the remaining ingredients. Pour over salad and toss to coat. **Yield:** 7 servings.

Pork Noodle Soup

Prep/Total Time: 30 min.

My daughter created this delicious, satisfying soup when she needed to use up some leftover pork, and I'm glad she shared the recipe with me. Add more water if you like your soup thinner...or use less water if you want a noodle side dish. I've substituted mushroom-flavored ramen noodles for the pork-flavored ones with equally tasty results.
—Eleanor Niska, Twin Falls, Idaho

1/2 cup chopped celery
1/2 cup chopped onion
1/2 teaspoon minced garlic
  1 tablespoon olive oil
  7 cups water
1-1/2 cups cut fresh asparagus (1-inch pieces)
1/2 cup chopped cabbage
1-1/2 teaspoons minced fresh parsley
3/4 teaspoon dried tarragon
Dash cayenne pepper, optional
  2 packages (3 ounces *each*) pork ramen noodles
  2 cups cubed cooked pork

In a large soup kettle, saute the celery, onion and garlic in oil until tender. Stir in the water, asparagus, cabbage, parsley, tarragon and cayenne if desired; bring to a boil.

Coarsely crush the noodles. Add the noodles with the contents of the seasoning packets to the kettle. Bring to a boil. Reduce heat; simmer, uncovered, for 3-5 minutes or until the noodles and vegetables are tender. Add the pork; heat through. **Yield:** 10 servings (2-1/2 quarts).

Ham 'n' Onion Gravy

Prep/Total Time: 30 min.

I cook for my husband and son, and they love this hearty dish. A homemade cream gravy is served with hot mashed potatoes and leftover ham for a stick-to-your-ribs meal. My family always makes short work of this comforting food. —Elsie Epp, Newton, Kansas

```
  4 thick ham slices (about 1 pound)
  3 tablespoons vegetable oil
  1 large onion, halved and thinly sliced
  3 tablespoons all-purpose flour
1/4 teaspoon salt
1/4 teaspoon pepper
1-1/2 cups milk
1/2 cup water
Hot mashed potatoes
```

In a large skillet, brown ham in oil; remove and keep warm. In the same skillet, saute onion until tender. Stir in the flour, salt and pepper until blended. Gradually stir in milk and water. Bring to a boil; cook and stir for 2 minutes or until thickened. Serve with ham and mashed potatoes. **Yield:** 4 servings.

Cashew Chicken Wraps

Prep/Total Time: 20 min.

Do you have extra cooked chicken on hand? Combine it with crunchy cashews, celery and an easy mayo dressing, then wrap it in a flour tortilla. This is a very refreshing sandwich on a hot summer day. It's great for picnics served with coleslaw and fruit. —Janet Goins Mesa, Arizona

```
1/2 cup mayonnaise
  6 tablespoons honey mustard
  1 tablespoon red wine vinegar
1/2 teaspoon salt
Dash pepper
  3 cups cubed cooked chicken
  2 celery ribs, thinly sliced
1/2 cup chopped cashews
1/4 cup chopped red onion
  4 flour tortillas (6 inches), warmed
1/2 cup shredded cheddar cheese
```

In a bowl, combine mayonnaise, mustard, vinegar, salt and pepper. Stir in chicken, celery, cashews and onion. Spoon about 1 cup down the center of each tortilla; sprinkle each with 2 tablespoons cheese. Roll up. **Yield:** 4 servings.

Shredded Beef Nachos

(Pictured below)

Prep/Total Time: 15 min.

After ordering nachos in a couple of restaurants, I figured they would be a snap to make at home. This version, which calls for leftover roast, is also good with bell peppers. I like to serve salsa, sour cream and guacamole on the side.
—Donna McFarland, Eugene, Oregon

```
  7 cups tortilla or nacho chips
  1 cup shredded cooked beef
  2 cups (8 ounces) shredded cheddar cheese
  2 medium plum tomatoes, diced
  1 can (2-1/4 ounces) sliced ripe olives, drained
  4 green onions, chopped
Salsa, sour cream and guacamole, optional
```

Arrange the chips in an ungreased broiler-safe platter or 15-in. x 10-in. x 1-in. baking pan. Top with beef, cheese, tomatoes, olives and onions. Broil 6 in. from the heat for 3-5 minutes or until cheese is melted. Serve with salsa, sour cream and guacamole if desired. **Yield:** 6-8 servings.

Shredded Beef Nachos

Chapter 8

⏱ *Speedy Side Dishes*

WHO SAYS quick side dishes need to be routine? You'll discover that it's a cinch to serve your family exciting new creations—just turn to the time-saving recipes here.

Try jazzed-up mashed potatoes...cheesy green beans...peppery pasta and rave-winning rice. Because every dish requires a mere 30 minutes—or less—of prep work, you'll have plenty of time to make your main course and even dessert, too.

Are you serving holiday dinner? Keep these delights in mind as a way to put a variety of impressive side dishes on the table in record time.

You may just discover that these on-the-side sensations end up taking center stage!

SENSATIONAL SIDES. Creamy Zucchini (p. 121), Bacon Mashed Potatoes (p. 122), Spicy Asparagus Spears (p. 122) and Tomatoes with Horseradish Sauce (p. 121).

Crumb-Covered Sprouts

Lemon-Butter Snow Peas

(Pictured below)

Prep/Total Time: 10 min.

A handful of ingredients and a microwave are all our Test Kitchen home economists needed to create this terrific treatment for fresh snow peas. A bit of lemon juice, some minced garlic and a dash of Italian seasoning make it a perfect addition to any meal.

✓ Uses less fat, sugar or salt. Includes Nutritional Analysis and Diabetic Exchanges.

    1/2 pound fresh snow peas
      1 tablespoon water
      1 teaspoon minced garlic
      1 tablespoon butter, melted
      1 teaspoon lemon juice
    1/2 teaspoon Italian seasoning

In a microwave-safe dish, combine the peas, water and garlic. Cover and microwave on high for 3-4 minutes or until crisp-tender; drain. Combine the butter, lemon juice and Italian seasoning; drizzle over peas and toss to coat. **Yield:** 2 servings.

Nutritional Analysis: 3/4 cup (prepared with reduced-fat butter) equals 76 calories, 3 g fat (2 g saturated fat), 10 mg cholesterol, 40 mg sodium, 9 g carbohydrate, 3 g fiber, 4 g protein. **Diabetic Exchanges:** 2 vegetable, 1/2 fat.

Editor's Note: This recipe was tested in a 1,100-watt microwave.

Crumb-Covered Sprouts

(Pictured above)

Prep/Total Time: 25 min.

I love brussels sprouts, but my family does not, so I dress up the steamed sprouts with crunchy bread crumbs, smoky bacon and cheddar cheese. When I prepare them this way, everyone comes back for seconds!
—Anne Baines
Kennesaw, Georgia

    12 fresh brussels sprouts, trimmed and halved
      2 tablespoons sesame seeds
      1 teaspoon minced garlic
      2 tablespoons olive oil
      1 tablespoon butter
    1/2 cup soft bread crumbs
      2 tablespoons real bacon bits
    1/2 cup shredded cheddar cheese
Salt and pepper to taste

Place brussels sprouts in a steamer basket; place in a saucepan over 1 in. of water. Bring to a boil; cover and steam for 15-20 minutes or until crisp-tender.

Meanwhile, in a large skillet over medium heat, cook and stir the sesame seeds and garlic in oil and butter for 2-3 minutes or until sesame seeds are lightly browned. Add the bread crumbs and bacon; cook and stir for 1-2 minutes or until crumbs are golden brown. Add the brussels sprouts, cheese, salt and pepper. **Yield:** 2-3 servings.

Lemon-Butter Snow Peas

Creamy Zucchini

(Pictured on page 118)

Prep/Total Time: 20 min.

Here's a different treatment for zucchini that's a favorite in our home. Even though the creamy Parmesan sauce is homemade, the cooking time is short.
—Marguerite Shaeffer, Sewell, New Jersey

   4 medium zucchini, julienned
1-1/2 teaspoons minced garlic
   2 tablespoons olive oil
   2 packages (3 ounces *each*) cream cheese,
      cubed
   1 cup half-and-half cream
1/2 cup shredded Parmesan cheese
1/4 teaspoon salt
1/8 teaspoon coarsely ground pepper
Dash ground nutmeg
Shredded Swiss cheese

In a large skillet, saute zucchini and garlic in oil for 3-5 minutes or until tender. Drain; remove zucchini mixture with a slotted spoon and keep warm.

In the same skillet, combine the cream cheese and cream; cook and stir over low heat until smooth. Stir in the Parmesan cheese. Return zucchini mixture to the pan. Cook and stir 1-2 minutes longer or until heated through. Sprinkle with salt, pepper, nutmeg and Swiss cheese. **Yield:** 6 servings.

Tomatoes with Horseradish Sauce

(Pictured on page 119)

Prep/Total Time: 15 min.

This warm dish of lightly sauteed tomatoes and tangy sauce is very tasty and quick to make. I occasionally use both red and green tomatoes to add even more color.
—Phyllis Shaughnessy, Livonia, New York

✓ Uses less fat, sugar or salt. Includes Nutritional Analysis and Diabetic Exchanges.

Refrigerated butter-flavored spray
   4 large tomatoes, sliced
   3 tablespoons mayonnaise
   2 tablespoons half-and-half cream
   1 tablespoon prepared horseradish
Minced fresh parsley

Coat a large skillet with refrigerated butter-flavored spray. Heat skillet over medium heat. Add tomato slices; cook for 2-3 minutes on each side or until edges begin to brown. In a bowl, whisk the mayonnaise, cream and horseradish. Spoon over tomatoes. Sprinkle with parsley. **Yield:** 4 servings.

Nutritional Analysis: 1 serving (prepared with fat-free mayonnaise and half-and-half) equals 53 calories, 1 g fat (trace saturated fat), 1 mg cholesterol, 124 mg sodium, 11 g carbohydrate, 2 g fiber, 2 g protein. **Diabetic Exchange:** 2 vegetable.

Editor's Note: This recipe was tested with I Can't Believe It's Not Butter Spray.

Herbed Potatoes and Veggies

Herbed Potatoes and Veggies

(Pictured above)

Prep/Total Time: 25 min.

I came up with this family favorite when I needed to use up leftover baked potatoes and extra produce from our garden. It's a great-tasting side dish. My husband requests it all the time and brags about it to company.
—Jenelle Parks, Hayfield, Minnesota

   4 medium baking potatoes
1-1/2 cups diced zucchini
   3 tablespoons olive oil
   2 tablespoons plus 1 teaspoon savory herb
      with garlic soup mix
1/4 teaspoon pepper
  10 cherry tomatoes, halved

Scrub and pierce potatoes; place on a microwave-safe plate. Microwave on high for 10-12 minutes or until tender, turning once. When potatoes are cool enough to handle, cut into cubes.

In a large skillet, saute potatoes and zucchini in oil for 5 minutes. Sprinkle with soup mix and pepper. Cook until heated through, stirring occasionally. Add tomatoes; cook for 1 minute. **Yield:** 6 servings.

Editor's Note: This recipe was tested in a 1,100-watt microwave.

Bacon Mashed Potatoes

(Pictured on page 119)

Prep/Total Time: 25 min.

Featuring cheddar cheese, bacon and chives, these rich and hearty potatoes go well with just about anything.
—Pat Mathison, Meadowlands, Minnesota

 2-1/2 cups cubed peeled potatoes (3/4 pound)
 1/4 cup milk
 1/4 cup mayonnaise
 4-1/2 teaspoons minced chives
 1/8 teaspoon garlic powder
 1/8 teaspoon pepper
 1/2 cup shredded cheddar cheese
 3 bacon strips, cooked and crumbled

Place potatoes in a large saucepan and cover with water. Bring to a boil. Reduce heat; cover and cook for 15-20 minutes or until tender. Drain. Add the milk, mayonnaise, chives, garlic powder and pepper; mash potatoes. Stir in cheese and bacon. **Yield:** 3 servings.

Blue Cheese Green Beans

(Pictured below)

Prep/Total Time: 20 min.

Bacon, blue cheese and chopped nuts make this my mom's favorite way to enjoy green beans. I always pre-pare this side dish when she's coming for dinner. The recipe is also a great way to use fresh-picked green beans from your garden.
—Kate Hilts, Grand Rapids, Michigan

 6 bacon strips, diced
 1 pound fresh green beans, cut into 2-inch pieces
 1/2 cup crumbled blue cheese
 1/3 cup chopped pecans, toasted
Pepper to taste

In a large skillet, cook bacon over medium heat until crisp. Using a slotted spoon, remove to paper towels. Drain, reserving 2 tablespoons drippings. In the drippings, cook and stir the beans for 8-10 minutes or until crisp-tender. Add the blue cheese, pecans, pepper and bacon. Cook for 2 minutes or until heated through. **Yield:** 6 servings.

Spicy Asparagus Spears

(Pictured on page 118)

Prep/Total Time: 15 min.

This no-fuss dish gets its zippy taste from Cajun seasoning and crushed red pepper flakes. Even those who don't like asparagus will enjoy these buttery spears.
—Marlies Kinnell, Barrie, Ontario

✓ Uses less fat, sugar or salt. Includes Nutritional Analysis and Diabetic Exchanges.

 2 tablespoons butter
 1/2 teaspoon onion powder
 1/2 teaspoon seasoned salt
 1/2 teaspoon Cajun seasoning
Crushed red pepper flakes to taste
 1-3/4 pounds fresh asparagus, trimmed

In a large skillet, melt butter. Stir in the onion powder, seasoned salt, Cajun seasoning and red pepper flakes. Add asparagus spears, stirring gently to coat. Cover and cook for 5-7 minutes or until crisp-tender, stirring occasionally. **Yield:** 6 servings.

Nutritional Analysis: 1 serving (prepared with reduced-fat butter) equals 26 calories, 2 g fat (1 g saturated fat), 7 mg cholesterol, 210 mg sodium, 2 g carbohydrate, 1 g fiber, 1 g protein. **Diabetic Exchange:** 1 vegetable.

Spanish Squash Medley

Prep/Total Time: 25 min.

This fresh-tasting combination of summer squash and zucchini goes well with a variety of main courses, from chicken and pork to steak. But this medley is so colorful and flavorful that it might steal the spotlight from your entree.
—Regina Gutierrez, San Antonio, Texas

✓ Uses less fat, sugar or salt. Includes Nutritional Analysis and Diabetic Exchanges.

 2 medium summer squash, halved and sliced
 2 medium zucchini, halved and sliced
 1/3 cup chopped onion

Blue Cheese Green Beans

Herbed Rice

1/2 teaspoon dried thyme
1/2 teaspoon dried marjoram
1/4 teaspoon dried rosemary, crushed
1-1/2 cups uncooked instant rice

In a large saucepan, bring water to a boil. Add the bouillon, onion, thyme, marjoram and rosemary; stir until the bouillon is dissolved. Stir in the rice. Cover and remove from the heat; let stand for 5 minutes. Fluff with a fork. **Yield:** 3 servings.

Feta Veggie Salad

(Pictured below)

Prep/Total Time: 15 min.

If you're tired of the same old green salads, try this medley I came up with after tasting something similar at a restaurant. It makes a wonderful meal paired with grilled chicken and steamed rice. —Kristen Zayon
Anchorage, Alaska

2 cups sliced fresh mushrooms
1 large green pepper, coarsely chopped
1 medium cucumber, seeded and chopped
1 large tomato, seeded and chopped
1 small red onion, coarsely chopped
1 cup (4 ounces) crumbled tomato and basil feta cheese
1 teaspoon minced garlic
2/3 cup Greek vinaigrette

In a large salad bowl, combine the first seven ingredients. Drizzle with vinaigrette and toss to coat. Chill until serving. **Yield:** 9 servings.

1-1/2 teaspoons olive oil
1 large plum tomato, diced
1 tablespoon butter
1/2 teaspoon lemon-pepper seasoning
1/4 teaspoon garlic powder
1/8 teaspoon salt
1/2 cup shredded Monterey Jack cheese

In a large skillet, saute the squash, zucchini and onion in oil for 8 minutes or until crisp-tender. Stir in the tomato, butter, lemon-pepper, garlic powder and salt. Cook for 2 minutes or until heated through. Remove from the heat; sprinkle with cheese. Cover for 1 minute or until cheese is melted. **Yield:** 8 servings.
Nutritional Analysis: 3/4 cup (prepared with reduced-fat butter and cheese) equals 55 calories, 3 g fat (2 g saturated fat), 8 mg cholesterol, 123 mg sodium, 5 g carbohydrate, 2 g fiber, 3 g protein. **Diabetic Exchanges:** 1 vegetable, 1/2 fat.

Herbed Rice

(Pictured above)

Prep/Total Time: 15 min.

My mom shared this recipe. It requires almost no preparation and makes a delicious addition to just about any main course. Try it with beef bouillon instead of chicken bouillon if that's a better fit with your meal.
—Valerie Meldrum, Taylorsville, Utah

1-1/2 cups water
2 teaspoons chicken bouillon granules
1 teaspoon dried minced onion

Feta Veggie Salad

Cranberry Apple Saute

1/2 cup water
3 tablespoons butter
3 tablespoons all-purpose flour
1/2 teaspoon salt
1/2 teaspoon pepper
1/2 teaspoon ground mustard
1/4 teaspoon chili powder
3/4 cup milk
1-1/4 cups shredded cheddar cheese
2 tablespoons salsa

Place cauliflower and water in a microwave-safe bowl. Cover and microwave on high for 8-10 minutes or until tender.

Meanwhile, in a small saucepan, melt the butter. Stir in flour and seasonings until smooth. Gradually stir in milk. Bring to a boil; cook and stir for 2 minutes. Reduce heat; stir in cheese and salsa until cheese is melted. Drain cauliflower well; drizzle with cheese sauce. **Yield:** 8 servings.

Editor's Note: This recipe was tested in a 1,100-watt microwave.

Fruited Broccoli Salad

(Pictured below)

Prep/Total Time: 20 min.

My husband is not usually a salad eater. When I developed this sweet dressing and salad for him, he loved it, and so have many others at church dinners, picnics and family gatherings. Sometimes we eat this by itself as a vegetarian meal.
—*Jad Monson, Spooner, Wisconsin*

Cranberry Apple Saute

(Pictured above)

Prep/Total Time: 30 min.

My husband came up with this recipe by adding cranberries to fried green apples. We thought the colors were perfect for the holidays, and the flavor went well with our Christmas ham. —*Rea Newell, Decatur, Illinois*

1/2 cup sugar
1/4 cup butter, cubed
1/2 teaspoon ground cinnamon
1/8 teaspoon ground nutmeg
Dash salt
4 medium unpeeled tart apples, thickly sliced
1 cup fresh *or* frozen cranberries

In a large saucepan, combine all ingredients. Cook over medium heat for 15-17 minutes or until the apples are tender and the sauce is slightly thickened, stirring occasionally. **Yield:** 6 servings.

Zippy Cauliflower

Prep/Total Time: 25 min.

I made up this recipe one night when I decided to have cauliflower with our supper. I used my mother-in-law's basic cheese sauce, added the spices, then stirred in some salsa left over from tacos the night before. It ended up being delightful. —*Shawntel Wiederholt, Layton, Utah*

1 medium head cauliflower, broken into florets (about 7-1/2 cups)

Fruited Broccoli Salad

1 can (8 ounces) pineapple chunks
4 cups fresh broccoli florets (about 1 large
   bunch)
2 celery ribs, chopped
1 cup seedless red grapes, halved
1 cup green grapes, halved
1 cup slivered almonds
1/4 cup snipped chives
1 cup mayonnaise
1/3 cup sugar

Drain pineapple, reserving 1 tablespoon juice (discard remaining juice or save for another use). In a large bowl, combine the pineapple, broccoli, celery, grapes, almonds and chives. In a small bowl, combine the mayonnaise, sugar and reserved juice. Pour over broccoli mixture and toss to coat. Refrigerate until serving. **Yield:** 8-10 servings.

Country Corn

Prep/Total Time: 20 min.

I cook church dinners for 120 people, so I'm always looking for fast, inexpensive menu items. After watching a chef put this corn dish together, I prepared it at church several times. There was never any left over.

—Kathleen Mancuso, Niskayuna, New York

6 green onions, chopped
3 tablespoons butter
1 package (16 ounces) frozen corn, thawed
2 teaspoons cornstarch
1/2 cup half-and-half cream
1/4 cup water
1/2 teaspoon salt
1/4 to 1/2 teaspoon pepper
1 cup grape tomatoes, halved

In a large skillet, saute the onions in butter for 2-3 minutes or until tender. Stir in the corn; cover and cook for 4-5 minutes or until heated through.

Meanwhile, in a small bowl, combine the cornstarch, cream, water, salt and pepper until smooth. Stir into corn mixture. Bring to a boil. Cook, uncovered, for 2 minutes or until thickened. Stir in the tomatoes. **Yield:** 6 servings.

Golden Diced Potatoes

(Pictured above right)

Prep: 15 min. **Cook:** 30 min.

My aunt once made potatoes like these for us. When I couldn't remember her exact recipe, I created this version. The lightly seasoned coating on the potatoes cooks to a pretty golden brown. —*Tiffany Wegerer Colwich, Kansas*

3/4 cup all-purpose flour
1 teaspoon seasoned salt
1/2 teaspoon onion powder
1/4 teaspoon garlic powder
1/4 teaspoon pepper

Golden Diced Potatoes

4 medium potatoes, peeled and cut into
   1/2-inch pieces
1/2 cup butter

In a large resealable plastic bag, combine the first five ingredients. Add 1/2 cup potatoes at a time; shake to coat. In two large skillets, melt butter. Add potatoes; cook and stir over medium heat for 25-30 minutes or until potatoes are tender. **Yield:** 6 servings.

More Spud Specialties

- When I need potato wedges for fries, I use my apple corer/slicer. Simply peel each potato if desired, stand it on a flat end and place the apple slicer on top. Then push down, and you'll have thick french fries. This is very fast and easy. —*Barbara Stewart Garland, Texas*

- To make instant mashed potatoes more flavorful, add chicken-flavored soup base. Just stir a tablespoon of the paste into the potatoes when you add the milk and butter. The mashed potatoes are so delicious that my grandchildren eat them without gravy. —*Saundra Meese, Bowerston, Ohio*

- I use leftover scalloped potatoes to make a quick potato soup. Combine a few cups of scalloped potatoes with mixed veggies and cream of mushroom, chicken or celery soup. Stir in enough milk to get the desired consistency, then heat through. —*Stephanie Wedland, Yates Center, Kansas*

Grilled Vegetable Medley

(Pictured below and on cover)

Prep: 15 min. **Grill:** 20 min.

This side dish is our favorite way to fix summer vegetables. Cleanup is a breeze because it cooks in foil. It goes from garden to table in under an hour and makes a great accompaniment to grilled steak or chicken.

—Lori Daniels, Beverly, West Virginia

 1/4 cup olive oil
 1 teaspoon salt
 1 teaspoon dried parsley flakes
 1 teaspoon dried basil
 3 large ears fresh corn on the cob, cut into 3-inch pieces
 2 medium zucchini, cut into 1/4-inch slices
 1 medium yellow summer squash, cut into 1/4-inch slices
 1 medium sweet onion, sliced
 1 large green pepper, diced
 10 cherry tomatoes
 1 jar (4-1/2 ounces) whole mushrooms, drained
 1/4 cup butter

In a large bowl, combine the oil, salt, parsley and basil. Add vegetables and toss to coat. Place on a double thickness of heavy-duty foil (about 28 in. x 18 in.). Dot with butter. Fold foil around vegetables and seal tightly. Grill, covered, over medium heat for 20-25 minutes or until corn is tender, turning once. **Yield:** 8 servings.

Skillet Sausage Stuffing

Prep/Total Time: 25 min.

I dressed up a package of stuffing mix with pork sausage, mushrooms, celery and onion to make this stuffing. It impressed my in-laws at a family gathering and has since become a popular side dish with my husband and children.

—Jennifer Lynn Cullen, Taylor, Michigan

 1 pound bulk pork sausage
 1-1/4 cups chopped celery
 1/2 cup chopped onion
 1/2 cup sliced fresh mushrooms
 1-1/2 teaspoons minced garlic
 1-1/2 cups reduced-sodium chicken broth
 1 teaspoon rubbed sage
 1 package (6 ounces) stuffing mix

In a large skillet, cook the sausage, celery, onion, mushrooms and garlic over medium heat until meat is no longer pink and vegetables are tender; drain. Stir in the broth and sage. Bring to a boil. Stir in stuffing mix. Cover and remove from the heat; let stand for 5 minutes. Fluff with a fork. **Yield:** 8 servings.

Vegetarian Penne

Prep/Total Time: 30 min.

My husband and I love pasta and vegetables, so I created this dish that combines penne with onion, zucchini, squash and more. It serves as dinner for the two of us or as an impressive side dish when we're entertaining. —Gail Cawsey
Fawnskin, California

 2 cups uncooked penne *or* medium tube pasta
 1/3 cup finely chopped onion
 1 small yellow summer squash, sliced
 1 small zucchini, sliced
 1/2 cup sliced fresh mushrooms
 1 teaspoon minced garlic
 3 tablespoons butter
 1 tablespoon all-purpose flour
 1/2 teaspoon salt
 1/4 teaspoon dried parsley flakes
 1/4 teaspoon dried thyme
 1/4 teaspoon pepper
 1/4 cup heavy whipping cream

Cook pasta according to package directions. Meanwhile, in a large skillet, saute the onion, summer squash, zucchini, mushrooms and garlic in butter until tender.

In a bowl, whisk the flour, seasonings and cream until smooth; add to the skillet. Cook for 2-3 minutes or until thickened. Drain pasta and add to vegetable mixture. Cook for 2-3 minutes or until heated through. **Yield:** 6-8 servings.

Grilled Vegetable Medley

fresh flavor. I like to serve them with grilled steak or my favorite roast. —Florence Palmer, Marshall, Illinois

   4 large tomatoes
Dash salt
   1 pound sliced fresh mushrooms
1/4 cup butter
   2 tablespoons all-purpose flour
   1 cup half-and-half cream
   2 tablespoons soft bread crumbs
3/4 cup minced fresh parsley
2/3 cup shredded cheddar cheese, *divided*

Cut tomatoes in half; scoop out and discard pulp, leaving a thin shell. Sprinkle lightly with salt; invert on paper towels to drain for 15 minutes.

In a large skillet, saute mushrooms in butter until most of liquid has evaporated, about 5 minutes. Sprinkle with flour; stir in cream. Bring to a boil; cook and stir for 2 minutes or until thickened.

Remove from the heat. Stir in the bread crumbs, parsley and 1/3 cup of cheese. Spoon into tomato cups; sprinkle with remaining cheese. Place in a greased 13-in. x 9-in. x 2-in. baking dish. Bake, uncovered, at 400° for 10 minutes or until cheese is melted. **Yield:** 8 servings.

Lemon Corn and Zucchini

(*Pictured above*)

Prep/Total Time: 15 min.

This is a delicious veggie accompaniment to most meals. A combination of lemon and dill offers an elegant taste that's simple to achieve. The colorful medley is great for special occasions or weeknight meals.
—*Linda Massicotte-Black, Coventry, Connecticut*

   1 small zucchini, halved lengthwise and thinly sliced
1/3 cup chopped onion
1/4 teaspoon dill weed
   1 tablespoon butter
   1 can (15-1/4 ounces) whole kernel corn, drained
   2 teaspoons lemon juice

In a skillet, saute the zucchini, onion and dill in butter until onion is tender. Add corn and lemon juice; cook and stir until heated through. **Yield:** 4 servings.

Stuffed Tomatoes

(*Pictured at right*)

Prep: 30 min. **Bake:** 10 min.

This special-looking side dish is inexpensive, quick to prepare and always a favorite. With plenty of sliced mushrooms, the cheesy mixture stuffed into tomatoes has

Stuffed Tomatoes

Ginger Garlic Linguine

2 medium onions, sliced
1 tablespoon brown sugar
2 tablespoons butter
2 large tart apples, peeled and sliced
1/4 teaspoon salt
1/8 teaspoon white pepper

In a small saucepan, cook the onions and brown sugar in butter over medium-low heat until onions are tender, about 8 minutes. Stir in the apples, salt and pepper; cover and simmer for 10 minutes or until apples are tender. **Yield:** 3-4 servings.

Sweet Pepper Skillet

(Pictured below)

Prep/Total Time: 20 min.

If you're looking for a tasty accompaniment for spaghetti or meat loaf, this is it. The easy pepper medley is a snap to saute on the stovetop. —*Sundra Hauck
Bogalusa, Louisiana*

✓ Uses less fat, sugar or salt. Includes Nutritional Analysis and Diabetic Exchanges.

2 teaspoons olive oil
2 medium green peppers, thinly sliced
1 medium sweet yellow pepper, thinly sliced
1 medium sweet red pepper, thinly sliced
1 medium onion, cut into wedges
2 teaspoons minced garlic

Ginger Garlic Linguine

(Pictured above)

Prep/Total Time: 25 min.

While this recipe's ginger sauce was designed for pasta, it's also good over green beans, pierogies or salmon. I often triple the sauce, then freeze the extra so I can whip this dish up even faster on busy nights. —*Julie Miske
Acworth, Georgia*

12 ounces uncooked linguine
1/2 cup butter
4 green onions, finely chopped
2 tablespoons minced fresh gingerroot
2 teaspoons minced garlic
1 teaspoon dried basil
1/4 teaspoon cayenne pepper
1/4 cup grated Parmesan cheese

Cook linguine according to package directions. Meanwhile, in a large skillet, melt butter. Stir in the onions, ginger, garlic, basil and cayenne. Cook and stir over medium heat for 3-4 minutes or until onions are tender. Drain the linguine; add to skillet and toss to coat. Sprinkle with the Parmesan cheese. **Yield:** 6 servings.

Apple Onion Saute

Prep/Total Time: 30 min.

This tasty combination makes a comforting side dish. My husband requests it whenever we have pork chops or pork roast. I've used a variety of apples, but we prefer a tart cooking apple, such as Granny Smith. —*Katie Crill
Priest River, Idaho*

Sweet Pepper S

1/4 teaspoon salt
1/4 teaspoon pepper

In a large skillet, heat oil. Stir in the remaining ingredients; saute for 5-7 minutes or until peppers are crisp-tender. **Yield:** 4 servings.

Nutritional Analysis: 1 cup equals 69 calories, 2 g fat (trace saturated fat), 0 cholesterol, 151 mg sodium, 12 g carbohydrate, 3 g fiber, 2 g protein. **Diabetic Exchanges:** 2 vegetable, 1/2 fat.

Veggie Rice Bowl

Prep/Total Time: 20 min.

This quick-and-easy recipe makes a lot, so it's great for potlucks, church suppers and other large gatherings. The buttery rice medley includes a colorful variety of vegetables. I've found that leftovers reheat well in the microwave.
—Sherry Hulsman, Elkton, Florida

　1 package (6.2 ounces) fast-cooking long grain and wild rice mix
　2 cups uncooked instant rice
1/2 cup chopped green onions
1/2 cup chopped celery
1/2 cup chopped fresh mushrooms
1/2 cup chopped carrot
　3 tablespoons butter
　1 cup frozen peas

Prepare rice mix and instant rice separately according to package directions. Meanwhile, in a large skillet, saute the onions, celery, mushrooms and carrot in butter for 4-6 minutes or until tender. Stir in peas and prepared rice; cook for 2-4 minutes or until heated through. **Yield:** 12 servings.

Creamed Spinach

Prep/Total Time: 20 min.

This flavorful side dish is so tasty, people forget that they're eating nutritious spinach. It's long been a family favorite, especially for holidays and special occasions. We've enjoyed this creamy creation with a variety of meats—roasted turkey, chicken, ham and brisket.
—Elizabeth Hunter, Flower Mound, Texas

　2 packages (10 ounces *each*) frozen chopped spinach
　1 tablespoon dried minced onion
　1 tablespoon all-purpose flour
　1 can (10-3/4 ounces) condensed cream of celery soup, undiluted
1/4 cup butter, cubed
1/4 teaspoon garlic powder
Dash pepper

Cook spinach according to package directions; drain and squeeze dry. Add onion; set aside. In a large saucepan, combine the flour, soup, butter and garlic powder. Bring to a boil over medium heat; cook and stir for 1 minute or until thickened. Stir in the spinach mixture and pepper. **Yield:** 3-4 servings.

Olive and Red Pepper Linguine

Olive and Red Pepper Linguine

(Pictured above)

Prep/Total Time: 20 min.

With 16 grandchildren, I find that there's always someone around who is hungry. This is a quick, satisfying dish I like to fix when I'm busy. I sometimes serve it along with slices of garlic bread for an easy meatless meal. —Betty Carpenter
Hookstown, Pennsylvania

　　8 ounces uncooked linguine
　　1 medium sweet red pepper, chopped
　3/4 cup sliced fresh mushrooms
　1/2 cup chopped onion
1-1/2 teaspoons minced garlic
　　1 tablespoon vegetable oil
　15 stuffed olives, sliced
　　1 tablespoon butter

Cook linguine according to package directions. Meanwhile, in a large skillet, saute the red pepper, mushrooms, onion and garlic in oil. Drain linguine; add to the skillet. Stir in the olives and butter. **Yield:** 8 servings.

Perk Up Pasta and Rice

If you're short on time but still want to round out a meal with rice or pasta, try this idea. When cooking the rice or pasta, add bouillion granules or instant soup mix to the water and omit the salt. I've found that it's an easy way to add extra flavor along with the sodium we like for good taste. —Lyne Shaffer
Redgranite, Wisconsin

Chapter 9

IT'S IRRESISTIBLE—the aroma of golden brown, tender, delectable baked goods fresh from the oven. And the taste of these tempting treats is even better!

With the fast-to-fix recipes here, you and your family can enjoy tantalizing breads, rolls, muffins, biscuits and other baked sensations whenever you like...even on the most hectic nights of the week.

You'll find it's a snap to whip up any of these time-saving delights—from Spiced Walnut Loaf and Garlic Herb Twists to Afternoon Tea Scones and Coconut-Chip Coffee Cake.

So put one of these fuss-free recipes on today's dinner menu and thrill everyone at the table.

GOLDEN GOODIES. Chocolate Chip Muffins (p. 137), Sweet Potato Quick Bread (p. 134), Garlic Herb Twists (p. 140) and Marmalade Monkey Bread (p. 134).

Afternoon Tea Scones

Winter Squash Bread

Prep: 15 min. **Bake:** 55 min. + cooling

My family loves this nutty bread that uses squash in place of zucchini. —*Violet Rundels, Waverly, Ohio*

3 cups all-purpose flour
2 cups sugar
2 teaspoons baking soda
2 teaspoons ground allspice
1-1/2 teaspoons baking powder
1 teaspoon salt
3 eggs
1 cup vegetable oil
2 teaspoons vanilla extract
1 cup frozen cooked winter squash, thawed
1 cup mashed ripe bananas (about 2 medium)
1 cup chopped walnuts

In a large bowl, combine flour, sugar, baking soda, all-spice, baking powder and salt. In another bowl, beat the eggs, oil and vanilla; add squash and bananas. Stir into dry ingredients just until moistened. Fold in walnuts.

Pour into two greased 8-in. x 4-in. x 2-in. loaf pans. Bake at 350° for 55-60 minutes or until a toothpick inserted near the center comes out clean. Cool for 10 minutes before removing from pans to wire racks. **Yield:** 2 loaves.

Gingerbread Loaf

(Pictured below right)

Prep: 10 min. **Bake:** 3 hours

As a diabetic, I tend to stick with tried-and-true recipes. I added spices to a well-liked oatmeal bread to make this loaf. —*Barbara Severson, Tularosa, New Mexico*

✓ Uses less fat, sugar or salt. Includes Nutritional Analysis and Diabetic Exchanges.

1 cup plus 1 tablespoon water (70° to 80°)
1/2 cup molasses
1 tablespoon canola oil
3 cups bread flour
1 cup old-fashioned oats
1-1/2 teaspoons ground cinnamon
1 to 1-1/2 teaspoons ground ginger
1 teaspoon salt
1/2 teaspoon grated orange peel
1/4 teaspoon ground nutmeg
1/4 teaspoon ground cloves
1 package (1/4 ounce) active dry yeast

In bread machine pan, place all ingredients in order suggested by manufacturer. Select basic bread setting. Choose crust color and loaf size if available. Bake according to bread machine directions (check dough after 5 minutes of mixing; add 1 to 2 tablespoons of water or flour if needed). **Yield:** 1 loaf (about 2 pounds, 16 slices).

Nutritional Analysis: 1 slice equals 131 calories, 1 g fat (trace saturated fat), 0 cholesterol, 152 mg sodium, 27 g carbohydrate, 1 g fiber, 4 g protein. **Diabetic Exchange:** 2 starch.

Afternoon Tea Scones

(Pictured above)

Prep/Total Time: 30 min.

My guests always enjoy these scones served with butter, jam or jelly. Or try them as an addition to a weeknight meal. —*Ruth Ann Stelfox, Raymond, Alberta*

✓ Uses less fat, sugar or salt. Includes Nutritional Analysis.

1-3/4 cups all-purpose flour
1/4 cup sugar
2 teaspoons baking powder
3/4 teaspoon baking soda
1/2 teaspoon salt
2 tablespoons cold butter
1 egg, beaten
3/4 cup sour cream
1/2 cup dried currants *or* raisins
1 teaspoon grated lemon peel
1 teaspoon grated orange peel
1 egg yolk
2 tablespoons water

In a large bowl, combine the flour, sugar, baking powder, baking soda and salt; cut in butter until mixture resembles coarse crumbs. Stir in the egg, sour cream, currants, lemon peel and orange peel.

Turn onto a well-floured surface. Roll into a 7-in. circle. In a small bowl, beat egg yolk and water. Brush over dough. Cut into six wedges. Transfer to a greased baking sheet. Bake at 400° for 15 minutes or until golden brown. Serve warm. **Yield:** 6 scones.

Nutritional Analysis: 1 scone (prepared with reduced-fat sour cream) equals 295 calories, 8 g fat (5 g saturated fat), 91 mg cholesterol, 559 mg sodium, 47 g carbohydrate, 2 g fiber, 8 g protein.

Raspberry Cream Muffins

(Pictured at right)

Prep: 15 min. **Bake:** 25 min.

It took me a couple of batches to perfect these muffins, but my family thinks this version is the best. And, since they always gobble them up fast, I have to agree. Stir the raspberries into the batter gently so they don't break apart.

—Stephanie Moon, Nampa, Idaho

1 cup fresh raspberries
3/4 cup plus 2 tablespoons sugar, *divided*
1/4 cup butter, softened
1 egg
1/2 teaspoon almond extract
1/2 teaspoon vanilla extract
2-1/4 cups all-purpose flour
3 teaspoons baking powder
1/2 teaspoon salt
1 cup half-and-half cream
1 cup finely chopped vanilla *or* white chips
2 tablespoons brown sugar

In a small bowl, toss raspberries with 1/4 cup sugar; set aside. In a large mixing bowl, cream butter and 1/2 cup sugar. Beat in egg and extracts. Combine the flour, baking powder and salt; add to creamed mixture alternately with cream. Stir in chopped vanilla chips and reserved raspberries.

Fill greased or paper lined muffin cups three-fourths full. Combine brown sugar and remaining sugar; sprinkle over batter. Bake at 375° for 25-30 minutes or until a toothpick comes out clean. Cool for 5 minutes before removing from pan to a wire rack. Serve warm. **Yield:** 1 dozen.

Vidalia Onion Custard Bread
Raspberry Cream Muffins

Vidalia Onion Custard Bread

(Pictured above)

Prep: 20 min. **Bake:** 30 min. + cooling

As a Vidalia onion broker, I'm always trying to find new ways to serve those sweet onions to family, friends and customers. Their sweetness comes through nicely in these moist wedges. Serve them with soups and stews at dinner or with your favorite egg dishes at brunch.

—Libby Beese, St. Augustine, Florida

1 large Vidalia *or* sweet onion, halved and sliced
3 tablespoons butter, *divided*
1-3/4 cups all-purpose flour
2-1/2 teaspoons baking powder
1/2 teaspoon salt
1 egg
1-1/4 cups milk
3/4 cup shredded cheddar cheese, *divided*
1 teaspoon poppy seeds

In a large skillet, cook onion in 2 tablespoons butter over medium-low heat until very tender and lightly browned, about 15 minutes.

In a large bowl, combine the flour, baking powder and salt. Beat egg and milk; stir into dry ingredients just until moistened. Set aside 2 tablespoons onion mixture; fold remaining mixture into batter. Fold in 1/2 cup cheese. Pour into a greased 9-in. pie plate. Top with remaining cheese and reserved onion mixture. Sprinkle with poppy seeds.

Melt remaining butter; drizzle over the top. Bake at 400° for 30-35 minutes or until a knife inserted near the center comes out clean. Cool for 10 minutes on a wire rack. Cut into wedges; serve warm. Refrigerate leftovers. **Yield:** 8-10 servings.

Gingerbread Loaf

Sweet Potato Quick Bread

(Pictured below and on page 131)

Prep: 20 min. **Bake:** 65 min. + cooling

I enjoy making this bread because it lets me use sweet potatoes in something besides pie. I found the recipe in an old Southern cookbook, but I changed a few things. The orange juice in the glaze adds a nice citrus flavor to the loaves. —Ann Jovanovic, Chicago, Illinois

```
3-1/2 cups all-purpose flour
    2 teaspoons baking soda
    1 teaspoon baking powder
    1 teaspoon ground cinnamon
    1 teaspoon ground nutmeg
  1/2 teaspoon salt
  1/2 teaspoon ground cloves
    2 cups mashed canned sweet potatoes
    3 eggs
    1 cup vegetable oil
    3 cups sugar
    1 cup chopped walnuts
    1 cup raisins
GLAZE:
1-1/2 cups confectioners' sugar
    4 to 5 teaspoons orange juice
    1 teaspoon grated orange peel
  1/3 cup chopped walnuts
```

In a large bowl, combine the first seven ingredients. In another bowl, whisk the sweet potatoes, eggs and oil. Add sugar; whisk until smooth. Stir into dry ingredients just until combined. Fold in walnuts and raisins (batter will be thick). Transfer to two greased 9-in. x 5-in. x 3-in. loaf pans.

Sweet Potato Quick Bread

Bake at 350° for 65-70 minutes or until a wooden skewer inserted almost to the bottom of the pan comes out clean. Cool for 10 minutes before removing from pans to wire racks to cool completely. For glaze, combine the confectioners' sugar, orange juice and orange peel until blended; drizzle over loaves. Sprinkle with walnuts. **Yield:** 2 loaves.

Buttons and Bows

Prep: 20 min. **Bake:** 10 min.

Biscuit mix speeds up these nutmeg-spiced buttons and bowknots. The recipe remains a Saturday morning favorite at our house. Serve the sugar-topped treats with hot coffee for dunking. —Marcie Holladay, Irving, Texas

```
    2 cups biscuit/baking mix
    2 tablespoons plus 1/4 cup sugar, divided
    1 teaspoon ground nutmeg
  1/8 teaspoon ground cinnamon
    1 egg
  1/3 cup milk
  1/4 cup butter, melted
```

In a bowl, combine the biscuit mix, 2 tablespoons sugar, nutmeg and cinnamon. Combine egg and milk; stir into dry ingredients just until moistened. Turn onto a heavily floured surface; knead 5-6 times. Roll out to 1/4-in. thickness. Cut with a floured 2-1/2-in. doughnut cutter; set centers aside for buttons.

For bows, twist each circle to form a figure eight; place on a greased baking sheet. Bake at 400° for 8-10 minutes or until golden brown. Place buttons on another greased baking sheet. Bake for 6-7 minutes. Brush tops with butter; sprinkle with remaining sugar. Remove from pans to wire racks. **Yield:** 1 dozen each buttons and bows.

Marmalade Monkey Bread

(Pictured above right and on page 131)

Prep: 15 min. **Bake:** 30 min.

We love this pretty pull-apart bread, and drop-in company just raves about it. Because it uses refrigerated biscuits, it's so easy and quick to fix. You can try whatever jam you have on hand in place of the marmalade. —Delia Kennedy, Deer Park, Washington

```
  2/3 cup orange marmalade
  1/2 cup chopped pecans or walnuts
  1/4 cup honey
    2 tablespoons butter, melted
    2 tubes (7-1/2 ounces each) refrigerated
      buttermilk biscuits
```

In a small bowl, combine the marmalade, pecans, honey and butter. Cut each biscuit into four pieces. Layer half of the pieces in a greased 10-in. tube pan; top with half of the marmalade mixture. Repeat.

Bake at 375° for 27-30 minutes or until golden brown. Cool in pan for 5 minutes before inverting onto a serving plate. Serve warm. **Yield:** 8 servings.

Marmalade Monkey Bread

Rosemary Cheddar Bread

(Pictured below)

Prep: 10 min. **Bake:** 3-4 hours

My husband and I love rosemary- and cheddar-crusted potatoes, so I adapted a potato bread recipe to include our favorite flavors. The bread machine makes this herbed loaf a snap to prepare. Everyone who has tasted it asks for the recipe. —Tammy Perrault, Lancaster, Ohio

> 1 cup water (70° to 80°)
> 3 tablespoons olive oil
> 1/2 cup mashed potato flakes
> 7-1/2 teaspoons sugar
> 3 teaspoons dried rosemary, crushed
> 1 teaspoon salt
> 3 cups bread flour
> 2-1/4 teaspoons active dry yeast
> 1-1/4 cups finely shredded cheddar cheese

In bread machine pan, place the first eight ingredients in order suggested by manufacturer. Select basic bread setting. Choose crust color and loaf size if available. Bake according to bread machine directions (check dough after 5 minutes of mixing; add 1 to 2 tablespoons of water or flour if needed).

Just before the final kneading (your machine may audibly signal this), add the cheese. **Yield:** 1 loaf (about 1-1/2 pounds).

Editor's Note: If your bread machine has a time-delay feature, we recommend you do not use it for this recipe.

Banana-Toffee Muffin Tops

(Pictured at right)

Prep/Total Time: 25 min.

Toffee bits and bananas give a delightful flavor to these moist breakfast treats. I sometimes sprinkle coarse sugar crystals on top for a special look. If you prefer, use miniature semisweet chocolate chips instead of English toffee bits. —Betty Kleberger, Florissant, Missouri

> 2-1/2 cups biscuit/baking mix
> 1/3 cup English toffee bits *or* almond brickle chips
> 1/4 cup sugar
> 1 egg
> 1/4 cup heavy whipping cream
> 1/2 teaspoon vanilla extract
> 1 cup mashed ripe bananas (about 2 medium)
> Additional sugar

In a bowl, combine the biscuit mix, toffee bits and sugar. In another bowl, combine the egg, cream and vanilla; stir in the bananas. Stir into the dry ingredients just until combined.

Drop by tablespoonfuls onto greased baking sheets. Sprinkle with additional sugar. Bake at 425° for 11-13 minutes or until golden brown. Remove to wire racks. Serve warm. **Yield:** about 1-1/2 dozen.

Rosemary Cheddar Bread
Banana-Toffee Muffin Tops

Breads in a Jiffy **135**

Cinnamon-Nut Coffee Cake

350° for 40-45 minutes or until a toothpick inserted near center comes out clean. Cool on a wire rack.

In a bowl, combine confectioners' sugar and butter flavoring; add enough milk to achieve desired consistency. Drizzle over coffee cake. **Yield:** 12 servings.

Lemon Blueberry Muffins

Prep/Total Time: 30 min.

When my sister and I spent the night at our grandmother's house, we often requested these muffins for breakfast. Today, I bake them for my kids. The very aroma is a trip down memory lane.
—*Kris Michels*
Walled Lake, Michigan

✓ Uses less fat, sugar or salt. Includes Nutritional Analysis and Diabetic Exchanges.

- 2 cups biscuit/baking mix
- 1/2 cup plus 2 tablespoons sugar, *divided*
- 1 egg
- 1 cup (8 ounces) sour cream
- 1 cup fresh *or* frozen blueberries
- 2 teaspoons grated lemon peel

In a large bowl, combine the biscuit mix and 1/2 cup sugar. Whisk the egg and sour cream; stir into dry ingredients just until moistened. Fold in blueberries.

Fill greased or paper-lined muffin cups half full. Combine the lemon peel and remaining sugar; sprinkle over batter. Bake at 400° for 20-25 minutes or until a toothpick comes out clean. Cool for 5 minutes before removing from pan to a wire rack. Serve warm. **Yield:** 1 dozen.

Nutritional Analysis: 1 muffin (prepared with reduced-fat baking mix and reduced-fat sour cream) equals 154 calories, 3 g fat (2 g saturated fat), 24 mg cholesterol, 251 mg sodium, 28 g carbohydrate, 1 g fiber, 3 g protein. **Diabetic Exchanges:** 1 starch, 1 fruit, 1/2 fat.

Editor's Note: If using frozen blueberries, do not thaw before adding to batter.

Cinnamon-Nut Coffee Cake

(Pictured above)

Prep: 15 min. **Bake:** 40 min. + cooling

With its simple glaze and layer of raisins and nuts, this buttery coffee cake tastes like a popular store-bought variety. I found the recipe in a church cookbook.
—*Maxine Winternheimer, Scottsdale, Arizona*

- 1 cup chopped pecans, *divided*
- 1/4 cup sugar
- 1/4 cup raisins
- 2 teaspoons ground cinnamon
- 1 package (18-1/4 ounces) yellow cake mix
- 1 package (3.4 ounces) instant vanilla pudding mix
- 4 eggs
- 3/4 cup water
- 3/4 cup vegetable oil
- 3 teaspoons butter flavoring
- 3 teaspoons vanilla extract

GLAZE:
- 1 cup confectioners' sugar
- 1/2 teaspoon butter flavoring
- 4 to 5 teaspoons milk

In a small bowl, combine 1/2 cup pecans, sugar, raisins and cinnamon; set aside. In a large mixing bowl, combine the cake mix, pudding mix, eggs, water, oil, butter flavoring, vanilla and remaining pecans. Beat on low speed just until blended; beat on medium speed for 2 minutes.

Pour half of the batter into a greased 13-in. x 9-in. x 2-in. baking pan. Sprinkle with reserved pecan mixture. Carefully spread remaining batter over top. Bake at

Coconut-Chip Coffee Cake

Prep: 15 min. **Bake:** 25 min. + cooling

I love the combination of chocolate, coconut and walnuts in this coffee cake. I serve it warm alongside a cup of coffee or hot cocoa. Using a biscuit mix really saves time when stirring up the batter.
—*Pauletta Bushnell*
Lebanon, Oregon

- 2 cups biscuit/baking mix
- 1/2 cup sugar, *divided*
- 1 egg
- 3/4 cup milk
- 3 tablespoons butter, melted, *divided*
- 1/3 cup semisweet chocolate chips, melted
- 1/3 cup flaked coconut
- 1/4 cup chopped walnuts

In a large bowl, combine the biscuit mix and 1/4 cup sugar. Whisk the egg, milk and 2 tablespoons butter; stir into dry ingredients just until moistened. Pour into a greased 8-in. square baking dish. Pour melted chocolate over the batter; cut through batter with a knife to swirl the chocolate.

Combine the coconut, walnuts, and remaining sugar and butter; sprinkle over the top. Bake at 400° for 25-30 minutes or until a toothpick inserted near the center comes out clean. Cool on a wire rack. **Yield:** 9 servings.

Chocolate Chip Muffins

(Pictured below and on page 130)

Prep: 15 min. **Bake:** 25 min.

Muffins are one of my favorite things to bake, and these are the best. I always keep some in the freezer for breakfast on the run. I can zap one in the microwave before I head out the door. —Kelly Kirby, Westville, Nova Scotia

  1/2 **cup butter, softened**
    1 **cup sugar**
    2 **eggs**
    1 **cup (8 ounces) plain yogurt**
    1 **teaspoon vanilla extract**
    2 **cups all-purpose flour**
    1 **teaspoon baking soda**
  1/2 **teaspoon baking powder**
  1/2 **teaspoon salt**
  3/4 **cup semisweet chocolate chips**
TOPPING:
  1/4 **cup semisweet chocolate chips**
    2 **tablespoons brown sugar**
    2 **tablespoons chopped walnuts, optional**
    1 **teaspoon ground cinnamon**

In a large mixing bowl, cream butter and sugar. Add eggs, one at a time, beating well after each addition.

Oregano-Swiss Bread Slices

Add yogurt and vanilla; mix well. Combine the flour, baking soda, baking powder and salt; add to the creamed mixture just until moistened. Fold in chocolate chips. Fill paper-lined muffin cups two-thirds full.

Combine the topping ingredients; sprinkle over batter. Bake at 350° for 25-30 minutes or until a toothpick inserted near the center comes out clean. Cool for 5 minutes before removing from the pans to wire racks. **Yield:** 1 dozen.

Oregano-Swiss Bread Slices

(Pictured above)

Prep/Total Time: 30 min.

I like to serve slices of this dressed-up French bread with a chef's salad. It's also a great complement to soup on a cold day. Sometimes I hollow out the loaf and fill it with the creamy mixture before baking. —Laura Murphy, Ventura, California

    2 **cups (8 ounces) shredded Swiss cheese**
  1/3 **cup mayonnaise**
    1 **tablespoon minced fresh oregano**
    1 **tablespoon grated onion**
    1 **tablespoon cider vinegar**
    1 **loaf (1 pound) unsliced French bread, halved lengthwise**

In a bowl, combine the cheese, mayonnaise, oregano, onion and vinegar. Spread over cut sides of bread. Place on an ungreased baking sheet. Bake at 400° for 8-10 minutes or until cheese is melted and lightly browned. Serve warm. **Yield:** 16 slices.

Chocolate Chip Muffins

Orange Cranberry Bread

(Pictured below)

Prep: 20 min. **Bake:** 50 min. + cooling

With this recipe, you and your family can enjoy two moist loaves of bread that are packed with the wonderful taste of cranberries, chopped apple and orange peel. I suggest serving toasted slices with butter or cream cheese.
—Ron Gardner, Grand Haven, Michigan

2-3/4 cups all-purpose flour
2/3 cup sugar
2/3 cup packed brown sugar
3-1/2 teaspoons baking powder
1 teaspoon salt
1/2 teaspoon ground cinnamon
1/4 teaspoon ground nutmeg
1 egg
1 cup milk
1/2 cup orange juice
3 tablespoons vegetable oil
2 to 3 teaspoons grated orange peel
2 cups coarsely chopped fresh *or* frozen cranberries
1 large apple, peeled and chopped

In a large bowl, combine the flour, sugars, baking powder, salt, cinnamon and nutmeg. Combine the egg, milk, orange juice, oil and orange peel; stir into dry ingredients just until blended. Fold in the cranberries and apple.

Pour into two greased 8-in. x 4-in. x 2-in. loaf pans. Bake at 350° for 50-55 minutes or until a toothpick inserted near the center comes out clean. Cool for 10 minutes before removing from the pans to wire racks. **Yield:** 2 loaves.

Pumpkin Ginger Scones

(Pictured below)

Prep/Total Time: 30 min.

I made these lovely scones one day when looking for a way to use up leftover pumpkin, and I was not disappointed. I often use my food processor to stir up the dough just until it comes together. It's so simple to prepare this way.
—Brenda Jackson, Garden City, Kansas

2 cups all-purpose flour
7 tablespoons plus 1 teaspoon sugar, *divided*
2 teaspoons baking powder
1 teaspoon ground cinnamon
1/2 teaspoon salt
1/2 teaspoon ground ginger
1/4 teaspoon baking soda
5 tablespoons cold butter, *divided*
1 egg, lightly beaten

Pumpkin Ginger Scones
Orange Cranberry Bread

Walnut Cocoa Bread

In bread machine pan, place the first eight ingredients in order suggested by manufacturer. Select basic bread setting. Choose crust color and loaf size if available. Bake according to bread machine directions (check dough after 5 minutes of mixing; add 1 to 2 tablespoons of water or flour if needed).

Just before the final kneading (your bread machine may audibly signal this), add the walnuts. **Yield:** 1 loaf (1-1/2 pounds).

Editor's Note: If your bread machine has a time-delay feature, we recommend you do not use it for this recipe.

Mushroom Cheese Bread

(Pictured below)

Prep/Total Time: 15 min.

This savory grilled bread is delightful with barbecued steak, baked potatoes and corn on the cob. My family prefers it instead of rolls at Sunday dinners. For variation, we use half cheddar cheese and half mozzarella.
—Dolly McDonald, Edmonton, Alberta

    1 cup (4 ounces) shredded mozzarella cheese
    1 can (4 ounces) mushroom stems and pieces, drained
  1/3 cup mayonnaise
    2 tablespoons shredded Parmesan cheese
    2 tablespoons chopped green onion
    1 loaf (1 pound) unsliced French bread

In a bowl, combine the mozzarella cheese, mushrooms, mayonnaise, Parmesan cheese and onion. Cut bread in half lengthwise; spread cheese mixture over cut sides. Grill, covered, over indirect heat or broil 4 in. from the heat for 5-10 minutes or until lightly browned. Slice and serve warm. **Yield:** 10-12 servings.

1/4 cup canned pumpkin
1/4 cup sour cream

In a large bowl, combine the flour, 7 tablespoons sugar, baking powder, cinnamon, salt, ginger and baking soda. Cut in 4 tablespoons butter until mixture resembles coarse crumbs. Combine the egg, pumpkin and sour cream; stir into crumb mixture just until moistened.

Turn onto a floured surface; knead 10 times. Pat into an 8-in. circle. Cut into eight wedges. Separate wedges and place on a greased baking sheet. Melt remaining butter; brush over dough. Sprinkle with remaining sugar. Bake at 425° for 15-20 minutes or until golden brown. Serve warm. **Yield:** 8 scones.

Walnut Cocoa Bread

(Pictured above)

Prep: 10 min. **Bake:** 3 hours

I let my bread machine do the work when making this tender, chocolatey loaf. Its 10-minute preparation time and combination of brown sugar, walnuts and cocoa will help make it a favorite in your home, too.
—Margaret Beyersdorf Kissimmee, Florida

  2/3 cup warm milk (70° to 80°)
  1/3 cup water (70° to 80°)
    5 tablespoons butter, softened
  1/3 cup packed brown sugar
    1 teaspoon salt
    3 cups bread flour
    5 tablespoons baking cocoa
2-1/4 teaspoons active dry yeast
  2/3 cup chopped walnuts, toasted

Mushroom Cheese Bread

Garlic Herb Twists

People especially like the topping that's slightly crunchy with brown sugar, cinnamon and walnuts.
—Kristine Skinner, Marion, New York

  2 cups all-purpose flour
  1 teaspoon baking soda
  1/2 teaspoon baking powder
  1/2 teaspoon ground cinnamon
  1/4 teaspoon salt
  1/4 teaspoon ground allspice
  1/4 teaspoon ground nutmeg
  2 eggs, lightly beaten
  1-1/4 cups unsweetened applesauce
  1 cup sugar
  1/2 cup vegetable oil
  3 tablespoons milk
  1/2 cup chopped walnuts
TOPPING:
  1/4 cup chopped walnuts
  1/4 cup packed brown sugar
  1/2 teaspoon ground cinnamon

In a bowl, combine the first seven ingredients. Combine the eggs, applesauce, sugar, oil and milk; add to the dry ingredients just until moistened. Fold in walnuts. Transfer to a greased and floured 9-in. x 5-in. x 3-in. loaf pan.

Combine topping ingredients; sprinkle over batter. Bake at 350° for 1 hour or until a toothpick inserted near the center comes out clean. Cool for 10 minutes before removing from pan to a wire rack. **Yield:** 1 loaf.

Pumpkin Coffee Cake

Prep: 15 min. **Bake:** 35 min. + cooling

It's tough to resist a second helping of this delightful, comforting treat. It's a breeze to throw together because the recipe calls for pound cake mix and canned pumpkin. On cool autumn days, a piece is wonderful with a hot cup of coffee.
    —Sarah Steele, Moulton, Alabama

  1 package (16 ounces) pound cake mix
  3/4 cup canned pumpkin
  6 tablespoons water
  2 eggs
  2 teaspoons pumpkin pie spice
  1 teaspoon baking soda
TOPPING:
  1/2 cup chopped walnuts
  1/2 cup packed brown sugar
  1/4 cup all-purpose flour
  3 teaspoons butter, melted

In a large mixing bowl, combine the first six ingredients. Beat on medium speed for 3 minutes. Pour half of the pumpkin mixture into a greased 9-in. square baking pan.

Combine the topping ingredients; sprinkle half over the batter. Carefully spread with remaining batter. Sprinkle with remaining topping (pan will be full). Bake at 350° for 35-40 minutes or until a toothpick inserted near center comes out clean. Cool on a wire rack. **Yield:** 9 servings.

Garlic Herb Twists

(Pictured above and on page 130)

Prep/Total Time: 25 min.

I'm a busy wife, mother and grandmother who also works full time as an accounts payable clerk, so I need quick dinner ideas. These three-ingredient breadsticks are nice for church meetings, at potlucks or anytime.
    —Peggy Rosamond, Jacksonville, Texas

  1 tube (8 ounces) refrigerated crescent rolls
  1/3 cup sour cream
  1 to 2 tablespoons herb with garlic soup mix

Unroll crescent dough into one long rectangle; seal seams and perforations. Combine sour cream and soup mix; spread over dough. Cut into 1-in. strips. Loosely twist strips and place on an ungreased baking sheet. Bake at 375° for 11-13 minutes or until golden brown. Serve warm. **Yield:** 1 dozen.

Spiced Walnut Loaf

Prep: 15 min. **Bake:** 1 hour + cooling

I received the recipe for this delicious bread from a co-worker years ago. Many friends have asked for it since then.

Berry Bread with Spread

(Pictured below)

Prep: 20 min. **Bake:** 50 min. + cooling

The recipe for these two loaves and the creamy strawberry spread came from my mother's collection. I added macadamia nuts to give the fruit bread a fun crunch and tropical flair. —Pat Stewart, Lees Summit, Missouri

    1 package (8 ounces) cream cheese, softened
    2 packages (10 ounces *each*) frozen
        sweetened sliced strawberries, thawed
    3 cups all-purpose flour
    2 cups sugar
    1 teaspoon salt
    1 teaspoon baking soda
    4 eggs
    1 cup vegetable oil
    1 jar (3-1/4 ounces) macadamia nuts, chopped

For strawberry spread, in a small mixing bowl, beat cream cheese until smooth. Drain strawberries, reserving 1/4 cup juice for bread batter. Add 6 tablespoons of berries to the cream cheese; beat well. Set remaining berries aside. Chill spread until serving.

In a large bowl, combine the flour, sugar, salt and baking soda. Combine the eggs, oil, and reserved berries and juice; stir into dry ingredients just until moistened. Fold in nuts (batter will be stiff). Transfer to two greased 8-in. x 4-in. x 2-in. loaf pans.

Bake at 350° for 50-55 minutes or until a toothpick inserted near the center comes out clean. Cool for 10 minutes before removing from pans to wire racks to cool completely. Serve with spread. **Yield:** 2 loaves and about 1 cup spread.

Mini Italian Biscuits

Mini Italian Biscuits

(Pictured above)

Prep/Total Time: 20 min.

I tasted biscuits like these at a seafood restaurant and really liked them. I experimented in my kitchen until I was able to get the same flavor in these fast little bites. —Elaine Whiting, Salt Lake City, Utah

    2 cups biscuit/baking mix
    1/2 cup finely shredded cheddar cheese
    1/2 teaspoon garlic powder
    1/2 teaspoon dried oregano
    1/2 teaspoon dried basil
    2/3 cup milk

In a bowl, combine the biscuit mix, cheese, garlic powder, oregano and basil. With a fork, stir in milk just until moistened. Drop by rounded teaspoonfuls onto a lightly greased baking sheet. Bake at 450° for 7-8 minutes or until golden brown. Serve warm. **Yield:** about 3 dozen.

Berry Bread with Spread

Make Baking a Breeze

THE NEXT TIME you'd like to prepare a batch of golden brown baked goods for your family or friends, keep these handy tips in mind.

- To save time down the road, freeze the wrappers from sticks of butter in a plastic bag. They make it a cinch to grease loaf pans, muffin tins, etc.
- Using a spoon to fill muffin cups with batter can get messy. Instead, try an ice cream scoop with a quick release, or pour batter from a measuring cup.
- Out of baking powder? No problem! In place of 1 teaspoon baking powder, substitute 1/2 teaspoon cream of tartar and 1/4 teaspoon baking soda.

Chapter 10

Slow-Cooked & Make-Ahead Marvels

HOW NICE it is to arrive home at night to a dinner that's already started...or even ready to put on the table for your hungry family.

With these make-in-advance recipes, you can begin a meal well ahead of time to ease the evening rush on your most hectic days.

Combine ingredients in the slow cooker, then just switch it on and let supper cook all day while you're out.

Chill a prepared dessert in the refrigerator until it's mealtime...or freeze a casserole for an evening when you need to quickly pop a main course in the oven.

All of these terrific dishes can be started at convenient times and taken advantage of when time's tight.

MADE IN ADVANCE. Flavorful Pot Roast (p. 147).

Cranberry Pork Tenderloin

Cranberry Pork Tenderloin

(Pictured at left)

Prep: 10 min. **Cook:** 5 hours

I rely on a can of cranberry sauce to create the sweet sauce for this flavorful pork entree. I add orange juice and ground cloves to the mixture to season it nicely as it simmers.
—*Betty Helton, Melbourne, Florida*

  1 pork tenderloin (1 pound)
  1 can (16 ounces) whole-berry cranberry sauce
1/2 cup orange juice
1/4 cup sugar
  1 tablespoon brown sugar
  1 teaspoon ground mustard
1/4 to 1/2 teaspoon ground cloves
  2 tablespoons cornstarch
  3 tablespoons cold water

Place the tenderloin in a 3-qt. slow cooker. Combine the cranberry sauce, orange juice, sugars, mustard and cloves; pour over pork. Cover and cook on low for 5-6 hours or until a meat thermometer reads 160°.

Remove pork and keep warm. In a small saucepan, combine cornstarch and cold water until smooth; stir in cranberry mixture. Bring to a boil; cook and stir for 2 minutes or until thickened. Serve with the pork. **Yield:** 4 servings.

Hearty Hash Brown Dinner

Prep: 15 min. **Cook:** 4-1/2 hours

This meal-in-one with vegetables and ground beef is frequent fare in my house. It's great for potlucks and other gatherings, too. French-fried onions sprinkled on this dish after cooking create a crispy topping that everyone likes.
—*Marge Berg*
Gibbon, Minnesota

  3 cups frozen shredded hash brown potatoes, thawed
1/2 teaspoon salt
1/4 teaspoon pepper
  1 pound ground beef
1/2 cup chopped onion
  1 package (16 ounces) frozen California-blend vegetables
  1 can (10-3/4 ounces) condensed cream of chicken soup, undiluted
  1 cup milk
 12 ounces process cheese (Velveeta), cubed
  1 can (2.8 ounces) french-fried onions

Place potatoes in a lightly greased 5-qt. slow cooker; sprinkle with salt and pepper. In a skillet, cook beef and onion over medium heat until meat is no longer pink; drain. Spoon over potatoes. Top with vegetables. Combine soup and milk; pour over vegetables. Cover and cook on low for 4 to 4-1/2 hours.

Top with cheese; cover and cook 30 minutes longer or until cheese is melted. Just before serving, sprinkle with french-fried onions. **Yield:** 4 servings.

Slow-Cooked Specialties

FOR ON-THE-GO FAMILIES, cooking food slowly can actually save time when it's needed most—at the hectic supper hour. All you have to do is take advantage of a favorite kitchen appliance: the slow cooker.

By putting together these mouth-watering main courses, side dishes and appetizers well ahead of time and letting them simmer in the slow cooker for a few hours or more, you'll take a lot of the last-minute fuss out of dinner preparations.

So when you come home at the end of a busy day and hear the question, "How soon can we eat?", it won't take long to serve up a delicious, comforting meal that's sure to satisfy everyone at the table.

Lemonade Chicken

Prep: 10 min. **Cook:** 3 hours

I don't know where this recipe originally came from, but my mother used to prepare it for our family when I was little, and now I love to make it. A sweet and tangy sauce nicely coats chicken that's ready to serve in just a few hours. —Jenny Cook, Eau Claire, Wisconsin

✓ Uses less fat, sugar or salt. Includes Nutritional Analysis and Diabetic Exchanges.

```
6 boneless skinless chicken breast halves
  (4 ounces each)
3/4 cup lemonade concentrate
3 tablespoons ketchup
2 tablespoons brown sugar
1 tablespoon cider vinegar
2 tablespoons cornstarch
2 tablespoons cold water
```

Place chicken in a 5-qt. slow cooker. Combine the lemonade, ketchup, brown sugar and vinegar; pour over chicken. Cover and cook on low for 2-1/2 hours or until chicken juices run clear.

Remove chicken and keep warm. For gravy, combine cornstarch and water until smooth; stir into cooking juices. Cover and cook on high for 30 minutes or until thickened. Return chicken to the slow cooker; heat through. **Yield:** 6 servings.

Nutritional Analysis: 1 chicken breast half with 1/4 cup sauce equals 208 calories, 3 g fat (1 g saturated fat), 63 mg cholesterol, 147 mg sodium, 22 g carbohydrate, trace fiber, 23 g protein. **Diabetic Exchanges:** 3 very lean meat, 1-1/2 fruit.

Hot Fruit Salad

(Pictured at right)

Prep: 10 min. **Cook:** 2 hours

This comforting side dish is convenient to make in the slow cooker when your oven and stovetop are occupied with other dishes. The warm medley also can be served over sliced pound cake for dessert. —Debbie Kimbrough, Lexington, Mississippi

```
3/4 cup sugar
1/2 cup butter, melted
1/4 teaspoon ground cinnamon
1/4 teaspoon ground nutmeg
1/8 teaspoon salt
2 cans (15-1/4 ounces each) sliced peaches,
  drained
2 cans (15-1/4 ounces each) sliced pears,
  undrained
1 jar (23 ounces) chunky applesauce
1/2 cup dried apricots, chopped
1/4 cup dried cranberries
```

In a 3-qt. slow cooker, combine the sugar, butter, cinnamon, nutmeg and salt. Stir in the remaining ingredients. Cover and cook on high for 2 hours or until heated through. **Yield:** 10 servings.

Freezing Slow-Cooked Foods

ONCE FROZEN, cooked foods can quickly lose their distinctive flavor and texture. Because foods prepared in the slow cooker are cooked until they are well done, freezing will accelerate this process. So when slow-cooked foods are frozen and then reheated for a later meal, they can have an overcooked flavor and a mushy texture.

In general, when freezing leftovers from the slow cooker, stay away from those that contain potatoes, noodles or rice, because these ingredients have a greater chance of becoming soft.

It's also a good idea to avoid putting leftover slow-cooked sauces and gravies that were thickened with eggs, flour or cornstarch in the freezer. These foods can break down and separate after they've been frozen and reheated.

For the best results, freeze portions of slow-cooked beef roasts, pork roasts or poultry in their cooking liquid. This way, you can make gravy from the cooking liquid just before serving. Store the meat and liquid in freezer containers or resealable plastic freezer bags and use them within 2-3 months.

Hot Fruit Salad

Hearty Chicken Noodle Soup

(Pictured below)

Prep: 20 min. **Cook:** 5-1/2 hours

This satisfying homemade soup with a hint of cayenne is chock-full of vegetables, chicken and noodles. I revised a recipe from my father-in-law to come up with this version. It's great with a salad and crusty bread.

—Norma Reynolds, Overland Park, Kansas

    12 fresh baby carrots, cut into 1/2-inch pieces
     4 celery ribs, cut into 1/2-inch pieces
    3/4 cup finely chopped onion
     1 tablespoon minced fresh parsley
    1/2 teaspoon pepper
    1/4 teaspoon cayenne pepper
  1-1/2 teaspoons mustard seed
     2 garlic cloves, peeled and halved
  1-1/4 pounds boneless skinless chicken breast
        halves
  1-1/4 pounds boneless skinless chicken thighs
     4 cans (14-1/2 ounces *each*) chicken broth
     1 package (9 ounces) refrigerated linguine

In a 5-qt. slow cooker, combine the first six ingredients. Place mustard seed and garlic on a double thickness of cheesecloth; bring up corners of cloth and tie with kitchen string to form a bag. Place in slow cooker. Add chicken and broth. Cover and cook on low for 5-6 hours or until chicken juices run clear.

Discard spice bag. Remove chicken; cool slightly. Stir linguine into soup; cover and cook for 30 minutes or until tender. Cut chicken into pieces and return to soup; heat through. **Yield:** 12 servings (3 quarts).

Spicy Seafood Stew

(Pictured below left)

Prep: 30 min. **Cook:** 4-3/4 hours

This zippy stew is very easy and quick to prepare. The hardest part is peeling and dicing the potatoes, and even that can be done the night before. Just place the diced potatoes in a bowl of water in the refrigerator overnight to speed up assembly the next day.

—Bonnie Marlow
Ottoville, Ohio

✓ Uses less fat, sugar or salt. Includes Nutritional Analysis and Diabetic Exchanges.

     2 pounds potatoes, peeled and diced
     1 pound carrots, sliced
     1 jar (26 ounces) spaghetti sauce
     2 jars (6 ounces *each*) sliced mushrooms,
        drained
  1-1/2 teaspoons ground turmeric
  1-1/2 teaspoons minced garlic
     1 teaspoon cayenne pepper
    3/4 teaspoon salt
  1-1/2 cups water
     1 pound sea scallops
     1 pound uncooked medium shrimp, peeled
        and deveined

In a 5-qt. slow cooker, combine the first eight ingredients. Cover and cook on low for 4-1/2 to 5 hours or until potatoes are tender.

Stir in the water, scallops and shrimp. Cover and cook for 15-20 minutes or until scallops are opaque and shrimp turn pink. **Yield:** 9 servings.

Nutritional Analysis: 1 cup equals 261 calories, 4 g fat (1 g saturated fat), 93 mg cholesterol, 958 mg sodium, 35 g carbohydrate, 5 g fiber, 22 g protein. **Diabetic Exchanges:** 3 very lean meat, 2 starch, 1 vegetable.

Cranberry Meatballs

Prep: 20 min. **Cook:** 6 hours

Whether you serve them as appetizers or a main course, these tasty meatballs are sure to be popular. Cranberry and chili sauces combine to give these morsels a nice sweetness. They're very good over egg noodles.

—Nina Hall
Citrus Heights, California

     2 eggs, beaten
     1 cup dry bread crumbs

Spicy Seafood Stew
Hearty Chicken Noodle Soup

Flavorful Pot Roast

1/3 cup minced fresh parsley
2 tablespoons finely chopped onion
1-1/2 pounds lean ground beef
1 can (16 ounces) jellied cranberry sauce
1 bottle (12 ounces) chili sauce
1/3 cup ketchup
2 tablespoons brown sugar
1 tablespoon lemon juice

In a large bowl, combine the eggs, bread crumbs, parsley and onion. Crumble beef over mixture and mix well. Shape into 1-1/2-in. balls. Place in a 3-qt. slow cooker.

In a small bowl, combine cranberry sauce, chili sauce, ketchup, brown sugar and lemon juice; mix well. Pour over the meatballs. Cover and cook on low for 6 hours or until the meat is no longer pink. **Yield:** 6 servings.

Ham and Lentil Soup

Prep: 10 min. **Cook:** 4 hours

Lentil lovers will enjoy a big batch of this satisfying soup. Just pop it in the slow cooker after lunch, and it will be ready by supper time. —Connie Jones Pixley
Roxboro, North Carolina

1 cup chopped celery
1 cup chopped carrots
1/2 cup chopped onion
1 tablespoon butter
8 cups water
2 cups dried lentils, rinsed
1 cup cubed fully cooked ham
2 teaspoons salt

1 teaspoon dried marjoram
1/2 teaspoon pepper

In a large skillet, saute the celery, carrots and onion in butter for 3-4 minutes or until crisp-tender. In a 5-qt. slow cooker, combine the water, lentils, ham, salt, marjoram and pepper. Stir in the celery mixture. Cover and cook on low for 4 hours or until lentils are tender. **Yield:** 11 servings.

Flavorful Pot Roast

(Pictured above and on page 142)

Prep: 10 min. **Cook:** 7 hours

I season this tender pot roast with convenient envelopes of salad dressing and gravy mixes. For a delicious side dish to accompany the roast, thicken the flavorful cooking juices to create a gravy and serve it over mashed potatoes.
—Arlene Butler, Ogden, Utah

2 boneless beef chuck roasts (2-1/2 pounds *each*)
1 envelope ranch salad dressing mix
1 envelope Italian salad dressing mix
1 envelope brown gravy mix
1/2 cup water

Place the chuck roasts in a 5-qt. slow cooker. In a small bowl, combine the salad dressing and gravy mixes; stir in water. Pour over meat. Cover and cook on low for 7-8 hours or until tender. If desired, thicken cooking juices for gravy. **Yield:** 12-15 servings.

Sweet-and-Sour Chicken

1-1/2 cups fresh *or* frozen snow peas
Hot cooked rice

In a large skillet, saute chicken in oil for 4-5 minutes; drain. Sprinkle with salt and pepper. Drain pineapple, reserving juice; set pineapple aside. In a 5-qt. slow cooker, combine the chicken, water chestnuts, carrots, soy sauce and pineapple juice. Cover and cook on low for 3 hours.

In a small bowl, combine the cornstarch, sweet-and-sour sauce, water and ginger until smooth. Stir into the slow cooker. Add onions and pineapple; cover and cook on high for 15 minutes or until thickened. Add peas and cook 5 minutes longer. Serve with rice. **Yield:** 5 servings.

Pork Chops with Sauerkraut

Prep: 15 min. **Cook:** 3 hours

I pair tender pork chops with tangy sauerkraut in this filling main dish. It's so quick and easy to put together.
—Stephanie Miller, Omaha, Nebraska

  4 bone-in center-cut pork loin chops (8 ounces *each* and 1/2 inch thick)
  2 tablespoons vegetable oil
  1 jar (32 ounces) sauerkraut, undrained
3/4 cup packed brown sugar
  1 medium green pepper, sliced
  1 medium onion, sliced

In a large skillet, brown pork chops in oil over medium heat for 3-4 minutes on each side; drain. In a 5-qt. slow cooker, combine the sauerkraut and brown sugar. Top with pork chops, green pepper and onion. Cover and cook on low for 3 to 3-1/2 hours. Serve with a slotted spoon. **Yield:** 4 servings.

Sweet-and-Sour Chicken

(Pictured above)

Prep: 15 min. **Cook:** 3 hours 20 min.

I use a skillet and my slow cooker to fix this stir-fry-like chicken supper. It's perfect served over hot rice. Adding the onions, pineapple and snow peas later in the process keeps them from becoming overcooked.
—Dorothy Hess
Hartwell, Georgia

1-1/4 pounds boneless skinless chicken breasts, cut into 1-inch strips
  1 tablespoon vegetable oil
Salt and pepper to taste
  1 can (8 ounces) pineapple chunks
  1 can (8 ounces) sliced water chestnuts, drained
  2 medium carrots, sliced
  2 tablespoons soy sauce
  4 teaspoons cornstarch
  1 cup sweet-and-sour sauce
1/4 cup water
1-1/2 teaspoons ground ginger
  3 green onions, cut into 1-inch pieces

Onion Meat Loaf

Prep: 10 min. **Cook:** 5 hours

My husband and I really enjoy this delicious meat loaf. I need just five ingredients to assemble the easy entree before popping it in the slow cooker. —Rhonda Cowden
Paducah, Kentucky

  2 eggs
1/2 cup ketchup
3/4 cup quick-cooking oats
  1 envelope onion soup mix
  2 pounds ground beef

In a large bowl, combine the eggs, ketchup, oats and soup mix. Crumble beef over mixture; mix well. Shape into a round loaf.

Cut three 20-in. x 3-in. strips of heavy-duty aluminum foil. Crisscross the strips so they resemble the spokes of a wheel. Place meat loaf in the center of the strips; pull the strips up and bend the edges to form handles. Grasp the foil handles to transfer loaf to a 3-qt. slow cooker. (Leave the foil in while meat loaf cooks.)

Cover and cook on low for 5-6 hours or until a meat thermometer reaches 160°. Using foil strips, lift meat loaf out of slow cooker. **Yield:** 8 servings.

Swiss Steak Supper

Prep: 20 min. **Cook:** 5-1/2 hours

When I need a satisfying supper, I can always rely on this simple slow cooker recipe that takes advantage of prepared beef gravy. To save a little time, I keep peppered seasoned salt on hand to use instead of the seasoned salt and pepper.
—*Kathleen Romaniuk, Laval, Quebec*

1-1/2 pounds boneless beef top round steak
1/2 teaspoon seasoned salt
1/4 teaspoon coarsely ground pepper
1 tablespoon vegetable oil
6 to 8 medium potatoes, quartered
1-1/2 cups fresh baby carrots
1 medium onion, sliced
1 can (14-1/2 ounces) Italian diced tomatoes
1 jar (12 ounces) home-style beef gravy
1 tablespoon minced fresh parsley

Cut steak into six serving-size pieces; flatten to 1/4-in. thickness. Rub with seasoned salt and pepper. In a large skillet, brown beef in oil on both sides.

In a 5-qt. slow cooker, layer the potatoes, carrots, beef and onion. Combine tomatoes and gravy; pour over the top. Cover and cook on low for 5-1/2 to 6 hours or until meat and vegetables are tender. Sprinkle with parsley. **Yield:** 6 servings.

Throw-Together Short Ribs

(Pictured below)

Prep: 15 min. **Cook:** 4 hours 10 min.

This recipe takes no time to prepare and results in the most delicious, fall-off-the-bone short ribs. The longer you cook them, the better they get! Serve them on a bed of rice.
—*Lamya Asiff, Delburne, Alberta*

1/3 cup water
1/4 cup tomato paste
3 tablespoons brown sugar
1 tablespoon prepared mustard
2 teaspoons seasoned salt
2 teaspoons cider vinegar
1 teaspoon Worcestershire sauce
1 teaspoon beef bouillon granules
2 pounds beef short ribs
1 small tomato, chopped
1 small onion, chopped
1 tablespoon cornstarch
1 tablespoon cold water

In a 3-qt. slow cooker, combine the first eight ingredients. Add the ribs, tomato and onion. Cover and cook on low for 4-5 hours or until meat is tender.

In a small bowl, combine cornstarch and cold water until smooth; gradually stir into cooking juices. Cover and cook for 10-15 minutes or until thickened. **Yield:** 4-5 servings.

Throw-Together Short Ribs

Marmalade-Glazed Carrots

(Pictured below)

Prep: 10 min. **Cook:** 5-1/2 hours

This side dish is ideal when you'd like to serve your vegetables in a different way for a special dinner. Cinnamon and nutmeg season baby carrots that are simmered with orange marmalade and brown sugar. —Barb Rudyk
Vermilion, Alberta

     1 package (2 pounds) fresh baby carrots
   1/2 cup orange marmalade
     3 tablespoons cold water, *divided*
     2 tablespoons brown sugar
     1 tablespoon butter, melted
   1/2 teaspoon ground cinnamon
   1/4 teaspoon salt
   1/4 teaspoon ground nutmeg
   1/8 teaspoon pepper
     1 tablespoon cornstarch

In a 3-qt. slow cooker, combine the carrots, marmalade, 1 tablespoon water, brown sugar, butter and seasonings. Cover and cook on low for 5-6 hours or until carrots are tender.

Combine cornstarch and remaining water until smooth; stir into carrot mixture. Cover and cook on high for 30 minutes or until thickened. Serve with a slotted spoon. **Yield:** 6 servings.

Garlic-Apple Pork Roast

(Pictured below)

Prep: 10 min. **Cook:** 8 hours

This is the meal I have become known for among family and friends, and it is so simple. The garlic and apple flavors really complement the pork. It's great with steamed fresh asparagus and roasted red potatoes. —Jennifer Loos
Washington Boro, Pennsylvania

✓ Uses less fat, sugar or salt. Includes Nutritional Analysis and Diabetic Exchanges.

     1 boneless whole pork loin roast (3-1/2 to 4 pounds)
     1 jar (12 ounces) apple jelly
   1/2 cup water

Marmalade-Glazed Carrots
Garlic-Apple Pork Roast

2-1/2 teaspoons minced garlic
1 tablespoon dried parsley flakes
1 to 1-1/2 teaspoons seasoned salt
1 to 1-1/2 teaspoons pepper

Cut the roast in half; place in a 5-qt. slow cooker. In a bowl, combine the jelly, water and garlic; pour over roast. Sprinkle with parsley, salt and pepper. Cover and cook on low for 8 to 8-1/2 hours or until a meat thermometer reads 160° and meat is tender.

Let stand for 5 minutes before slicing. Serve with cooking juices if desired. **Yield:** 12 servings.

Nutritional Analysis: 3 ounces cooked meat (prepared with 1 teaspoon seasoned salt) equals 236 calories, 6 g fat (2 g saturated fat), 66 mg cholesterol, 165 mg sodium, 19 g carbohydrate, trace fiber, 26 g protein. **Diabetic Exchanges:** 3 lean meat, 1 fruit.

Creamy Bratwurst Stew

Smoked Beef Brisket

Prep: 10 min. **Cook:** 8 hours

Tender slices of this slow-cooked beef brisket have a sensational smoky flavor. This main dish is one of my family's favorites. —Dana Cebolski, Bessemer, Michigan

1 fresh beef brisket (2-1/2 pounds)
1 tablespoon Liquid Smoke
1 teaspoon salt
1/2 teaspoon pepper
1/2 cup chopped onion
1/2 cup ketchup
2 teaspoons Dijon mustard
1/2 teaspoon celery seed

Cut the brisket in half; rub with Liquid Smoke, salt and pepper. Place in a 3-qt. slow cooker. Top with onion. Combine the ketchup, mustard and celery seed; spread over meat. Cover and cook on low for 8-9 hours. Remove brisket and keep warm. Transfer cooking juices to a blender; cover and process until smooth. Serve with brisket. **Yield:** 4-6 servings.

Editor's Note: This is a fresh beef brisket, not corned beef.

Southern Pot Roast

Prep: 10 min. **Cook:** 5 hours

Cajun seasoning adds a kick to this beef roast that's served with a corn and tomato mixture. It's an unusual dish but full of flavor. —Amber Zurbrugg, Alliance, Ohio

1 boneless beef chuck roast (2-1/2 pounds)
1 tablespoon Cajun seasoning
1 package (9 ounces) frozen corn, thawed
1/2 cup chopped onion
1/2 cup chopped green pepper
1 can (14-1/2 ounces) diced tomatoes, undrained
1/2 teaspoon pepper
1/2 teaspoon hot pepper sauce

Cut roast in half; place in a 5-qt. slow cooker. Sprinkle with Cajun seasoning. Top with corn, onion and green pepper. Combine the tomatoes, pepper and hot pepper sauce; pour over vegetables. Cover and cook on low for 5-6 hours or until meat is tender. Serve corn mixture with a slotted spoon. **Yield:** 5 servings.

Creamy Bratwurst Stew

(Pictured above)

Prep: 20 min. **Cook:** 7-1/2 hours

A rich sauce coats this hearty combination of potatoes, carrots and bratwurst chunks. To create it, I adapted a baked stew recipe that appeared in a newspaper. This is so comforting on cold winter evenings. —Susan Holmes Germantown, Wisconsin

4 medium potatoes, cubed
2 medium carrots, coarsely chopped
2 celery ribs, chopped
1 cup chopped onion
3/4 cup chopped green pepper
2 pounds fresh bratwurst links, cut into 1-inch slices
1/2 cup chicken broth
1 teaspoon salt
1 teaspoon dried basil
1/2 teaspoon pepper
2 cups half-and-half cream
3 tablespoons cornstarch
3 teaspoons cold water

In a 5-qt. slow cooker, combine the potatoes, carrots, celery, onion and green pepper. Top with bratwurst slices. Combine the broth, salt, basil and pepper; pour over top. Cover and cook on low for 7 hours or until vegetables are tender and sausage is no longer pink.

Stir in the cream. Combine the cornstarch and water until smooth; stir into the stew. Cover and cook on high for 30 minutes or until the gravy is thickened. **Yield:** 8 servings.

Pizza Dip

Prep: 10 min. **Cook:** 1-1/2 hours

Everybody loves this simple dip. If you have any left over, spoon it on toasted English muffins for a great open-faced sandwich. —Sara Nowacki, Franklin, Wisconsin

 2 packages (8 ounces *each*) cream cheese, cubed
 1 can (14 ounces) pizza sauce
 1 package (8 ounces) sliced pepperoni, chopped
 1 can (3.8 ounces) chopped ripe olives, drained
 2 cups (8 ounces) shredded mozzarella cheese
Bagel chips *or* garlic toast

Place the cream cheese in a 3-qt. slow cooker. Combine the pizza sauce, pepperoni and olives; pour over cream cheese. Top with mozzarella cheese. Cover and cook on low for 1-1/2 to 2 hours or until cheese is melted. Stir; serve warm with bagel chips or garlic toast. **Yield:** 5-1/2 cups.

Sweet Pepper Chicken

(Pictured below)

Prep: 10 min. **Cook:** 4 hours

Sweet red and green pepper strips add attractive color to this delicious chicken. Put it in the slow cooker before getting ready for church on Sunday morning, and it'll be ready to eat when you get home. —Ann Johnson Dunn, North Carolina

 6 bone-in chicken breast halves, skin removed
 1 tablespoon vegetable oil
 2 cups sliced fresh mushrooms

Sweet Pepper Chicken

 1 medium onion, halved and sliced
 1 medium green pepper, julienned
 1 medium sweet red pepper, julienned
 1 can (10-3/4 ounces) condensed cream of chicken soup, undiluted
 1 can (10-3/4 ounces) condensed cream of mushroom soup, undiluted
Hot cooked rice

In a large skillet, brown chicken in oil on both sides. Transfer to a 5-qt. slow cooker. Top with mushrooms, onion and peppers. Combine the soups; pour over vegetables. Cover and cook on low for 4-5 hours or until the chicken juices run clear. Serve with rice. **Yield:** 6 servings.

Burgundy Lamb Shanks

Prep: 10 min. **Cook:** 8-1/4 hours

For those who love fall-from-the-bone lamb, this recipe fills the bill. Burgundy wine adds a special touch to the sauce that's served alongside. —Val Creutz Southold, New York

 4 lamb shanks (about 20 ounces *each*)
Salt and pepper to taste
 2 tablespoons dried parsley flakes
 2 teaspoons minced garlic
 1/2 teaspoon dried oregano
 1/2 teaspoon grated lemon peel
 1/2 cup chopped onion
 1 medium carrot, chopped
 1 teaspoon olive oil
 1 cup burgundy wine *or* beef broth
 1 teaspoon beef bouillon granules

Sprinkle lamb shanks with salt and pepper. Place in a 5-qt. slow cooker. Sprinkle with parsley, garlic, oregano and lemon peel.

In a small saucepan, saute the onion and carrot in oil for 3-4 minutes or until tender. Stir in wine or broth and bouillon. Bring to a boil, stirring occasionally. Pour over lamb. Cover and cook on low for 8 hours or until meat is tender.

Remove lamb and keep warm. Strain cooking juices and skim fat. In a small saucepan, bring juices to a boil; cook until liquid is reduced by half. Serve with lamb. **Yield:** 4 servings.

Tender Beef 'n' Bean Stew

(Pictured above right)

Prep: 15 min. **Cook:** 8-1/2 hours

I often whip up this easy stew on days when I am juggling a lot of the kids' sports schedules. Add a green salad and some corn bread or homemade rolls for a perfect meal. —Juline Goelzer, Arroyo Grande, California

✓ Uses less fat, sugar or salt. Includes Nutritional Analysis and Diabetic Exchanges.

 1 pound lean beef stew meat, cut into 1-inch cubes

Tender Beef 'n' Bean Stew

Citrus Turkey Roast

(Pictured below)

Prep: 15 min. **Cook:** 5-1/4 hours

I was skeptical at first about fixing turkey in a slow cooker. But once I tasted this dish, I was hooked. With a little cornstarch to thicken the juices, the gravy is easily made.
                                                    —Kathy Kittell, Lenexa, Kansas

   1 frozen boneless turkey roast (3 pounds), thawed
   1 tablespoon garlic powder
   1 tablespoon paprika
   1 tablespoon olive oil
   2 teaspoons Worcestershire sauce
1/2 teaspoon salt
1/2 teaspoon pepper
   8 garlic cloves, peeled
   1 cup chicken broth, *divided*
1/4 cup water
1/4 cup white wine *or* additional chicken broth
1/4 cup orange juice
   1 tablespoon lemon juice
   2 tablespoons cornstarch

Cut roast in half. Combine the garlic powder, paprika, oil, Worcestershire sauce, salt and pepper; rub over turkey. Place in a 5-qt. slow cooker. Add the garlic, 1/2 cup broth, water, wine or additional broth, orange juice and lemon juice. Cover and cook on low for 5-6 hours or until a meat thermometer reads 170°.

Remove turkey and keep warm. Discard garlic cloves. For gravy, combine cornstarch and remaining broth until smooth; stir into cooking juices. Cover and cook on high for 15 minutes or until thickened. Slice turkey; serve with gravy. **Yield:** 12 servings.

   2 cans (16 ounces *each*) kidney beans, rinsed and drained
   1 can (14-1/2 ounces) diced tomatoes, undrained
1-1/2 cups frozen corn
   1 cup hot water
   1 cup chopped onion
   2 celery ribs, chopped
   1 can (4 ounces) chopped green chilies
   1 can (2-1/4 ounces) sliced ripe olives, drained
   2 tablespoons uncooked long grain rice
   1 to 2 tablespoons chili powder
   2 teaspoons beef bouillon granules
1/4 teaspoon salt
   1 can (8 ounces) tomato sauce
Shredded cheddar cheese and sour cream, optional

In a 5-qt. slow cooker, combine the first 13 ingredients. Cover and cook on low for 8-9 hours or until beef is tender. Stir in the tomato sauce; cover and cook for 30 minutes or until heated through. Garnish with cheese and sour cream if desired. **Yield:** 10 servings.

Nutritional Analysis: 1 cup (prepared with reduced-sodium bouillon; calculated without cheese and sour cream) equals 209 calories, 4 g fat (1 g saturated fat), 28 mg cholesterol, 558 mg sodium, 28 g carbohydrate, 7 g fiber, 17 g protein. **Diabetic Exchanges:** 2 starch, 1-1/2 lean meat.

Citrus Turkey Roast

Cabbage Patch Stew

Prep: 20 min. **Cook:** 6 hours

Our family loves this hearty stew. I like to serve steaming helpings in old-fashioned soup plates with thick crusty slices of homemade bread. To get the 11 cups of chopped cabbage for this stew, you'll need to start with a small head of cabbage, about 2 to 2-1/2 pounds. Or for quicker prep, substitute coleslaw mix from the produce department.
—*Karen Ann Bland, Gove, Kansas*

✓ Uses less fat, sugar or salt. Includes Nutritional Analysis and Diabetic Exchanges.

> 1 pound ground beef
> 1 cup chopped onion
> 2 celery ribs, chopped
> 11 cups chopped cabbage
> 2 cans (14-1/2 ounces *each*) stewed tomatoes
> 1 can (15 ounces) pinto beans, rinsed and drained
> 1 can (10 ounces) diced tomatoes with green chilies
> 1/2 cup ketchup
> 1 to 1-1/2 teaspoons chili powder
> 1/2 teaspoon dried oregano
> 1/2 teaspoon pepper
> 1/4 teaspoon salt
> Shredded cheddar cheese and sour cream, optional

In a large skillet, cook beef, onion and celery over medium heat until meat is no longer pink and vegetables are tender; drain. Transfer to a 5-qt. slow cooker. Stir in cabbage, stewed tomatoes, beans, diced tomatoes, ketchup, chili powder, oregano, pepper and salt.

Cover and cook on low for 6-8 hours or until the cabbage is tender. Serve with shredded cheddar cheese and sour cream if desired. **Yield:** 8 servings.

Nutritional Analysis: 1-1/2 cups (prepared with lean ground beef; calculated without salt and optional toppings) equals 214 calories, 5 g fat (2 g saturated fat), 28 mg cholesterol, 642 mg sodium, 29 g carbohydrate, 6 g fiber, 16 g protein. **Diabetic Exchanges:** 2 lean meat, 2 vegetable, 1 starch.

Round Steak Sauerbraten

Prep: 20 min. **Cook:** 7 hours

It takes less than half an hour to prepare this round steak for the slow cooker. Then I simply let it simmer to a tasty tenderness most of the day. The flavorful beef strips and sauce are especially good served over hot rice.
—*Linda Bloom McHenry, Illinois*

> 1 envelope brown gravy mix
> 2 tablespoons plus 1-1/2 teaspoons brown sugar
> 2-1/2 cups cold water, *divided*
> 1 cup chopped onion
> 2 tablespoons white vinegar
> 2 teaspoons Worcestershire sauce
> 4 bay leaves
> 2-1/2 pounds boneless beef top round steak, cut into 3-inch x 1/2-inch strips
> 2 teaspoons salt
> 1 teaspoon pepper
> 1/4 cup cornstarch

In a 5-qt. slow cooker, combine the gravy mix, brown sugar, 2 cups water, onion, vinegar, Worcestershire sauce and bay leaves. Sprinkle beef with salt and pepper; stir into gravy mixture. Cover and cook on low for 6-1/2 to 7 hours or until tender.

Combine cornstarch and remaining water until smooth; stir into beef mixture. Cover and cook on high for 30 minutes or until thickened. Discard bay leaves. **Yield:** 8-10 servings.

Turkey Thigh Supper

(Pictured at left)

Prep: 10 min. **Cook:** 7 hours

This family-pleasing meal-in-one has it all—tender turkey thighs, tasty vegetables and a homemade sauce. I like to cook chicken breasts the same way. It's also good with honey-flavored barbecue sauce poured over the meat instead of the soup mixture.
—*Betty Gingrich Oxford, Arkansas*

> 3 medium red potatoes, cut into chunks
> 1/2 pound fresh baby carrots
> 2 medium onions, cut into chunks
> 4 turkey thighs, skin removed
> 1 can (10-3/4 ounces) condensed tomato soup, undiluted
> 1/3 cup water
> 1 teaspoon minced garlic

Turkey Thigh Supper

Italian Sausage Hoagies
Scalloped Taters

1 teaspoon Italian seasoning
1/2 to 1 teaspoon salt

In a 5-qt. slow cooker, layer the potatoes, carrots and onions. Top with turkey. Combine the soup, water, garlic, Italian seasoning and salt; pour over turkey. Cover and cook on high for 7-8 hours or until a meat thermometer reads 170° and vegetables are tender. **Yield:** 4 servings.

Italian Sausage Hoagies

(Pictured above)

Prep: 15 min. **Cook:** 4 hours

In southeastern Wisconsin, our cuisine is influenced by both Germans and Italians who immigrated to this area. When preparing this recipe, we usually substitute German bratwurst for the Italian sausage, so we blend the two influences with delicious results. —*Craig Wachs*
Racine, Wisconsin

10 uncooked Italian sausage links
2 tablespoons olive oil
1 jar (26 ounces) meatless spaghetti sauce
1/2 medium green pepper, julienned
1/2 medium sweet red pepper, julienned
1/2 cup water
1/4 cup grated Romano cheese
2 tablespoons dried oregano
2 tablespoons dried basil
2 loaves French bread (20 inches *each*)

In a large skillet over medium-high heat, brown sausage in oil; drain. Transfer to a 5-qt. slow cooker. Add the spaghetti sauce, peppers, water, cheese, oregano and basil. Cover and cook on low for 4 hours or until sausage is no longer pink.

Slice both loaves of French bread lengthwise but not all of the way through; cut each widthwise into five pieces. Fill each with sausage, peppers and sauce. **Yield:** 10 servings.

Scalloped Taters

(Pictured above)

Prep: 10 min. **Cook:** 4-1/2 hours

This creamy and comforting side dish tastes great with almost any dish and is a snap to assemble with convenient frozen hash browns. This is a good way to make potatoes when your oven is busy with other dishes.
—*Lucinda Walker, Somerset, Pennsylvania*

1 package (2 pounds) frozen cubed hash brown potatoes
1 can (10-3/4 ounces) condensed cream of chicken soup, undiluted
1-1/2 cups milk
1 cup (4 ounces) shredded cheddar cheese
1/2 cup plus 1 tablespoon butter, melted, *divided*
1/4 cup dried minced onion
1/2 teaspoon salt
1/8 teaspoon pepper
3/4 cup crushed cornflakes

In a large bowl, combine hash browns, soup, milk, cheese, 1/2 cup butter, onion, salt and pepper. Pour into a greased 5-qt. slow cooker. Cover and cook on low for 4-1/2 to 5 hours or until potatoes are tender.

Just before serving, combine the cornflake crumbs and remaining butter in a pie plate. Bake at 350° for 4-6 minutes or until golden brown. Stir the potatoes; sprinkle with crumb topping. **Yield:** 12 servings.

Grilled Pork Chops

In a large resealable plastic bag, combine the first eight ingredients; add pork chops. Seal bag and turn to coat; refrigerate for 8 hours or overnight.

Drain and discard marinade. Grill pork chops, covered, over medium heat for 10-15 minutes on each side or until juices run clear and a meat thermometer reads 160°. **Yield:** 4 servings.

Ice Cream Pretzel Cake

(Pictured below)

Prep: 30 min. + freezing

Our family loved a dessert we had at a local restaurant, so I invented my own version for a birthday party.
—Monica Rush, Reading, Pennsylvania

1-1/4 cups crushed pretzels
6 tablespoons cold butter
3/4 cup hot fudge ice cream topping, warmed
2 packages (7-1/2 ounces *each*) chocolate-covered miniature pretzels
1/2 gallon vanilla ice cream, softened
1/4 cup caramel ice cream topping

Place crushed pretzels in a small bowl; cut in butter until crumbly. Press onto the bottom of a greased 9-in. springform pan. Cover and freeze for at least 30 minutes. Spread fudge topping over crust; cover and freeze.

Set aside 16 chocolate-covered pretzels for garnish. Place remaining pretzels in a food processor; cover and process until crumbly. Transfer to a large bowl; stir in ice cream. Spread over the fudge topping. Drizzle with the caramel topping. Garnish with the reserved pretzels. Cover and freeze for at least 8 hours or overnight. **Yield:** 16 servings.

Editor's Note: If you are unable to find chocolate-coated pretzels, use 1 package (11-1/2 ounces) milk chocolate chips, 4 teaspoons shortening and about 110 miniature pretzel twists. In a microwave, melt chips and shortening; stir until blended. With a fork, dip pretzels into chocolate mixture to evenly coat, reheating chocolate if needed. Let stand on waxed paper until set.

Make-Ahead Marvels

THE KITCHEN is a busy place in many households during the dinner hour, with the kids' homework being done while the mail is opened and meal preparation gets under way.

To cut down on the commotion, cooks often turn to recipes like these that can be readied ahead of time. Trimming time before supper can make your meal more relaxing for everyone.

Grilled Pork Chops

(Pictured above and on cover)

Prep: 5 min. + marinating **Grill:** 20 min.

I start preparing this sensational entree the night before I want to grill it. The marinade is fabulous and gives the meat great flavor. —Erica Svejda, Janesville, Wisconsin

1/2 cup Worcestershire sauce
1/4 cup minced fresh parsley
1/4 cup balsamic vinegar
1/4 cup soy sauce
2 tablespoons olive oil
1 teaspoon minced garlic
1/2 teaspoon pepper
1/4 teaspoon cayenne pepper
4 boneless pork loin chops (1 inch thick)

Ice Cream Pretzel Cake

Three-Meat Spaghetti Sauce

Three-Meat Spaghetti Sauce

(Pictured above)

Prep: 10 min. **Cook:** 55 min. + freezing

I simmer this hearty sauce in large batches, freeze it and use it for spaghetti, lasagna, mostaccioli and pizza.
—Ellen Stringer, Fairmont, West Virginia

 1 **pound ground beef**
 1 **pound bulk Italian sausage**
 1 **cup chopped onion**
 1 **can (28 ounces) crushed tomatoes**
 3 **cups water**
 2 **cans (6 ounces *each*) tomato paste**
 2 **jars (4-1/2 ounces *each*) sliced mushrooms,**
   drained
 1 **cup chopped pepperoni**
 2 **tablespoons grated Parmesan cheese**
 1 **tablespoon sugar**
 2 **tablespoons Italian seasoning**
 2 **teaspoons garlic salt**
 1 **teaspoon pepper**
 1 **teaspoon dried parsley flakes**
Hot cooked spaghetti

In a soup kettle or Dutch oven, cook beef, sausage and onion over medium heat until meat is no longer pink; drain. Stir in tomatoes, water, tomato paste, mushrooms, pepperoni, Parmesan cheese, sugar and seasonings. Bring to a boil. Reduce heat; cover and simmer for 30 minutes. Cool. Freeze in serving-size portions.
Yield: 11-1/2 cups.

To use frozen spaghetti sauce: Thaw in the refrigerator overnight. Heat in a saucepan; serve over spaghetti.

Pumpkin Cake Roll

(Pictured at right)

Prep: 30 min. **Bake:** 15 min. + freezing

This is great to keep in the freezer for a quick dessert for my family. —Erica Berchtold, Freeport, Illinois

 3 **eggs,** *separated*
 1 **cup sugar,** *divided*
2/3 **cup canned pumpkin**
3/4 **cup all-purpose flour**
 1 **teaspoon baking soda**
1/2 **teaspoon ground cinnamon**
1/8 **teaspoon salt**
FILLING:
 1 **package (8 ounces) cream cheese, softened**
 2 **tablespoons butter, softened**
 1 **cup confectioners' sugar**
3/4 **teaspoon vanilla extract**
Additional confectioners' sugar, optional

Line a 15-in. x 10-in. x 1-in. baking pan with waxed paper; grease the waxed paper and set aside. In a large mixing bowl, beat the egg yolks on high speed until thick and lemon-colored. Gradually add 1/2 cup sugar and the pumpkin, beating on high until the sugar is almost dissolved.

In a small mixing bowl, beat egg whites until soft peaks form. Gradually add the remaining sugar, beating until stiff peaks form. Fold into the egg yolk mixture. Combine the flour, baking soda, cinnamon and salt; gently fold into the pumpkin mixture. Spread into the prepared pan.

Bake at 375° for 12-15 minutes or until the cake springs back when lightly touched. Cool for 5 minutes. Turn cake onto a kitchen towel dusted with confectioners' sugar. Gently peel off waxed paper. Roll up cake in the towel jelly-roll style, starting with a short side. Cool completely on a wire rack.

In a mixing bowl, combine cream cheese, butter, confectioners' sugar and vanilla; beat until smooth. Unroll cake; spread filling evenly to within 1/2 in. of edges. Roll up again. Cover and freeze until firm. May be frozen for up to 3 months. Remove from freezer 15 minutes before cutting. Dust with confectioners' sugar if desired.
Yield: 10 servings.

Pumpkin Cake Roll

Zucchini Quiche

(Pictured below)

Prep: 25 min. **Bake:** 35 min.

A few years ago, I found this zucchini recipe that's quick to prepare and freezes well, too. Just put it in the refrigerator to thaw in the morning and pop it into the oven when you get home!
—Karen Howard
Lakeville, Massachusetts

   4 cups thinly sliced zucchini
   1 large onion, thinly sliced
   3 tablespoons butter
   2 eggs
   2 teaspoons dried parsley flakes
1/2 teaspoon salt
1/2 teaspoon *each* garlic powder, dried basil and
     oregano
1/4 teaspoon pepper
   2 cups (8 ounces) shredded mozzarella cheese
   2 teaspoons prepared mustard
   1 pastry shell (9 inches)

In a large skillet, saute the zucchini and onion in butter until tender; drain. In a large bowl, whisk the eggs, parsley, salt, garlic powder, basil, oregano and pepper. Stir in cheese and zucchini mixture. Spread mustard over pastry shell; add egg mixture.

Cover and freeze for up to 2 months. Or bake, uncovered, at 400° for 35-40 minutes or until a knife inserted near the center comes out clean and crust is golden brown (cover loosely with foil after 25 minutes if needed to prevent overbrowning). Let stand for 5 minutes before cutting.

To use frozen quiche: Thaw in the refrigerator. Bake, uncovered, at 400° for 50-55 minutes or until a knife inserted near the center comes out clean and crust is golden brown (cover loosely with foil after 35 minutes

Grilled Flank Steak Salad

if needed to prevent overbrowning). Let stand for 5 minutes before cutting. **Yield:** 6-8 servings.

Grilled Flank Steak Salad

(Pictured above)

Prep: 10 min. + marinating **Grill:** 25 min.

This super steak-and-veggie salad is one of our family's favorite recipes. The marinade gives the meat such a wonderful flavor. All you need to complete this meal is some good bread or a basket of dinner rolls.
—Mitzi Sentiff
Alexandria, Virginia

1/4 cup olive oil
1/3 cup balsamic vinegar
   1 tablespoon brown sugar
   1 tablespoon Dijon mustard
1/2 teaspoon minced garlic
1/2 teaspoon pepper
   1 beef flank steak (3/4 pound)
   1 package (5 ounces) spring mix salad greens
   1 plum tomato, cut into wedges
1/4 cup sliced radishes
1/4 cup chopped celery
   2 green onions, cut into 1-inch strips

In a bowl, whisk the first six ingredients. Pour 1/3 cup into a large resealable plastic bag; add steak. Seal bag and turn to coat; refrigerate for 3 hours. Cover and refrigerate the remaining marinade for dressing.

Drain and discard marinade from steak. Grill, covered, over indirect medium heat for 11-12 minutes on each side or until meat reaches desired doneness (for medium-rare, a meat thermometer should read 145°; medium, 160°; well-done, 170°). Cut across the grain into thin slices.

In a large serving bowl, combine the greens, tomato, radishes, celery, onions and beef. Drizzle with reserved marinade and toss to coat. **Yield:** 4 servings.

Zucchini Quiche

Pineapple Sirloin Skewers

(Pictured below)

Prep: 10 min. + marinating **Cook:** 10 min.

This is a tasty treatment for beef that relies on a made-in-moments marinade. I like to add mushrooms to the skewers and serve the yummy kabobs over hot cooked rice.
—Karen Hamlin, Marysville, Washington

  1 can (8 ounces) pineapple chunks
  6 tablespoons soy sauce
  2 tablespoons brown sugar
  2 tablespoons vegetable oil
  2 teaspoons ground ginger
  1 teaspoon minced garlic
1/2 teaspoon pepper
  1 pound boneless beef sirloin steak, cut
     into 1-inch cubes

Drain pineapple, reserving juice. Refrigerate the pineapple. In a small bowl, combine the pineapple juice, soy sauce, brown sugar, oil, ginger, garlic and pepper. Reserve 1/3 cup marinade for basting and 1/3 cup for serving; cover and refrigerate.

Pour the remaining marinade into a large resealable plastic bag; add beef cubes. Seal bag and turn to coat; refrigerate for 8 hours or overnight.

Drain and discard marinade from beef. On metal or soaked wooden skewers, alternately thread beef and pineapple chunks. Grill, uncovered, over medium heat for 5 minutes on each side or broil 4-6 in. from the heat until beef reaches desired doneness, basting frequently with one portion of reserved marinade. Serve with remaining marinade. **Yield:** 4 servings.

Toffee Apple French Toast

Pineapple Sirloin Skewers

Toffee Apple French Toast

(Pictured above)

Prep: 25 min. + chilling **Bake:** 35 min.

I love quick breakfast recipes that can be assembled the night before, saving time on busy mornings. I created this dish by incorporating my family's favorite apple dip with French toast. The winning combination is perfect for overnight guests.
—Reneé Endress, Galva, Illinois

  8 cups cubed French bread (1-inch cubes)
  2 medium tart apples, peeled and chopped
  1 package (8 ounces) cream cheese, softened
3/4 cup packed brown sugar
1/4 cup sugar
1-3/4 cups milk, *divided*
  2 teaspoons vanilla extract, *divided*
1/2 cup English toffee bits *or* almond brickle
     chips
  5 eggs

Place half of the bread cubes in a greased 13-in. x 9-in. x 2-in. baking dish; top with apples. In a mixing bowl, beat the cream cheese, sugars, 1/4 cup milk and 1 teaspoon vanilla until smooth; stir in toffee bits. Spread over apples. Top with remaining bread cubes. In another mixing bowl, beat the eggs and remaining milk and vanilla; pour over bread. Cover and refrigerate overnight.

Remove from the refrigerator 30 minutes before baking. Bake, uncovered, at 350° for 35-45 minutes or until a knife inserted near the center comes out clean. **Yield:** 8 servings.

Chili Tots

Kitchen home economists. Bake two loaves today and stash one (or both!) in the freezer to share with holiday company or at a last-minute get-together. You can also bake the bread in miniature pans to create three smaller loaves that make festive gifts when wrapped in plastic wrap and tied with ribbon.

      3-1/3 cups all-purpose flour
          3 cups sugar
          4 teaspoons pumpkin pie spice
          2 teaspoons baking soda
          1 teaspoon salt
      1/2 teaspoon baking powder
          4 eggs
          1 can (15 ounces) solid-pack pumpkin
      2/3 cup water
      2/3 cup vegetable oil
          2 cups (12 ounces) semisweet chocolate chips
          1 cup sliced almonds, toasted

In a large bowl, combine the first six ingredients. In another bowl, combine the eggs, pumpkin, water and oil; stir into dry ingredients just until moistened. Stir in chocolate chips and almonds.

Pour into two greased 9-in. x 5-in. x 3-in. loaf pans. Bake at 350° for 70-75 minutes or until a toothpick inserted near the center comes out clean. Cool for 10 minutes before removing from pans to wire racks to cool completely. Wrap the loaves in foil and freeze for up to 3 months.

To use frozen bread: Thaw at room temperature. **Yield:** 2 loaves.

Chili Tots

(Pictured above)

Prep: 15 min. **Bake:** 35 min.

I bake these tots in a 9- by 13-inch pan, but you can also use two smaller pans so you can enjoy one casserole tonight and freeze the other for another night.
                    —*Linda Baldwin, Long Beach, California*

      1 pound ground beef
      2 cans (15 ounces *each*) chili without beans
      1 can (8 ounces) tomato sauce
      1 can (2-1/4 ounces) sliced ripe olives, drained
      1 can (4 ounces) chopped green chilies
      2 cups (8 ounces) shredded cheddar cheese
      1 package (32 ounces) frozen Tater Tots

In a large skillet, cook the beef over medium heat until no longer pink; drain. Stir in the chili, tomato sauce, olives and chilies. Transfer to two greased 8-in. square baking dishes. Sprinkle with cheese; top with Tater Tots.

Cover and freeze one casserole for up to 3 months. Cover and bake the remaining casserole at 350° for 35-40 minutes or until heated through.

To use frozen casserole: Remove from the freezer 30 minutes before baking (do not thaw). Cover and bake at 350° for 1-1/4 to 1-1/2 hours or until heated through. **Yield:** 2 casseroles (6 servings each).

Chocolate Pumpkin Bread

(Pictured at right)

Prep: 15 min. **Bake:** 70 min. + cooling

Trim time during the busy holiday season with this recipe for moist pumpkin-flavored bread from our Test

Chocolate Pumpkin Bread

Potluck Lasagna

utes longer or until edges are bubbly. Let stand for 10 minutes before cutting. **Yield:** 12-15 servings.

To use frozen lasagna: Thaw in refrigerator overnight. Bake as directed.

Pistachio Eclair Dessert

(Pictured below)

Prep: 20 min. + chilling

This yummy dessert whips up in minutes and can be chilled until ready to serve. It's scrumptious and easy to fix. I often bring it to family gatherings and office parties, and it's always the first to go. —Lisa Givens
Austin, Texas

    3 cups cold milk
    1 package (3.4 ounces) instant pistachio
      pudding mix
    1 package (3.4 ounces) instant French vanilla
      pudding mix
    1 carton (8 ounces) frozen whipped topping,
      thawed
    1 package (14.4 ounces) graham crackers
    1 can (16 ounces) chocolate frosting

In a large bowl, whisk milk and pudding mixes for 2 minutes. Let stand for 2 minutes or until soft-set. Fold in whipped topping. In a 13-in. x 9-in. x 2-in. dish, layer a third of the graham crackers and half of the pudding mixture. Repeat layers. Top with remaining graham crackers. Refrigerate for at least 1 hour.

Spoon frosting into a microwave-safe bowl. Cover and microwave on high for 15-20 seconds or until softened, stirring once. Spread over graham crackers. Chill for at least 20 minutes or until frosting is set. **Yield:** 15-20 servings.

Potluck Lasagna

(Pictured above)

Prep: 30 min. **Bake:** 55 min. + standing

This is a variation on a lasagna dish a co-worker made for a company potluck. I usually double the recipe. When I was expecting our third son, I often prepared meals and froze them. It was so nice to have a substantial entree like this one ready to bake. —Colleen Wolfisberg
Everson, Washington

    1 pound ground beef
    1 can (14-1/2 ounces) Italian stewed
      tomatoes, cut up
    1 can (6 ounces) tomato paste
    1 tablespoon minced fresh parsley
  1/2 teaspoon minced garlic
    2 eggs
1-1/2 cups small-curd cottage cheese
1-1/2 cups ricotta cheese
    1 cup grated Parmesan cheese
    1 teaspoon salt
    1 teaspoon pepper
    6 lasagna noodles, cooked and drained
    2 cups (8 ounces) shredded mozzarella cheese

In a large skillet, cook beef over medium heat until no longer pink; drain. Stir in the tomatoes, tomato paste, parsley and garlic; remove from the heat. In a large bowl, combine the eggs, cheeses, salt and pepper. Layer three noodles in a greased 13-in. x 9-in. x 2-in. baking dish. Top with half of cottage cheese mixture, 1 cup mozzarella cheese and half of the meat sauce. Repeat layers.

Cover and freeze for up to 3 months. Or cover and bake at 375° for 30 minutes. Uncover; bake 25-30 min-

Pistachio Eclair Dessert

Chapter 11

Breakfast & Brunch Favorites

RISE AND SHINE for a tasty home-cooked breakfast! It's easy to do when you take advantage of the quick morning-meal recipes here.

So forget about stopping at the drive-thru window to get fast food on your way to work or other activities. Instead, let the whole family sit down to these sunrise sensations that start off your day in a wholesome, energizing way.

Each one can be put together either the night before or just before breakfast time. You'll be amazed at the fantastic feasts you can enjoy, from pancakes and sausages to egg bakes and sweet rolls.

And when you're planning to serve weekend brunch, rely on these done-in-a-dash dishes to impress your guests.

EARLY-DAY DELIGHTS. Cherry Berry Smoothies (p. 175), Florentine Egg Bake (p. 167), Caramel Sweet Rolls (p. 171) and Chocolate Croissants (p. 172).

Pancake Stack with Syrup

(Pictured at right)

Prep/Total Time: 20 min.

Who has time to make from-scratch pancakes and home-made syrup? You do, thanks to this easy recipe. My husband and I enjoy these pancakes with crisp bacon or sausages. —Joan Baskin, Black Creek, British Columbia

- 1-1/3 cups all-purpose flour
- 2 tablespoons sugar
- 3 teaspoons baking powder
- 1/2 teaspoon salt
- 1 egg
- 1 cup milk
- 3 tablespoons vegetable oil
SYRUP:
- 1 cup packed brown sugar
- 1/2 cup water
- 2 teaspoons butter
- 1/2 teaspoon rum extract

In a small bowl, combine the flour, sugar, baking powder and salt. Combine the egg, milk and oil; stir into dry ingredients just until combined. Pour batter by 1/3 cupfuls onto a lightly greased hot griddle. Turn when bubbles form on top of the pancake; cook until second side is golden brown.

Meanwhile, in a small saucepan, combine syrup ingredients. Cook until sugar is dissolved. Serve with pancakes. **Yield:** 6 pancakes and 1 cup syrup.

Monterey Turkey Omelet

(Pictured at right)

Prep/Total Time: 20 min.

Our Test Kitchen home economists use deli turkey, onion, garlic and green pepper to give a twist to a sunrise staple. The cheesy omelet looks special enough for company but leaves brunch hosts plenty of time to relax.

- 4 ounces thinly sliced deli smoked turkey, chopped
- 1/3 cup chopped onion
- 1/4 cup diced green pepper
- 1/2 teaspoon minced garlic
- 3 tablespoons butter, *divided*
- 6 eggs
- 3 tablespoons water
- 1/2 cup shredded Monterey Jack cheese

In a large skillet, cook the turkey, onion, green pepper and garlic in 2 tablespoons butter until vegetables are tender. Remove and keep warm.

In the same skillet, melt remaining butter. In a bowl, beat the eggs and water. Pour into skillet; cook over medium heat. As eggs set, lift the edges, letting uncooked portion flow underneath. When eggs are nearly set, spoon turkey mixture over half of the omelet. Fold omelet over filling. Sprinkle with cheese. Cover and let stand for 1-2 minutes or until the cheese is melted. **Yield:** 2-3 servings.

Tropical Smoothies

(Pictured at right)

Prep/Total Time: 10 min.

We like to experiment with different kinds of smoothies, and this refreshing creation is our favorite so far. The thick creamy blend has fabulous fruit flavors.
—Wendy Thomas, Pickens, South Carolina

✓ Uses less fat, sugar or salt. Includes Nutritional Analysis and Diabetic Exchanges.

- 2 cartons (6 ounces *each*) pina colada or pineapple yogurt
- 1 cup milk
- 1 can (11 ounces) mandarin oranges, drained
- 1/2 small ripe banana
- 1/2 cup frozen peach slices
- 2 tablespoons plus 1-1/2 teaspoons instant vanilla pudding mix
- 17 to 20 ice cubes

In a blender, combine first six ingredients; cover and process until smooth. While processing, add a few ice cubes at a time until mixture achieves desired thickness. Pour into chilled glasses; serve immediately. **Yield:** 5 servings.

Nutritional Analysis: 1 cup (prepared with reduced-fat yogurt, fat-free milk and sugar-free pudding) equals 150 calories, 1 g fat (1 g saturated fat), 4 mg cholesterol, 415 mg sodium, 30 g carbohydrate, 1 g fiber, 5 g protein. **Diabetic Exchanges:** 1 fat-free milk, 1 fruit.

Reuben Brunch Bake

Prep: 15 min. + chilling **Bake:** 40 min. + standing

I created this for a graduation brunch for two of our sons. When I realized I had most of the ingredients on hand for the Reuben dip I usually make, I decided to use them in a casserole instead! Everyone asked for the recipe.
—Janelle Reed, Merriam, Kansas

- 8 eggs, lightly beaten
- 1 can (14-1/2 ounces) sauerkraut, rinsed and well drained
- 2 cups (8 ounces) shredded Swiss cheese
- 1 package (2-1/2 ounces) deli corned beef, cut into 1-inch pieces
- 1/2 cup chopped green onions
- 1/2 cup milk
- 1 tablespoon Dijon mustard
- 1/4 teaspoon salt
- 1/4 teaspoon pepper
- 3 slices rye bread, toasted and coarsely chopped
- 1/4 cup butter, melted

In a large bowl, combine the first nine ingredients. Pour into a greased 11-in. x 7-in. x 2-in. baking dish. Cover and refrigerate overnight.

Remove from the refrigerator 30 minutes before baking. Toss crumbs and butter; sprinkle over casserole. Bake, uncovered, at 350° for 40-45 minutes or until a knife inserted near the center comes out clean. Let stand for 10 minutes before serving. **Yield:** 8-12 servings.

Pancake Stack with Syrup
Tropical Smoothies
Monterey Turkey Omelet

floured surface; knead 6-8 times.

On a greased baking sheet, pat the dough into a 10-1/2-in. circle, about 3/4 in. thick. Cut into eight wedges. Beat remaining egg; brush over dough. Slightly separate wedges. Bake at 425° for 10-15 minutes or until golden brown. Serve warm. **Yield:** 8 servings.

Peach Coffee Cake

(Pictured below)

Prep: 20 min. **Bake:** 20 min. + cooling

This from-scratch coffee cake is quick to put together, and it easily serves a crowd. While it's delicious with peach or apricot pie filling, I like to make it with cherry or strawberry filling during the holidays. —*Diana Krol Nickerson, Kansas*

    1 cup butter, softened
1-3/4 cups sugar
    4 eggs
    3 cups all-purpose flour
1-1/2 teaspoons salt
1-1/2 teaspoons baking powder
    1 can (21 ounces) peach pie filling
ICING:
1-1/4 cups confectioners' sugar
  1/2 teaspoon almond extract
    3 to 4 tablespoons milk

In a large mixing bowl, cream the butter and sugar until light and fluffy. Add the eggs, one at a time, beating well after each addition. Combine the flour, salt and baking powder; add to the creamed mixture and

Almond Chip Scones

Almond Chip Scones

(Pictured above)

Prep/Total Time: 30 min.

For bridal showers or other special occasions, I often triple the recipe for these moist scones. You can try blueberries instead of the chocolate chips and almonds. Or cut the dough into strips like biscotti, bake them and dip them into coffee. —*Heidi Rowley, Baton Rouge, Louisiana*

3-1/2 cups all-purpose flour
    2 tablespoons sugar
    5 teaspoons baking powder
    1 teaspoon salt
  1/2 cup cold butter
    4 eggs
    1 cup heavy whipping cream
1-1/2 to 2 teaspoons almond extract
    1 cup (6 ounces) semisweet chocolate chips
  1/2 cup slivered almonds, toasted

In a large bowl, combine the flour, sugar, baking powder and salt. Cut in the butter until the mixture resembles coarse crumbs. In a bowl, whisk 3 eggs, whipping cream and extract; add to crumb mixture just until moistened. Gently stir in chocolate chips and almonds. Turn onto a

Peach Coffee Cake

beat just until combined.

Spread 3-3/4 cups of batter into a greased 15-in. x 10-in. x 1-in. baking pan. Carefully spoon the pie filling to within 1 in. of edges. Spoon remaining batter over filling. Bake at 350° for 20-25 minutes or until a toothpick inserted near center comes out clean (cover loosely with foil if edges brown too quickly). Cool on a wire rack.

In a small bowl, combine the icing ingredients. Drizzle over coffee cake. **Yield:** 16-20 servings.

Florentine Egg Bake

(Pictured on page 162)

Prep: 30 min. **Bake:** 50 min. + standing

This flavorful breakfast bake comes together quickly using handy convenience foods, including refrigerated hash browns, biscuit mix and store-bought pesto. For a seafood variation, replace the ham with crabmeat.
   —Patricia Harmon, Economy Borough, Pennsylvania

   1 package (20 ounces) refrigerated shredded
      hash brown potatoes
   1 tablespoon olive oil
   1 package (10 ounces) frozen chopped
      spinach, thawed and squeezed dry
   4 ounces Swiss cheese, cubed
   4 ounces thinly sliced deli ham, coarsely
      chopped
   8 eggs
 1/2 cup buttermilk
   1 tablespoon prepared pesto
   1 cup biscuit/baking mix
 1/4 teaspoon salt
 1/8 teaspoon pepper
 1-1/2 cups shredded Asiago cheese
   2 tablespoons minced fresh basil

In a large bowl, combine the hash browns and oil. Press into a 13-in. x 9-in. x 2-in. baking dish coated with nonstick cooking spray. Bake at 350° for 25-30 minutes or until edges are golden brown.

Combine the spinach and Swiss cheese; sprinkle over crust. Top with ham. In a large bowl, whisk the eggs, buttermilk and pesto. Combine the biscuit mix, salt and pepper; add to egg mixture. Stir in the Asiago cheese. Pour over ham.

Bake, uncovered, for 25-30 minutes or until a knife inserted near the center comes out clean. Let stand for 10-15 minutes before cutting. Sprinkle with the basil. **Yield:** 8 servings.

Pumpkin Pancakes

(Pictured above right)

Prep/Total Time: 20 min.

With four small children, I am always looking for simple, quick and tasty recipes that they'll enjoy. They love pancakes, and these are great with breakfast sausage. I usually double or triple the recipe, depending on how hungry they are.   —Megan Schwartz, Burbank, Ohio

Pumpkin Pancakes

   1 cup complete buttermilk pancake mix
 1/2 teaspoon ground cinnamon
 1/8 teaspoon ground ginger
 2/3 cup cold water
 1/3 cup canned pumpkin
   1 cup maple syrup, warmed
 1/4 cup chopped pecans, toasted

In a bowl, combine the mix, cinnamon and ginger. In a small bowl, whisk water and pumpkin until blended; stir into dry ingredients just until moistened.

Pour batter by 1/4 cupfuls onto a hot griddle coated with nonstick cooking spray. Flatten with the back of a spoon. When underside is browned, turn pancakes and cook until second side is browned. Top with syrup and pecans. **Yield:** 6 pancakes.

When Egg Bakes Are Done

MOST RECIPES for baked egg dishes will say to bake until a knife inserted near the center comes out clean. However, that doesn't mean that the knife will be dry. Typically, the knife will be wet but not have a coating of egg on it.

It may be difficult to determine the doneness of egg dishes containing cheese or heavy cream because those ingredients may cling to the knife. When unsure of an egg bake's doneness, insert a thermometer near the center. It should register 160° or higher.

Very Vanilla French Toast

(Pictured at right)

Prep/Total Time: 10 min.

These French toast slices have creamy vanilla flavor from convenient pudding mix, plus a hint of cinnamon. We like to top them with syrup or powdered sugar and fresh berries. As a change of pace, try butterscotch pudding instead of vanilla.

—Linda Bernhagen, Plainfield, Illinois

1 cup milk
1 package (3 ounces) cook-and-serve vanilla pudding mix
1 egg
1/2 teaspoon ground cinnamon
8 slices Texas toast
2 teaspoons butter

In a bowl, whisk the milk, pudding mix, egg and cinnamon for 2 minutes or until well blended. Dip toast in pudding mixture, coating both sides. Melt butter on a griddle; cook French toast for 2-4 minutes on each side or until golden brown. **Yield:** 4 servings.

Honey Fruit Salad

(Pictured at right)

Prep/Total Time: 10 min.

Though fresh fruit steals the show in this morning medley, the subtle honey sauce makes it an especially sweet treat. It takes just 10 minutes to assemble this easy salad, which tastes so good with brunch. If you like, replace some of these fruits with blackberries, mangoes or peaches.

—Dorothy Dinnean, Harrison, Arkansas

2 medium firm bananas, chopped
2 cups fresh blueberries
2 cups fresh raspberries
2 cups sliced fresh strawberries
5 tablespoons honey
1 teaspoon lemon juice
3/4 teaspoon poppy seeds

In a large bowl, combine the bananas and berries. In a small bowl, combine the honey, lemon juice and poppy seeds. Pour over fruit and toss to coat. **Yield:** 8 servings.

Fiesta Scrambled Eggs

(Pictured at right)

Prep/Total Time: 30 min.

I love to fix this spicy scrambled egg dish for friends and family. It's a meal in itself, but I usually serve it with muffins or biscuits, fresh fruit, juice and coffee. For a milder breakfast dish that's still very flavorful, just eliminate the jalapeno peppers.

—Kay Kropff, Canyon, Texas

1/2 cup chopped onion
1/4 cup chopped sweet red pepper
1 jalapeno pepper, seeded and chopped
8 bacon strips, cooked and crumbled
8 eggs, lightly beaten
1 cup (4 ounces) shredded cheddar cheese, *divided*
1/2 teaspoon salt
1/8 teaspoon pepper
Salsa

In a large nonstick skillet coated with nonstick cooking spray, saute the onion and peppers until tender. Sprinkle with bacon. Pour eggs over the top; sprinkle with 1/2 cup cheese, salt and pepper. Cook over medium heat, stirring occasionally, until eggs are completely set. Sprinkle with the remaining cheese. Serve with salsa. **Yield:** 6 servings.

Editor's Note: When cutting or seeding hot peppers, use rubber or plastic gloves to protect your hands. Avoid touching your face.

Blueberry Blintz Souffle

Prep: 10 min. **Bake:** 65 min.

Store-bought blintzes speed up the preparation of this rich blueberry souffle. The wonderful brunch entree tastes great served alongside just about any breakfast meat. Additional sour cream and ice cream make yummy toppings.

—Iris Katz, Pompano Beach, Florida

3 tablespoons butter, melted
2 packages (13 ounces *each*) frozen blueberry blintzes
4 eggs, lightly beaten
1-1/2 cups (12 ounces) sour cream
1/4 cup sugar
1 tablespoon orange juice
1 teaspoon vanilla extract
Confectioners' sugar, optional

Place the butter in a 13-in. x 9-in. x 2-in. baking dish. Top with blueberry blintzes. In a bowl, combine the eggs, sour cream, sugar, orange juice and vanilla. Pour over the blintzes.

Cover and bake at 350° for 55 minutes. Uncover; bake 10-15 minutes longer or until lightly browned and a knife inserted in the egg mixture comes out clean. Sprinkle the souffle with confectioners' sugar if desired. **Yield:** 6 servings.

Outstanding Scrambled Eggs

When camping, my husband and I often host breakfast for 20 people or more. Needless to say, we need a fast strategy for feeding a hungry crowd.

So I use a wok to make a big batch of scrambled eggs cooked with ham and cheese. Then I transfer the eggs to a heated slow cooker. It keeps them nice and hot while everyone helps themselves to the feast.

—Betty Wilber, Rogue River, Oregon

Very Vanilla French Toast
Honey Fruit Salad
Fiesta Scrambled Eggs

Apple Puff Pancake

Pecan-Stuffed Waffles

(Pictured below)

Prep/Total Time: 15 min.

This is a great recipe for entertaining because it's easy yet extremely impressive. Whenever I serve it, no one guesses that it takes a mere 15 minutes to prepare. The creamy brown sugar and pecan filling between the waffles is delectable, and strawberries make a pretty, fresh-tasting garnish. —Jenny Flake, Gilbert, Arizona

    8 frozen waffles
    2 packages (3 ounces *each*) cream cheese, softened
  1/2 cup packed brown sugar
1-1/2 teaspoons ground cinnamon
    1 teaspoon vanilla extract
  1/2 cup chopped pecans
    1 cup maple syrup
Confectioners' sugar
    4 fresh strawberries, cut in half

Toast waffles according to package directions. In a small mixing bowl, beat the cream cheese, brown sugar, cinnamon and vanilla until smooth. Stir in pecans. Spread over four waffles; top with remaining waffles. Drizzle with maple syrup. Sprinkle with sugar; garnish each with a strawberry. **Yield:** 4 servings.

Apple Puff Pancake

(Pictured above)

Prep/Total Time: 25 min.

This thick and puffy pancake has such a pretty presentation that it gets high praise from family and company alike. For an extra-special touch, try topping each serving with warm pancake syrup and a dollop of whipped cream. —Linda Hubbuch, Versailles, Kentucky

  1/3 cup butter
    1 cup all-purpose flour
    4 eggs
    1 cup milk
Dash salt
    1 can (21 ounces) apple *or* peach pie filling
Toasted walnuts, optional

Place butter in a 10-in. ovenproof skillet. Place in a 425° oven until melted. In a large mixing bowl, beat the flour, eggs, milk and salt until smooth. Leaving 1 tablespoon melted butter in the skillet, pour the remaining butter into the batter; mix until blended. Pour batter into hot skillet. Bake for 15-20 minutes or until edges are golden brown.

    In a small saucepan, warm pie filling over low heat until heated through. Pour into center of puff pancake. Sprinkle with walnuts if desired. Serve immediately. **Yield:** 4 servings.

Pecan-Stuffed Waffles

Caramel Sweet Rolls

(Pictured on page 163)

Prep: 10 min. **Bake:** 25 min.

This is my favorite recipe for sweet rolls because it calls for a tube of ready-made breadstick dough. They take just minutes to assemble but taste like you spent hours making them. —Krista Smith, Mentone, California

1/2 cup packed brown sugar
1/3 cup heavy whipping cream
1/4 cup chopped walnuts
1 tube (11 ounces) refrigerated breadsticks
2 tablespoons sugar
1 teaspoon ground cinnamon

In a small bowl, combine brown sugar and cream until sugar is dissolved. Spread into a greased 8-in. square baking dish. Sprinkle with walnuts.

On a lightly floured surface, unroll breadstick dough (do not separate). Combine sugar and cinnamon; sprinkle over dough. Reroll, starting with a short end. Cut along breadstick scored lines. Place cut side down in prepared pan.

Bake at 350° for 25-30 minutes or until golden brown. Cool for 1 minute before inverting onto a serving plate. Serve warm. **Yield:** 6 servings.

Maple-Granola Trail Mix

Prep: 10 min. **Bake:** 30 min. + cooling

This crunchy mix is wonderful any time of day. It's great sprinkled over yogurt at breakfast or packed into a lunch box. —Malone Davidson, Landrum, South Carolina

4 cups old-fashioned oats
1/2 cup vegetable oil
1/2 cup maple syrup
1/2 cup slivered almonds
3 teaspoons vanilla extract
1/2 teaspoon ground cinnamon
1/3 cup *each* dried cranberries, chopped dried apples and chopped dried apricots
1/4 cup milk chocolate chips
1/4 cup butterscotch chips

In a large bowl, combine the oats, oil, syrup, almonds, vanilla and cinnamon. Spread in a 15-in. x 10-in. x 1-in. baking pan. Bake at 325° for 10-15 minutes. Stir; bake 20 minutes longer or until golden brown. Cool completely. Add the dried fruit and chips; toss to combine. Store in an airtight container. **Yield:** about 6 cups.

French Toast Supreme

(Pictured above right)

Prep/Total Time: 15 min.

I often use thick slices of French bread or homemade white bread when fixing these sandwiches. I served them with a fresh fruit salad at brunch, and everyone asked me for the recipe. It's easy to double or triple for a hungry crowd. —Elaine Bonica, Bethel, Maine

French Toast Supreme

8 slices Texas toast
4 slices Canadian bacon
4 slices Monterey Jack cheese
1 egg
1/2 cup refrigerated French vanilla nondairy creamer
Confectioners' sugar, optional
1/4 cup seedless raspberry jam

On four slices of Texas toast, place one slice of bacon and one slice of cheese; top with remaining Texas toast. In a shallow bowl, whisk egg and creamer. Dip sandwiches into egg mixture.

On a hot griddle or large skillet coated with nonstick cooking spray, cook the sandwiches for 2-3 minutes on each side or until golden brown. Sprinkle with confectioners' sugar if desired. Serve with jam. **Yield:** 4 servings.

Clues About Confectioners' Sugar

ALSO CALLED powdered sugar, confectioners' sugar is granulated sugar that has been crushed into a fine powder with about 3 percent cornstarch added to prevent clumping. It creates a pretty presentation when sprinkled on breakfast dishes like French Toast Supreme and Pecan-Stuffed Waffles.

Confectioners' sugar comes in three degrees of fineness, but only 10x, the most finely ground, is available in supermarkets. (Both 6x and 4x are only available commercially.) All *Quick Cooking* recipes are tested using 10x confectioners' sugar.

Pecan Pancake Pizza

(Pictured at right)

Prep/Total Time: 15 min.

Want to feed your family without flipping griddle after griddle of flapjacks? Try this big pancake pizza from our Test Kitchen home economists that bakes in the oven in minutes. Topped with granola and nuts, the wedges are wonderful served with syrup.

    2 cups pancake mix
    2 eggs, beaten
1-3/4 cups milk
    2 tablespoons vegetable oil
    1 teaspoon maple flavoring
    3/4 cup granola cereal without raisins
    3/4 cup pecan halves
Maple syrup, optional

Place pancake mix in a bowl. Combine the eggs, milk, oil and maple flavoring; add to pancake mix and mix well. Pour onto a greased 14-in. pizza pan; sprinkle with granola and pecans. Bake at 425° for 10-12 minutes or until a toothpick comes out clean. Cut into wedges. Serve with syrup if desired. **Yield:** 6-8 servings.

Spiced Fruit Compote

(Pictured at right)

Prep/Total Time: 25 min.

Cinnamon, cloves and ginger spice up convenient canned fruit in this warm medley that's ideal for a cool morning.
        —Thelma Hale, Osborne, Kansas

    2 cinnamon sticks (2 inches)
  12 whole cloves
1-1/2 cups orange juice
    2/3 cup raisins
    1/3 cup packed brown sugar
    1/2 teaspoon salt
    1/4 teaspoon ground ginger
    1 can (15-1/4 ounces) apricot halves, drained
    1 can (15-1/4 ounces) sliced pears, drained
    1 can (15-1/4 ounces) sliced peaches, drained
    1 can (15 ounces) pitted dark sweet cherries, drained

Place cinnamon sticks and cloves on a double thickness of cheesecloth; bring up corners of cloth and tie with kitchen string to form a bag.

In a large saucepan, combine the orange juice, raisins, brown sugar, salt and ginger. Add spice bag; bring to a boil. Reduce heat and simmer for 8 minutes. Add fruit; simmer for 3 minutes. Discard spice bag. Serve fruit warm or cold with a slotted spoon. **Yield:** 8 servings.

Strawberry Butter

Prep/Total Time: 10 min.

You'll need only three ingredients to whip up this fruit-filled breakfast spread. It's terrific on plain bread or toast, but I think it's especially good on pancakes and waffles.   *—Irene Marquardt, Peshtigo, Wisconsin*

    1 package (10 ounces) frozen sweetened sliced strawberries, thawed
    1 cup butter, softened
    1 cup confectioners' sugar
Bagels, English muffins or toast

In a blender or food processor, combine the strawberries, butter and sugar; cover and process for 3 minutes or until completely blended. Serve with bagels, English muffins or toast. **Yield:** 2-3/4 cups.

Chocolate Croissants

(Pictured on page 162)

Prep/Total Time: 25 min.

From time to time, we have stuffed French toast made from rich buttery brioche. One Father's Day when I wanted to make it for my husband, the store was out of brioche, so I tried croissants instead. They turned out to be even simpler to use.
        —Phyllis Johnston
        Fayetteville, Tennessee

  12 unsliced croissants
    2 cups milk chocolate chips
1/3 cup sugar
    1 teaspoon cornstarch
    1 teaspoon ground cinnamon
    1 cup milk
    4 eggs, lightly beaten
1/2 cup half-and-half cream
    3 teaspoons vanilla extract

Cut a slit into the side of each croissant; fill each with about 2 tablespoons chocolate chips. In a shallow bowl, combine the sugar, cornstarch and cinnamon; whisk in milk until smooth. Whisk in the eggs, cream and vanilla.

Dip croissants into egg mixture. Place in two greased 15-in. x 10-in. x 1-in. baking pans. Bake at 400° for 7-9 minutes or until golden brown. Serve warm. **Yield:** 1 dozen.

Freezing Flapjacks

FOR a family-pleasing pancake breakfast that requires almost no prep work in the morning, simply make extra pancakes ahead of time and freeze them. Try the following easy method:

After cooking the pancakes, let them cool. Then arrange them on baking sheets and freeze them, uncovered, until firm. Place them in resealable plastic freezer bags or airtight freezer containers before storing. They'll keep for up to 3 months.

To use the frozen pancakes, there's no need to thaw them before heating. Simply remove the number of pancakes that you want from the freezer and heat them in the oven, microwave or toaster oven until warm. Then just add maple syrup and enjoy!

Pecan Pancake Pizza
Spiced Fruit Compote

Pear-Pecan Sausage Quiche

nutmeg. Stir in cheese. Pour over sausage mixture.

Bake at 350° for 35-40 minutes or until a knife inserted near the center comes out clean and crust is golden brown. Garnish with pecan halves. Let stand for 5 minutes before slicing. **Yield:** 8 servings.

Christmas Cocoa

(Pictured below)

Prep/Total Time: 15 min.

A sprinkling of crushed candy canes gives a festive touch to this creamy hot cocoa...or place a chocolate mint candy cane in each mug as a stirrer. Serve this heartwarming beverage with Christmas cookies to welcome friends in from the cold after skating, sledding or caroling.
—Lori Daniels, Beverly, West Virginia

    4 cups milk
  2/3 cup instant chocolate drink mix
    5 chocolate mint candy canes, crushed, *divided*
1-1/2 cups heavy whipping cream
  1/4 cup confectioners' sugar
  1/2 teaspoon vanilla extract

In a large saucepan, combine the milk and drink mix. Cook and stir over medium heat until heated through. Remove from the heat. Set aside 1 tablespoon crushed candy canes for garnish. Stir remaining candy canes into cocoa; keep warm.

In a small mixing bowl, beat cream until it begins to

Christmas Cocoa

Pear-Pecan Sausage Quiche

(Pictured above)

Prep: 15 min. **Bake:** 35 min.

This quiche is a delightful addition to brunch, especially during the holiday season. It's savory from the spicy sausage yet sweet from the sliced pear.
—Patricia Harmon, Baden, Pennsylvania

  1/2 pound bulk hot Italian sausage
  1/3 cup chopped sweet onion
    1 medium pear, sliced
    1 unbaked pastry shell (9 inches)
  1/3 cup chopped pecans
    4 eggs
1-1/2 cups half-and-half cream
  1/2 teaspoon salt
  1/2 teaspoon dried thyme
  1/8 teaspoon ground nutmeg
    1 cup (4 ounces) shredded cheddar cheese
    8 pecan halves

In a large skillet, cook sausage and onion over medium heat for 4-5 minutes or until meat is no longer pink; drain. Arrange pear slices in pastry shell; top with the sausage mixture. Sprinkle with chopped pecans. In a large bowl, whisk the eggs, cream, salt, thyme and

thicken. Add confectioners' sugar and vanilla; beat until stiff peaks form. Ladle cocoa into mugs. Top with whipped cream; sprinkle with reserved crushed candy canes. **Yield:** 4 servings.

Mint-Cream Fruit Topping

(Pictured at right)

Prep: 15 min. + chilling

For a different spin on a typical fruit salad, try this creamy mint sauce. It's delicious dolloped on orange slices and other fresh fruit. In summer, it's very refreshing served over melon, strawberries, and red and green grapes.
—*Diane Hixon, Niceville, Florida*

  1 cup (8 ounces) sour cream
  2 tablespoons confectioners' sugar
  2 to 3 teaspoons minced fresh mint
1/4 teaspoon ground cardamom
  2 medium star fruit, sliced
  3 large navel oranges, peeled and sliced
  3 large kiwifruit, peeled and sliced
1/4 cup dried cranberries

In a small bowl, combine the sour cream, confectioners' sugar, mint and cardamom. Chill for at least 30 minutes. Just before serving, arrange star fruit, oranges and kiwi on salad plates or a serving platter; sprinkle with cranberries and dollop with the cream topping. **Yield:** 8 servings.

Cherry Berry Smoothies

(Pictured on page 163)

Prep/Total Time: 5 min.

You need just four ingredients to blend together these super-fast smoothies for breakfast. Try whipping them up on a hot summer day for a cool and refreshing treat.
—*Macy Plummer, Avon, Indiana*

1-1/2 cups unsweetened apple juice
  1 cup frozen unsweetened raspberries
  1 cup frozen pitted dark sweet cherries
1-1/2 cups raspberry sherbet

In a blender, combine the apple juice, raspberries and cherries. Add sherbet; cover and process until well blended. Pour into chilled glasses; serve immediately. **Yield:** 4 servings.

Speedy Sausage Squares

Prep: 15 min. **Bake:** 30 min.

Whenever I want to serve something special for a family brunch, this is usually what I prepare. I'll get the ingredients together the night before, so it's a snap to bake the next morning. —*Miriam Yoder, Houstonia, Missouri*

1 tube (8 ounces) refrigerated crescent rolls
1 pound bulk pork sausage
1/4 cup chopped onion

Mint-Cream Fruit Topping

  6 eggs, lightly beaten
3/4 cup milk
  2 tablespoons chopped green pepper
1/2 teaspoon dried oregano
1/2 teaspoon pepper
1/4 teaspoon garlic salt
  1 cup (4 ounces) shredded mozzarella cheese

Unroll crescent dough into a greased 13-in. x 9-in. x 2-in. baking dish; seal seams and perforations. Bake at 375° for 6 minutes or until golden brown.

Meanwhile, in a skillet, cook sausage and onion over medium heat until meat is no longer pink; drain. In a bowl, combine the eggs, milk, green pepper, oregano, pepper and garlic salt; pour over crust. Sprinkle with sausage mixture. Bake for 15-20 minutes. Sprinkle with cheese; bake 5 minutes longer or until cheese is melted. **Yield:** 12 servings.

One-Step Sausages

My family enjoys link sausages with breakfast, but I don't like taking the time needed to fry them up on a busy morning.

Instead, I buy several packages of sausage when they're on sale. I fry them all at once and freeze them for up to 2 months in a resealable storage bag. Whenever we want sausage, we just reheat as many links as we'd like. —*Mary Geisler, Lincoln, Nebraska*

Chapter 12

Snappy Soups, Salads & Sandwiches

SOMETIMES the perfect solution to a lunch or dinner dilemma is a steaming batch of hearty soup, a bowl chock-full of salad or a platter of super sandwiches. When that's the case, you'll want to make the most of this wide variety of winning recipes.

Not only are they delicious and satisfying, they can be put together in a snap. So they're perfect for speedy suppers and in-a-rush lunches—as well as parties, potluck gatherings and take-along meals.

Try comforting Chunky Potato Soup...out-of-the-ordinary Peachy Tossed Salad...flavor-packed Pork Vegetable Hero or any other crowd-pleasing creation. You'll have fantastic fare in no time flat.

FILLING FEAST. Pepper Artichoke Stromboli, Mosaic Salad and Zucchini Bisque (all recipes on p. 190).

Tangy Barbecued Beef

(Pictured at right)

Prep/Total Time: 30 min.

Families are sure to enjoy these hearty sandwiches. Convenient deli roast beef is jazzed up with a flavorful sauce that simmers swiftly on the stovetop.
—Nancye Thompson, Paducah, Kentucky

1-1/2 cups ketchup
1/2 cup water
2 tablespoons brown sugar
2 tablespoons chopped onion
2 tablespoons lemon juice
1 tablespoon cider vinegar
1 tablespoon Worcestershire sauce
1/2 teaspoon minced garlic
1/4 teaspoon ground mustard
1/4 to 1/2 teaspoon hot pepper sauce
Dash pepper
3 cups thinly sliced deli roast beef, cut into strips
6 sandwich rolls, split

In a large saucepan, combine the first 11 ingredients; bring to a boil. Reduce heat; cover and simmer for 15 minutes, stirring occasionally. Stir in beef; cover and simmer 5-10 minutes longer or until heated through. Serve on rolls. **Yield:** 6 servings.

Pesto Minestrone

(Pictured at right)

Prep/Total Time: 30 min.

I rely on store-bought pesto to provide mild flavor to this chunky tortellini and vegetable soup. It's been a favorite in my house ever since I first made a batch. If you don't like zucchini, simply substitute a different vegetable. —Natalie Cataldo
Des Moines, Iowa

1/2 cup chopped onion
1 teaspoon minced garlic
2 teaspoons olive oil
2-1/4 cups water
2 cups frozen mixed vegetables
1 can (14-1/2 ounces) vegetable broth
3/4 teaspoon dried oregano
1/2 teaspoon salt
1/2 teaspoon pepper
1 package (9 ounces) refrigerated cheese tortellini
2 cups diced zucchini
2 tablespoons prepared pesto

In a large saucepan, saute the onion and garlic in oil until tender. Stir in the water, mixed vegetables, broth, oregano, salt and pepper. Bring to a boil. Reduce heat; cover and simmer for 3 minutes. Add the tortellini, zucchini and pesto. Simmer, uncovered, 6-8 minutes longer or until pasta and vegetables are tender. **Yield:** 4 servings.

Mixed Green Salad

(Pictured at right)

Prep/Total Time: 20 min.

I often toss together this pretty medley of greens, mushrooms, red pepper, onion and oranges. I use raspberry vinegar in the homemade dressing, but cider vinegar works nicely in a pinch.
—Brenda Lancaster
Grand Blanc, Michigan

✓ Uses less fat, sugar or salt. Includes Nutritional Analysis and Diabetic Exchanges.

3-1/2 cups baby spinach
2 cups torn leaf lettuce
1/2 cup chopped sweet red pepper
1/2 cup sliced red onion
1/4 cup mandarin oranges
1/4 cup sliced fresh mushrooms
DRESSING:
2 tablespoons olive oil
1 tablespoon raspberry vinegar
1 teaspoon sugar
1/4 teaspoon minced fresh parsley
1/4 teaspoon minced fresh basil
Pepper to taste

In a large salad bowl, combine spinach, lettuce, red pepper, onion, oranges and mushrooms. In a jar with a tight-fitting lid, combine the dressing ingredients; shake well. Drizzle over salad; toss to coat. **Yield:** 4 servings.
Nutritional Analysis: 1 serving equals 96 calories, 7 g fat (1 g saturated fat), 0 cholesterol, 25 mg sodium, 8 g carbohydrate, 2 g fiber, 2 g protein. **Diabetic Exchanges:** 1 vegetable, 1 fat.

Cheesy Taco Chili

Prep/Total Time: 25 min.

My husband, Ron, and I farm. I prepare this chili and take it out to the field during harvest. It's filling, warm and satisfies the hungry workers' appetites. —Chris Severson
Emerson, Nebraska

1-1/2 pounds ground beef
1/2 cup chopped onion
1 pound process cheese (Velveeta), cubed
1 jar (16 ounces) salsa
1 can (16 ounces) red beans, rinsed and drained
1 can (14-1/2 ounces) stewed tomatoes, undrained
1 can (10 ounces) diced tomatoes and green chilies, undrained
1/2 teaspoon chili powder
1 cup (8 ounces) sour cream

In a large saucepan or Dutch oven, cook the beef and onion over medium heat until meat is no longer pink; drain. Stir in the cheese, salsa, beans, tomatoes and chili powder. Cook for 10 minutes or until cheese is melted. Remove from the heat; stir in sour cream. **Yield:** 10 servings.

Tangy Barbecued Beef
Pesto Minestrone
Mixed Green Salad

Ham and Bean Soup

1 cup (4 ounces) shredded Colby cheese
1 cup (4 ounces) shredded Monterey Jack cheese
Shredded lettuce, chopped tomatoes, guacamole and sour cream

In a large skillet, cook the beef and onion over medium heat until meat is no longer pink; drain. Stir in the taco seasoning, olives and taco sauce.

Unroll crescent dough; separate into eight rectangles. Seal seams and perforations. Place meat mixture in the center of each rectangle; sprinkle with cheeses. Fold dough over filling and pinch to seal. Place seam side down on an ungreased baking sheet.

Bake at 375° for 15-20 minutes or until golden brown. Layer lettuce, tomatoes, guacamole and sour cream on four serving plates; top each with two bundles. **Yield:** 4 servings.

Ham and Bean Soup

(Pictured above)

Prep/Total Time: 30 min.

If you like ham and bean soup but don't want to spend hours in the kitchen, this tasty and timely version prepared by our Test Kitchen will leave you with a satisfied smile.

> 2 medium carrots, sliced
> 2 celery ribs, chopped
> 1/2 cup chopped onion
> 2 tablespoons butter
> 4 cans (15-1/2 ounces *each*) great northern beans, rinsed and drained
> 4 cups chicken broth
> 2 cups cubed fully cooked ham
> 1 teaspoon chili powder
> 1/2 teaspoon minced garlic
> 1/4 teaspoon pepper
> 1 bay leaf

In a large saucepan, saute the carrots, celery and onion in butter until tender. Stir in the remaining ingredients; cook for 15 minutes or until heated through. Discard bay leaf before serving. **Yield:** 7 servings.

Taco Bundles

Prep: 25 min. **Bake:** 15 min.

I had so much fun in a gourmet Mexican cooking class that I developed many of my own recipes, including these easy sandwiches that kids especially love.
—GaleLynn Peterson, Long Beach, California

> 3/4 pound ground beef
> 1/3 cup chopped onion
> 2 tablespoons taco seasoning
> 2 tablespoons sliced ripe olives, drained
> 2 tablespoons taco sauce
> 2 tubes (8 ounces *each*) refrigerated crescent rolls

Sauerkraut Slaw

Prep: 15 min. + chilling

This sweet crunchy combination marinates overnight, so it's handy to make ahead of time. I often serve it at family barbecues and picnics. —Frances Campbell
Austin, Texas

> 2 cans (14 ounces *each*) sauerkraut, rinsed and drained
> 2 cups chopped celery
> 1 cup chopped onion
> 1 jar (2 ounces) diced pimientos, drained
> 1 medium green pepper, chopped
> 1/2 cup julienned carrot
> 1-1/2 cups sugar
> 1/3 cup cider vinegar

In a bowl, combine the sauerkraut, celery, onion, pimientos, green pepper and carrot. In another bowl, combine the sugar and vinegar until sugar is dissolved. Pour over the vegetable mixture. Cover and refrigerate for 8 hours or overnight. **Yield:** 6 servings.

Simple Spinach Salad

Prep/Total Time: 20 min.

This lovely spinach salad is tossed with chopped cucumber, broccoli, mushrooms and raisins. It's coated in a sweet homemade dressing that's very tasty. If you prefer, substitute red and green grapes for the spinach.
—Glenna Petersen, Wellsville, Utah

> 1 package (6 ounces) fresh baby spinach
> 1 cup chopped cucumber
> 1 cup fresh broccoli florets
> 1/2 cup golden raisins
> 1/2 cup real bacon bits
> 1/4 cup slivered almonds
> 1/4 cup sliced fresh mushrooms
> 1/4 cup chopped red onion
> DRESSING:
> 1/3 cup mayonnaise

1/4 cup sugar
2 tablespoons red wine vinegar

In a large salad bowl, combine the spinach, cucumber, broccoli, raisins, bacon, almonds, mushrooms and onion. In a small bowl, whisk the dressing ingredients until smooth. Drizzle over salad and toss to coat. **Yield:** 9 servings.

Chicken Caesar Sandwiches

(Pictured below)

Prep: 15 min. **Bake:** 25 min.

I came up with this easy sandwich recipe after eating something similar at a local restaurant. Mayonnaise keeps the chicken so moist, and Parmesan cheese gives it a delightful tang. Serve it with some crispy chips for a satisfying yet not-too-heavy Sunday lunch.
—Sara Schurtz Gonzalez, Phoenix, Arizona

✓ Uses less fat, sugar or salt. Includes Nutritional Analysis.

    4 boneless skinless chicken breast halves
      (4 ounces *each*)
1/3 cup mayonnaise
1/2 cup seasoned bread crumbs
1/2 cup grated Parmesan cheese
    2 teaspoons minced fresh parsley
1/4 cup Caesar salad dressing
    4 hard rolls, split
    4 romaine leaves
    1 medium tomato, sliced

Flatten chicken to 1/4-in. thickness; spread mayonnaise over both sides. Combine the bread crumbs, Parmesan

Sausage Cheese Snacks

cheese and parsley; sprinkle over chicken. Place in a greased 11-in. x 7-in. x 2-in. baking dish. Bake, uncovered, at 375° for 25-30 minutes or until juices run clear.

Spread salad dressing over cut sides of rolls. Place romaine on roll bottoms; top with chicken, tomato and roll tops. **Yield:** 4 servings.

Nutritional Analysis: 1 sandwich (prepared with fat-free mayonnaise and fat-free dressing) equals 435 calories, 10 g fat (3 g saturated fat), 73 mg cholesterol, 1,110 mg sodium, 50 g carbohydrate, 3 g fiber, 36 g protein.

Sausage Cheese Snacks

(Pictured above)

Prep: 20 min. **Bake:** 20 min.

When I was growing up, my mother often made these open-faced sandwiches as a special treat on cold Friday nights. I now make them for my family. They're a great change of pace on pizza night. —Melissa Fowlkes
Streamwood, Illinois

    1 pound bulk Italian sausage *or* pork sausage
1/2 cup chopped onion
    1 can (15 ounces) pizza sauce
1/2 pound sliced fresh mushrooms
    1 loaf (16 ounces) French bread, cut into 22 slices
    1 package (8 ounces) sliced mozzarella cheese, halved

In a large skillet, cook sausage and onion over medium heat until meat is no longer pink; drain. Stir in pizza sauce and mushrooms.

Place bread slices on a 15-in. x 10-in. x 1-in. baking pan; spoon 2 heaping tablespoons of sausage mixture on each. Top each with a half slice of cheese. Bake at 350° for 20-25 minutes or until the cheese is melted. **Yield:** 22 slices.

Chicken Caesar Sandwiches

Macaroni Vegetable Soup

(Pictured at right)

Prep/Total Time: 30 min.

I created this colorful veggie soup with a hint of cayenne. A nice change of pace from heavy cream soups, this hearty yet healthy combination can be served as a side dish...or as a light meal paired with your favorite bread or salad.
—Edna Hoffman, Hebron, Indiana

 Uses less fat, sugar or salt. Includes Nutritional Analysis and Diabetic Exchanges.

- 1 medium zucchini, julienned
- 1/2 cup finely chopped onion
- 1 medium carrot, halved and thinly sliced
- 1 tablespoon butter
- 2 cans (14-1/2 ounces *each*) chicken broth
- 1 cup tomato *or* vegetable juice
- 1/2 cup uncooked elbow macaroni
- 1/8 to 1/4 teaspoon cayenne pepper
- 1 can (15 ounces) white kidney *or* cannellini beans, rinsed and drained
- 1/2 cup frozen corn

In a large saucepan, saute the zucchini, onion and carrot in butter until tender. Add broth and tomato juice. Bring to a boil; stir in macaroni and cayenne. Cook for 10 minutes or until macaroni is tender. Stir in the beans and corn and heat through. **Yield:** 8 servings (2 quarts).

Nutritional Analysis: 1 cup (prepared with reduced-fat butter and reduced-sodium broth) equals 96 calories, 1 g fat (1 g saturated fat), 3 mg cholesterol, 325 mg sodium, 18 g carbohydrate, 3 g fiber, 5 g protein. **Diabetic Exchange:** 1 starch.

Garbanzo Bean Salad

(Pictured at right)

Prep/Total Time: 15 min.

Gonzo for garbanzos, I found a way to duplicate a favorite restaurant recipe at home. It's excellent as a side dish, as an appetizer or spooned over a tossed salad. It keeps for days in the fridge, but it rarely lasts that long! —Eleanor Glofka
Mountain Top, Pennsylvania

- 2 cans (15 ounces *each*) garbanzo beans *or* chickpeas, rinsed and drained
- 1/2 cup chopped sweet onion
- 1/2 cup whole ripe olives, halved
- 1/4 cup chopped sweet red pepper
- 1/4 cup chopped green pepper
- 1 celery rib, chopped
- 1/4 cup shredded Parmesan cheese
- 1/2 cup olive oil
- 3 tablespoons balsamic vinegar
- 2 tablespoons minced fresh parsley
- 1 tablespoon sugar
- 1/4 teaspoon onion powder

- 1/8 teaspoon dried basil
- Dash dried oregano

In a bowl, combine the beans, onion, olives, peppers, celery and Parmesan cheese. In a jar with a tight-fitting lid, combine the remaining ingredients; shake well. Pour over the bean mixture and toss to coat. **Yield:** 6 servings.

Crab Salad on Croissants

(Pictured at right)

Prep/Total Time: 20 min.

These seafood-filled croissants will leave you anything but crabby! We'd used the filling as an appetizer but found it makes a quick-and-easy sandwich, too. —Kari Moore
West Plains, Missouri

- 2 packages (8 ounces *each*) imitation crabmeat, flaked
- 2 celery ribs, chopped
- 1/4 cup chopped green onions
- 1/4 cup shredded cheddar cheese
- 3 tablespoons mayonnaise
- 3 tablespoons plain yogurt
- 8 croissants, split
- Lettuce leaves and tomato slices

In a bowl, combine the crab, celery, onions and cheese. Combine the mayonnaise and yogurt until blended; add to crab mixture and toss to coat. Line croissants with lettuce; top with crab salad and tomato slices. **Yield:** 8 servings.

Fancy Green Salad

Prep/Total Time: 20 min.

This festive salad adds color and berry flavor to any table. A lady brought this to a church gathering, and it was so wonderful that I just had to have the recipe. Instead of sunflower kernels, I often use pine nuts I toast in a dry skillet. —Diana Smith, Wesson, Mississippi

- 1 package (10 ounces) mixed salad greens
- 1/2 cup dried cranberries
- 1/2 cup crumbled blue cheese
- 1/3 cup sunflower kernels, toasted
- RASPBERRY VINAIGRETTE:
- 5 tablespoons olive oil
- 2 tablespoons plus 2 teaspoons raspberry vinegar
- 3 to 4 teaspoons sugar
- 2 teaspoons chopped green onion
- 1/4 teaspoon poppy seeds
- 1/8 teaspoon salt
- 1/8 teaspoon pepper

In a large salad bowl, combine the greens, cranberries, blue cheese and sunflower kernels. In a jar with a tight-fitting lid, combine the vinaigrette ingredients; shake well. Drizzle over the salad and toss to coat. **Yield:** 8 servings.

Macaroni Vegetable Soup
Garbanzo Bean Salad
Crab Salad on Croissants

Artichoke Pasta Salad

the right amount of onion flavor, it's both delicious and crowd-pleasing.   —*Janet James, Bluff City, Tennessee*

> 4 cups chopped onions
> 3-1/3 cups water
> 6 celery ribs, chopped
> 4 teaspoons beef bouillon granules
> 1-1/2 teaspoons salt
> 1/2 teaspoon pepper
> 1/2 cup all-purpose flour
> 1 cup milk
> 1 cup (4 ounces) shredded Mexican cheese blend

In a large saucepan, combine onions, water, celery, bouillon, salt and pepper. Bring to a boil. Reduce heat; cover and simmer for 10 minutes or until vegetables are tender.

Combine the flour and milk until smooth; gradually stir into onion mixture. Bring to a boil; cook and stir for 2 minutes or until thickened. Reduce heat; stir in cheese until melted. **Yield:** 7 servings.

Sausage Minestrone

Prep: 10 min. **Cook:** 20 min. + standing

Experimenting with recipes, especially soups, is my favorite hobby. We love this easy, healthier minestrone variety that features turkey kielbasa, egg noodles and plenty of vegetables. I've made it often when time is at a premium.
            —*Judy Wolters, Atchison, Kansas*

✓ Uses less fat, sugar or salt. Includes Nutritional Analysis and Diabetic Exchanges.

> 1/2 cup chopped onion
> 1/2 cup chopped celery
> 1-3/4 cups water, *divided*
> 1/4 teaspoon garlic powder
> 1 can (14-1/2 ounces) diced tomatoes, undrained
> 1 cup uncooked fine egg noodles
> 1 cup chopped cabbage
> 1-1/2 teaspoons beef bouillon granules
> 1/2 teaspoon dried basil
> 1/2 teaspoon dried oregano
> Pinch sugar
> 1/2 pound fully cooked turkey kielbasa, halved lengthwise and sliced

In a 3-qt. microwave-safe dish, combine the onion, celery, 1/4 cup water and garlic powder. Cover and microwave on high for 3 minutes.

Stir in the diced tomatoes, egg noodles, cabbage, beef bouillon granules, basil, oregano, sugar and remaining water. Cover the soup and microwave on high for 11-13 minutes or until the noodles are tender, stirring twice. Add the sliced sausage; cook 2 minutes longer. Cover the soup and let stand for 10 minutes before serving. **Yield:** 4 servings.

Nutritional Analysis: 1-1/4 cups (prepared with yolk-free noodles) equals 161 calories, 3 g fat (1 g saturated fat), 25 mg cholesterol, 935 mg sodium, 23 g carbohydrate, 3 g fiber, 10 g protein. **Diabetic Exchanges:**

Artichoke Pasta Salad

(Pictured above)

Prep/Total Time: 20 min.

I've made this flavorful and fetching macaroni medley many times for my husband. We like it for lunch with pineapple-topped ham slices and sweet potatoes. Or you can stir a can of tuna into the salad for a complete meal.
            —*Nancy Adams, Las Vegas, Nevada*

> 1 cup uncooked elbow macaroni
> 1 cup halved grape tomatoes
> 1 cup sliced ripe olives
> 1 jar (6-1/2 ounces) marinated artichoke hearts, undrained
> 1 tablespoon minced fresh parsley
> 1/4 teaspoon salt
> 1/4 teaspoon pepper

Cook the macaroni according to package directions; drain and rinse in cold water. Place in a bowl; add the remaining ingredients and toss gently. Cover and refrigerate until serving. **Yield:** 6-8 servings.

Cream of Celery Soup

Prep: 15 min. **Cook:** 25 min.

This rich and creamy celery soup will warm up any family gathering or even a quiet evening at home. With just

1 starch, 1 lean meat, 1 vegetable.

Editor's Note: This recipe was tested in a 1,100-watt microwave.

Oriental Shrimp Soup

(Pictured below)

Prep/Total Time: 15 min.

A package of ramen noodles speeds up assembly of this soup that gets color from green onions, shrimp and carrot.
—Donna Hellinger, Lorain, Ohio

✓ Uses less fat, sugar or salt. Includes Nutritional Analysis and Diabetic Exchanges.

3-1/2 cups water
  1 package (3 ounces) Oriental ramen noodles
  1 cup frozen cooked small shrimp
1/2 cup chopped green onions
  1 medium carrot, julienned
  2 tablespoons soy sauce

In a large saucepan, bring water to a boil. Set aside seasoning packet from noodles. Add the noodles to boiling water; cook and stir for 3 minutes. Add the shrimp, onions, carrot, soy sauce and contents of seasoning packet. Cook 3-4 minutes longer or until heated through. **Yield:** 4 servings.

Nutritional Analysis: 1 cup (prepared with reduced-sodium soy sauce) equals 148 calories, 4 g fat (2 g saturated fat), 83 mg cholesterol, 857 mg sodium, 17 g carbohydrate, 1 g fiber, 12 g protein. **Diabetic Exchanges:** 1 starch, 1 lean meat.

Chicken Cucumber Boats

Oriental Shrimp Soup

Chicken Cucumber Boats

(Pictured above)

Prep/Total Time: 20 min.

These refreshing cucumber creations will make your next lunch seem special. This is a cool dish when days get warm. Try it with tuna or turkey salad as the filling instead.
—Sue Ross, Casa Grande, Arizona

✓ Uses less fat, sugar or salt. Includes Nutritional Analysis and Diabetic Exchanges.

  2 medium cucumbers
  1 cup cubed cooked chicken breast
3/4 cup shredded cheddar cheese
1/2 cup finely chopped celery
1/3 cup mayonnaise
  2 tablespoons sweet pickle relish
  1 tablespoon chopped onion
  1 teaspoon lemon juice
1/4 teaspoon salt
1/8 teaspoon pepper

Cut cucumbers in half lengthwise; remove seeds. With a sharp knife, cut a thin slice from the bottom of each cucumber half so it sits flat. In a bowl, combine the remaining ingredients. Spoon into cucumber boats. Refrigerate until serving. **Yield:** 4 servings.

Nutritional Analysis: 1 stuffed cucumber half (prepared with reduced-fat cheese and fat-free mayonnaise) equals 164 calories, 6 g fat (3 g saturated fat), 44 mg cholesterol, 540 mg sodium, 12 g carbohydrate, 2 g fiber, 17 g protein. **Diabetic Exchanges:** 2 very lean meat, 2 vegetable, 1 fat.

Taco Avocado Wraps

(Pictured at right)

Prep/Total Time: 30 min.

I came up with this sandwich one summer evening when we wanted a light supper and didn't want to turn on the oven. Serve the wraps for lunch, as a snack or paired with refried beans for dinner. —Renee Rutherford
Andover, Minnesota

  1 package (8 ounces) cream cheese, softened
1/2 cup sour cream
  1 can (4 ounces) chopped green chilies, drained
  1 tablespoon taco seasoning
  4 flour tortillas (10 inches), warmed
  2 medium ripe avocados, peeled and sliced
  2 plum tomatoes, thinly sliced
  5 green onions, sliced
  1 can (4 ounces) sliced ripe olives, drained

In a small bowl, combine the cream cheese, sour cream, chilies and taco seasoning. Spread about 1/2 cup over each tortilla. Top with avocados, tomatoes, onions and olives; roll up. **Yield:** 4 servings.

Bacon-Chive Tossed Salad

(Pictured at right)

Prep/Total Time: 10 min.

Fresh chives and crispy bacon really dress up this salad and make it a guaranteed winner. I think this salad is especially good with grilled hamburgers. —Maria Regakis
Somerville, Massachusetts

1/2 cup creamy Parmesan Romano salad
    dressing
  2 tablespoons snipped chives
  4 cups torn Bibb *or* Boston lettuce
  1 medium red onion, thinly
    sliced and separated into rings
  1 cup (4 ounces) shredded cheddar cheese
1/4 cup real bacon bits

In a small bowl, combine salad dressing and chives. In a salad bowl, toss lettuce, onion, cheese and bacon. Serve with dressing. **Yield:** 6 servings.

Vegetable Cheese Soup

(Pictured at right)

Prep/Total Time: 30 min.

This recipe originally came from my pastor's wife. I've made a few changes for convenience, and now it's a snap to whip up. It tastes even better the next day. —Michelle Isenhoff, Wayland, Michigan

  2 tablespoons chopped onion
1/4 cup butter, cubed
1/4 cup all-purpose flour
  3 cups milk
1-1/2 cups chicken broth

  1 package (16 ounces) frozen California-blend vegetables, thawed
1-1/2 cups (6 ounces) shredded cheddar cheese
3/4 cup process cheese sauce

In a large saucepan, saute onion in butter until tender. Stir in the flour until blended. Gradually add milk. Bring to a boil; cook and stir for 2 minutes or until thickened.

Stir in the broth and vegetables. Reduce heat; cover and simmer for 15-20 minutes until vegetables are crisp-tender. Stir in cheddar cheese and cheese sauce; cook until heated through and cheese is melted. **Yield:** 7 servings.

Pork Vegetable Hero

Prep: 25 min. **Bake:** 10 min.

Tender pork, green and red peppers and melted mozzarella cheese come together in this fantastic family-size sandwich. For extra flavor, I sometimes add Italian seasoning to the meat and vegetables. —Jane Ulness
Edmonds, Washington

  1 loaf French bread (1 pound)
  3 tablespoons olive oil
  2 pounds pork tenderloin, cubed
  1 cup julienned green pepper
  1 cup julienned sweet red pepper
1/2 cup chopped celery
  1 small onion, sliced
  2 teaspoons garlic powder
  1 teaspoon onion powder
  1 teaspoon pepper
1/2 cup chicken broth
  2 cups sliced plum tomatoes
  1 cup (4 ounces) shredded mozzarella cheese

Cut the top fourth off of the loaf of French bread; carefully hollow out the top and bottom, leaving a 1-in. shell (save the removed bread for another use). Set the bread shell aside.

In a large skillet, heat oil. Add pork, green and red peppers, celery, onion, garlic powder, onion powder and pepper; cook and stir until pork is browned and vegetables are tender. Add broth; simmer until mixture is reduced. Spoon into bread shell; top with tomatoes and cheese. Replace bread top.

Wrap in a large piece of heavy-duty foil; seal tightly. Bake at 400° for 10-15 minutes or until heated through and cheese is melted. **Yield:** 8 servings.

Timely Tortilla Tip

WHEN you need tortillas for a recipe like Taco Avocado Wraps but can't use the whole package at once, freezing is a great way to store the extras for future use. Just stack tortillas between waxed paper and store them in resealable freezer bags. Tortillas can be kept this way in the freezer for up to 3 months.

Bacon-Chive Tossed Salad
Vegetable Cheese Soup
Taco Avocado Wraps

Pumpernickel Turkey Hero

2 medium cantaloupe
1 cup cubed salami
1 medium cucumber, halved, seeded and sliced
3 tablespoons lemon juice
2 tablespoons honey
1/4 teaspoon minced fresh marjoram

Cut each cantaloupe in half; scoop out and discard seeds. Cut melon into cubes; place in a large bowl. Cut a thin slice off the bottom of each cantaloupe half so the shell sits level; pat dry and set aside.

Add salami and cucumber to melon cubes. In a jar with a tight-fitting lid, combine the lemon juice, honey and marjoram; shake well. Drizzle over cantaloupe mixture and toss to coat. Serve in cantaloupe shells. **Yield:** 4 servings.

Nutritional Analysis: 1/2 filled cantaloupe (prepared with turkey salami) equals 196 calories, 4 g fat (1 g saturated fat), 27 mg cholesterol, 386 mg sodium, 35 g carbohydrate, 3 g fiber, 9 g protein. **Diabetic Exchanges:** 2-1/2 fruit, 1 lean meat, 1/2 fat.

Kidney Bean Coleslaw

Prep: 15 min. + chilling

My mom gave me the recipe for this salad, and my family really enjoys it. The make-ahead medley is easy to toss together and great at picnics and backyard barbecues.
—*Sandra Lee Espig, Paso Robles, California*

4 cups shredded cabbage
1/2 cup real bacon bits
1 can (16 ounces) kidney beans, rinsed and drained
2 celery ribs, thinly sliced
2/3 cup chopped onion
4 teaspoons minced fresh parsley
1/2 cup mayonnaise
2 tablespoons cider vinegar
1/4 teaspoon pepper
1/8 teaspoon salt

In a large bowl, combine the cabbage, bacon, beans, celery, onion and parsley. In a small bowl, combine the mayonnaise, vinegar, pepper and salt; pour over cabbage mixture and toss to coat. Cover and refrigerate for 2-3 hours. Stir before serving. **Yield:** 6-8 servings.

Pumpernickel Turkey Hero

(Pictured above)

Prep/Total Time: 10 min.

Thousand Island dressing lends flavor to each bite of this hearty turkey and Swiss sandwich. A friend brought this impressive pumpernickel loaf to a sandwich luncheon, and I asked for the recipe so I could serve it to my family. They liked it, too. —*Mildred Sherrer, Bay City, Texas*

1 loaf (1 pound) unsliced pumpernickel bread
1/3 cup Thousand Island salad dressing
6 lettuce leaves
2 medium tomatoes, sliced
3 slices red onion, separated into rings
6 slices Swiss cheese
1 package (12 ounces) thinly sliced deli turkey

Cut bread in half horizontally; spread salad dressing over cut sides. On the bottom half, layer the lettuce, tomatoes, onion, half of the cheese and half of the turkey. Top with remaining cheese and turkey. Replace bread top. Slice before serving. **Yield:** 6 servings.

Cantaloupe Salami Salad

Prep/Total Time: 30 min.

I need just six ingredients to toss together this unusual salad. I serve it in the cantaloupe shells for summer brunches. It's delicious and very easy to make.
—*Barbara Nowakowski, North Tonawanda, New York*

Beer Cheese Soup

Prep/Total Time: 20 min.

A family friend used to invite us for Sunday supper and served this savory soup several times. It was so simple and good that I couldn't resist asking for the recipe. This soup is easy to double for a crowd and will keep warm in a slow cooker set on low for 3-6 hours.
—*Sharon Lock Forman, North Dakota*

2 tablespoons finely chopped onion
1/2 teaspoon butter

2 cans (10-3/4 ounces *each*) condensed cream
   of celery soup, undiluted
1 cup beer *or* nonalcoholic beer
1 cup milk
1 teaspoon Worcestershire sauce
1/2 teaspoon dried parsley flakes
1/4 teaspoon paprika
3/4 pound process cheese (Velveeta), cubed

In a large saucepan, saute onion in butter. Stir in soup, beer, milk, Worcestershire sauce, parsley and paprika. Reduce heat; stir in cheese until melted. Heat through (do not boil). **Yield:** 6 servings.

Peachy Tossed Salad

Pepper Pork Pockets

(Pictured below)

Prep/Total Time: 25 min.

I accompany these pita pockets with pasta salad and sliced tomatoes, carrots and cucumbers. To save time, you can make the garlic sauce up to 2 days in advance and refrigerate it. —*Paula Marchesi, Lenhartsville, Pennsylvania*

1 pound boneless pork loin chops, cut into
   thin 2-inch strips
1 teaspoon pepper
1/2 teaspoon salt
1 tablespoon olive oil
1 jar (7 ounces) roasted sweet red peppers,
   drained and coarsely chopped
1/2 cup mayonnaise
2 tablespoons milk
1 teaspoon minced garlic

6 lettuce leaves
3 pita breads (6 inches), halved and warmed

Sprinkle pork with pepper and salt. In a large skillet, saute pork in oil until juices run clear. Add red peppers; cook and stir until heated through. Remove from the heat.

In a large bowl, combine the mayonnaise, milk and garlic. Spoon pork mixture into lettuce-lined pita halves. Drizzle with dressing. **Yield:** 3 servings.

Peachy Tossed Salad

(Pictured above)

Prep/Total Time: 20 min.

A sweet homemade dressing flecked with poppy seeds coats this green salad. The combination of sweet peaches, salty feta cheese, and crunchy onion and cucumber offers an array of tastes and textures. —*Tonia Booker
Gilbert, Arizona*

1 package (10 ounces) ready-to-serve salad
   greens
1 to 2 medium fresh peaches, cut into wedges
1/2 cup thinly sliced cucumber
1/2 cup crumbled feta cheese
1/4 cup thinly sliced red onion, separated into
   rings
CREAMY POPPY SEED DRESSING:
2/3 cup vegetable oil
1/4 cup sugar
1/4 cup white vinegar
1/4 cup sour cream
2 teaspoons poppy seeds
1/2 teaspoon salt

In a large salad bowl, combine the greens, peaches, cucumber, feta cheese and onion. In a jar with a tight-fitting lid, combine the dressing ingredients; shake well. Serve with salad. **Yield:** 8 servings.

Pepper Pork Pockets

Macaroni Bean Salad

Prep: 25 min. + chilling

Two types of store-bought beans, a can of ripe olives and lots of cubed cheese make this pasta salad a cinch to assemble. With its creamy dressing, the festive medley is sure to earn praise at potlucks. Try other small pasta noodles.
—Sandra Gordon, Emmett, Idaho

      2 cups uncooked elbow macaroni
      1 can (4-1/2 ounces) sliced ripe olives, drained
      2 celery ribs, sliced
    3/4 cup garbanzo beans
    3/4 cup kidney beans
    1/2 cup mayonnaise
    1/2 cup cubed Monterey Jack cheese
    1/2 cup cubed Colby-Monterey Jack cheese
    1/4 cup Italian salad dressing
      2 tablespoons white wine vinegar
      2 teaspoons seasoned salt
    1/4 teaspoon pepper

Cook macaroni according to package directions. Meanwhile, in a large bowl, combine all of the remaining ingredients. Drain the macaroni and rinse in cold water. Add to the bean mixture and toss to coat. Cover and refrigerate for 1-2 hours. Serve salad with a slotted spoon. **Yield:** 10 servings.

Zucchini Bisque

(Pictured at right and on page 176)

Prep/Total Time: 30 min.

Looking for an out-of-the-ordinary way to serve a bounty of garden zucchini? Try this deliciously different soup! A food processor hurries along preparation of the thick full-flavored blend that's accented by just a hint of nutmeg.
—Germaine Stank, Pound, Wisconsin

      4 medium zucchini, shredded
      1 medium onion, chopped
    1/2 cup butter, cubed
  2-1/2 cups chicken broth
      1 cup heavy whipping cream
    3/4 teaspoon salt
    1/2 teaspoon minced fresh basil
    1/2 teaspoon pepper
    1/4 teaspoon ground nutmeg
  Sour cream and additional nutmeg, optional

In a large saucepan, saute the zucchini and onion in butter for 5-6 minutes or until tender. Stir in broth. Bring to a boil. Reduce heat; cover and simmer for 12-15 minutes. Cool slightly.

Transfer to a food processor or blender; cover and process on low until smooth. Return to the pan. Stir in the cream, salt, basil, pepper and nutmeg. Bring to a boil. Reduce heat; simmer, uncovered, for 1-2 minutes or until heated through. Garnish with sour cream and additional nutmeg if desired. **Yield:** 6 servings.

Mosaic Salad

(Pictured at right and on page 177)

Prep/Total Time: 20 min.

This pretty salad combines garden-fresh ingredients to create a colorful side dish. It would be a great addition to a barbecue or picnic. You can serve it right away, but I like to chill it a few hours to blend the flavors.
—Maria Regakis, Somerville, Massachusetts

      1 medium cucumber, sliced
      2 medium yellow summer squash, sliced
      2 medium tomatoes, sliced
  DRESSING:
    1/4 cup vegetable oil
      3 tablespoons minced fresh basil *or* 1 tablespoon dried basil
      2 tablespoons lemon juice
      2 tablespoons cider vinegar
      1 teaspoon sugar
    1/2 teaspoon grated lemon peel
    1/4 teaspoon salt

Arrange the cucumber, squash and tomatoes on a large serving platter. In a jar with a tight-fitting lid, combine the dressing ingredients; shake well. Drizzle over salad. Serve immediately. **Yield:** 6-8 servings.

Pepper Artichoke Stromboli

(Pictured at right and on page 176)

Prep: 15 min. **Bake:** 15 min. + standing

This fun-to-eat stromboli is a snap to make, thanks to store-bought pizza dough...and the kids love it. You can use just about any pizza topping as filling to suit different tastes. For example, try mushrooms or onion.
—Andrea Jones, McKinney, Texas

      1 tube (13.8 ounces) refrigerated pizza crust
    1/2 cup shredded mozzarella cheese
    1/2 cup water-packed artichoke hearts, rinsed, drained and chopped
      1 jar (7 ounces) roasted sweet red peppers, drained
      2 slices turkey salami, cut in half
      1 egg white, lightly beaten

Unroll the pizza dough onto a lightly floured surface; roll into a 12-in. x 8-in. rectangle. Layer the cheese, artichokes, red peppers and salami lengthwise down the center of the dough rectangle. Fold one long side of the dough over the filling. Fold the other long side over the top; pinch the seams and ends to seal.

Place seam side down on a greased foil-lined baking sheet. Brush with egg white. Bake at 400° for 15-20 minutes or until browned. Let stand for 10 minutes before slicing. **Yield:** 4-6 servings.

Mosaic Salad
Pepper Artichoke Stromboli
Zucchini Bisque

Creamy Chicken Rice Soup

In a small bowl, combine the flour and milk until smooth; stir into soup. Bring to a boil; cook and stir for 2 minutes or until thickened. Stir in chicken; heat through. **Yield:** 5 servings.

Nutritional Analysis: 1 cup (prepared with reduced-sodium chicken broth and fat-free milk) equals 185 calories, 4 g fat (1 g saturated fat), 32 mg cholesterol, 617 mg sodium, 21 g carbohydrate, 1 g fiber, 17 g protein. **Diabetic Exchanges:** 2 lean meat, 1 starch, 1 vegetable.

Grilled Chicken Reubens

Prep/Total Time: 15 min.

I typically use my backyard grill to fix this recipe, but an indoor grill works well, too. Since we grill almost every meal in the summer, I thought we'd try these sandwiches. Serve them with coleslaw or a green salad.
—*Sharilyn Thompson, St. Paul Park, Minnesota*

> 2 boneless skinless chicken breast halves
>   (4 ounces *each*)
> 4 slices Swiss cheese
> 4 slices rye bread
> 3/4 cup sauerkraut, rinsed and well drained
> 1 tablespoon butter, softened

Place chicken on an indoor grill coated with nonstick cooking spray; grill for 3-4 minutes or until juices run clear. Place a slice of cheese on each of two bread slices. Slice chicken; place over cheese. Top with sauerkraut and remaining cheese and bread.

Spread butter over both sides of sandwiches. Cook on indoor grill until bread is browned and cheese is melted. **Yield:** 2 servings.

Chunky Potato Soup

Prep/Total Time: 30 min.

The first time I made this creamy satisfying soup, it instantly became our family's favorite. Even those who don't normally like Swiss cheese savor this delicious soup.
—*Stephanie Moon, Nampa, Idaho*

> 4 medium potatoes (about 2 pounds), peeled
>   and cubed
> 3/4 cup chopped onion
> 1 small carrot, chopped
> 1/4 cup chopped celery
> 1-1/2 cups chicken broth
> 3 tablespoons butter, cubed
> 3 tablespoons all-purpose flour
> 2-1/2 cups milk
> 1 tablespoon minced fresh parsley
> 3/4 teaspoon salt
> 1/2 teaspoon pepper
> 1 cup (4 ounces) shredded Swiss cheese

In a large saucepan, combine the potatoes, onion, carrot, celery and broth. Bring to a boil. Reduce heat; cover and simmer for 12-15 minutes or until vegetables are tender; lightly mash.

Meanwhile, in a small saucepan, melt butter; stir in

Creamy Chicken Rice Soup

(Pictured above)

Prep/Total Time: 30 min.

I came up with this thick flavorful soup while making adjustments to a favorite stovetop chicken dish. It goes together in short order using cooked chicken and a mini food processor to chop the veggies. We like this soup for lunch with crisp rolls and fresh fruit. To reduce the fat, use some broth instead of oil to saute the vegetables.
—*Janice Mitchell, Aurora, Colorado*

✓ Uses less fat, sugar or salt. Includes Nutritional Analysis and Diabetic Exchanges.

> 1/2 cup chopped onion
> 1 medium carrot, chopped
> 1 celery rib, chopped
> 1/2 teaspoon minced garlic
> 1 tablespoon canola oil
> 2 cans (14-1/2 ounces *each*) chicken broth
> 1/3 cup uncooked long grain rice
> 3/4 teaspoon dried basil
> 1/4 teaspoon pepper
> 3 tablespoons all-purpose flour
> 1 can (5 ounces) evaporated milk
> 1 package (9 ounces) frozen diced cooked
>   chicken, thawed

In a saucepan, saute the onion, carrot, celery and garlic in oil until tender. Stir in the broth, rice, basil and pepper. Bring to a boil. Reduce heat; cover and simmer for 15 minutes or until rice is tender.

flour until smooth. Gradually stir in milk. Bring to a boil; cook and stir for 2 minutes or until thickened. Stir into potato mixture. Cook and stir until thickened and bubbly. Add parsley, salt and pepper. Remove from the heat; stir in cheese until melted. **Yield:** 7 servings.

Tasty Burritos

(Pictured below)

Prep/Total Time: 30 min.

My cousin is of Mexican heritage, and I've watched her put together these crunchy burritos for years. When I made them for my family, they were a huge hit. Any leftovers are great reheated the next day. —Debi Lane
Chattanooga, Tennessee

    1 pound ground beef
    1 envelope taco seasoning
    1 can (16 ounces) refried beans
    6 flour tortillas (12 inches), warmed
    1 cup (4 ounces) shredded Colby-Monterey
       Jack cheese
    4 teaspoons vegetable oil
Sour cream and salsa

In a large skillet, cook beef over medium heat until no longer pink; drain. Stir in taco seasoning. In a small saucepan, cook refried beans over medium-low heat for 2-3 minutes or until heated through.

Spoon about 1/3 cup of the refried beans off-center on each tortilla; top with about 2 rounded tablespoons of the beef mixture. Sprinkle with the shredded cheese. Fold the sides and ends of the tortillas over the filling; roll up the tortillas. In a large skillet over medium-high heat, brown the burritos in oil on all sides. Serve with sour cream and salsa. **Yield:** 6 servings.

Tasty Burritos

Witch's Hat Soup

Witch's Hat Soup

(Pictured above)

Prep/Total Time: 30 min.

In autumn, you can get into the Halloween spirit with this thick soup that's topped with a cute crunchy garnish. Created by our Test Kitchen home economists, the vegetables, beans and seasonings are a hearty mixture that have a kick of spice to heat up Halloween menus.

    4 flour tortillas (8 inches)
    1 envelope taco seasoning, *divided*
    1 pound ground beef
 1/3 cup chopped onion
    2 cups water
    2 cups frozen mixed vegetables
    1 can (15-1/2 ounces) chili beans, undrained
    1 can (15 ounces) black beans, rinsed and
       drained
    1 can (14-1/2 ounces) diced tomatoes with
       mild green chilies, undrained
 1/2 teaspoon sugar
Canned pasteurized cheddar cheese snack

Spritz tortillas with nonstick cooking spray; sprinkle with 1/2 teaspoon taco seasoning. With a 2-1/2-in. round cookie cutter, cut out four circles from each tortilla (discard scraps). Cut a slit into the center of eight circles; shape each into a cone and secure with toothpicks. Place circles and cones on an ungreased baking sheet. Bake at 400° for 8-10 minutes or until crisp.

Meanwhile, in a large saucepan, cook beef and onion over medium heat until meat is no longer pink; drain. Stir in the water, vegetables, beans, tomatoes, sugar and remaining taco seasoning. Cover and simmer for 10 minutes or until heated through, stirring occasionally.

Discard toothpicks from cones. To assemble hats, place cones on circles; pipe a band of cheese around bases of cones. Ladle soup into bowls and top with hats. **Yield:** 8 servings (2 quarts).

Chapter 13

MAIN DISHES are undoubtedly the focal point of any meal. But that doesn't mean they have to take more time and effort to prepare than the other items on your menu.

Here, you'll discover flavor-packed, impressive entrees that get to the table in a flash. In fact, every recipe can be prepared from start to finish in a mere 30 minutes...or less!

Choose from a wide variety of tasty main courses—beef, pork, poultry, seafood and meatless. No matter what you fix for your family, they'll be savoring a hot entree in no more than a half hour.

Many of these supper sensations are so hearty and filling, you won't even need to serve up a side dish!

MADE IN MINUTES. Corn Bread Chicken (p. 199).

Pork Cabbage Saute

Black Bean Spinach Pizza

Prep/Total Time: 30 min.

A relative brought this vegetarian pizza to a family gathering, and everyone enjoyed it. It's great right out of the oven, but I think leftovers are even better reheated the next day. —Kim Balvance, Shakopee, Minnesota

- 1 prebaked Italian bread shell crust (10 ounces)
- 1 can (15 ounces) black beans, rinsed, drained and mashed
- 1/3 cup chopped onion
- 2 teaspoons chili powder
- 1 teaspoon ground cumin
- 1/2 teaspoon minced garlic
- 1/2 cup salsa
- 1/2 cup frozen chopped spinach, thawed and squeezed dry
- 2 tablespoons minced fresh cilantro
- 1/2 teaspoon hot pepper sauce
- 1/2 cup shredded Monterey Jack cheese
- 1/2 cup shredded sharp cheddar cheese

Place the crust on an ungreased 12-in. pizza pan. Combine the beans, onion, chili powder, cumin and garlic; spread over crust. Layer with salsa, spinach and cilantro. Sprinkle with hot pepper sauce and cheeses. Bake at 450° for 8-10 minutes or until golden brown. **Yield:** 6 slices.

Pork Cabbage Saute

(Pictured above)

Prep/Total Time: 25 min.

I mildly season pork slices and cabbage strips to create this main dish. I like to make this one-pan meal because it's fast and easy. —Rosemary Gisin, Peekskill, New York

✓ Uses less fat, sugar or salt. Includes Nutritional Analysis and Diabetic Exchanges.

- 1 pound boneless pork loin, cut into 2-inch strips
- 1 tablespoon canola oil
- 1/2 medium head cabbage, shredded
- 1 medium onion, thinly sliced
- 1/2 teaspoon minced garlic
- 2 bay leaves
- 2 tablespoons butter
- 1/2 teaspoon salt
- 1/2 teaspoon pepper

In a large skillet, cook and stir the pork in oil over medium heat until no longer pink; remove and keep warm. In the same skillet, saute the cabbage, onion, garlic and bay leaves in butter until vegetables are tender. Discard bay leaves. Stir in the pork, salt and pepper. **Yield:** 4 servings.

Nutritional Analysis: 1 cup (prepared with reduced-fat butter) equals 251 calories, 13 g fat (5 g saturated fat), 65 mg cholesterol, 383 mg sodium, 10 g carbohydrate, 3 g fiber, 24 g protein. **Diabetic Exchanges:** 3 lean meat, 2 vegetable, 1 fat.

Salmon Supper

Prep/Total Time: 30 min.

With a husband and four children to cook for, I'm always on the lookout for quick recipes. This one was given to me by my mother-in-law many years ago. The creamy salmon casserole is topped with crescent roll dough and baked until golden brown. —Debra Knippel Medford, Wisconsin

- 1/3 cup chopped green pepper
- 3 tablespoons chopped onion
- 2 tablespoons vegetable oil
- 1/4 cup all-purpose flour
- 1/2 teaspoon salt
- 1-1/2 cups milk
- 1 can (10-3/4 ounces) condensed cream of celery soup, undiluted
- 2 pouches (3 ounces *each*) boneless skinless pink salmon
- 1 cup frozen peas
- 2 teaspoons lemon juice
- 1 tube (8 ounces) refrigerated crescent rolls

In a large skillet, saute green pepper and onion in oil for 3-4 minutes or until crisp-tender. In a small bowl, combine flour, salt, milk and soup until blended. Add to the skillet. Bring to a boil. Reduce heat; cook and stir for 2 minutes or until smooth. Stir in the salmon, peas and lemon juice.

Pour into an ungreased 11-in. x 7-in. x 2-in. baking dish. Do not unroll crescent dough; cut into eight equal slices. Arrange over salmon mixture. Bake, uncovered, at 375° for 10-12 minutes or until golden brown. **Yield:** 4 servings.

Hamburger Supper

(Pictured below)

Prep/Total Time: 30 min.

I have good memories of eating this meal-in-one often while growing up. We all loved the flavor and seldom had leftovers. Instead of sprinkling it with cheddar, I sometimes create a cheese sauce using American cheese and milk. It makes it so cheesy!
—Andrea Brandt
Newton, Kansas

      1 **pound ground beef**
 1-1/2 **cups water**
   1/2 **teaspoon poultry seasoning**
   1/4 **teaspoon pepper**
      1 **envelope brown gravy mix**
      1 **medium onion, sliced and separated into**
        rings
      1 **medium carrot, sliced**
      2 **medium potatoes, sliced**
      1 **cup (4 ounces) shredded cheddar cheese**

In a large skillet, cook beef over medium heat until no longer pink; drain. Stir in the water, poultry seasoning and pepper. Bring to a boil. Stir in gravy mix. Cook and stir for 2 minutes or until slightly thickened.

Arrange the onion, carrot and potatoes over beef. Reduce heat; cover and simmer for 10-15 minutes or until vegetables are tender. Sprinkle with cheese. Cover and cook 3-5 minutes longer or until cheese is melted. **Yield:** 4 servings.

Sausage-Stuffed Squash

Hamburger Supper

Sausage-Stuffed Squash

(Pictured above)

Prep/Total Time: 20 min.

I tuck a flavorful sausage mixture into colorful acorn squash halves for a special-looking meal. Cooking the squash in the microwave means this entree is done in minutes. I like to use maple-flavored bulk pork sausage.
—Mary Magner
Cedar Rapids, Iowa

    2 **medium acorn squash**
    1 **pound bulk pork sausage**
  1/2 **cup finely chopped celery**
  1/2 **cup finely chopped onion**
  1/3 **cup sour cream**

Cut squash in half; remove and discard seeds. Place squash cut side down in a microwave-safe dish.

Cover and microwave on high for 10-12 minutes or until tender.

Meanwhile, crumble sausage into a large skillet; add celery and onion. Cook over medium heat until meat is no longer pink; drain. Remove from the heat; stir in sour cream. Spoon into squash halves. Cover and microwave for 1 minute or until heated through. **Yield:** 4 servings.

Editor's Note: This recipe was tested in a 1,100-watt microwave.

Almond Cranberry Chicken

Beef 'n' Gravy on Potatoes

Prep/Total Time: 20 min.

My husband was raised on meat-and-potato meals, and this quick main dish is one of his all-time favorites. Complete this hearty dinner in a jiffy by zapping some frozen vegetables in the microwave. —Michelle Hallock Warwick, Rhode Island

      3 medium potatoes, peeled and cut
        into 1-inch cubes
    1/3 cup water
      1 pound ground beef
      1 teaspoon garlic powder
      1 teaspoon onion powder
      1 envelope brown gravy mix
    1/4 cup milk
      3 tablespoons butter, softened
    1/8 teaspoon salt
    1/8 teaspoon pepper

Place potatoes and water in a microwave-safe dish. Cover and microwave on high for 8-10 minutes or until tender. Meanwhile, in a large skillet, cook beef over medium heat until no longer pink; drain. Stir in garlic powder and onion powder.

Prepare gravy according to package directions. Place the potatoes in a mixing bowl; add milk, butter, salt and pepper. Beat on medium speed until smooth. Serve the beef and gravy over the mashed potatoes. **Yield:** 4 servings.

Editor's Note: This recipe was tested in a 1,100-watt microwave.

Almond Cranberry Chicken

(Pictured above)

Prep/Total Time: 25 min.

Our Test Kitchen staff adds seasonal flair to everyday chicken with this flavorful sauce that showcases fresh cranberries. It's a snap to prepare on the stovetop. Round out the meal deliciously with side dishes of steamed broccoli and buttered couscous.

      6 boneless skinless chicken breast halves
        (4 ounces *each*)
    1/2 cup all-purpose flour
    1/2 teaspoon salt
    1/4 teaspoon cayenne pepper
    1/4 cup butter
      1 cup fresh *or* frozen cranberries
      1 cup water
    1/2 cup packed brown sugar
      1 tablespoon red wine vinegar
    1/4 to 1/2 teaspoon grated orange peel
    1/4 cup slivered almonds, toasted

Flatten chicken to 1/4-in. thickness. In a large resealable bag, combine the flour, salt and cayenne; add chicken, a few pieces at a time, and shake to coat.

In a large skillet, brown chicken in butter over medium heat for 10-12 minutes or until juices run clear. Remove and keep warm.

In the same skillet, combine the cranberries, water, brown sugar, vinegar and orange peel. Bring to a boil; cook for 10 minutes or until thickened, stirring occasionally. Spoon over chicken; sprinkle with almonds. **Yield:** 6 servings.

Taco-Stuffed Pepper Cups

Prep/Total Time: 30 min.

When green, red or yellow bell peppers are plentiful, they create colorful containers for this spicy taco mixture that's ready in record time. —Pat Habiger, Spearville, Kansas

 Uses less fat, sugar or salt. Includes Nutritional Analysis and Diabetic Exchanges.

      2 medium green peppers
    1/2 pound ground beef *or* lean ground turkey
      2 tablespoons chopped onion
      1 can (16 ounces) kidney beans, rinsed and
        drained
      1 can (8 ounces) tomato sauce
      3 tablespoons taco seasoning
    1/4 cup sour cream
    1/4 cup shredded cheddar cheese
    1/4 cup chopped tomato

Cut the peppers in half lengthwise and remove the seeds. Cook in boiling water for 5 minutes; drain and set aside. In a large skillet, cook the beef and onion over medium heat until the meat is no longer pink; drain. Add the kidney beans, tomato sauce and taco seasoning; bring to a boil. Reduce heat; simmer, uncovered, for 5 minutes.

Place pepper halves in an ungreased 8-in. square baking dish. Fill with meat mixture. Bake, uncovered, at

350° for 10 minutes or until peppers are tender. Top with sour cream, cheese and tomato. **Yield:** 4 servings.

Nutritional Analysis: 1 stuffed pepper half (prepared with ground turkey, fat-free sour cream and reduced-fat cheddar cheese) equals 261 calories, 6 g fat (2 g saturated fat), 52 mg cholesterol, 823 mg sodium, 31 g carbohydrate, 7 g fiber, 21 g protein. **Diabetic Exchanges:** 2 lean meat, 2 vegetable, 1-1/2 starch, 1 fat.

Salmon Linguine Alfredo

Prep/Total Time: 25 min.

Jars of prepared Alfredo sauce and a can of salmon speed up this creamy pasta dish. You can drain two 6-ounce cans of crabmeat and use them instead of the salmon.
—Arlene Mackun, St. George, Utah

  1 package (16 ounces) linguine
1/4 cup chopped green onions
  1 tablespoon butter
  1 can (12 ounces) skinless boneless pink
    salmon, drained
  2 jars (17 ounces *each*) Alfredo sauce
  2 tablespoons sherry *or* chicken broth
  1 teaspoon celery salt
  1 teaspoon dried parsley flakes
1/4 teaspoon pepper

Cook pasta according to package directions. Meanwhile, in a large skillet, cook the onions in butter over medium heat for 2 minutes. Add salmon; cook for 5 minutes or until heated through.

Stir in the Alfredo sauce, sherry or broth, celery salt, parsley and pepper; cook for 5 minutes or until heated through. Drain linguine; top with the salmon mixture. **Yield:** 6 servings.

Corn Bread Chicken

(Pictured on page 194)

Prep/Total Time: 25 min.

Just five ingredients are required to make this easy-to-assemble entree. I'm not sure how this recipe found its way into my kitchen, but I'm glad it did! We eat a lot of chicken, and this is a family favorite.
—Dawn d'Hooghe
Concord, North Carolina

  1 package (8-1/2 ounces) corn bread/muffin
    mix
  1 envelope ranch salad dressing mix
  1 cup milk
  6 boneless skinless chicken breast halves
    (4 ounces *each*)
  2 tablespoons vegetable oil

In a large resealable plastic bag, combine corn bread mix and salad dressing mix. Pour milk into a shallow bowl. Dip chicken in milk, then place in bag and shake to coat.

In a large skillet or Dutch oven over medium-high heat, brown chicken in oil on both sides. Cook, uncovered, over medium heat for 6-7 minutes on each side or until juices run clear. **Yield:** 6 servings.

Pronto Prosciutto Pasta

(Pictured below)

Prep/Total Time: 15 min.

With lots of flavor from prosciutto, feta and seasonings, this impressive pasta is quick and easy. It's a tasty entree for two on a busy weeknight. Or you can double the recipe for a family. —Jill Conley, Chicago, Illinois

  5 ounces uncooked spaghetti
  2 teaspoons minced garlic
1/4 cup olive oil
1/4 cup chopped prosciutto
  1 tablespoon chopped ripe olives
  1 teaspoon onion powder
1/2 teaspoon dried basil
1/2 teaspoon dried parsley flakes
1/2 teaspoon pepper
1/8 teaspoon salt
1/4 cup crumbled feta cheese

Cook spaghetti according to package directions. Meanwhile, in a large skillet, saute garlic in oil until tender. Stir in the prosciutto, olives, onion powder, basil, parsley, pepper and salt. Cook, uncovered, over medium heat for 3-4 minutes or until heated through. Drain spaghetti; toss with prosciutto mixture. Sprinkle with feta cheese. **Yield:** 2 servings.

Pronto Prosciutto Pasta

Asparagus Beef Lo Mein

boil; add ramen noodles and contents of remaining seasoning packet. Cook for 3 minutes. Remove from the heat; cover and let stand until noodles are tender. Serve with beef mixture. **Yield:** 4 servings.

Cajun Pork

Prep/Total Time: 30 min.

It took me a few tries to perfect this recipe, and now it's requested regularly. More Cajun seasoning can be added, but it tends to make the dish too hot for children. Chicken breasts can be substituted for the pork tenderloin and rice can be used instead of the noodles. —Tina Gantner
Matthews, Missouri

  2 pounds pork tenderloin, cut into 2-inch strips
  3 teaspoons Cajun seasoning
  3 teaspoons minced garlic
  2 teaspoons Italian seasoning
1/3 cup butter, cubed
 12 ounces uncooked fine egg noodles
3/4 cup chicken broth
  2 teaspoons Worcestershire sauce
  2 large tomatoes, chopped

In a large skillet over medium heat, cook and stir the pork, Cajun seasoning, garlic and Italian seasoning in butter for 8-10 minutes or until meat is no longer pink. Meanwhile, cook noodles according to package directions.

Stir broth and Worcestershire sauce into pork mixture. Bring to a boil. Reduce heat; simmer, uncovered, for 5 minutes. Stir in tomatoes; cook 1-2 minutes longer or until heated through. Drain noodles. Use a slotted spoon to serve pork mixture over noodles; drizzle with pan juices. **Yield:** 4 servings.

Pesto Chicken 'n' Ravioli

Prep/Total Time: 20 min.

Calling for several convenience products, this easy-to-assemble main course has a delightful taste pesto lovers especially will enjoy. Serve it with Caesar salad and garlic bread, and it's sure to get rave reviews.
—Andrea Fishlock, Barto, Pennsylvania

  1 package (9 ounces) refrigerated cheese
     ravioli
  1 pound boneless skinless chicken breasts, cut
     into 2-inch strips
  1 teaspoon minced garlic
  1 tablespoon olive oil
  1 jar (7-1/4 ounces) roasted sweet red
     peppers, drained
3/4 cup prepared pesto

Cook ravioli according to package directions. Meanwhile, in a large skillet, cook and stir the chicken and garlic in oil over medium heat until chicken is no longer pink. Add roasted peppers; cook for 1-2 minutes or until heated through. Remove from the heat. Drain ravioli; add to the chicken mixture. Add pesto; toss gently to coat. **Yield:** 4 servings.

Asparagus Beef Lo Mein

(Pictured above)

Prep/Total Time: 20 min.

This flavorful stir-fry is easy and relatively inexpensive. It's served over ramen noodles, which is a nice change from the rice we usually have. To simplify preparation, I use store-bought garlic-infused olive oil instead of minced garlic and olive oil. —Dottie Wanat, Modesto, California

  1 boneless beef sirloin steak (1 pound), thinly
     sliced
1/4 teaspoon minced garlic
  2 tablespoons olive oil
  1 pound fresh asparagus, trimmed and cut
     into 2-1/2-inch pieces
2-1/4 cups water, *divided*
  2 packages (3 ounces *each*) beef ramen
     noodles
2/3 cup hoisin sauce

In a large skillet or wok, stir-fry beef and garlic in oil for 5 minutes or until meat is no longer pink. Add the asparagus; stir-fry for 2 minutes or until crisp-tender.

In a small bowl, combine 1/4 cup water and 1/2 teaspoon seasoning from one ramen noodle seasoning packet; stir until dissolved. Add hoisin sauce; stir into the beef mixture. Bring to a boil; cook and stir for 2 minutes or until thickened. (Discard remaining seasoning from opened packet.)

In a large saucepan, bring the remaining water to a

Broccoli Turkey Roll-Ups

(Pictured below)

Prep/Total Time: 15 min.

I rely on my microwave and six ingredients to fix this quick-and-easy main dish. It would be great for a Sunday lunch or dinner. Garnish with a dollop of light salad dressing and sliced pimiento. —Mary Beth Jordan Collinsville, Virginia

- 2 packages (9 ounces *each*) frozen broccoli spears
- 1/3 cup mayonnaise
- 1/3 cup plain yogurt
- 6 green onions, finely chopped
- 8 slices Swiss cheese
- 8 thick slices deli smoked turkey breast

Cook broccoli according to package directions; drain. In a small bowl, combine the mayonnaise, yogurt and onions. Place a cheese slice on each turkey slice; spread with 1 tablespoon mayonnaise mixture. Top with broccoli spears. Set remaining mayonnaise mixture aside.

Roll turkey up and place seam side down in a greased microwave-safe 11-in. x 7-in. x 2-in. dish. Microwave, uncovered, on high for 1-2 minutes or until heated through. Top with remaining mayonnaise mixture. **Yield:** 4 servings.

Editor's Note: This recipe was tested in a 1,100-watt microwave.

Creamy Tortellini

Broccoli Turkey Roll-Ups

Creamy Tortellini

(Pictured above)

Prep/Total Time: 25 min.

An envelope of vegetable soup mix lends flavor to the simple cream sauce that coats this rich pasta entree. I like to garnish it with additional mozzarella cheese and parsley. —Janice Plourde, Smooth Rock Falls, Ontario

- 3 cups refrigerated cheese tortellini
- 2 teaspoons minced garlic
- 2 tablespoons vegetable oil
- 1 envelope vegetable soup mix
- 2 cups half-and-half cream
- 1/4 cup minced fresh parsley
- 1/4 cup shredded mozzarella cheese
- 1/4 teaspoon pepper

Cook tortellini according to package directions. Meanwhile, in a large skillet, saute garlic in oil until tender. In a small bowl, combine the soup mix and cream; stir into skillet.

Drain tortellini; add to cream mixture. Bring to a boil. Reduce heat; simmer, uncovered, for 4-5 minutes or until heated through, stirring occasionally. Add the parsley, cheese and pepper. Cook 3-4 minutes longer or until cheese is melted. **Yield:** 6-8 servings.

Ginger Beef Stir-Fry

(Pictured below)

Prep/Total Time: 30 min.

This stir-fry is so colorful and delicious. Vary the recipe by substituting chicken or using vegetables you have on hand. The quickest version uses prepared veggies from our grocery store's salad bar.
—Linda Murray
Allenstown, New Hampshire

    1 teaspoon cornstarch
1/4 cup cold water
1/4 cup plum sauce
    1 tablespoon grated fresh gingerroot
    1 tablespoon soy sauce
1/4 teaspoon crushed red pepper flakes
    1 pound boneless beef sirloin steak, cut into thin 2-inch strips
    1 to 2 tablespoons vegetable oil
    1 medium sweet red pepper, julienned
1-1/2 cups fresh broccoli florets
    2 medium carrots, thinly sliced
    4 green onions, chopped
    1 teaspoon minced garlic
    3 tablespoons salted peanuts, chopped
Hot cooked rice, optional
    2 tablespoons sesame seeds, toasted

In a small bowl, whisk cornstarch and cold water until smooth. Stir in the plum sauce, ginger, soy sauce and pepper flakes; set aside. In a large skillet or wok, stir-fry beef in oil until no longer pink; remove and keep warm.

In the same pan, stir-fry the vegetables and garlic until tender. Return beef to the pan. Whisk the plum sauce mixture; stir into skillet. Cook and stir until slightly thickened. Stir in peanuts. Serve over rice if desired. Sprinkle with sesame seeds. **Yield:** 4 servings.

Tangy Almond Chicken

Prep/Total Time: 30 min.

With its appealing presentation, this scrumptious chicken dish will wow them at your next gathering. This is a very attractive entree to serve, and the sauce is delectable!
—Michelle Krzmarzick, Redondo Beach, California

    6 boneless skinless chicken breast halves (4 ounces *each*)
    3 tablespoons butter
    1 jar (12 ounces) currant jelly
1/2 cup prepared mustard
1/2 cup slivered almonds, toasted
    3 tablespoons brown sugar
    2 tablespoons lemon juice
1/2 teaspoon ground cinnamon

In a large skillet, brown chicken in butter for 4 minutes on each side. Remove and keep warm. Add the remaining ingredients to the skillet. Cook and stir until jelly is melted and mixture is smooth, about 2 minutes. Bring to a boil. Return chicken to pan. Reduce heat; cover and simmer for 12-15 minutes or until chicken juices run clear. **Yield:** 6 servings.

Kielbasa with Pasta

Prep/Total Time: 25 min.

One weekend while my husband was out of town, I came up with this recipe by using ingredients that I thought only I would enjoy. But to my surprise, my husband—who came home in time for supper—loved it.
—Ann Dee Bent
Sullivan, Missouri

    1 pound smoked kielbasa *or* Polish sausage, cut into 1/4-inch slices
1/2 cup chopped green pepper
1/4 cup chopped onion
1/2 teaspoon minced garlic
    2 tablespoons vegetable oil
    2 cans (14-1/2 ounces *each*) stewed tomatoes
    1 package (9 ounces) refrigerated angel hair pasta
1/2 cup grated Parmesan cheese
    2 tablespoons butter, melted

In a large skillet, saute the kielbasa, green pepper, onion and garlic in oil until sausage is lightly browned. Stir in tomatoes. Bring to a boil. Reduce heat; simmer, uncovered, for 10 minutes.

Meanwhile, cook pasta according to package directions; drain. Stir in Parmesan cheese and butter. Serve with kielbasa mixture. **Yield:** 4 servings.

Ginger Beef Stir-Fry

Swiss Cheese Chicken

Prep/Total Time: 30 min.

I tuck a little cheese into tender chicken cutlets, then top them with a savory sauce. I like to serve this with a four-bean salad and finish up with a pineapple dessert for a meal in minutes. —Nicole Pickett, Oro Valley, Arizona

✓ Uses less fat, sugar or salt. Includes Nutritional Analysis and Diabetic Exchanges.

  4 boneless skinless chicken breast halves
    (4 ounces *each*)
  2 tablespoons all-purpose flour
3/4 teaspoon pepper
1/4 teaspoon salt
  2 slices Swiss cheese, cut in half
  1 tablespoon butter
1/2 cup chicken broth
1/4 cup white wine *or* additional chicken broth
1/4 teaspoon dried oregano

Flatten chicken to 1/4-in. thickness. In a shallow bowl, combine the flour, pepper and salt. Place a piece of cheese on each piece of chicken; tuck in ends and roll up. Secure with toothpicks. Roll in flour mixture.

In a large nonstick skillet, brown roll-ups in butter on each side over medium heat. Stir in the broth, wine or additional broth and oregano; bring to a boil. Reduce heat; simmer, uncovered, for 10-12 minutes or until chicken juices run clear. Remove toothpicks before serving. **Yield:** 2 servings.

Nutritional Analysis: 2 roll-ups (prepared with reduced-fat cheese, reduced-fat butter and reduced-sodium chicken broth) equals 383 calories, 12 g fat (6 g saturated fat), 145 mg cholesterol, 626 mg sodium, 8 g carbohydrate, trace fiber, 55 g protein. **Diabetic Exchanges:** 6 lean meat, 1/2 starch.

Creamy Turkey Cleanup

Prep/Total Time: 15 min.

I first made this mostly microwaved medley when I was home on maternity leave with my third child. I needed to rely on quick-and-easy recipes that were kid-friendly, too. We all loved this supper in a dish, and it cleared up a bunch of turkey leftovers. —Julia Hainsworth Mt. Morris, New York

1-1/2 cups uncooked instant rice
  1 cup fresh broccoli florets
  1 medium carrot, coarsely chopped
  2 tablespoons water
  2 cups cubed cooked turkey
  1 can (10-3/4 ounces) condensed cream of
    mushroom soup, undiluted
3/4 cup milk
  3 tablespoons grated Parmesan cheese
1/2 teaspoon salt
1/2 teaspoon pepper

Cook rice according to package directions. Meanwhile, in a large microwave-safe bowl, combine the broccoli, carrot and water. Cover and microwave on high for 2-4 minutes or until crisp-tender; drain. Stir in the turkey, soup, milk, Parmesan cheese, salt, pepper and rice. Microwave, uncovered, for 2-3 minutes or until heated through, stirring twice. **Yield:** 4 servings.

Editor's Note: This recipe was tested in a 1,100-watt microwave.

Cheese Ravioli with Veggies

Cheese Ravioli with Veggies

(Pictured above)

Prep/Total Time: 30 min.

This pasta dish went over big when I served it to friends who dropped by and stayed for dinner. Since then, I've modified the recipe to include some vegetables, so it's a complete meal by itself. My sons ask for it all the time. —Amy Burns, Charleston, Illinois

  6 quarts water
  1 package (16 ounces) frozen California-blend
    vegetables
  1 package (25 ounces) frozen cheese ravioli
1/4 cup butter, melted
1/4 teaspoon salt-free seasoning blend
1/4 cup shredded Parmesan cheese

In a large saucepan or Dutch oven, bring the water to a boil. Add the vegetables; cook for 5 minutes. Add the ravioli. Cook 5 minutes longer or until vegetables and ravioli are tender; drain. Gently stir in butter. Sprinkle with seasoning blend and Parmesan cheese. **Yield:** 6 servings.

Garden Ham 'n' Noodles

Creamed Chicken 'n' Veggies

Prep/Total Time: 20 min.

I discovered this delicious skillet dish quite by accident one night when combining different ingredients. Now, everyone requests it. Serve the saucy entree with rice or your favorite quick biscuits for a wonderful hot meal. —Nina Steinman Golden, Colorado

> 2 cups frozen mixed vegetables
> 2 cups frozen broccoli cuts
> 2 tablespoons olive oil
> 4 cups cubed cooked chicken
> 1 jar (16 ounces) roasted garlic Parmesan Alfredo sauce
> 1/2 teaspoon salt
> 1/4 teaspoon pepper
> Hot cooked rice

In a large skillet, saute the mixed vegetables and broccoli in oil until tender. Stir in the chicken, Alfredo sauce, salt and pepper; heat through. Serve with rice. **Yield:** 6 servings.

Pronto Beef and Rice

Prep/Total Time: 30 min.

This stovetop meal is simple yet satisfying, especially when it's served with a tossed green salad and pinto beans. You could also use this dish as a tasty make-ahead filling for stuffed peppers or cabbage rolls.
—Steve Nieswiadomy, Fort Worth, Texas

> 1-1/2 pounds ground beef
> 2 cans (14-1/2 ounces *each*) chicken broth
> 1-1/2 cups uncooked long grain rice
> 1 can (8 ounces) tomato sauce
> 1/3 cup diced onion
> 1 small green pepper, diced
> 1 jalapeno pepper, seeded and diced

In a large skillet, cook beef over medium heat until no longer pink; drain. Stir in the remaining ingredients. Bring to a boil. Reduce heat; cover and simmer for 15 minutes or until rice is tender. **Yield:** 6 servings.

Editor's Note: When cutting or seeding hot peppers, use rubber or plastic gloves to protect your hands. Avoid touching your face.

Chops in Mushroom Gravy

Prep/Total Time: 20 min.

Although I love to cook, some days I just don't have a lot of time, so I keep boneless pork chops in my freezer for this quick dinner. My husband and children love the gravy. This recipe is easy to double if unexpected company drops by. —Karen Ehatt, Chester, Maryland

> 4 boneless pork loin chops (3/4 inch thick)
> 3/4 cup chopped onion
> 2 tablespoons butter

Garden Ham 'n' Noodles

(Pictured above)

Prep/Total Time: 30 min.

This blend of ingredients makes a very filling and comforting dish. I especially like to make it in summer when there's an abundance of fresh zucchini and carrots.
—Adena Foster, Kernersville, North Carolina

> 4 quarts water
> 2 medium carrots, diced
> 6 cups uncooked wide egg noodles
> 1 medium zucchini, halved and thinly sliced
> 1 cup heavy whipping cream
> 1 cup milk
> 1/2 to 1 teaspoon salt
> 1/2 pound fully cooked ham, cubed
> 1 can (15-1/4 ounces) whole kernel corn, drained
> 1 cup shredded Parmesan cheese

In a large saucepan or Dutch oven, bring water to a boil. Add carrots; cook for 1 minute. Add noodles; cook for 2 minutes. Add zucchini; cook 4-5 minutes longer or until noodles and vegetables are tender.

Meanwhile, in a large skillet, bring the cream, milk and salt to a boil. Reduce heat; simmer, uncovered, for 5 minutes. Stir in ham and corn; heat through. Drain noodle mixture; stir into ham mixture. Sprinkle with Parmesan cheese and toss to coat. **Yield:** 6-8 servings.

1 can (10-3/4 ounces) condensed cream of
    mushroom soup, undiluted
1/2 cup milk
Salt and pepper to taste

In a large skillet, brown pork chops and onion in butter
until onion is tender. Stir in the soup, milk, salt and
pepper. Bring to a boil. Reduce heat; cover and simmer
for 15-20 minutes or until meat juices run clear. **Yield:**
4 servings.

Colorful Chicken Pasta

(Pictured below)

Prep/Total Time: 30 min.

*I'm tired at the end of the workday, so fast meals are al-
ways appreciated. I came up with this pasta dish one night
using ingredients we happened to have on hand. I knew
it was a success when my husband, who doesn't even
like chicken, couldn't stop eating it!* —Shannon Mink
Columbus, Ohio

1-1/2 pounds boneless skinless chicken breasts, cut
        into 3-inch strips
    2   tablespoons olive oil
    1   teaspoon lemon-pepper seasoning
    1   package (16 ounces) frozen California-blend
        vegetables
    1   can (14-1/2 ounces) diced tomatoes,
        undrained
1/2 cup chopped onion

Glazed Salmon

    1   teaspoon dried basil
1/2 teaspoon onion powder
    1   package (16 ounces) angel hair pasta
Shredded Parmesan cheese, optional

In a large skillet, saute the chicken in oil until lightly
browned; sprinkle with the lemon-pepper. Add the
frozen vegetables, tomatoes, onion, basil and onion
powder. Bring to a boil. Reduce heat; cover and simmer for 6-8 minutes or until chicken juices run clear
and vegetables are tender.

Meanwhile, cook pasta according to package directions; drain. Top with chicken mixture. Serve with
Parmesan cheese if desired. **Yield:** 6 servings.

Glazed Salmon

(Pictured above)

Prep/Total Time: 20 min.

*After I grilled this for my boss and her husband, I was
swamped with calls asking for the recipe the next day at
work. My boss said she'd never tasted such delicious
salmon. And it takes only minutes to prepare.*
—Naomi Mahoney, Oakville, Ontario

1/2 cup olive oil
1/3 cup molasses
    2   teaspoons minced garlic
1-1/2 teaspoons grated lemon peel
    4   salmon fillets (6 ounces *each*)

In a small bowl, combine the oil, molasses, garlic and
lemon peel; set aside half of the mixture for serving.
Before starting grill, coat grill rack with nonstick cooking
spray. Grill salmon, uncovered, over medium heat for
6-8 minutes on each side or until fish flakes easily with
a fork, basting frequently with molasses mixture. Serve
with reserved molasses mixture. **Yield:** 4 servings.

Colorful Chicken Pasta

Vegetarian Spaghetti

(Pictured below)

Prep/Total Time: 25 min.

Who says spaghetti needs meat to be tasty? I stream-lined the original recipe for this deliciously different dish to reduce its 2-hour simmer time to just 10 minutes.
—*Margaret Wilson, Hemet, California*

  1 package (16 ounces) spaghetti
  1 cup chopped onion
1/2 cup chopped celery
  1 teaspoon garlic powder
  3 tablespoons vegetable oil
  1 jar (26 ounces) meatless spaghetti sauce
  1 can (16 ounces) garbanzo beans *or* chickpeas, rinsed and drained
  1 can (14-1/2 ounces) diced tomatoes with garlic and onion, undrained
  1 teaspoon sugar
1/2 teaspoon salt
1/2 teaspoon dried oregano
  1 bay leaf
1/4 cup grated Parmesan cheese

Cook spaghetti according to package directions. Mean-while, in a large skillet, saute the onion, celery and gar-lic powder in oil until tender. Add the spaghetti sauce, beans, tomatoes, sugar, salt, oregano and bay leaf.

Bring to a boil; cover and simmer for 10 minutes. Discard bay leaf. Drain spaghetti; top with sauce and Parmesan cheese. **Yield:** 6 servings.

Mushroom Oven Omelet

Prep/Total Time: 30 min.

If you're looking for an entree that can be served for break-fast, lunch or dinner, try this recipe. My versatile egg bake picks up flavor from the cheese, mushrooms and bacon.
—*Barbara Nowakowski*
North Tonawanda, New York

1/2 pound sliced fresh mushrooms
  2 tablespoons butter
  2 tablespoons all-purpose flour
  6 eggs
1/3 cup milk
1/8 teaspoon pepper
1-1/2 cups (6 ounces) shredded cheddar cheese, *divided*
1/2 cup real bacon bits

In a small skillet, saute mushrooms in butter until tender; drain. In a bowl, combine the flour, eggs, milk and pepper until smooth. Stir in 1 cup cheese, bacon and mushrooms. Pour into a greased 8-in. square baking dish. Sprinkle with remaining cheese. Bake, uncovered, at 375° for 18-20 minutes or until eggs are completely set. **Yield:** 4 servings.

Stovetop Bratwurst Dinner

Prep/Total Time: 30 min.

For a lip-smacking alternative to plain brats, I combine them with green beans and a mild cheese sauce for a swift skillet supper. I round out the menu with cauliflower cashew salad and brownies for dessert.
—*Darcy Dougherty, Postville, Iowa*

1-1/2 cups milk
  1 can (10-3/4 ounces) condensed cream of mushroom soup, undiluted
  1 pound fully cooked bratwurst links, cut into 1/2-inch pieces
  2 cups frozen cut green beans
  4 ounces process cheese (Velveeta), cubed
  6 cups hot cooked noodles

In a large saucepan, combine the milk and soup until blended. Add bratwurst and beans. Bring to a boil. Re-duce heat; cover and simmer for 15 minutes or until heated through. Stir in cheese until melted. Serve over noodles. **Yield:** 4-6 servings.

Blue Cheese Pork Chops

Prep/Total Time: 30 min.

This recipe makes the most delicious creamy gravy to serve over pork chops. With just a hint of blue cheese flavor, it

Vegetarian Spaghetti

tastes like something from a fancy restaurant. I like to serve this special dish with sauteed mushrooms.
—*Linda Foreman, Locust Grove, Oklahoma*

    1 cup heavy whipping cream
    4 bone-in pork loin chops (1 inch thick)
    2 tablespoons vegetable oil
    1/2 teaspoon garlic powder
    1/4 teaspoon pepper
    2 ounces crumbled blue cheese

In a small saucepan, bring cream to a boil. Reduce heat; simmer, uncovered, for 15-20 minutes or until thickened. Meanwhile, in a large skillet, brown pork chops in oil over medium heat until juices run clear, about 20 minutes. Sprinkle with garlic powder and pepper.

Stir the blue cheese into the cream; cook and stir over medium heat for 2-3 minutes or until cheese is softened. Pour over pork chops. **Yield:** 4 servings.

Raisin Sauce for Ham

Spinach Sole Roll-Ups

Prep/Total Time: 30 min.

This is an unusual but delicious combination of ingredients. For a great company meal, I serve it with a chilled green bean salad and sliced French bread that's been spread with butter and dried basil, then baked.
—*Dixie Terry Marion, Illinois*

✓ Uses less fat, sugar or salt. Includes Nutritional Analysis and Diabetic Exchanges.

    1 package (10 ounces) frozen leaf spinach,
      thawed and squeezed dry
    1/2 cup sliced green onions
    1/3 cup sour cream
  1-1/4 pounds sole fillets
Lemon-pepper seasoning
    1 tablespoon cornstarch
    1 tablespoon water
    1 can (14-1/2 ounces) stewed tomatoes,
      undrained

In a small bowl, combine the spinach, onions and sour cream. Spread into an ungreased 13-in. x 9-in. x 2-in. baking dish. Cut sole fillets into 6-in. x 2-in. strips; carefully roll up and secure with toothpicks.

Place over spinach mixture. Sprinkle with lemon-pepper. Bake, uncovered, at 350° for 15-20 minutes or until fish flakes easily with a fork.

In a saucepan, combine the cornstarch and water until smooth. Gradually add tomatoes. Bring to a boil over medium heat; cook and stir for 2 minutes or until thickened. Discard toothpicks from roll-ups. Spoon tomato sauce over roll-ups and spinach mixture. **Yield:** 4 servings.

Nutritional Analysis: 1 serving (prepared with reduced-fat sour cream) equals 213 calories, 4 g fat (2 g saturated fat), 75 mg cholesterol, 388 mg sodium, 14 g carbohydrate, 3 g fiber, 31 g protein. **Diabetic Exchanges:** 5 very lean meat, 1 vegetable, 1/2 starch.

Raisin Sauce for Ham

(Pictured above)

Prep/Total Time: 15 min.

This fruity rum sauce can make ordinary ham something to celebrate! If you don't have rum extract, use a tablespoon of rum instead...or eliminate it altogether.
—*Elizabeth Halls, Courtenay, British Columbia*

✓ Uses less fat, sugar or salt. Includes Nutritional Analysis and Diabetic Exchanges.

    1/4 cup raisins
    5 tablespoons water, *divided*
    1/2 cup orange juice
    2 tablespoons unsweetened crushed
      pineapple, undrained
    1 tablespoon cornstarch
    1/2 teaspoon rum extract, optional
    1 boneless fully cooked ham steak (1 pound)

In a large saucepan, combine the raisins, 4 tablespoons water, orange juice and pineapple. Bring to a boil. Combine cornstarch and remaining water until smooth; gradually stir into raisin mixture. Cook and stir for 2 minutes or until thickened. Remove from the heat; stir in extract if desired.

Cut the ham steak into four pieces. In a large skillet coated with nonstick cooking spray, cook ham over medium heat for 1-2 minutes on each side or until browned. Serve with raisin sauce. **Yield:** 4 servings.

Nutritional Analysis: 3 ounces cooked ham with 1/4 cup raisin sauce equals 237 calories, 10 g fat (3 g saturated fat), 60 mg cholesterol, 1,451 mg sodium, 16 g carbohydrate, trace fiber, 21 g protein. **Diabetic Exchanges:** 3 lean meat, 1 fruit.

Chapter 14

ALMOST EVERYONE loves to top off a tasty dinner or lunch with a sweet homemade treat. But who has the time needed to make one? You do—thanks to the rapid recipes here!

While these special confections may look impressive and complicated, they're actually easy to prepare on a moment's notice and serve as a delightful surprise for family and friends.

Everyone with a sweet tooth will be satisfied when they sample tantalizing temptations like Raspberry Lemon Torte, Black Forest Cheesecake and Chocolate Walnut Tart.

These luscious cakes, candies, pies, cookies and more prove it's true—you'll always have time to whip up a delectable dessert.

SIMPLY SCRUMPTIOUS. Candy Bar Cheesecake (p. 210), Fresh Fruit Tartlets (p. 212) and Pineapple Crunch (p. 210).

Cranberry Cornmeal Cake

Pineapple Crunch

(Pictured on page 209)

Prep: 15 min. **Bake:** 10 min. + cooling

This crunchy pineapple dessert offers quick refreshment. The recipe was given to me years ago by a co-worker.
—*Betty Wiersma, Sherwood Park, Alberta*

- 1 cup crushed cornflakes
- 2 tablespoons sugar
- 1/3 cup butter, melted
- 2 tablespoons cornstarch
- 2 cans (8 ounces *each*) crushed pineapple, undrained
- 2 cups vanilla ice cream, softened
- 1 package (3.4 ounces) instant vanilla pudding mix

In a bowl, combine the cornflake crumbs, sugar and butter. Press into a greased 9-in. square baking dish. Bake at 350° for 10 minutes. Cool on a wire rack.

In a saucepan, combine the cornstarch and pineapple until blended. Bring to a boil; cook and stir for 2 minutes or until thickened. Cool. In a mixing bowl, beat the ice cream and pudding mix on low speed for 2 minutes or until blended and thickened. Spoon over crust. Top with pineapple mixture. Refrigerate until serving. **Yield:** 9-12 servings.

Cranberry Cornmeal Cake

(Pictured above)

Prep: 15 min. **Bake:** 55 min. + cooling

Cornmeal gives a pleasant texture to this moist golden cake. With colorful cranberries and raisins on top, it's a delicious dessert that's perfect for the holidays. Friends and family will never guess it's so quick to put together.
—*Emma Magielda, Amsterdam, New York*

- 3/4 cup butter, softened, *divided*
- 1-1/2 cups packed brown sugar, *divided*
- 1-1/2 cups fresh *or* frozen cranberries, thawed
- 1/2 cup golden raisins
- 2 eggs
- 3 teaspoons vanilla extract
- 1-1/4 cups all-purpose flour
- 1/3 cup cornmeal
- 1-1/2 teaspoons baking powder
- 2/3 cup milk

Melt 1/4 cup butter; pour into an ungreased 9-in. round baking pan. Tilt to grease sides of pan. Sprinkle with 3/4 cup brown sugar. Top with cranberries and raisins; set aside.

In a large mixing bowl, cream the remaining butter and brown sugar until light and fluffy. Add eggs, one at a time, beating well after each addition. Beat in vanilla. Combine the flour, cornmeal and baking powder; add to creamed mixture alternately with milk. Carefully spread over cranberries and raisins.

Bake at 350° for 55-60 minutes or until a toothpick inserted near the center of cake comes out clean. Cool for 10 minutes before inverting onto a serving platter. Serve warm. **Yield:** 10-12 servings.

Candy Bar Cheesecake

(Pictured on page 208)

Prep: 25 min. **Bake:** 1-1/4 hours + chilling

With this recipe, you can easily create a cheesecake that tastes like a fancy store-bought treat. It's always requested when I'm asked to bring dessert to a function.
—*Julie Cervenka, Ballwin, Missouri*

- 1-3/4 cups crushed chocolate wafers (about 28 wafers)
- 1/4 cup sugar
- 1/3 cup butter, melted
- 3 packages (8 ounces *each*) cream cheese, softened
- 1 can (14 ounces) sweetened condensed milk
- 1 cup chocolate syrup
- 2 teaspoons vanilla extract
- 3 eggs, lightly beaten
- 6 Snickers candy bars (2.07 ounces *each*), coarsely chopped, *divided*

Additional chocolate syrup

In a small bowl, combine wafer crumbs and sugar; stir in butter. Press onto the bottom and 1-1/2 in. up the sides of a greased 9-in. springform pan. Place pan on a baking sheet. Bake at 325° for 12 minutes. Cool on a wire rack.

In a large mixing bowl, beat cream cheese, milk, chocolate syrup and vanilla until smooth. Add eggs; beat just until combined. Stir in 2-1/2 cups chopped candy bars. Pour into crust.

Place pan on a double thickness of heavy-duty foil

(about 18 in. square); securely wrap foil around pan. Place in a large baking pan. Add 1 in. of hot water to larger pan.

Bake for 75-80 minutes or until center is just set. Cool on a wire rack for 10 minutes. Carefully run a knife around the edge of pan to loosen; cool 1 hour longer. Refrigerate overnight. Top with remaining chopped candy bars; drizzle with additional chocolate syrup. **Yield:** 12-14 servings.

Star-Spangled Shortcake

Mint Cookie Candies

(Pictured below)

Prep/Total Time: 30 min.

These yummy chocolate mint bites from our Test Kitchen home economists are so delightful, you'll find it difficult to stop at one. With an attractive two-tone look, they're pretty on a cookie tray. Try topping them with crushed candy canes when giving them as gifts.

- 12 **ounces white candy coating, coarsely chopped**
- 6 **teaspoons shortening,** *divided*
- 1/4 **teaspoon green food coloring**
- 4 **mint cream-filled chocolate sandwich cookies, crushed**
- 2 **packages (4.67 ounces** *each***) mint Andes candies**

In a microwave-safe bowl, melt candy coating and 4 teaspoons shortening; stir until smooth. Stir in food coloring. Pour evenly into miniature muffin cup liners. Sprinkle with cookie crumbs. In a microwave-safe bowl, melt mint candies and remaining shortening; stir until smooth. Pour over cookie crumbs. Let stand until set. **Yield:** 4 dozen.

Mint Cookie Candies

Star-Spangled Shortcake

(Pictured above)

Prep/Total Time: 30 min.

Celebrate Independence Day with this patriotic dessert dreamed up by our Test Kitchen staff. The star-shaped corn muffins are wonderful when topped with vanilla ice cream and colorful berries.

- 1 **package (8-1/2 ounces) corn bread/muffin mix**
- 2 **cups halved fresh strawberries**
- 2 **cups fresh** *or* **frozen blueberries, thawed**
- 1/3 **cup sugar**
- 5 **teaspoons balsamic vinegar**

Vanilla ice cream

Prepare corn bread batter according to package directions. Fill six greased star-shaped cups or muffin cups two-thirds full. Bake at 350° for 12-15 minutes or until a toothpick comes out clean. Meanwhile, in a bowl, combine the strawberries and blueberries; sprinkle with sugar and gently toss to coat.

Cool shortcakes for 10 minutes before carefully removing from pan to a wire rack. Drizzle vinegar over berries; toss to coat. Top each shortcake with a scoop of ice cream and berry mixture. **Yield:** 6 servings.

Orange Dream Torte

(Pictured at right)

Prep: 20 min. + chilling

Our Test Kitchen staff came up with this fancy-looking torte. The fluffy filling is encircled by store-bought ladyfingers and topped with mandarin oranges.

✓ Uses less fat, sugar or salt. Includes Nutritional Analysis and Diabetic Exchanges.

1 package (3 ounces) orange gelatin
2/3 cup boiling water
1/2 cup cold water
1 carton (16 ounces) frozen whipped topping, thawed, *divided*
1 package (8 ounces) cream cheese, softened
1/4 cup sugar
1/4 cup milk
1/4 cup graham cracker crumbs
1 package (3 ounces) ladyfingers, split
1 can (11 ounces) mandarin oranges, drained

In a large bowl, dissolve gelatin in boiling water. Stir in cold water. Cover and refrigerate for 30 minutes or until syrupy. Fold in 3 cups whipped topping; set aside. In a small mixing bowl, beat the cream cheese and sugar until smooth; gradually beat in the milk. Fold in remaining whipped topping.

Grease the bottom of a 9-in. springform pan; sprinkle with crumbs. Arrange ladyfingers around edge of pan. Set aside 1-1/2 cups of orange mixture. Alternately spoon cream cheese mixture and remaining orange mixture into pan. Spread reserved orange mixture over top. Refrigerate for 1 hour or until set. Remove sides of pan. Garnish with oranges. **Yield:** 12 servings.

Nutritional Analysis: 1 serving (prepared with sugar-free gelatin, reduced-fat whipped topping, reduced-fat cream cheese and fat-free milk) equals 193 calories, 9 g fat (7 g saturated fat), 39 mg cholesterol, 120 mg sodium, 21 g carbohydrate, trace fiber, 4 g protein. **Diabetic Exchanges:** 2 fat, 1 starch, 1/2 fruit.

Honey Lemon Cookies

(Pictured at right)

Prep: 15 min. **Bake:** 10 min.

*Grated lemon peel in the batter and on the icing of these soft cake-like cookies gives them their fresh citrus flavor.
—Betty Thompson, La Porte, Texas*

7 tablespoons butter, softened
1/2 cup sugar
1 egg
1-3/4 cups all-purpose flour
1 teaspoon baking powder
1/2 teaspoon salt
1/3 cup honey
1/4 cup plain yogurt
2 teaspoons grated lemon peel
1/2 teaspoon lemon extract
ICING:
1 cup confectioners' sugar
2 tablespoons lemon juice
2 teaspoons grated lemon peel

In a small mixing bowl, cream butter and sugar. Beat in egg. Combine flour, baking powder and salt. Combine honey, yogurt, peel and extract. Add dry ingredients to creamed mixture alternately with honey mixture.

Drop by tablespoonfuls 2 in. apart onto greased baking sheets. Bake at 350° for 10-12 minutes or until golden brown. Remove to wire racks. In a small bowl, combine the confectioners' sugar and lemon juice until smooth. Brush over the warm cookies; sprinkle with lemon peel. **Yield:** about 3 dozen.

Chocolate Chip Cookie Pizza

(Pictured at right)

Prep: 25 min. **Bake:** 15 min. + cooling

*Prepared cookie dough and pudding mix speed up this yummy treat. It's a favorite at our house. —Mary White
Lincoln, Nebraska*

1 tube (18 ounces) chocolate chip cookie dough
1 package (8 ounces) cream cheese, softened
1/3 cup sugar
2 cups cold half-and-half cream
1 package (3.9 ounces) instant chocolate pudding mix
1/4 cup chopped pecans *or* walnuts

Press cookie dough onto an ungreased 12-in. pizza pan. Bake at 350° for 13-16 minutes or until center is set and cookie is lightly browned. Cool for 5 minutes; gently run a flexible metal spatula under crust to loosen. Cool completely.

In a small mixing bowl, beat cream cheese and sugar until blended. Spread over crust. In a bowl, whisk cream and pudding mix for 2 minutes. Let stand for 2 minutes or until soft-set. Spread over cream cheese mixture; sprinkle with nuts. Refrigerate until serving. **Yield:** 14-16 slices.

Fresh Fruit Tartlets

(Pictured on page 208)

Prep/Total Time: 20 min.

These mini tarts are perfect for showers, parties or whenever you need a pretty dessert. Top them with just about any fruit. —Shelly Forslund, Delafield, Wisconsin

1 envelope whipped topping mix
1/2 cup cold milk
1 teaspoon vanilla extract
1 package (8 ounces) cream cheese, softened
1/2 cup confectioners' sugar
10 individual graham cracker tart shells
Assorted fresh fruit

In a small mixing bowl, beat topping mix, milk and vanilla on low speed until blended. Beat on high until soft peaks form, about 4 minutes. In a large mixing bowl, beat cream cheese and confectioners' sugar until smooth. Fold in the whipped topping mixture. Spoon into tart shells; top with fruit. Refrigerate leftovers. **Yield:** 10 servings.

Orange Dream Torte
Chocolate Chip Cookie Pizza
Honey Lemon Cookies

Apple Pie in a Goblet

(Pictured below)

Prep: 10 min. **Cook:** 25 min.

This dessert is not only easy but very elegant. I got the recipe from a church cooking class and now fix it often, always with rave reviews. You can serve it in dessert bowls, but I get more oohs and aahs when I put it in goblets.
—*Reneé Zimmer, Gig Harbor, Washington*

- 3 large tart apples, peeled and coarsely chopped
- 1/4 cup sugar
- 1/4 cup water
- 3/4 teaspoon ground cinnamon
- 1/4 teaspoon ground nutmeg
- 12 shortbread cookies, crushed
- 2 cups vanilla ice cream

Whipped cream

In a large saucepan, combine the apples, sugar, water, cinnamon and nutmeg. Bring to a boil. Reduce heat; cover and simmer for 10 minutes or until apples are tender. Uncover; cook 9-11 minutes longer or until most of the liquid has evaporated. Remove from the heat.

In each of four goblets or parfait glasses, layer 1 tablespoon cookie crumbs, 1/2 cup ice cream and a fourth of the apple mixture. Top with remaining cookie crumbs and whipped cream. Serve immediately. **Yield:** 4 servings.

Ribbon Crispies

Apple Pie in a Goblet

Ribbon Crispies

(Pictured above)

Prep: 10 min. **Cook:** 10 min. + cooling

These dressed-up rice cereal bars are a great-tasting twist on a longtime favorite. They're perfect for buffet tables and meals eaten on the run. Kids from age 1 to 101 love them, and they're always a huge hit no matter where or when I share them. —*Nancy Baker, Boonville, Missouri*

- 1/2 cup butter, cubed
- 2 jars (7 ounces *each*) marshmallow creme
- 11 cups crisp rice cereal
- 1 to 1-1/2 cups peanut butter
- 1 to 1-1/2 cups hot fudge ice cream topping, warmed

In a large saucepan, melt butter over medium-low heat. Stir in the marshmallow creme until smooth. Remove from the heat; stir in cereal until blended.

Press half of the mixture into a greased 15-in. x 10-in. x 1-in. pan; spread with peanut butter. Carefully spread with hot fudge topping. Press the remaining cereal mixture over fudge layer (pan will be full). Cool for 10 minutes before cutting. **Yield:** 3 dozen.

Raspberry Coconut Cookies

Prep: 30 min. **Bake:** 10 min.

With their yummy raspberry centers, these chewy cookies will disappear from your picnic table fast. My mother used to make these, and they were always my favorite. Now my

family enjoys them, too. Store the cooled cookies in a sealed container to keep them soft. —Cheryl Giroux
Amherstburg, Ontario

1/2 cup shortening
1/2 cup packed brown sugar
6 tablespoons sugar
1 egg
1/4 cup water
1/2 teaspoon almond extract
1-1/2 cups plus 2 tablespoons all-purpose flour
1/2 teaspoon baking soda
1/2 teaspoon salt
1 cup flaked coconut
1/3 cup seedless raspberry jam

In a large mixing bowl, cream shortening and sugars. Add egg; beat well. Beat in water and extract. Combine the flour, baking soda and salt; gradually add to creamed mixture. Stir in the coconut (dough will be sticky).

Roll into 1-in. balls. Using the end of a wooden spoon handle, make a deep indentation in the center of each. Fill each with 1/2 teaspoon jam. Cover jam with a teaspoonful of dough; seal and reshape into balls.

Place 2 in. apart on ungreased baking sheets. Bake at 375° for 10-12 minutes or until lightly browned. Remove to wire racks to cool. **Yield:** about 2-1/2 dozen.

Strawberry Angel Delight

Prep/Total Time: 30 min.

For a nice ending to a barbecue, offer slices of this tempting tunnel cake. I found the recipe in an old cookbook. When making the filling, use any type of fruit you prefer.
—Jean King, Anderson, California

2 cups heavy whipping cream
1/4 cup confectioners' sugar
1/2 cup miniature marshmallows
1/2 cup chopped fresh strawberries
1/3 cup crushed pineapple, drained
1 prepared angel food cake (8 inches)

In a large mixing bowl, beat the cream until it begins to thicken. Add confectioners' sugar; beat until stiff peaks form. In a large bowl, combine the marshmallows, strawberries, pineapple and 1-1/2 cups whipped cream.

Cut a 1-in. slice off the top of the cake; set aside. Carefully hollow out bottom of cake, leaving a 1-in. shell. Set aside 1/2 cup strawberry mixture. Fill tunnel in cake with remaining strawberry mixture; replace cake top. Spread remaining whipped cream over top and sides of cake. Spread reserved strawberry mixture over the top. Store in the refrigerator. **Yield:** 10-12 servings.

Mud Pie

(Pictured at right)

Prep: 15 min. + chilling

Coming from the South, we fell in love with mud pie—a chocolate dessert that's filled with pecans. Some versions

take all day to put together, but mine takes just 15 minutes of preparation. Then store it in the refrigerator until you're ready to serve it. —Deboraha Woolard
Las Vegas, Nevada

3 squares (1 ounce *each*) semisweet chocolate
1/4 cup sweetened condensed milk
1 chocolate crumb crust (8 inches)
1/2 cup chopped pecans
2 cups cold milk
2 packages (3.9 ounces *each*) instant chocolate pudding mix
1 carton (8 ounces) frozen whipped topping, thawed, *divided*

In a microwave or heavy saucepan, melt chocolate; stir in condensed milk until smooth. Pour into crust; sprinkle with pecans.

In a small bowl, whisk milk and pudding mixes for 2 minutes. Let stand for 2 minutes or until soft-set. Carefully spread 1-1/2 cups of pudding mixture over pecans. Fold 1/2 cup whipped topping into the remaining pudding mixture; spoon over pudding layer. Top with the remaining whipped topping. Chill until set. Refrigerate leftovers. **Yield:** 8 servings.

Mud Pie

Coffee Ice Cream Pie

Streusel Rhubarb Dessert

Prep: 15 min. **Bake:** 1 hour + cooling

This old-fashioned dessert has a sweet crumb topping and pleasantly tart rhubarb filling that guests are sure to love. —Shelley Balint, Cordova, Alaska

   1 cup all-purpose flour
 1/3 cup confectioners' sugar
 1/3 cup cold butter
FILLING:
1-1/4 cups sugar
 1/4 cup all-purpose flour
 1/2 teaspoon salt
   2 eggs, lightly beaten
   3 cups chopped fresh *or* frozen rhubarb
TOPPING:
 3/4 cup all-purpose flour
 1/2 cup sugar
 1/4 teaspoon ground cinnamon
 1/3 cup cold butter

In a bowl, combine flour and confectioners' sugar. Cut in butter until crumbly. Press into a greased 9-in. square baking dish. Bake at 350° for 15-18 minutes or until brown around the edges.

Meanwhile, in a large bowl, combine the sugar, flour and salt. Add eggs; mix well. Fold in the rhubarb. Pour over crust.

For topping, combine the flour, sugar and cinnamon in a small bowl; cut in the butter until crumbly. Sprinkle over the filling. Bake at 350° for 45-50 minutes or until the rhubarb is bubbly. Cool on a wire rack. **Yield:** 12 servings.

Editor's Note: If using frozen rhubarb, measure rhubarb while still frozen, then thaw completely. Drain in a colander, but do not press liquid out.

Coffee Ice Cream Pie

(Pictured above)

Prep: 25 min. + freezing

I stir mini marshmallows, mini chocolate chips and crushed sandwich cookies into coffee ice cream to create this irresistible frozen dessert. The fancy look is a snap to achieve by pulling a toothpick through lines of ice cream topping. —Cherron Nagel, Columbus, Ohio

1-1/2 cups crushed cream-filled chocolate
      sandwich cookies, *divided*
 1/4 cup butter, melted
   2 pints coffee ice cream, softened
   1 cup miniature marshmallows
   1 cup miniature semisweet chocolate chips
   2 cups whipped topping
   2 tablespoons caramel ice cream topping
   2 tablespoons hot fudge ice cream topping,
      warmed
Additional cream-filled chocolate sandwich cookies,
   optional

In a small bowl, combine 1-1/4 cups crushed cookies and butter. Press onto the bottom and up the sides of a 9-in. pie plate. In a large bowl, combine the ice cream, marshmallows, chocolate chips and remaining crushed cookies. Spoon into crust. Freeze for 30 minutes.

Spread whipped topping over pie. Alternately pipe thin lines of caramel topping and hot fudge topping over pie; gently pull a toothpick or sharp knife through lines in one direction. Cover and freeze overnight. May be frozen for up to 2 months. Remove from the freezer 10-15 minutes before cutting. Garnish with additional cookies if desired. **Yield:** 6-8 servings.

Zucchini Cake

Prep: 30 min. **Bake:** 20 min. + cooling

I frequently fix this moist snack cake topped with sweet cream cheese frosting. Squares of this cake freeze extremely well. —Cindy West, Marshalltown, Iowa

   3 eggs
 3/4 cup vegetable oil
   2 cups all-purpose flour
   2 cups sugar
   2 teaspoons baking powder
1-1/2 teaspoons salt
   1 teaspoon ground cinnamon
   2 cups shredded zucchini
FROSTING:
   1 package (3 ounces) cream cheese, softened
   2 tablespoons butter, softened
   1 teaspoon vanilla extract
   3 cups confectioners' sugar
   2 to 3 tablespoons milk

In a mixing bowl, beat eggs and oil. Combine flour, sugar, baking powder, salt and cinnamon; add to egg mixture and mix well. Stir in zucchini. Spread into a greased

15-in. x 10-in. x 1-in. baking pan. Bake at 350° for 20-25 minutes or until a toothpick inserted near the center comes out clean. Cool completely on a wire rack.

In a small mixing bowl, beat cream cheese, butter and vanilla until smooth. Gradually beat in confectioners' sugar. Add enough milk to achieve spreading consistency. Frost cake and cut into squares. Store leftovers in the refrigerator. **Yield:** about 24 servings.

Blueberry Peach Cobbler

(Pictured below)

Prep: 20 min. **Bake:** 25 min.

This delicious cobbler smells so good while it's in the oven, your mouth will be watering before it's finished baking. Believe me—there will be no leftovers! Serve it warm with cream...or ice cream, my family's favorite.
—*Roni Goodell, Spanish Fork, Utah*

- 1/2 cup packed brown sugar
- 3 tablespoons cornstarch
- 1/4 teaspoon ground mace
- 1/4 cup sherry *or* unsweetened apple juice
- 5 cups sliced peeled peaches
- 1 cup fresh *or* frozen blueberries
- 1/2 cup chopped pecans
- 1 tablespoon butter
- 1 tablespoon lemon juice

TOPPING:
- 1 cup all-purpose flour
- 1/3 cup sugar
- 1-1/2 teaspoons baking powder

Dash salt
- 1/4 cup cold butter
- 1/4 cup milk
- 1 egg, lightly beaten

In a large saucepan, combine the brown sugar, cornstarch and mace. Stir in sherry or juice until blended. Bring to a boil; cook and stir for 1-2 minutes or until thickened. Add the peaches, blueberries, pecans, butter and lemon juice. Pour into a greased shallow 2-qt. baking dish.

For topping, in a small bowl, combine the flour, sugar, baking powder and salt. Cut in butter until coarse crumbs form. Stir in milk and egg. Spoon over fruit mixture. Bake at 400° for 25-30 minutes or until bubbly and a toothpick inserted in the topping comes out clean. Serve warm. **Yield:** 6-8 servings.

Glazed Apricot Sorbet

(Pictured above)

Prep: 10 min. + freezing

This fruity dessert is refreshingly cool and light with a hint of richness. It's just right for a company meal or a pleasant afternoon treat. I like to serve it in sherbet glasses with mint sprigs for an elegant look.
—*Nina Rohlfs*
Unadilla, Nebraska

- 1 can (20 ounces) apricot halves, drained
- 1 jar (10 ounces) apricot preserves
- 1-1/2 teaspoons grated orange peel
- 2 tablespoons lemon juice
- 5 tablespoons heavy whipping cream

In a food processor or blender, combine the apricots, preserves, orange peel and lemon juice; cover and process until smooth. Pour into a freezer container; cover and freeze for at least 3 hours. May be frozen for up to 3 months.

Remove from the freezer at least 15 minutes before serving. Scoop into dessert dishes; drizzle with cream. **Yield:** 5 servings.

Blueberry Peach Cobbler

Raspberry Lemon Torte

(Pictured at right and on cover)

Prep: 15 min. **Bake:** 25 min. + cooling

A box of lemon cake mix, raspberry jam and canned frosting make it a breeze to assemble this lovely layered torte from our Test Kitchen staff. To split each cake layer evenly, insert toothpicks into the side of the cake layer to mark the halfway point. Wrap a length of dental floss around the cake, resting it on the toothpicks. Cross the ends of the floss and pull gently to split the cake.

    1 package (18-1/4 ounces) lemon cake mix
    1 tablespoon poppy seeds
    1 tablespoon grated lemon peel
    1 jar (12 ounces) seedless raspberry jam
2-3/4 cups vanilla frosting
Fresh raspberries

Grease two 9-in. round baking pans and line with waxed paper; grease and flour the paper. Prepare cake batter according to package directions; stir in poppy seeds and lemon peel. Pour into prepared pans. Bake at 350° for 21-26 minutes or until a toothpick inserted near the center comes out clean. Cool for 10 minutes before removing from pans to wire racks to cool completely.

Split each cake into two horizontal layers. Place one bottom layer on a serving plate; top with half of the jam. Top with a second layer; spread with 3/4 cup frosting. Top with third layer and remaining jam. Top with remaining layer; spread remaining frosting over top and sides of cake. Sprinkle with raspberries. **Yield:** 12 servings.

Peanut Lover's Pie

(Pictured at right)

Prep: 30 min. + freezing

I add peanut butter, honey roasted peanuts and peanut butter cups to this yummy chocolate ice cream pie. It tastes like a specialty dessert from an ice cream shop. Since this pie is kept in the freezer, it can easily be made ahead and frozen.
—Lori Hunter, Poca, West Virginia

    6 tablespoons honey roasted peanuts, *divided*
1-1/2 cups graham cracker crumbs
    7 tablespoons butter, melted
    3 pints chocolate ice cream, softened
    1 cup plus 1 tablespoon peanut butter, *divided*
3/4 cup coarsely chopped peanut butter cups, *divided*
1/2 cup caramel ice cream topping

Chop 1 tablespoon of peanuts; set aside. Place the remaining peanuts in a food processor; cover and process until ground. In a small bowl, combine the ground nuts, cracker crumbs and butter. Press onto the bottom and up the sides of an ungreased 9-in. pie plate. Freeze until firm, about 30 minutes.

In a large bowl, combine the ice cream and 1 cup peanut butter until blended. Spoon half into crust. Re-

turn remaining ice cream mixture to the freezer. Cover and freeze pie until almost firm, about 1 hour. Sprinkle with about two-thirds of the chopped peanut butter cups. Freeze for 30 minutes.

Meanwhile, resoften remaining ice cream mixture. Spread over peanut butter cups (pie will be very full). Cover and freeze for at least 2 hours or until almost firm. Sprinkle with reserved chopped peanuts and remaining chopped peanut butter cups. Cover and freeze until firm, about 1 hour longer.

Remove pie from the freezer 15 minutes before serving. Combine caramel topping and remaining peanut butter; drizzle some over dessert plates. Top each with a piece of pie; drizzle with remaining caramel mixture. **Yield:** 8 servings.

Peach Strawberry Sundaes

(Pictured at right)

Prep/Total Time: 10 min.

There is something special that happens when you combine fresh lime juice with peaches and strawberries—talk about a burst of flavor! This simple yet elegant treat is fabulous on a hot summer day.
—Kathy Clement
Apex, North Carolina

☑ Uses less fat, sugar or salt. Includes Nutritional Analysis and Diabetic Exchanges.

2-1/2 cups chopped peeled fresh peaches
    1 cup fresh strawberries, quartered
4-1/2 teaspoons sugar
    1 tablespoon lime juice
Vanilla ice cream

In a large bowl, combine peaches and strawberries. Combine the sugar and lime juice; pour over fruit and gently toss to coat. Serve over ice cream. **Yield:** 6 servings.

Nutritional Analysis: 1/2 cup fruit mixture over 1/2 cup reduced-fat frozen yogurt equals 142 calories, 1 g fat (1 g saturated fat), 5 mg cholesterol, 59 mg sodium, 29 g carbohydrate, 2 g fiber, 5 g protein. **Diabetic Exchanges:** 1-1/2 fruit, 1/2 reduced-fat milk.

Pineapple Berry Breeze

Prep/Total Time: 10 min.

This fruit-filled sherbet with crunchy pecans is so refreshing. I recommend tucking a few wafer creme cookies alongside each serving of the frosty dessert.
—Jan Ashworth, Santa Clara, Utah

    1 package (12 ounces) frozen unsweetened raspberries
    2 quarts pineapple sherbet, slightly softened
    2 medium bananas, diced
1/2 cup chopped pecans, toasted

Thaw raspberries on paper towels; set aside. In a large mixing bowl, beat sherbet until smooth. Fold in bananas and pecans. Gently fold in raspberries. Serve immediately or spoon into a freezer container and freeze. **Yield:** about 2-1/2 quarts.

Raspberry Lemon Torte
Peanut Lover's Pie
Peach Strawberry Sundaes

Pumpkin Torte

Bake at 350° for 25-30 minutes or until a toothpick comes out clean. Cool 10 minutes before removing from pans to wire racks. Cool completely.

Beat cream cheese, sugar, and remaining pumpkin and pie spice until smooth. Fold in whipped topping. Split each cake horizontally. Place a layer on a plate; spread with a fourth of filling. Repeat layers three times. Top with caramel topping and pecans. Chill. **Yield:** 10-12 servings.

Black Forest Cheesecake

(Pictured below)

Prep: 20 min. + chilling

I created this recipe about 10 years ago, and my family has been requesting it ever since. I'm asked to take this popular no-bake cheesecake to every gathering. In fact, when I was ill at Thanksgiving last year, my sister made it so the family could still enjoy it.
—*Christine Ooyen, Winnebago, Illinois*

    1 package (8 ounces) cream cheese, softened
 1/3 cup sugar
    1 cup (8 ounces) sour cream
    2 teaspoons vanilla extract
    1 carton (8 ounces) frozen whipped topping, thawed
    1 chocolate crumb crust (8 inches)
 1/4 cup baking cocoa
    1 tablespoon confectioners' sugar
    1 can (21 ounces) cherry pie filling

Black Forest Cheesecake

Pumpkin Torte

(Pictured above)

Prep: 30 min. **Bake:** 25 min. + cooling

This beautiful layered cake has a creamy filling with a mild pumpkin flavor and a little spice. It's quick and always turns out well. The caramel topping and nuts add a nice finishing touch, but you can also try other toppings as a variation. —*Trixie Fisher, Piqua, Ohio*

    1 package (18-1/4 ounces) yellow cake mix
    1 can (15 ounces) solid-pack pumpkin, *divided*
 1/2 cup milk
 1/3 cup vegetable oil
    4 eggs
1-1/2 teaspoons pumpkin pie spice, *divided*
    1 package (8 ounces) cream cheese, softened
    1 cup confectioners' sugar
    1 carton (16 ounces) frozen whipped topping, thawed
 1/4 cup caramel ice cream topping
 1/3 cup chopped pecans, toasted

In a mixing bowl, combine the dry cake mix, 1 cup pumpkin, milk, oil, eggs and 1 teaspoon pumpkin pie spice; beat on low speed for 30 seconds. Beat on medium for 2 minutes. Pour into two greased and floured 9-in. round baking pans.

In a large mixing bowl, beat cream cheese and sugar until smooth. Beat in the sour cream and vanilla. Fold in whipped topping. Spread half of the mixture evenly into crust. Fold cocoa and confectioners' sugar into remaining whipped topping mixture; carefully spread over cream cheese layer. Refrigerate for at least 4 hours.

Cut into slices; top each slice with cherry pie filling. Refrigerate leftovers. **Yield:** 6-8 servings.

Chocolate Walnut Tart

Prep: 20 min. **Bake:** 25 min. + cooling

You'll have no hassle, no fuss and no leftovers with this dessert! It looks impressive, but it's so simple to make. It can be prepared in a 9- or 11-inch tart pan and tastes wonderful served warm with ice cream or whipped cream.
—*Sue Shank, Harrisonburg, Virginia*

  1 sheet refrigerated pie pastry
  1 cup (6 ounces) semisweet chocolate chips
  1 cup coarsely chopped walnuts
  3 eggs, lightly beaten
3/4 cup dark corn syrup
1/2 cup packed brown sugar
1/4 cup butter, melted
  1 teaspoon vanilla extract
Whipped cream, optional

On a lightly floured surface, roll out pastry to fit an 11-in. tart pan with a removable bottom. Transfer pastry to pan; trim edges. Sprinkle with chocolate chips and walnuts. In a small bowl, whisk the eggs, corn syrup, brown sugar, butter and vanilla. Pour over chips and nuts.

Bake at 350° for 25-30 minutes or until a knife inserted near the center comes out clean. Cool on a wire rack. Serve with whipped cream if desired. **Yield:** 8-10 servings.

Fruity Rhubarb Sauce

(Pictured above right)

Prep/Total Time: 30 min.

Rhubarb, pineapple, strawberries and raisins create this speedy sauce that's perfect on vanilla ice cream. We also like it over pound cake, and it's wonderful simply served with a dollop of whipped cream.   —*Lorraine Darocha Berkshire, Massachusetts*

  4 cups chopped fresh *or* frozen rhubarb
  1 cup raisins
2/3 cup sugar
1/2 cup water
  1 can (8 ounces) unsweetened crushed
     pineapple, undrained
  1 cup sliced fresh strawberries
Vanilla ice cream

In a large saucepan, combine rhubarb, raisins, sugar and water. Bring to a boil. Reduce heat; simmer, uncovered, for 20-22 minutes or until rhubarb is tender. Remove from the heat. Fold in pineapple and strawberries. Serve warm or chilled over ice cream. **Yield:** 5 cups.

Fruity Rhubarb Sauce

Shipping Gifts of Goodies

IF YOU'D like to send a package of home-baked treats to someone far away, keep in mind the following tips.

When choosing recipes, look for bars, drop cookies, slice-and-bake cookies and sandwich cookies, because they are fairly sturdy. Avoid delicate cutout and shaped cookies, which may break during shipping; chocolate, since it will melt easily; and items with perishable frostings or fillings.

When packaging, wrap bars individually in plastic wrap. Drop cookies can be bundled back-to-back in packages of two. Slice-and-bake and sandwich cookies can be wrapped in bundles of two or three.

Pack soft cookies in containers separate from crisp cookies. If combined, the moisture from the soft ones will make the others lose their crispness. Also, to help retain flavor, don't pack strong-flavored cookies like gingersnaps with mild ones like sugar cookies.

Line the containers with crumpled waxed paper to help cushion the cookies. Snugly pack cookies to within 1 inch of the top. Use crumpled waxed paper or bubble wrap to fill any gaps between cookies, and add more over the last layer to cushion the cookies and prevent shifting during shipping.

Place a layer of crumpled paper, bubble wrap or foam shipping peanuts in the bottom of a sturdy corrugated box that is slightly larger than your cookie container. Set the container on top, then add more paper, bubble wrap or peanuts.

Chapter 15

⊙ *Fast Kid-Friendly Fare*

IT'S CHILD'S PLAY to serve your children home-cooked, wholesome food they'll love. Just turn to the kid-pleasing recipes here!

Young eyes are sure to light up when they see fun fare like Wagon Train Pasta, Santa Pancakes, Sloppy Dogs and Owl Cookies. Even picky eaters will dig into these youthfully appealing dishes.

And when the kids are clamoring for something yummy, they won't have to wait long. Each of these tasty recipes can be prepared in just minutes, so you'll have a satisfying meal on the table soon after you hear, "I'm hungry!"

These delightful dishes are so appetizing and delicious, you'll want to make them as a feast for the whole family.

FUN-FILLED FOOD. Mac 'n' Cheese Soup and Fish Stick Sandwiches (recipes on p. 225).

Wagon Train Pasta

(Pictured below)

Prep/Total Time: 20 min.

Our three kids just love the fun wagon wheel shapes in this quick-and-easy recipe. The mildly seasoned sauce is something that even the pickiest eaters enjoy. For variety, try it with Italian sausage instead of ground beef.

—Janine Freeman, Blaine, Washington

    3 cups uncooked wagon wheel pasta
    1 egg
1/2 teaspoon salt
1/8 teaspoon minced garlic
1/8 teaspoon coarsely ground pepper
1/2 pound ground beef
    2 tablespoons grated Parmesan cheese
    2 tablespoons seasoned bread crumbs
1-1/2 cups meatless spaghetti sauce
    1 cup (4 ounces) shredded mozzarella cheese,
       divided

Cook pasta according to package directions. Meanwhile, in a large bowl, beat the egg, salt, garlic and pepper. Add beef and mix well. Sprinkle with Parmesan cheese

Patriotic Cupcakes

and bread crumbs; mix gently.

Crumble beef mixture into a large skillet. Cook over medium-high heat until meat is no longer pink; drain. Stir in the spaghetti sauce. Reduce heat; cover and simmer for 2-4 minutes or until heated through.

Drain pasta; place in a serving bowl. Add beef mixture; sprinkle with 1/2 cup mozzarella cheese. Toss until pasta is well coated and cheese is melted. Sprinkle with remaining mozzarella. **Yield:** 5 servings.

Patriotic Cupcakes

(Pictured above)

Prep: 15 min. **Bake:** 20 min. + cooling

These festive cupcakes are sure to be the star of your Fourth of July menu. One year, I divided the batter from regular cupcakes into portions and used food coloring to make red, white and blue treats. Our kids loved helping prepare them. — Jodi Rugg
Aurora, Illinois

    1 package (18-1/4 ounces) white cake mix
1/2 teaspoon blue food coloring
1/2 teaspoon red food coloring
    1 can (16 ounces) vanilla frosting
Red, white and blue sprinkles

Wagon Train Pasta

Prepare the cake batter according to package directions. In a small bowl, combine 1-1/3 cups batter and blue food coloring. In another bowl, combine 1-1/3 cups batter and red food coloring. Leave remaining batter plain.

Fill paper-lined muffin cups with 2 tablespoons red batter, 2 tablespoons plain batter and 2 tablespoons blue batter. Bake at 350° for 20-24 minutes or until a toothpick comes out clean. Cool for 10 minutes before removing from pans to wire racks to cool completely. Frost with vanilla frosting; decorate with sprinkles. **Yield:** 1-1/2 dozen.

Fish Stick Sandwiches

(Pictured on page 222)

Prep/Total Time: 25 min.

Make the most of convenient frozen fish sticks with these fun family-pleasing sandwiches. My mom whipped these up whenever she wanted fish in a hurry.
—*Cherie Durbin, Hickory, North Carolina*

  1/4 cup butter, melted
    2 tablespoons lemon juice
    1 package (11.4 ounces) frozen breaded fish sticks
    2 tablespoons mayonnaise
    6 hot dog buns, split
Shredded lettuce, chopped onion and chopped tomato, optional

In a shallow bowl, combine butter and lemon juice. Coat fish sticks with butter mixture. Place in a single layer in an ungreased baking pan. Bake at 400° for 15-18 minutes or until crispy. Spread mayonnaise on cut side of buns; add fish sticks. Top with lettuce, onion and tomato if desired. **Yield:** 6 servings.

Mac 'n' Cheese Soup

(Pictured on page 222)

Prep/Total Time: 30 min.

I found this recipe a few years ago and made a few changes to suit our tastes. We love this creamy soup. Because it starts with a package of macaroni and cheese, it's ready in a jiffy. —*Nancy Daugherty, Cortland, Ohio*

    1 package (14 ounces) deluxe macaroni and cheese dinner mix
    9 cups water, divided
    1 cup fresh broccoli florets
    2 tablespoons finely chopped onion
    1 can (10-3/4 ounces) condensed cheddar cheese soup, undiluted
2 1/2 cups milk
    1 cup chopped fully cooked ham

Set aside cheese sauce packet from macaroni and cheese mix. In a large saucepan, bring 8 cups water to a boil. Add macaroni; cook for 8-10 minutes or until tender.

Meanwhile, in another large saucepan, bring remaining water to a boil. Add broccoli and onion; cook for 3 minutes. Stir in soup, milk, ham and contents of cheese sauce packet; heat through. Drain macaroni; stir into soup. **Yield:** 8 servings.

Confetti Snack Mix

(Pictured below)

Prep/Total Time: 10 min.

I've assembled this party mix for many years, and I usually prepare a double batch. It makes a wonderful gift that always results in recipe requests. —*Jane Bray*
Temple Terrace, Florida

    4 cups Golden Grahams
    1 cup dry roasted peanuts
    1 cup dried banana chips
    1 cup raisins
    1 cup milk chocolate M&M's

In a large bowl, combine all ingredients. Store in an airtight container. **Yield:** 7 cups.

Confetti Snack Mix

Sweet Popcorn Snack Mix

1/2 cup butter, softened
  1 cup confectioners' sugar
  1 cup chopped peanut butter-filled sandwich
    cookies

In a bowl, whisk milk and pudding mix for 2 minutes; let stand for 2 minutes or until soft-set. Fold in whipped topping; set aside.

In a large mixing bowl, beat cream cheese, butter and confectioners' sugar until smooth. Fold in pudding mixture. Spoon into an ungreased 13-in. x 9-in. x 2-in. dish. Sprinkle with cookie crumbs. Cover and refrigerate overnight. Cut into squares. **Yield:** 12-15 servings.

Sweet Popcorn Snack Mix

(Pictured above)

Prep/Total Time: 15 min.

Pack a sandwich bag of this treat in each of your children's lunches and watch their eyes light up. Coated with cocoa and cinnamon-sugar, the munchable medley also is a yummy after-school snack. —Shirley Glaab
Hattiesburg, Mississippi

  8 cups popped popcorn
  2 tablespoons cinnamon-sugar
  1 tablespoon baking cocoa
  1 cup bear-shaped graham snacks
  1 cup broken thin pretzel sticks
1/2 cup milk chocolate M&M's

Place popcorn in a large bowl. Combine cinnamon-sugar and cocoa; sprinkle over popcorn and toss to coat. Stir in the graham snacks, pretzels and M&M's. Store in an airtight container. **Yield:** about 2-1/2 quarts.

Peanut Butter Cream Dessert

Prep: 25 min. + chilling

With a few minor changes to the original cookies-and-cream recipe, I can please the peanut butter lovers in my family. I use instant pudding mix, frozen whipped topping and store-bought sandwich cookies to hurry along preparation. —Mary Ann Saam, Cridersville, Ohio

2-1/4 cups cold milk
  2 packages (3.3 ounces each) instant white
    chocolate pudding mix
2-1/2 cups whipped topping
  1 package (8 ounces) cream cheese, softened

Supreme Bagel Pizzas

(Pictured below)

Prep/Total Time: 30 min.

We used to enjoy pizza bagel bites from the freezer section but found they weren't filling unless we made quite a few. Now we use whole bagels to prepare a heartier meal that's ready in a jiffy. It's nice that we can each add our favorite toppings.
—Michele Potter, Caledonia, Michigan

  2 plain bagels, split
1/2 cup pizza sauce
 20 pepperoni slices
3/4 cup diced fully cooked ham
1/4 cup real bacon bits
1/4 cup chopped green pepper
  1 cup (4 ounces) shredded mozzarella cheese

Place bagels on a baking sheet. Spread with pizza sauce. Arrange five slices of pepperoni on each, covering the bagel hole with one slice. Top each with ham, bacon, green pepper and cheese. Bake at 400° for 12-14 minutes or until cheese is melted. **Yield:** 4 servings.

Supreme Bagel Pizzas

Crescent Butterflies
Cheesy Chicken Supper

Cheesy Chicken Supper

(Pictured above)

Prep/Total Time: 20 min.

I'm always looking for quick-and-easy dishes. I came up with this one by modifying several casserole recipes. It's simple, cooks on the stovetop and is ready in less than half an hour. —Waldron Upham, Eagle River, Alaska

    2 cups frozen broccoli florets, thawed
    1 teaspoon vegetable oil
    2 cups cubed cooked chicken breast
    1 can (10-3/4 ounces) condensed broccoli
       cheese soup, undiluted
  1/2 cup milk
Dash pepper
  1/2 cup shredded cheddar cheese
  1/2 cup french-fried onions
Hot cooked rice

In a large skillet, cook and stir the broccoli in oil for 2 minutes or until crisp-tender. Stir in the chicken, soup, milk and pepper; bring to a boil. Reduce heat; cover and simmer for 5 minutes or until the chicken is heated through.

    Top with the cheese and onions. Remove from the heat; cover and let stand for 2 minutes or until cheese is melted. Serve with rice. **Yield:** 4 servings.

Crescent Butterflies

(Pictured above)

Prep/Total Time: 30 min.

Our Test Kitchen home economists created these savory snacks that kids will enjoy dipping in marinara sauce. A cookie cutter makes it easy to cut the butterfly shapes from crescent roll dough.

    1 tube (8 ounces) refrigerated crescent rolls
    2 giant Slim Jim snack sticks, cut into 2-inch
       pieces
    2 tablespoons butter, melted
    1 tablespoon grated Parmesan cheese
    1 tablespoon Italian seasoning
    1 cup marinara sauce, warmed

Unroll the crescent dough on a lightly floured surface; roll into a 12-in. x 9-in. rectangle. Seal seams. Cut with a butterfly cookie cutter dipped in flour. Place 1 in. apart on an ungreased baking sheet. Press a snack piece in the middle of each butterfly; carefully pinch dough around long sides of each snack piece.

    Brush wings with butter. Sprinkle with Parmesan cheese and Italian seasoning. Bake at 375° for 10-12 minutes or until golden brown. Cool for 10 minutes before removing to a wire rack. Serve warm with marinara sauce. **Yield:** 1 dozen.

Creamy Beef Sandwiches

Prep/Total Time: 20 min.

This is a quick way to create special sandwiches that both kids and adults will enjoy. With dried beef, cheddar cheese and ranch salad dressing, the filling is delicious. I often turn to this recipe when I need lunches on the go. —Doris Byerly Mondovi, Wisconsin

- 1/2 cup salad dressing *or* mayonnaise
- 2 to 3 tablespoons prepared ranch salad dressing
- 2 packages (2-1/2 ounces *each*) thinly sliced dried beef, chopped
- 1 cup (4 ounces) shredded cheddar cheese
- 12 slices white bread
- 1-1/2 cups shredded lettuce

In a small bowl, combine the salad dressing or mayonnaise and ranch dressing. Stir in the beef and cheese. Spread about 1/3 cup each on six slices of bread; top with lettuce and remaining bread. **Yield:** 6 servings.

Fudge Pops

(Pictured below)

Prep: 15 min. + freezing

Living on the equator, we experience warm weather year-round. These cold sweets are a favorite after-nap treat with my four children. I like how these pops are easy to make in large quantities. —Sally Jo Stensaas, Masaka, Uganda

Fudge Pops

Doughnut Parfaits

- 3/4 cup sugar
- 3 tablespoons all-purpose flour
- 3 tablespoons baking cocoa
- 4 cups milk
- 10 Popsicle molds *or* plastic cups (3 ounces) and Popsicle sticks

In a saucepan, combine the sugar, flour and cocoa. Gradually stir in milk until smooth. Bring to a boil over medium heat; cook and stir for 2 minutes or until thickened. Cool slightly. Pour 1/4 cup into each mold or plastic cup; top with holders or insert Popsicle sticks. Freeze until set. May be frozen for up to 3 months. **Yield:** 10 servings.

Doughnut Parfaits

(Pictured above)

Prep/Total Time: 20 min.

I was in a hurry to make a quick dessert, so I threw together a few items from the grocery store. My whole family raved about the results. To serve a big group, I increase the ingredients and layer them in a large glass trifle bowl.
—Christine Delili, Avon Lake, Ohio

- 2 cups cold milk
- 1 package (3.4 ounces) instant vanilla pudding mix
- 16 powdered sugar doughnut holes, halved

1 to 2 medium firm bananas, cut into 1/4-inch slices
2 cups whipped topping
Chopped nuts and maraschino cherries

In a bowl, whisk the milk and pudding mix for 2 minutes. Let stand for 2 minutes or until soft-set. Place four doughnut hole halves in each of four parfait glasses. Top with half of the pudding, bananas and whipped topping. Repeat the layers. Garnish with nuts and cherries. **Yield:** 4 servings.

Chicken Fingers

Prep/Total Time: 30 min.

These homemade chicken fingers, with their crispy breading and moist interior, are a snap to put together. You can prepare them in minutes for a snack or meal, and they're always a hit. I serve them with ranch dressing on the side. —Catherine Starbird, Warrenton, Virginia

1 cup seasoned bread crumbs
1 envelope ranch salad dressing mix
1/4 teaspoon pepper
2 eggs
1-1/2 pounds boneless skinless chicken breasts, cut into 1-inch strips
1/4 cup vegetable oil

In a shallow bowl, combine the bread crumbs, salad dressing mix and pepper. In another shallow bowl, beat the eggs. Dip chicken strips in eggs, then coat with crumb mixture. In a large skillet, cook chicken in oil in batches for 10-12 minutes or until chicken juices run clear, turning once. Drain on paper towels. **Yield:** 6 servings.

Santa Pancakes

(Pictured at right)

Prep/Total Time: 30 min.

For a breakfast sure to make little eyes shine bright, try this recipe from our Test Kitchen staff. Cinnamon pancakes are dressed up with cherry pie filling and whipped cream to look like the jolly ol' elf himself. Garnish plates with red and green sugar or sprinkles for a festive look.

2 cups biscuit/baking mix
1 teaspoon ground cinnamon
2 eggs, beaten
1 cup milk
1 teaspoon vanilla extract
2 medium bananas, sliced
18 semisweet chocolate chips
1 can (21 ounces) cherry pie filling
Whipped cream in a can

In a large bowl, combine baking mix and cinnamon. Combine the eggs, milk and vanilla; stir into dry ingredients just until moistened. Pour batter by 1/4 cupfuls onto a greased hot griddle. Turn when bubbles form on top; cook until second side is golden brown.

Place the pancakes on individual plates. For Santa's eyes, place two banana slices on each pancake; top each with a chocolate chip. For ears, cut remaining banana slices in half; place on either side of pancake. For nose, remove nine cherries from pie filling; place one in the center of each pancake. Spoon 1/4 cup pie filling above pancake for hat. Use whipped cream to spray the beard, hat brim and pom-pom. **Yield:** 9 servings.

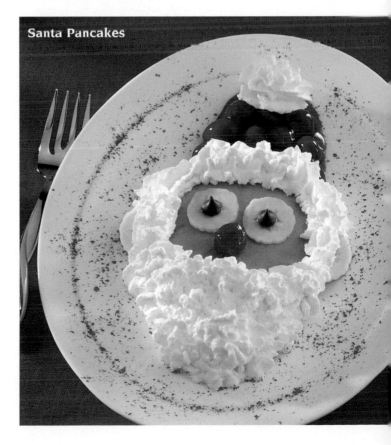

Santa Pancakes

trace fat (0 saturated fat), 0 cholesterol, 323 mg sodium, 4 g carbohydrate, 1 g fiber, 1 g protein. **Diabetic Exchange:** Free food.

Graham Cracker Cookies

Prep/Total Time: 30 min.

My brother and I enjoyed these peanut butter treats when we were young. I made these cookies for my children, and now I make them for my grandchildren.
—Lois McKnight, Freeport, Illinois

 1-1/2 cups sugar
  6 tablespoons butter, cubed
  1/3 cup evaporated milk
  1 cup marshmallow creme
  3/4 cup peanut butter
  1/3 cup chopped salted peanuts, optional
  1/2 teaspoon vanilla extract
  1 package (14.4 ounces) whole graham crackers

In a large saucepan, combine the sugar, butter and milk. Cook and stir over medium heat until mixture comes to a boil. Cook 4-5 minutes longer or until thickened and bubbly. Remove from the heat; stir in the marshmallow creme, peanut butter, peanuts if desired and vanilla.

 Break the graham crackers in half. Spread about 2 tablespoons filling each on half of the crackers; top with remaining crackers. **Yield:** 2-1/2 dozen.

Cheesy Sliced Potatoes

Prep/Total Time: 30 min.

Your microwave makes this rich and cheesy treatment for sliced potatoes quick to prepare. It is so delicious and a good change from plain scalloped potatoes.
—Jeannine Ricketson, Saugerties, New York

 6-1/2 cups thinly sliced potatoes (about 2 pounds)
  1/3 cup water
  2 tablespoons dried minced onion
  2 teaspoons chicken bouillon granules
  1 tablespoon all-purpose flour
  1/2 teaspoon salt
  1/8 teaspoon garlic powder
  3/4 cup milk
  3/4 cup sour cream
  1/2 cup shredded cheddar cheese

Place the potatoes, water, minced onion and chicken bouillon granules in an ungreased microwave-safe 2-1/2-qt. dish. Cover and microwave on high for 12-14 minutes until the potatoes are tender and the bouillon is dissolved, stirring once.

 In a small bowl, combine flour, salt and garlic powder; stir in milk until smooth. Pour over potatoes. Microwave, uncovered, on high for 4 minutes or until thickened, stirring twice. Stir in sour cream; sprinkle with cheese. Cook 3 minutes longer or until cheese is melted. **Yield:** 8 servings.

 Editor's Note: This recipe was tested in a 1,100-watt microwave.

Pantry Salsa

Pantry Salsa

(Pictured above)
Prep/Total Time: 5 min.

This homemade salsa is easy because it's made with canned tomatoes. Simply combine them with the seasonings for a flavorful salsa that's great with tortilla chips.
—Lois Wyant, Manassas, Virginia

✓ Uses less fat, sugar or salt. Includes Nutritional Analysis and Diabetic Exchanges.

 1 can (14-1/2 ounces) diced tomatoes with onion, drained
 1 can (14-1/2 ounces) diced tomatoes with green chilies, undrained
 3/4 teaspoon ground cumin
 1/2 teaspoon onion powder
 1/2 teaspoon garlic powder
 1/2 teaspoon sugar
 1/2 teaspoon seasoned salt
 1/4 teaspoon garlic salt
Tortilla chips

In a large bowl, combine the first eight ingredients. Serve with tortilla chips. **Yield:** 3 cups.

 Nutritional Analysis: 1/4 cup salsa equals 18 calories,

Owl Cookies

(Pictured below)

Prep/Total Time: 30 min.

"Who" wouldn't love these adorable cookies? Our Test Kitchen staff assembled them using refrigerated cookie dough, candy coating disks and chocolate chips for eyes, and candy corn for the beaks. If you don't have any chocolate chips on hand, use M&M's instead.

   1 tube (18 ounces) refrigerated peanut butter
      cookie dough
1/2 cup all-purpose flour
  18 yellow candy coating disks
  18 semisweet chocolate chips
   9 pieces candy corn

In a large mixing bowl, beat cookie dough and flour until combined. Set aside 4-1/2 teaspoons of dough for the ears. Drop dough by 1/4 cupfuls into nine mounds 2 in. apart on ungreased baking sheets. Coat the bottom of a glass with nonstick cooking spray; flatten dough with glass to about 1/8-in. thickness.

Position two candy coating disks on each cookie for eyes. Place a chocolate chip on each disk. Use 1/4 teaspoon of reserved dough to shape each ear; position on top of each head.

Bake at 350° for 8-10 minutes or until golden brown. Immediately position a piece of candy corn on each cookie for beak. Cool for 2 minutes before removing from pans to wire racks. **Yield:** 9 cookies.

Sloppy Dogs

Sloppy Dogs

(Pictured above)

Prep/Total Time: 30 min.

A can of sloppy joe sauce really speeds the preparation of these sassy saucy dogs. Sometimes we like to toast the buns and top the hot dogs with an Italian cheese blend for a slightly different taste. They're easy to freeze and heat up fast in the microwave for quick meals.
—Diane Halferty, Corpus Christi, Texas

1/2 pound ground turkey
   1 cup chopped onion
   2 teaspoons vegetable oil
   1 can (15-1/2 ounces) sloppy joe sauce
   8 hot dogs
   8 hot dog buns, split
1/2 cup shredded Mexican cheese blend

In a large skillet, cook turkey and onion in oil over medium heat for 5-6 minutes or until meat is no longer pink; drain. Stir in sloppy joe sauce. Bring to a boil. Reduce heat; simmer, uncovered, for 5-6 minutes or until heated through, stirring occasionally.

Meanwhile, cook hot dogs according to package directions. Place in buns; top with sloppy joe mixture. Sprinkle with cheese. **Yield:** 8 servings.

Creating Kid-Size Burgers

When my daughter was young, she loved hamburgers but could never finish a whole one. So I bought a pound of ground beef and patted out 3-inch burgers (I got about 10 burgers from a pound).

I served them on small bakery buns (you could also use a biscuit cutter to cut "buns" from bread). They were the perfect size for my daughter's small hands...and small appetite! —Amy Monfredi
Pittsburgh, Pennsylvania

Owl Cookies

Chapter 16

☉ *Stovetop Suppers and Casseroles*

STIRRING UP a quick dish on the stovetop and popping a fast casserole in the oven are two of the easiest ways to get a hearty home-cooked meal on the table pronto.

That's why cooks with non-stop schedules are sure to appreciate the supper sensations here. Each time-easing recipe either comes together in a rush on the range or is a breeze to assemble before baking.

Just pull out a skillet to prepare filling fare like Chops with Fried Rice...or use a baking dish to whip up tasty Veggie Turkey Casserole.

You could even choose one of the delicious side dishes you'll find among these casseroles, then bake it as you put together a stovetop entree.

FROM THE OVEN. Corny Chicken Bake (p. 246).

Macaroni Chicken Skillet

2 teaspoons chicken bouillon granules
1/2 teaspoon dried tarragon
1/4 teaspoon lemon-pepper seasoning
1 tablespoon all-purpose flour
1 cup milk
4 ounces process cheese (Velveeta), cubed

Cook macaroni according to package directions. Meanwhile, in a large skillet, saute the broccoli, red pepper, onion, carrots and garlic in oil until crisp-tender. Stir in the chicken, peas, bouillon, tarragon and lemon-pepper; reduce heat.

In a small bowl, combine flour and milk until smooth; stir into skillet. Bring to a boil; cook and stir for 2 minutes or until thickened. Reduce heat. Drain macaroni; stir into the chicken mixture. Add cheese and stir until melted. **Yield:** 4 servings.

Red Clam Sauce over Pasta

Prep/Total Time: 25 min.

This sensational basil-seasoned clam sauce will shake up supper time. It's a nice change from meat-based pasta sauces. —Laura Valdez, Lexington Park, Maryland

2 teaspoons minced garlic
2 tablespoons butter
1-1/2 teaspoons olive oil
1 can (15 ounces) tomato sauce
1 can (6-1/2 ounces) chopped clams, drained
1 tablespoon dried parsley flakes
1 tablespoon dried basil
1/8 teaspoon pepper
Hot cooked linguine

In a large saucepan, saute garlic in butter and oil for 30 seconds. Stir in the tomato sauce, clams, parsley, basil and pepper. Bring to a boil. Reduce heat; cover and simmer for 15 minutes, stirring occasionally. Serve over linguine. **Yield:** 4 servings.

Stovetop Suppers

IT'S EASY to pull dinner together quickly when all of the ingredients combine in a skillet or saucepan. Here, you'll find rangetop recipes that will come in handy again and again when time's tight.

Not only are these stovetop suppers fast to fix on hectic weeknights, they're proven family-pleasers. So go ahead—just pull out a skillet or saucepan, turn on a burner and start cooking!

Macaroni Chicken Skillet

(Pictured above)

Prep/Total Time: 30 min.

Our family loves this meal. I found the recipe on a box of pasta years ago, and I've used it many times since. —Edie DeSpain, Logan, Utah

1 cup uncooked elbow macaroni
2 cups fresh broccoli florets
1 medium sweet red pepper, chopped
1 cup chopped onion
2 medium carrots, cut into 1/4-inch slices
1/2 teaspoon minced garlic
2 tablespoons olive oil
1 package (9 ounces) frozen cubed cooked chicken, thawed
1/4 cup frozen peas

Curly Noodle Dinner

Prep/Total Time: 25 min.

Looking for a hearty meal that calls for only a few items? This beefy entree fits the bill. We have three active children, so this simple skillet dinner is ideal. —Joanne Shewchuk, St. Benedict, Saskatchewan

1 pound ground beef
1 can (14-1/2 ounces) diced tomatoes, undrained
1 can (11 ounces) whole kernel corn, drained
1 package (3 ounces) beef ramen noodles
1/4 to 1/2 cup water, optional

In a large skillet, cook beef over medium heat until no longer pink; drain. Stir in the tomatoes, corn and contents of noodle seasoning packet. Bring to a boil. Break noodles into small pieces; stir into beef mixture.

Reduce heat; cover and simmer for 10-12 minutes or until noodles are tender, adding water if desired. **Yield:** 6 servings.

Pork Cubes 'n' Stuffing

Prep/Total Time: 20 min.

This recipe is too good to keep to myself. I created the savory specialty when I had pork and stuffing mix on hand. My husband just raved about it.
—Heather Kirchkesner, Yaurep Station, Pennsylvania

1-1/2 pounds pork chop suey meat *or* boneless
    pork loin, cut into 1/2-inch cubes
  1/2 teaspoon pepper
    2 tablespoons vegetable oil
    1 cup plus 2 tablespoons water
2-1/4 cups crushed chicken stuffing mix
  1/2 cup shredded cheddar cheese

Season pork with pepper. In a large skillet, saute pork in oil for 5-6 minutes or until browned; drain. Add water; bring to a boil. Cover and cook for 2 minutes. Stir in stuffing mix. Cover and remove from heat; let stand for 5 minutes. Fluff with a fork. Sprinkle with cheese. Cover for 1 minute or until cheese begins to melt. **Yield:** 5 servings.

Kielbasa with Veggies

Prep/Total Time: 30 min.

The home economists in the Quick Cooking Test Kitchen whipped up this comforting combination that takes advantage of time-saving frozen vegetables and fully cooked sausage. A little soup mix lends a mild onion flavor to this winter warmer-upper.

  1 pound fully cooked kielbasa *or* Polish
    sausage, cut into 1/4-inch slices
  1 tablespoon vegetable oil
  1 package (16 ounces) frozen vegetables for
    beef stew
  1 cup beef broth
  1 tablespoon onion soup mix
  1 tablespoon cornstarch
  1 tablespoon cold water

In a large skillet, brown sausage in oil over medium-high heat. Remove with a slotted spoon and keep warm. Add the vegetables, broth and soup mix to skillet. Bring to a boil. Reduce heat; cover and simmer for 10-12 minutes or until vegetables are tender.

Return sausage to the pan. Combine cornstarch and cold water until smooth; stir into sausage mixture. Bring to a boil; cook and stir for 1 minute or until thickened. **Yield:** 4 servings.

Thai Shrimp and Noodles

(Pictured at right)

Prep/Total Time: 30 min.

Shrimp lovers will dive into this speedy dish that gets its Asian flavor from ginger, peanut butter, sesame oil, soy sauce and red pepper flakes. My family loves it.
—Ramona Heflin, Farmersville, Ohio

  1 pound cooked medium shrimp, peeled and
    deveined

  1/3 cup Italian salad dressing
    8 ounces uncooked angel hair pasta
  1/4 cup chicken broth
    2 tablespoons minced fresh cilantro
    2 tablespoons chunky peanut butter
    1 tablespoon honey
    1 tablespoon soy sauce
    1 teaspoon minced fresh gingerroot
  1/2 teaspoon crushed red pepper flakes
    1 cup julienned carrots
    1 cup chopped green onions
    2 tablespoons vegetable oil
    1 tablespoon sesame oil

In a large resealable plastic bag, combine shrimp and salad dressing. Seal bag and turn to coat; refrigerate for at least 15 minutes. Meanwhile, cook pasta according to package directions.

In a small bowl, combine broth, cilantro, peanut butter, honey, soy sauce, ginger and pepper flakes; set aside. In a large skillet, saute carrots and onions in vegetable and sesame oils for 2-3 minutes or until vegetables are crisp-tender.

Drain shrimp and discard marinade. Add shrimp to vegetables; cook for 2-3 minutes or until heated through. Drain pasta and place in a large bowl.

Add the shrimp mixture and the peanut butter mixture; toss to coat. **Yield:** 6 servings.

Thai Shrimp and Noodles

Jiffy Ground Pork Skillet

(Pictured below)

Prep/Total Time: 30 min.

Some people call it dinner hour, but many of us call it rush hour. You can slow down the pace with this super-quick, mouth-watering meal. The only thing you'll have left over is time to share with your family at the table.

—Brigitte Schaller, Flemington, Missouri

    1-1/2 cups uncooked penne *or* medium tube pasta
        1 pound ground pork
      1/2 cup chopped onion
        1 can (14-1/2 ounces) stewed tomatoes
        1 can (8 ounces) tomato sauce
        1 teaspoon Italian seasoning
        1 medium zucchini, cut into 1/4-inch slices

Cook pasta according to package directions. Meanwhile, in a large skillet, cook pork and onion over medium heat until meat is no longer pink; drain. Add the tomatoes, tomato sauce and Italian seasoning. Bring to a boil. Reduce heat; cover and cook for 5 minutes.

Drain pasta and add to the skillet. Stir in zucchini. Cover and cook for 3-5 minutes or until zucchini is crisp-tender. **Yield:** 6 servings.

Jiffy Ground Pork Skillet

One-Pot Pork Chops

Prep: 15 min. **Cook:** 35 min.

Years ago, one of my teenage daughters saw this recipe in a magazine and wanted to try it. It became a family favorite. Serve it with rolls and a lettuce salad.

—Doris Shoemaker, Dakota, Illinois

        4 bone-in pork loin chops (6 ounces *each*)
      1/4 cup all-purpose flour
        6 small potatoes, quartered
        1 cup fresh baby carrots
      1/2 cup water
        1 teaspoon Worcestershire sauce
      1/2 teaspoon salt
      1/4 teaspoon dried oregano
        1 can (10-3/4 ounces) condensed tomato
          soup, undiluted

Coat pork chops with flour. In a large skillet, brown chops on both sides. Add potatoes and carrots. In a small bowl, combine water, Worcestershire sauce, salt and oregano; pour over pork and vegetables. Cover and simmer for 25 minutes.

Stir in soup; cover and simmer 10-15 minutes longer or until meat and vegetables are tender. **Yield:** 4 servings.

Chicken Noodle Dinner

Prep/Total Time: 20 min.

This recipe warms friends and family with a flavorful blend of creamy chicken and vegetables over noodles. Round out the meal with a loaf of crusty French bread.

—Helen Higgins, Middle Musquodoboit, Nova Scotia

    1-1/2 cups cubed cooked chicken
        1 tablespoon vegetable oil
        1 package (16 ounces) frozen broccoli florets
        1 cup sliced carrots
        1 can (10-3/4 ounces) condensed cream of
          mushroom soup, undiluted
      1/2 cup milk
      1/2 teaspoon salt
      1/4 teaspoon pepper
        4 cups hot cooked egg noodles
      1/2 cup grated Parmesan cheese

In a large skillet, saute chicken in oil for 2 minutes. Add the broccoli and carrots; saute for 4-5 minutes or until crisp-tender. Stir in the soup, milk, salt and pepper; heat through. Serve over noodles. Sprinkle with Parmesan cheese. **Yield:** 4 servings.

Tasty Shrimp Penne

Prep/Total Time: 30 min.

This is a nutritious meal that's nice enough for company. Everybody asks for seconds. To make it more colorful, choose a variety of veggies.
—Dena Winner
Lansdale, Pennsylvania

    1-1/2 cups uncooked penne *or* medium tube
          pasta

1/2 cup *each* chopped broccoli, zucchini and
    carrot
1/2 pound deveined peeled cooked medium
    shrimp
1-1/2 teaspoons minced garlic
1/2 teaspoon dried basil
1-1/2 teaspoons olive oil
   1 cup spaghetti sauce
1/2 cup crumbled feta cheese
Salt and pepper to taste

Cook pasta according to package directions, adding the vegetables during the last 5 minutes of cooking.

Meanwhile, in a large skillet, cook the shrimp, garlic and basil in oil for 1-2 minutes or until heated through. Add spaghetti sauce; bring to a boil. Reduce heat to low. Drain pasta and vegetables; stir into shrimp mixture. Add feta cheese, salt and pepper. **Yield:** 6 servings.

Coconut Pineapple Chicken

Prep/Total Time: 30 min.

Pineapple, coconut and almonds dress up this pleasantly sweet treatment for cooked chicken. It's a great way to serve leftovers from a chicken dinner. Sometimes, I use turkey instead and enjoy it just as much. —Nyla Christensen
Rapid City, South Dakota

   1 can (20 ounces) pineapple chunks
   2 tablespoons cornstarch
   2 tablespoons sugar
   1 cup chicken broth
   1 tablespoon lemon juice
   1 teaspoon salt
   3 cups cubed cooked chicken
   1 medium green pepper, julienned
1/4 cup flaked coconut, toasted
1/2 cup slivered almonds, toasted, *divided*
   1 teaspoon rum extract

Drain pineapple, reserving juice; set the pineapple aside. In a large skillet, combine the cornstarch, sugar, broth, lemon juice, salt and reserved juice until smooth. Bring to a boil; cook and stir for 2 minutes or until thickened.

Stir in the chicken, green pepper, coconut, pineapple, 1/4 cup almonds and extract. Cook for 8-10 minutes or until chicken is heated through. Sprinkle with remaining almonds. **Yield:** 4-6 servings.

Curried Turkey Tacos

(Pictured above right)

Prep/Total Time: 25 min.

I give a twist to traditional tacos by adding curry powder, black beans and salsa to the ground turkey filling. This is simple, economical and very tasty. —Peggy Bailey
Covington, Kentucky

1-1/4 pounds ground turkey
1-1/2 teaspoons dried minced onion

Curried Turkey Tacos

   1 can (15 ounces) black beans, rinsed and
     drained
   1 cup salsa
   2 teaspoons taco seasoning
1/4 to 1/2 teaspoon curry powder
   2 cups (8 ounces) shredded Mexican blend
     cheese, *divided*
 12 taco shells, warmed
Shredded lettuce
Sour cream and additional salsa, optional

In a large skillet, cook turkey and onion over medium heat until meat is no longer pink; drain. Stir in beans, salsa, taco seasoning and curry powder; heat through. Stir in 1 cup cheese.

Spoon into taco shells. Sprinkle with remaining cheese; top with lettuce. Serve with sour cream and salsa if desired. **Yield:** 12 tacos.

Southwestern Supper

FOR Southwestern-style fare you can prepare on the stovetop, try the dish I call Fajita Salad. To assemble it, I warm sliced cooked beef, pork or poultry in a skillet with sliced onion, green pepper and a little Liquid Smoke. Then I set the warm mixture over salad greens and add shredded cheese.

Served with tortilla chips, this salad is a fast and filling meal. I make it all the time because my husband loves it. —Sandra Thompson, Lindale, Texas

Barbecue Sausage Skillet

Prep/Total Time: 25 min.

I came up with this when I had to bring a dish for a church supper. I got a lot of compliments on it—even our teenage boys requested I make it again. I usually serve it over a mixture of white and wild rice. —Janis Plourde
Smooth Rock Falls, Ontario

1 pound Italian sausage links
2 cups fresh broccoli florets
1 cup chopped onion
1/2 cup chopped celery
1/4 cup chopped sweet red pepper
1 tablespoon vegetable oil
1/2 cup water
1/2 to 2/3 cup barbecue sauce
1 envelope onion soup mix
1/2 teaspoon dried thyme
1/4 teaspoon salt
1/4 teaspoon pepper
Hot cooked noodles *or* rice

In a large skillet, cook sausage over medium heat until no longer pink. Meanwhile, in another skillet, stir-fry the broccoli, onion, celery and red pepper in oil until onion is tender. Stir in the water, barbecue sauce, soup mix, thyme, salt and pepper.

Cut sausage into 1/2-in. slices; add to vegetable mixture. Reduce heat; cook, uncovered, for 5-8 minutes, stirring occasionally. Serve over noodles or rice. **Yield:** 4-6 servings.

Shrimp Creole

Prep/Total Time: 30 min.

I give a mild Creole flavor to convenient cooked shrimp in this skillet supper that has been part of my recipe collection for years. It's quick and very good.
—W. Florence Johns, Houston, Texas

✓ Uses less fat, sugar or salt. Includes Nutritional Analysis and Diabetic Exchanges.

1/2 cup chopped onion
1/2 cup chopped green pepper
1 celery rib, chopped
1 teaspoon minced garlic
2 tablespoons vegetable oil
2 cans (8 ounces *each*) tomato sauce
1 teaspoon chili powder
1/2 teaspoon sugar
1/4 teaspoon cayenne pepper
1 pound frozen peeled cooked shrimp, thawed
Hot cooked rice, optional

In a large skillet, saute the onion, green pepper, celery and garlic in oil for 6 minutes. Stir in the tomato sauce, chili powder, sugar and cayenne. Bring to a boil. Reduce heat; simmer, uncovered, for 10 minutes. Add shrimp; cook and stir until heated through. Serve with rice if desired. **Yield:** 4 servings.

Nutritional Analysis: 3/4 cup (calculated without rice) equals 220 calories, 8 g fat (1 g saturated fat),

Veggie Ham Medley

Veggie Ham Medley

(Pictured above)

Prep/Total Time: 20 min.

Ever since a friend gave me the recipe for this macaroni dish, it has been my husband's favorite. I fix it for him every week. —Ida Mae White, Forsyth, Missouri

1 cup uncooked elbow macaroni
1 cup diced fully cooked ham
1 tablespoon minced fresh basil
1/4 teaspoon garlic powder
2 tablespoons butter
1 package (10 ounces) frozen mixed vegetables
1/4 cup sour cream
1/2 cup shredded cheddar cheese, *divided*

Cook macaroni according to package directions. Meanwhile, in a large skillet over medium heat, cook the ham, basil and garlic powder in butter for 5 minutes.

Add vegetables; cook until tender, stirring occasionally. Drain macaroni; add to the skillet. Stir in sour cream and 1/4 cup shredded cheese. Sprinkle with remaining cheese; cover and let stand until the cheese is melted. **Yield:** 3 servings.

221 mg cholesterol, 791 mg sodium, 10 g carbohydrate, 2 g fiber, 26 g protein. **Diabetic Exchanges:** 3 lean meat, 2 vegetable.

Chops with Fried Rice

Prep/Total Time: 25 min.

Looking for a last-minute dinner standout on a busy weeknight? Try these juicy pork chops and savory rice. This delicious dish is table-ready in less than half an hour.
—Donna Anderson, Amboy, Indiana

      4 boneless pork loin chops (3/4 inch thick)
      1 tablespoon vegetable oil
      1 package (6.2 ounces) fried rice and vermicelli mix
      2 tablespoons butter
      2 cups hot water
      1 jar (6 ounces) sliced mushrooms, drained
      1 tablespoon soy sauce

In a large skillet, brown the pork chops in oil on both sides; remove the chops and keep warm. In the same skillet, saute the rice mix in butter for 2 minutes. Stir in the hot water, sliced mushrooms and contents of rice seasoning packet.

Place pork chops over rice mixture; drizzle with soy sauce. Bring to a boil. Reduce heat; cover and simmer for 10 minutes. Uncover; simmer 2-5 minutes longer or until rice is tender and meat juices run clear. **Yield:** 4 servings.

Peanut Beef Stir-Fry

Prep/Total Time: 20 min.

Creamy peanut butter lends deliciously different flavor to this stir-fried beef dish that's ready in just 20 minutes. I think it tastes best served over hot noodles. For a change of pace, replace the sliced steak with ground beef. —Rita Reifenstein Evans City, Pennsylvania

      5 teaspoons cornstarch
      1 can (14-1/2 ounces) beef broth
      2 tablespoons soy sauce
      2 tablespoons creamy peanut butter
    1/2 teaspoon sugar
Dash pepper
      1 boneless beef sirloin steak (1 pound), thinly sliced
      1 cup sliced onion
      1 cup sliced celery
      1 teaspoon minced garlic
      2 tablespoons vegetable oil

In a bowl, combine cornstarch, broth, soy sauce, peanut butter, sugar and pepper until smooth; set aside. In a large skillet or wok, stir-fry the beef, onion, celery and garlic in oil for 5-8 minutes or until meat is no longer pink.

Stir the broth mixture and add to the pan. Bring to a boil; cook and stir for 1-2 minutes or until thickened. **Yield:** 4 servings.

Skillet Shepherd's Pie

(Pictured below)

Prep/Total Time: 30 min.

This is the best shepherd's pie I've ever tasted. It's very quick to make, and I usually have most—if not all—of the ingredients already on hand. Served with fruit, it's a complete meal. —Tirzah Sandt, San Diego, California

      1 pound ground beef
      1 cup chopped onion
      2 cups frozen corn, thawed
      2 cups frozen peas, thawed
      2 tablespoons ketchup
      1 tablespoon Worcestershire sauce
      2 teaspoons minced garlic
      1 teaspoon beef bouillon granules
    1/2 cup boiling water
      1 tablespoon cornstarch
    1/2 cup sour cream
  3-1/2 cups mashed potatoes (prepared with milk and butter)
    3/4 cup shredded cheddar cheese

In a large skillet, cook the beef and onion over medium heat until the meat is no longer pink; drain. Stir in the corn, peas, ketchup, Worcestershire sauce and garlic. Reduce heat; cover and simmer for 5 minutes.

Meanwhile, in a small bowl, dissolve bouillon in boiling water. Combine cornstarch and sour cream until smooth; stir into beef mixture. Add bouillon. Spread mashed potatoes over the top; sprinkle with cheese. Cover and cook until potatoes are heated through and cheese is melted. **Yield:** 6 servings.

Skillet Shepherd's Pie

Italian Chicken

(Pictured below)

Prep: 10 min. **Cook:** 45 min.

I simmer breaded chicken in a tomatoey sauce seasoned with garlic, oregano and basil. A sprinkling of cheeses gives it a fast final touch. —Bobby Taylor
Michigan City, Indiana

        1 egg
        1 tablespoon plus 1/4 cup water, *divided*
    1/2 cup seasoned bread crumbs
        1 broiler/fryer chicken (2 to 3 pounds), cut up
        2 tablespoons vegetable oil
        1 can (10-3/4 ounces) condensed tomato
          soup, undiluted
    1/4 cup chopped onion
    1/2 teaspoon garlic powder
    1/2 teaspoon dried basil
    1/2 teaspoon dried oregano
        1 cup (4 ounces) shredded mozzarella cheese
Shredded Parmesan cheese

In a shallow bowl, beat egg and 1 tablespoon water. Place the bread crumbs in another shallow bowl. Dip chicken in egg mixture, then coat with crumbs. In a large skillet, cook the chicken in oil over medium heat for 4-5 minutes or until browned; drain. Remove and keep warm.

In the same skillet, combine soup, onion, garlic powder, basil, oregano and remaining water. Return chicken to pan. Cover and simmer for 40-45 minutes or until chicken juices run clear. Sprinkle with mozzarella cheese; cover and cook for 1-2 minutes or until the cheese is melted. Sprinkle with Parmesan cheese. **Yield:** 4 servings.

Italian Chicken

Pierogi Supper

Prep/Total Time: 15 min.

My husband is a big fan of pierogies. So when I needed a fast meal, I decided to use frozen pierogies to create an all-in-one dinner. This dish is ready to eat in just 15 minutes. It's also very filling, so no one leaves the table hungry.
—Holly Bosworth, Ocala, Florida

        1 package (16.9 ounces) frozen pierogies
        2 cups cubed fully cooked ham
        1 medium yellow summer squash, cut
          into 1/4-inch slices
        1 medium zucchini, cut into 1/4-inch slices
    1/2 teaspoon garlic powder
        3 tablespoons butter

Cook pierogies according to package directions. In a large skillet, cook the ham, squash, zucchini and garlic powder in butter for 4 minutes or until squash is tender. Drain pierogies and add to skillet; heat through. **Yield:** 4 servings.

Scallops Alfredo

Prep/Total Time: 15 min.

When I went back to school while working full-time, fast-to-fix recipes like this one became a necessity. That's how this recipe evolved. While the pasta's cooking, I can quickly combine the scallops, veggies and Alfredo sauce in a skillet. —Georgia Stott, New Glarus, Wisconsin

    1/2 pound sea scallops *or* imitation scallops
    1/2 pound sliced fresh mushrooms
    1/2 cup chopped green onions
        1 tablespoon butter
        1 jar (16 ounces) Alfredo sauce with
          mushrooms
Hot cooked angel hair pasta

In a large skillet, saute the scallops, mushrooms and onions in butter for 4-6 minutes or until scallops are firm and opaque and mushrooms are tender. Stir in the Alfredo sauce. Cover and cook for 2-3 minutes or until heated through. Serve over pasta. **Yield:** 4 servings.

Sloppy Joes

Prep/Total Time: 25 min.

Here's a sophisticated twist on a family-favorite sandwich. My daughter Tiffany came up with this deliciously different version of traditional sloppy joes—and we all love it! The tangy meat mixture can be made ahead and frozen to use whenever you need it. —Suzanne McKinley
Lyons, Georgia

        1 pound ground beef
    1/3 cup chopped onion
        1 garlic clove, minced
        1 can (8 ounces) tomato sauce
    1/2 cup ketchup

1 teaspoon molasses
4 teaspoons Worcestershire sauce
1 teaspoon prepared mustard
1/2 teaspoon ground mustard
Pinch ground cloves
Pinch cayenne pepper
1/4 teaspoon grated orange peel, optional
6 whole wheat buns, split

In a saucepan, cook the beef, onion and garlic over medium heat until meat is no longer pink; drain. Stir in the tomato sauce, ketchup, molasses, Worcestershire sauce, prepared mustard, ground mustard, cloves, cayenne and orange peel if desired. Bring to a boil. Reduce heat; simmer, uncovered, for 5 minutes. Serve on buns. **Yield:** 6 servings.

Western Skillet

Prep: 5 min. **Cook:** 40 min.

Onion soup mix accents the flavor of this easy beef-and-rice combo. Just add a green salad, and your meal is ready. If you don't have these exact ingredients on hand, feel free to replace the frozen peas with corn or green beans, or use Swiss cheese instead of shredded cheddar.
—*Carol Trussler, Petersburg, Ontario*

1 pound ground beef
3 cups water
1 can (14-1/2 ounces) stewed tomatoes
1-1/2 cups uncooked long grain rice
1 cup frozen peas, thawed
1 envelope onion soup mix
1 cup (4 ounces) shredded cheddar cheese

In a large skillet, cook beef over medium heat until no longer pink; drain. Stir in the water, tomatoes, rice, peas and soup mix. Bring to a boil. Reduce heat; cover and simmer for 25 minutes or until rice is tender. Sprinkle with cheese. **Yield:** 4-6 servings.

Crab Lo Mein

(Pictured above right)

Prep/Total Time: 25 min.

I came up with this one night when I had some leftover spaghetti that I needed to use up. When stirring up the sauce, I like to use half soy sauce and half oyster sauce for a richer, more developed flavor. —*Laura Mryyan*
Topeka, Kansas

✓ Uses less fat, sugar or salt. Includes Nutritional Analysis and Diabetic Exchanges.

4 ounces uncooked angel hair pasta *or* thin spaghetti
1 medium onion, thinly sliced
1 medium green pepper, cut into 1-inch strips
1 package (8 ounces) frozen broccoli cuts, thawed
1/4 cup sliced fresh mushrooms
2 tablespoons canola oil
1 tablespoon cornstarch

Crab Lo Mein

1-1/4 cups chicken broth
1/4 cup water
1/4 cup soy sauce
12 ounces imitation crabmeat, cut into 1-inch pieces

Cook pasta according to package directions. Meanwhile, in a large skillet or wok, stir-fry the onion, green pepper, broccoli and mushrooms in oil for 3-4 minutes or until crisp-tender.

In a small bowl, combine the cornstarch, broth, water and soy sauce until smooth. Gradually stir into skillet. Bring to a boil; cook and stir for 2 minutes or until thickened. Stir in crab; cook 2-3 minutes longer or until heated through. Drain pasta; toss with crab mixture. **Yield:** 6 servings.

Nutritional Analysis: 1 cup (prepared with reduced-sodium chicken broth and reduced-sodium soy sauce) equals 218 calories, 5 g fat (1 g saturated fat), 28 mg cholesterol, 579 mg sodium, 29 g carbohydrate, 2 g fiber, 13 g protein. **Diabetic Exchanges:** 2 starch, 1-1/2 very lean meat.

Meat Loaf on the Stove

Here's a quick way to prepare meat loaf when you want a change of pace...or when you don't want to turn on the oven and heat up the kitchen on hot summer days.

I start by preparing my favorite meat loaf recipe. But instead of shaping the mixture into the usual loaf, I form serving-size patties and cook them in a skillet. I round out this simple supper with a side dish of mashed potatoes and gravy.

My family loves meat loaf made this way, and the patties also make super sandwiches.
—*Tammy Montenero, Yucaipa, California*

Sweet-and-Sour Pork

(Pictured below)

Prep: 15 min. + marinating **Cook:** 20 min.

I stir up a homemade sweet-and-sour sauce for this colorful combination of tender pork, crunchy vegetables and tangy pineapple. Serve it over hot rice, chow mein noodles or both. —Eleanor Dunbar, Peoria, Illinois

✓ Uses less fat, sugar or salt. Includes Nutritional Analysis.

    2/3 cup packed brown sugar
    2/3 cup cider vinegar
    2/3 cup ketchup
      2 teaspoons soy sauce
      1 pound boneless pork loin, cut into 1-inch
        cubes
      1 tablespoon canola oil
      1 medium onion, cut into chunks
      2 medium carrots, sliced
      1 medium green pepper, cut into 1-inch pieces
    1/2 teaspoon minced garlic
    1/4 teaspoon ground ginger
      1 can (8 ounces) pineapple chunks, drained
    Hot cooked rice, optional

In a small bowl, combine the brown sugar, vinegar, ketchup and soy sauce. Pour half into a large resealable plastic bag; add pork. Seal bag and turn to coat; refrigerate for 30 minutes. Set remaining marinade aside.

Drain and discard marinade from pork. In a large skillet, cook pork in oil for 3 minutes. Add the onion, carrots, green pepper, garlic and ginger; saute until pork is no longer pink. Add reserved marinade. Bring to a boil; cook for 1 minute. Stir in the pineapple. Serve with rice if desired. **Yield:** 4 servings.

Nutritional Analysis: 1-1/4 cups (prepared with reduced-sodium soy sauce; calculated without rice) equals 389 calories, 10 g fat (3 g saturated fat), 55 mg cholesterol, 490 mg sodium, 53 g carbohydrate, 3 g fiber, 24 g protein.

Gumbo Joes

Prep/Total Time: 20 min.

Just a few ingredients, including a convenient can of chicken gumbo soup, are needed to prepare this variation on traditional sloppy joe sandwiches. I made this speedy recipe often when I was working, and it's still one of my favorite supper dishes. —Wanda Stonebraker Wheatfield, Indiana

      1 pound ground beef
    1/3 cup chopped onion
      1 can (10-3/4 ounces) condensed chicken
        gumbo soup, undiluted
    3/4 cup ketchup
    1-1/2 teaspoons prepared mustard
      6 to 7 hamburger buns, split

In a large skillet, cook beef and onion over medium heat until meat is no longer pink; drain. Add the soup, ketchup and mustard; bring to a boil. Reduce heat; simmer, uncovered, for 5-10 minutes or until mixture reaches desired thickness. Serve on buns. **Yield:** 6-7 servings.

Chicken with Couscous

Prep/Total Time: 25 min.

My sister shared this recipe with me, and it's been a hit with me, my husband and our friends ever since. After working all day, I find this dish is fast to prepare. Plus, it tastes great. —Shari Ruffalo, Watertown, New York

✓ Uses less fat, sugar or salt. Includes Nutritional Analysis and Diabetic Exchanges.

    1-1/2 cups fresh broccoli florets
      1 package (5.8 ounces) roasted garlic and olive
        oil couscous
      1 cup water
      1 teaspoon plus 2 tablespoons olive oil, *divided*
      4 boneless skinless chicken breast halves
        (4 ounces *each*)
    1/2 teaspoon salt
    1/2 teaspoon pepper
      2 tablespoons lemon juice
      2 teaspoons minced garlic
    1/2 teaspoon dried oregano
      1 large tomato, seeded and chopped

In a large saucepan, combine the broccoli, contents of the couscous seasoning packet, water and 1 teaspoon oil. Bring to a boil. Stir in couscous. Cover and remove from the heat; let mixture stand for 5 minutes.

Meanwhile, flatten the chicken to 1/4-in. thickness.

Sweet-and-Sour Pork

Kielbasa with Baked Beans

casionally. Stir in the remaining ingredients. Bring to a boil. Reduce heat; cover and simmer for 10 minutes or until heated through. **Yield:** 4 servings.

Sausage 'n' Sauerkraut

(Pictured below)

Prep/Total Time: 30 min.

A new fan of sauerkraut, I discovered I like it best when served with meat and potatoes, so I created this quick-and-easy dish. Having three young children involved in different activities, I can throw this together in no time on busy nights. —Mary Lyon, Spotsylvania, Virginia

4 medium potatoes, peeled and cubed
2 tablespoons vegetable oil
1 small onion, halved and sliced
1 pound smoked sausage, cut into 1/4-inch pieces
1 package (16 ounces) sauerkraut, rinsed and well drained
1/4 teaspoon pepper
1/8 teaspoon salt

In a large skillet, saute the potatoes in oil for 5-6 minutes or until lightly browned. Stir in onion; saute for 3-4 minutes or until tender. Add the sausage, sauerkraut, pepper and salt. Cook, uncovered, over medium heat for 4-5 minutes or until heated through, stirring occasionally. **Yield:** 4 servings.

Sprinkle with salt and pepper. Combine the lemon juice, garlic and oregano; rub over chicken.

In a large skillet, brown chicken in remaining oil over medium heat for 8-10 minutes or until juices run clear. Stir tomato into the couscous; serve with chicken. **Yield:** 4 servings.

Nutritional Analysis: 1 chicken breast half with 1 cup couscous equals 357 calories, 12 g fat (2 g saturated fat), 63 mg cholesterol, 711 mg sodium, 35 g carbohydrate, 3 g fiber, 29 g protein. **Diabetic Exchanges:** 3 lean meat, 2 starch, 1 vegetable.

Kielbasa with Baked Beans

(Pictured above)

Prep/Total Time: 20 min.

I came up with this satisfying supper one night when I was in a hurry. My husband is a very picky eater, and he loves it. It's delicious with corn bread. —Vickie Wells Philadelphia, Tennessee

1/2 cup chopped onion
1 tablespoon butter
2 teaspoons vegetable oil
1 pound fully cooked kielbasa *or* Polish sausage, cut into 1/8-inch slices
1 can (28 ounces) pork and beans
1 cup ketchup
2 tablespoons Worcestershire sauce
1 tablespoon steak sauce

In a large skillet, saute the onion in butter and oil until tender. Add sausage; cook for 2-3 minutes, stirring oc-

Sausage 'n' Sauerkraut

Meat Lover's Pizza Bake

In a large skillet, cook beef and green pepper over medium heat until meat is no longer pink; drain. Stir in the pizza sauce, pepperoni and olives. Transfer to a greased 11-in. x 7-in. x 2-in. baking dish. Sprinkle with cheese.

In a small bowl, combine the biscuit mix, eggs and milk until blended. Pour evenly over cheese. Bake, uncovered, at 400° for 25-30 minutes or until golden brown. Let stand for 10 minutes before serving. **Yield:** 6 servings.

Deluxe Scalloped Corn

Prep: 10 min. **Bake:** 30 min.

I dress up canned corn with mushroom soup, sour cream and crackers. —Shawna Hull, Grovetown, Georgia

    4 cans (15-1/4 ounces *each*) whole kernel corn, drained
    1 can (10-3/4 ounces) condensed cream of mushroom soup, undiluted
    1 cup (8 ounces) sour cream
 1/4 cup all-purpose flour
 1/4 cup milk
    1 tablespoon dried minced onion
 1/4 teaspoon salt
 1/4 teaspoon pepper
1-3/4 cups crushed butter-flavored crackers (about 34 crackers)
    1 cup (4 ounces) shredded cheddar cheese

In a large bowl, combine the first eight ingredients. Transfer to a greased 13-in. x 9-in. x 2-in. baking dish. Combine cracker crumbs and cheese; sprinkle over the top. Bake, uncovered, at 350° for 30-35 minutes or until edges are bubbly. **Yield:** 8-10 servings.

Au Gratin Ham Potpie

Prep: 15 min. **Bake:** 40 min.

We first had this potpie at a family get-together, and we loved it. —Mary Zinsmeister, Slinger, Wisconsin

    1 package (4.9 ounces) au gratin potatoes
1-1/2 cups boiling water
    2 cups frozen peas and carrots
1-1/2 cups cubed fully cooked ham
    1 can (10-3/4 ounces) condensed cream of chicken soup, undiluted
    1 can (4 ounces) mushroom stems and pieces, drained
 1/2 cup milk
 1/2 cup sour cream
    1 jar (2 ounces) diced pimientos, drained
    1 sheet refrigerated pie pastry

In a large bowl, combine the potatoes, contents of sauce mix, boiling water, peas and carrots, ham, soup, mushrooms, milk, sour cream and pimientos. Pour into an ungreased 2-qt. round baking dish.

Roll out pastry to fit top of dish; place over potato mixture. Flute edges; cut slits in pastry. Bake at 400° for 40-45 minutes or until golden. Let stand 5 minutes before serving. **Yield:** 4-6 servings.

Catchall Casseroles

IS YOUR FAMILY fond of comforting casseroles? If so, you've turned to the right place. Hot from the oven, these delicious baked dishes are guaranteed to please...and don't take long to assemble before you pop them in the oven.

While the casserole cooks, toss together a simple green salad and whip up an easy dessert. You'll have a complete supper that'll fill 'em up fast.

Meat Lover's Pizza Bake

(Pictured above)

Prep: 20 min. **Bake:** 25 min. + standing

This yummy casserole is hearty with ground beef and pepperoni. Instead of a typical pizza crust, it features a crust-like topping. —Carol Oakes, Sturgis, Michigan

    1 pound ground beef
 1/2 cup chopped green pepper
    1 can (15 ounces) pizza sauce
    1 package (3-1/2 ounces) sliced pepperoni, chopped
    1 can (2-1/4 ounces) sliced ripe olives, drained
    2 cups (8 ounces) shredded mozzarella cheese
 3/4 cup biscuit/baking mix
    2 eggs
 3/4 cup milk

Cheesy Clam Manicotti

(Pictured below)

Prep: 30 min. **Bake:** 25 min.

I created this when I was having company and couldn't decide whether to serve seafood or Italian. It was a big hit! I usually add a little extra hot sauce to give it that special Louisiana kick. The cream cheese mixture can be stuffed in other types of pasta shells. —Kathy Kysar
St. Francisville, Louisiana

    1 jar (26 ounces) meatless spaghetti sauce
1/4 teaspoon hot pepper sauce
    2 cans (6-1/2 ounces *each*) minced clams
    1 carton (8 ounces) ricotta cheese
    4 ounces cream cheese, softened
1/4 cup spreadable chive and onion cream
        cheese
    2 cups (8 ounces) shredded mozzarella cheese
1/3 cup grated Parmesan cheese
    1 teaspoon minced garlic
1/2 teaspoon pepper
1/4 teaspoon dried oregano
    8 manicotti shells, cooked and drained

In a large saucepan, combine the spaghetti sauce and hot pepper sauce. Drain one can of clams; add clams to sauce. Stir in clams and juice from second can. Bring to a boil. Reduce heat; simmer, uncovered, for 20 minutes.

Meanwhile, in a large mixing bowl, beat ricotta and cream cheeses until smooth. Stir in the mozzarella, Parmesan, garlic, pepper and oregano. Stuff into manicotti shells.

Spread 3/4 cup clam sauce into a greased 11-in. x 7-in. x 2-in. baking dish. Arrange manicotti over sauce; top with remaining sauce. Bake, uncovered, at 350° for 25-

Cheesy Clam Manicotti

Coconut Sweet Potatoes

30 minutes or until bubbly. Let stand for 5 minutes before serving. **Yield:** 4 servings.

Coconut Sweet Potatoes

(Pictured above)

Prep: 50 min. **Bake:** 30 min.

I mash sweet potatoes with crushed pineapple, orange juice and spices. The coconut-pecan topping gives this dish a pretty look and sweet taste. I like to use chopped peanuts in place of pecans, so choose the type of nut your family prefers. —Hasel King, Nacogdoches, Texas

1-1/2 pounds sweet potatoes (about 6 medium)
    1/3 cup crushed pineapple
       2 tablespoons butter, melted
       1 tablespoon orange juice
       1 egg, beaten
       1 teaspoon salt
    1/4 teaspoon ground mace
    1/8 teaspoon ground ginger
    1/3 cup flaked coconut
    1/3 cup finely chopped pecans
       2 tablespoons brown sugar

Place sweet potatoes in a Dutch oven; cover with water. Bring to a boil. Reduce heat; cover and cook for 30-35 minutes or until tender. Drain; cool slightly.

Peel the potatoes and place in a large mixing bowl; mash. Add the pineapple, butter, orange juice, egg, salt, mace and ginger; mix well. Transfer to a greased 11-in. x 7-in. x 2-in. baking dish. Bake, uncovered, at 400° for 20-30 minutes or until heated through.

Combine the coconut, pecans and brown sugar; sprinkle over the top. Bake 8-10 minutes longer or until topping is lightly browned. **Yield:** 6-8 servings.

Hearty Maple Beans

cook the sausage and onion over medium-high heat until sausage is lightly browned. Stir in the bacon and remaining ingredients. Transfer to an ungreased 11-in. x 7-in. x 2-in. baking dish. Bake, uncovered, at 350° for 25-30 minutes or until bubbly. **Yield:** 8 servings.

Corny Chicken Bake

(Pictured on page 232)

Prep: 15 min. **Bake:** 25 min.

These glazed chicken breasts are baked with corn bread stuffing mix that's jazzed up with creamed corn, onion and celery. My mother gave me this quick and delicious recipe after she received it from a friend. The glaze recipe can be doubled for those who like a tangy taste.
—Barbara Ramstack, Fond du Lac, Wisconsin

   3 cups corn bread stuffing mix
   1 can (14-3/4 ounces) cream-style corn
1/3 cup finely chopped onion
   1 celery rib, diced
   4 boneless skinless chicken breast halves
    (4 ounces *each*)
1/4 cup packed brown sugar
1/4 cup butter, melted
   3 tablespoons spicy brown *or* horseradish
    mustard

In a large bowl, combine the stuffing mix, corn, onion and celery. Spoon into a greased 13-in. x 9-in. x 2-in. baking dish. Top with chicken. Combine the brown sugar, butter and mustard; drizzle over chicken. Bake, uncovered, at 400° for 25-30 minutes or until chicken juices run clear. **Yield:** 4 servings.

Hearty Maple Beans

(Pictured above)

Prep: 15 min. **Bake:** 25 min.

I modified this recipe to suit my family's taste. It's a great side dish for a backyard barbecue with hamburgers and hot dogs. Plus, it can be made in advance and kept warm in a slow cooker for hours without losing any flavor. —Marge Glassic
Easton, Pennsylvania

   6 bacon strips, diced
1/2 pound fully cooked kielbasa *or* Polish
    sausage, sliced
1/2 cup chopped onion
   1 can (16 ounces) pork and beans
   1 can (16 ounces) kidney beans, rinsed and
    drained
   1 can (15-1/2 ounces) butter beans *or* lima
    beans, rinsed and drained
1/2 cup maple syrup
   3 tablespoons white vinegar
   3 tablespoons ketchup
   3 tablespoons prepared mustard

In a large skillet, cook bacon over medium heat until crisp. Using a slotted spoon, remove to paper towels. Drain, reserving 1 tablespoon drippings. In the drippings,

Chicken Rice Casserole

Prep: 20 min. **Bake:** 20 min.

This heartwarming main course with lots of chicken, cheese and rice makes a quick and comforting weeknight meal. Requiring just 20 minutes to assemble, it's a great recipe for people who have full-time jobs.
—Donna Burnett, Baileyton, Alabama

   1 package (5.6 ounces) instant rice and
    chicken-flavored sauce mix
   2 cups cubed cooked chicken
   1 can (10-3/4 ounces) condensed cream of
    celery soup, undiluted
1/2 cup mayonnaise
1/2 teaspoon Worcestershire sauce
1/4 teaspoon pepper
   1 cup (4 ounces) shredded cheddar cheese

Cook rice mix according to package directions. In a bowl, combine the chicken, soup, mayonnaise, Worcestershire sauce and pepper. Stir in rice. Transfer to a greased 1-1/2-qt. baking dish. Sprinkle with cheese. Bake, uncovered, at 350° for 20-25 minutes or until heated through. **Yield:** 4 servings.

  Editor's Note: Reduced-fat or fat-free mayonnaise is not recommended for this recipe.

Veggie Turkey Casserole

(Pictured below)

Prep: 10 min. **Bake:** 30 min.

I rely on canned goods, frozen vegetables and leftover turkey to hurry along this creamy main-dish casserole. I like it so much that I've requested it for my birthday dinner. Just add a basket of rolls or biscuits for a supper your family will love.
—Michelle Summers
Chattanooga, Tennessee

- 3 cups cubed cooked turkey *or* chicken
- 2 cups frozen mixed vegetables
- 2 cups frozen broccoli florets
- 1 can (10-3/4 ounces) condensed cream of chicken soup, undiluted
- 1 can (10-3/4 ounces) condensed cream of mushroom soup, undiluted
- 1/2 cup chopped onion
- 1/4 teaspoon garlic powder
- 1/4 teaspoon celery seed

In a large bowl, combine all ingredients. Transfer to a greased 11-in. x 7-in. x 2-in. baking dish. Bake, uncovered, at 350° for 30-35 minutes or until heated through. Stir before serving. **Yield:** 4 servings.

Creative Casseroles

- In our house, my "Leftover Casserole" is popular. I store leftovers from other meals—even if it's just a spoonful of peas—in a container in the freezer. When the container is full, I combine the leftovers with a can of cream soup, cheese and onion or garlic powder. I put it in a casserole dish and top it with seasoned bread crumbs, potato chip crumbs or french-fried onions.
  —Elizabeth Beiler
  Paradise, Pennsylvania

- I spread extra mashed potatoes in a baking dish and add cheddar cheese, cracker crumbs and pats of butter. Then I pour about 1/2 cup of milk over it all and bake it until golden. Side dishes don't get much easier than this, and it's delicious.
  —Katherine Wisecarver, Berryville, Virginia

- When preparing a homemade chicken potpie made in a glass or ceramic pie plate, I cut slits in the top crust, then heat the pie in the microwave on high for 10 minutes, rotating it during cooking. Then I bake it in a 450° oven for 10 minutes more to brown and crisp the crust. It always turns out perfect and cuts the cooking time by 30 to 40 minutes.
  —Erika Shupe, Mt. Vernon, Washington

Veggie Turkey Casserole

Scalloped Chicken Supper

☑ Uses less fat, sugar or salt. Includes Nutritional Analysis and Diabetic Exchanges.

1 package (10 ounces) frozen chopped broccoli, thawed and drained
1/2 cup biscuit/baking mix
1 cup (8 ounces) sour cream
1 cup (8 ounces) small-curd cottage cheese
2 eggs
1/4 cup butter, melted
1/4 teaspoon salt
1 large tomato, thinly sliced and halved
1/4 cup grated Parmesan cheese

Arrange the broccoli in a greased 8-in. square baking dish. In a large mixing bowl, beat the biscuit mix, sour cream, cottage cheese, eggs, butter and salt; pour over broccoli. Arrange tomato slices over the top; sprinkle with Parmesan cheese.

Bake, uncovered, at 350° for 35-40 minutes or until a knife inserted near the center comes out clean. Let stand for 5 minutes before cutting. **Yield:** 9 servings.

Nutritional Analysis: 1 serving (prepared with reduced-fat baking mix, reduced-fat sour cream and fat-free cottage cheese) equals 158 calories, 9 g fat (6 g saturated fat), 72 mg cholesterol, 354 mg sodium, 10 g carbohydrate, 1 g fiber, 8 g protein. **Diabetic Exchanges:** 1-1/2 fat, 1 lean meat, 1/2 starch.

Scalloped Chicken Supper

(Pictured above)

Prep: 10 min. **Bake:** 45 min.

Canned soup and a package of scalloped potato mix hurry along this creamy and comforting casserole. You can use either leftover chicken or turkey. —Cheryl Maczko
Arthurdale, West Virginia

1 package (4.9 ounces) scalloped potatoes
1/8 teaspoon poultry seasoning
1-3/4 cups boiling water
1 can (10-3/4 ounces) condensed cream of chicken soup, undiluted
2 cups cubed cooked chicken
1 cup shredded carrots
1/2 cup chopped celery
1/4 cup finely chopped onion

Set the potatoes aside. Place the contents of the sauce mix in a large bowl; sprinkle with poultry seasoning. Whisk in the water and soup. Stir in the chicken, carrots, celery, onion and potatoes. Transfer to a greased 2-qt. baking dish. Bake, uncovered, at 400° for 45-50 minutes or until vegetables are tender. **Yield:** 4 servings.

Veggie Cheese Casserole

Prep: 10 min. **Bake:** 35 min.

This vegetable combination makes a delightful side dish or weekend brunch specialty. It's long been a favorite with my children. I like it because it's so easy to put together and can easily be lightened up by using reduced-fat ingredients. —Jacque Capurro, Anchorage, Alaska

Baked Mac and Cheese

(Pictured below)

Prep: 15 min. **Bake:** 30 min.

Even people who have had their own macaroni and cheese recipe for years ask for mine when they taste this crumb-

Baked Mac and Cheese

topped version. It's a good thing the recipe makes a lot, because it disappears fast! Use extra-sharp white cheddar cheese if you'd like more flavor. —Schelby Thompson
Dover, Delaware

4 cups uncooked elbow macaroni
3/4 cup finely chopped onion
3/4 cup butter, *divided*
6 tablespoons all-purpose flour
4-1/2 cups milk
4 cups (16 ounces) shredded sharp cheddar cheese
1 teaspoon ground mustard
1-1/2 teaspoons salt
1/4 teaspoon pepper
3/4 cup dry bread crumbs

Cook the macaroni according to the package directions. Meanwhile, in a saucepan, saute the onion in 1/2 cup butter. Add flour; whisk until blended. Gradually add the milk. Bring to a boil; cook and stir for 2 minutes or until thickened. Stir in the cheddar cheese, mustard, salt and pepper until smooth.

Drain macaroni and add to sauce; stir until coated. Transfer to a greased 13-in. x 9-in. x 2-in. baking dish. Melt the remaining butter; toss with bread crumbs. Sprinkle over macaroni mixture. Bake, uncovered, at 350° for 30-35 minutes or until heated through. **Yield:** 6-8 servings.

Black Bean Tamale Pie

Prep: 20 min. **Bake:** 20 min.

A packaged corn bread mix and canned beans speed the preparation of this winning Southwestern entree. My husband really likes it, and guests seem to enjoy it, too. For a change of pace, try topping it with shredded lettuce, guacamole or extra salsa. —Laura Morris
St. Joseph, Missouri

1/2 pound ground beef
1/2 cup chopped onion
1/2 cup chopped green pepper
1 can (15 ounces) black beans, rinsed and drained
1 cup salsa
1 package (8-1/2 ounces) corn bread/muffin mix
1/4 cup milk
1 egg
2 cups (8 ounces) shredded cheddar cheese, *divided*
Sour cream and sliced ripe olives, optional

In a large skillet, cook the beef, onion and green pepper over medium heat until the meat is no longer pink; drain. Stir in the black beans and salsa; set aside. In a bowl, combine the muffin mix, milk, egg and 1 cup cheese. Pour into a greased 9-in. pie plate. Bake at 375° for 5-6 minutes.

Spoon beef mixture over crust, leaving a 1/2-in. edge. Bake for 15-18 minutes or until crust is golden brown. Sprinkle with remaining cheese. Bake 1-2 minutes longer

Baked Spaghetti

or until cheese is melted. Serve with sour cream and olives if desired. **Yield:** 6-8 servings.

Baked Spaghetti

(Pictured above)

Prep: 25 min. **Bake:** 1 hour

A tasty twist on traditional spaghetti, this casserole will be requested again and again for potlucks, family gatherings and other get-togethers. It's especially popular with my grandchildren, who just love all the cheese. —Louise Miller
Westminster, Maryland

1 package (16 ounces) spaghetti
1 pound ground beef
1 medium onion, chopped
1 jar (26 ounces) meatless spaghetti sauce
1/2 teaspoon seasoned salt
2 eggs
1/3 cup grated Parmesan cheese
5 tablespoons butter, melted
2 cups (16 ounces) small-curd cottage cheese
4 cups (16 ounces) shredded mozzarella cheese

Cook spaghetti according to package directions. Meanwhile, in a large skillet, cook beef and onion over medium heat until meat is no longer pink; drain. Stir in the spaghetti sauce and seasoned salt; set aside.

In a large bowl, whisk eggs, Parmesan cheese and butter. Drain spaghetti; add to egg mixture and toss to coat.

Place half of the spaghetti mixture in a greased 13-in. x 9-in. x 2-in. baking dish. Top with half of the cottage cheese, meat sauce and mozzarella cheese. Repeat layers. Cover and bake at 350° for 40 minutes. Uncover; bake 20-25 minutes longer or until cheese is melted. **Yield:** 8-10 servings.

Chapter 17

⏱ *Time-Crunched Lunches*

WHEN NOONTIME arrives, you need filling fare that will ease your hunger until dinnertime. But with today's on-the-go lifestyles, there's rarely much time to even *eat* lunch, much less prepare it! So what's the solution?

You don't need to settle for takeout from a fast-food restaurant...or to skip lunch altogether. Instead, turn to the midday "menu" here—an array of quick-as-can-be recipes that are perfect for afternoon eating.

Whether you want to pack lunches-to-go in brown bags or to prepare a meal at noontime in your kitchen, these delicious homemade dishes will satisfy appetites in a snap so you and your family can get on with the rest of your day.

MIDDAY MEAL. Macaroni Bean Soup and Ham 'n' Swiss with a Twist (recipes on p. 252).

Mozzarella Wedges

(Pictured at left)

Prep/Total Time: 25 min.

I invented this recipe one night as an alternative to plain crescent rolls, and my family loved it. The cheesy wedges can be served as an appetizer or an accompaniment to soup or salad. —Lisa Keesee, Temperance, Michigan

　1 tube (8 ounces) refrigerated crescent rolls
　1 tablespoon butter, melted
　1/4 to 1/2 teaspoon garlic powder
　2 cups (8 ounces) shredded mozzarella cheese

Separate crescent dough into eight triangles; place on a greased 12-in. round pizza pan with points toward the center. Press dough onto the bottom and up the sides of pan; seal perforations. Brush with butter; sprinkle with garlic powder and cheese.

　Bake at 375° for 15-17 minutes or until crust is golden brown and cheese is lightly browned. Cut into wedges. **Yield:** 8 servings.

Ham 'n' Swiss with a Twist

(Pictured on page 251)

Prep/Total Time: 25 min.

To satisfy hearty appetites, try this deliciously different take on a grilled ham-and-cheese sandwich. The sliced apple and caramelized onion give it a sweet taste twist. For variation, use rye bread instead of the Texas toast.
—Marietta Slater, Augusta, Kansas

　1 large onion, sliced
　4 tablespoons butter, softened, *divided*
　8 slices Texas toast
　2 tablespoons spicy brown mustard
1/2 pound thinly sliced deli ham
　1 medium apple, sliced
　4 slices Swiss cheese

In a skillet, cook the onion in 1 tablespoon butter over medium heat for 8-10 minutes or until golden brown, stirring frequently.

　Spread remaining butter over one side of each slice of Texas toast. Place four slices, buttered side down, on a griddle. Spread with mustard; layer with ham, apple, onion and cheese. Top each with another slice of toast, buttered side up. Cook over medium heat for 3-4 minutes or until golden brown. Carefully turn; cook 2 minutes longer or until cheese is melted. **Yield:** 4 servings.

Macaroni Bean Soup

(Pictured on page 250)

Prep/Total Time: 25 min.

This chunky noodle soup makes a great meatless main course. Best of all, it's ready to serve in just 25 minutes. We like a lot of macaroni, so I often use more.
—Sundra Hauck, Bogalusa, Louisiana

Mozzarella Wedges
Taco Pasta Salad

Taco Pasta Salad

(Pictured above)

Prep/Total Time: 30 min.

I blend the best of two popular salads into one satisfying main dish. Serve taco or corn chips on the side, and you have a complete meal. —Gert Rosenau
Pewaukee, Wisconsin

　2 cups uncooked spiral pasta
　1 pound ground beef
　1 envelope taco seasoning
　3 cups shredded lettuce
　2 cups halved cherry tomatoes
　1 cup (4 ounces) shredded cheddar cheese
1/2 cup chopped onion
1/2 cup chopped green pepper
1/2 cup Catalina salad dressing
Tortilla chips

Cook pasta according to package directions. Meanwhile, in a skillet, cook beef over medium heat until no longer pink; drain. Stir in the taco seasoning; cool.

　Drain pasta and rinse in cold water; stir into meat mixture. Add the lettuce, tomatoes, cheese, onion, green pepper and dressing; toss to coat. Serve with tortilla chips. **Yield:** 6 servings.

4 cups chicken broth
2 cups tomato juice
1 cup uncooked elbow macaroni
1 cup sliced fresh carrots
1 teaspoon minced garlic
2 medium yellow summer squash, sliced
1 can (16 ounces) kidney beans, rinsed and drained
1 teaspoon seasoned salt
1/8 teaspoon pepper
1/4 cup grated Parmesan cheese
1 tablespoon lemon juice

In a large saucepan, bring the broth, tomato juice, macaroni, carrots and garlic to a boil. Reduce heat; cover and simmer for 5 minutes or until carrots are tender. Stir in the squash, beans, seasoned salt and pepper; simmer for 10 minutes or until macaroni and vegetables are tender. Remove from the heat; stir in the Parmesan cheese and lemon juice. **Yield:** 9 servings (about 2 quarts).

Feta-Olive Romaine Salad

(Pictured at right)

Prep/Total Time: 15 min.

With fresh feta cheese, colorful peppers and a homemade dressing, this easy Greek salad is loaded with flavor. To make this dish more authentic, use traditional Greek olives in place of ripe olives. —Anita Keppinger
Philomath, Oregon

6 cups torn romaine
2/3 cup diced sweet red pepper
1/3 cup diced green pepper
3 tablespoons chopped ripe olives
1/4 cup olive oil
1/4 cup balsamic vinegar
1/3 cup tomato and basil feta cheese, crumbled

In a salad bowl, toss the romaine, peppers and olives. In a jar with a tight-fitting lid, combine oil and vinegar; shake well. Drizzle over salad and toss to coat. Sprinkle with feta cheese. **Yield:** 4-6 servings.

Bread Bowl Chili

(Pictured at right)

Prep/Total Time: 30 min.

I like meals that are simple to prepare, yet offer maximum taste. Served in hollowed-out rolls, this zippy chili is hearty with beans and two kinds of meat. Sometimes I serve it in one large round bread loaf. —Tonya Burkhard
Cape Coral, Florida

1/2 pound ground beef
1/2 pound ground pork
2 cans (16 ounces *each*) kidney beans, rinsed and drained
2 cans (14-1/2 ounces *each*) diced tomatoes with garlic and onion, undrained
1 can (14-1/2 ounces) beef broth
1 can (8 ounces) tomato sauce

1 jalapeno pepper, seeded and chopped
2 tablespoons chili powder
12 hard rolls (about 4-1/2 inches)

In a large saucepan, cook beef and pork over medium heat until no longer pink; drain. Stir in the beans, tomatoes, broth, tomato sauce, jalapeno and chili powder. Bring to a boil. Reduce heat; cover and simmer for 20 minutes.

Meanwhile, cut the top fourth off of each roll; carefully hollow out the bottoms, leaving 1-1/2-in. shells. Cube the removed bread. Spoon the chili into bread bowls. Serve with cubed bread. **Yield:** 12 servings.

Editor's Note: When cutting or seeding hot peppers, use rubber or plastic gloves to protect your hands. Avoid touching your face.

Feta-Olive Romaine Salad
Bread Bowl Chili

Blue Cheese Ham Wraps

(Pictured at right)

Prep/Total Time: 20 min.

Bottled blue cheese salad dressing gives these wraps a burst of flavor. After topping the deli ham with the Swiss cheese, I like to melt the cheese in the microwave before quickly assembling the rest of the wrap. —Marie Yockel
Smyrna, Tennessee

> 4 flour tortillas (6 inches)
> 12 thin slices deli ham
> 4 thin slices Swiss cheese
> 1-1/2 cups shredded lettuce
> 1 medium tomato, diced
> 2 hard-cooked eggs, chopped
> 4 teaspoons blue cheese salad dressing

On each tortilla, layer a fourth of the ham, Swiss cheese, lettuce, tomato and eggs. Drizzle each with 1 teaspoon dressing; fold in sides. **Yield:** 4 wraps.

Spinach Feta Croissants

(Pictured below)

Prep/Total Time: 20 min.

I had this delicious sandwich in a local cafe and added my own twist to spruce it up. It would be lovely for a shower, a picnic or a special occasion. I often use mini croissants for pretty smaller-sized servings. —Dolores Brigham
Inglewood, California

Blue Cheese Ham Wraps

> 1/2 cup Italian salad dressing
> 6 croissants, split
> 3 cups fresh baby spinach
> 4 plum tomatoes, thinly sliced
> 1 cup (4 ounces) crumbled feta cheese

Brush salad dressing over the cut sides of croissants. On the bottom halves, layer the spinach, tomatoes and feta cheese; replace tops. **Yield:** 6 servings.

Cheddar Potato Wedges

Prep/Total Time: 20 min.

My aunt served this when we stopped in on short notice. The microwave hurries along preparation of these easy, cheesy potatoes. Our four children really like this fast snack, especially with ketchup. —Kathy Troyer
Gladys, Virginia

✓ Uses less fat, sugar or salt. Includes Nutritional Analysis and Diabetic Exchanges.

> 1/2 teaspoon garlic salt *or* garlic powder
> 1/2 teaspoon seasoned salt
> 1/2 teaspoon paprika
> 3 medium potatoes, *each* cut lengthwise into 8 wedges
> 2 tablespoons butter
> 1 cup (4 ounces) finely shredded cheddar cheese

In a large resealable plastic bag, combine the garlic salt, seasoned salt and paprika. Add potatoes; seal bag and toss to coat. Transfer potatoes to an ungreased microwave-safe dish. Dot with butter. Microwave, uncovered, on high for 3 minutes. Turn potatoes; cook 2-3 minutes longer or

Spinach Feta Croissants

until tender. Sprinkle with cheese; cover and let stand until cheese is melted. **Yield:** 4 servings.

Nutritional Analysis: 6 potato wedges (prepared with garlic powder, reduced-fat butter and reduced-fat cheese) equals 234 calories, 9 g fat (6 g saturated fat), 30 mg cholesterol, 417 mg sodium, 30 g carbohydrate, 3 g fiber, 11 g protein. **Diabetic Exchanges:** 2 starch, 2 fat.

Editor's Note: This recipe was tested in a 1,100-watt microwave.

Chocolate Toffee Cookies

Prep/Total Time: 20 min.

Friends and family will be surprised to learn that these rich cookies start from a boxed cookie mix. The sweet treats have crisp edges and a chewy interior. Enjoy them with hot coffee for an after-lunch pick-me-up.
—*Patricia Van Wyk, Newton, Iowa*

  1 package (17-1/2 ounces) chocolate chip cookie mix
1/4 cup vegetable oil
  1 egg
  2 tablespoons water
1/2 cup English toffee bits *or* almond brickle chips

In a large mixing bowl, beat the cookie mix, oil, egg and water. Stir in toffee bits. Drop by tablespoonfuls 2 in. apart onto parchment paper-lined baking sheets. Bake at 350° for 10-12 minutes or until set. Cool for 2 minutes before removing to wire racks. **Yield:** 2 dozen.

Pizza Burgers

(Pictured at right)

Prep/Total Time: 30 min.

The home economists in our Test Kitchen came up with this tasty switch from the usual burger. Italian-seasoned ground beef patties are stuffed with mozzarella cheese, then topped with pizza sauce and green pepper rings for a flavorful twist.

1/2 pound ground beef
1/2 teaspoon minced garlic
1/2 teaspoon beef bouillon granules
1/2 teaspoon Italian seasoning
1/4 teaspoon salt
  2 slices mozzarella cheese
  2 hamburger buns, split
  3 tablespoons pizza sauce, warmed
  4 green pepper rings

In a small bowl, combine the beef, garlic, bouillon, Italian seasoning and salt. Shape into four thin patties. Place a slice of cheese on two patties. Top each with another patty; press edges to seal.

Grill, uncovered, over medium-hot heat for 6-8 minutes on each side or until meat is no longer pink. Serve on buns with pizza sauce and green pepper rings. **Yield:** 2 servings.

Floret Pasta Toss

(Pictured below)

Prep/Total Time: 20 min.

This refreshing salad is fast to prepare because you can slice the vegetables while the penne pasta cooks. I just threw it together, adding flavors that suited my taste. Feel free to add a few of your own.
—*Kari Congenie*
Oakbrook Terrace, Illinois

✓ Uses less fat, sugar or salt. Includes Nutritional Analysis and Diabetic Exchanges.

  8 ounces uncooked penne *or* medium tube pasta
1-1/2 cups fresh cauliflowerets
1-1/2 cups fresh broccoli florets
  2 small tomatoes, seeded and chopped
  1 small onion, sliced
1/2 cup Italian salad dressing
  2 to 3 tablespoons balsamic vinegar
1/4 teaspoon salt
1/8 teaspoon pepper

Cook pasta according to package directions. Meanwhile, in a large bowl, combine the cauliflower, broccoli, tomatoes and onion. In a small bowl, whisk the salad dressing, vinegar, salt and pepper. Drain pasta and rinse in cold water; add to vegetable mixture. Drizzle with dressing and toss to coat. Chill until serving. **Yield:** 9 servings.

Nutritional Analysis: 3/4 cup (prepared with fat-free dressing) equals 116 calories, 1 g fat (trace saturated fat), trace cholesterol, 269 mg sodium, 24 g carbohydrate, 2 g fiber, 5 g protein. **Diabetic Exchanges:** 1-1/2 vegetable, 1 starch.

Pizza Burgers
Floret Pasta Toss

look, add a garnish of minced parsley or grated egg whites.
—Sandy Spackman, Trenton, Utah

✓ Uses less fat, sugar or salt. Includes Nutritional Analysis and Diabetic Exchanges.

  1 medium bunch broccoli, cut into spears
  2 tablespoons water
3-1/2 teaspoons cornstarch
  1/4 teaspoon garlic powder
  1/4 teaspoon onion powder
Dash white pepper
Dash ground nutmeg
  1 cup milk
  1 cup (4 ounces) shredded cheddar cheese
  1/2 teaspoon Worcestershire sauce

Place broccoli and water in a microwave-safe bowl. Cover and microwave on high for 3-5 minutes or until tender.

Meanwhile, in a small saucepan, whisk the cornstarch, seasonings and milk until smooth. Bring to a boil over medium heat; cook and stir for 1-2 minutes or until thickened. Stir in the cheddar cheese and Worcestershire sauce until cheese is melted. Drain the broccoli; top with cheese sauce. **Yield:** 4 servings.

Nutritional Analysis: 2 broccoli spears with about 2 tablespoons sauce (prepared with fat-free milk and reduced-fat cheese) equals 134 calories, 6 g fat (4 g saturated fat), 21 mg cholesterol, 241 mg sodium, 10 g carbohydrate, 2 g fiber, 11 g protein. **Diabetic Exchanges:** 1 vegetable, 1 fat, 1/2 reduced-fat milk.

Editor's Note: This recipe was tested in a 1,100-watt microwave.

Hawaiian Deli Sandwiches
Broccoli with Cheese Sauce

Hawaiian Deli Sandwiches

(Pictured above)

Prep/Total Time: 5 min.

When our kids were in sports, we were often on the road for meals. These easy sandwiches can be made ahead and travel well. —Tammy Blomquist, Taylorville, Illinois

  1 package (4.4 ounces) Hawaiian sweet rolls
  1 tablespoon ranch salad dressing
  1 tablespoon prepared mustard
  2 slices deli ham
  4 slices hard salami
  2 slices deli turkey

Leaving the rolls attached, cut in half horizontally; remove top. Spread ranch dressing over cut side of top; spread mustard over cut side of bottom. Layer with ham, salami and turkey; replace top. Cut into four sandwiches. **Yield:** 2 servings.

Broccoli with Cheese Sauce

(Pictured above)

Prep/Total Time: 15 min.

This creamy cheese sauce is a great way to jazz up ordinary vegetables. Try any cheese you like. For an elegant

Beef Sandwiches Au Jus

Prep/Total Time: 30 min.

I serve these stovetop sandwiches with individual ramekins of well-seasoned bouillon for dipping. This recipe is a favorite of ours when we want a hot meal but time is of the essence. Nobody leaves the table hungry.
—Marge Miller
Atlantic Mine, Michigan

  2 cups water
  1 tablespoon beef bouillon granules
  1/2 teaspoon pepper, *divided*
  1/4 teaspoon crushed red pepper flakes
  1/8 teaspoon garlic salt
  1 medium onion, thinly sliced
  1 small green pepper, thinly sliced
  4 tablespoons butter, *divided*
  1/4 teaspoon salt
  1 pound boneless beef sirloin steak, cut into 1/2-inch strips
  4 French rolls, split
  4 slices provolone cheese

In a large saucepan, combine the water, bouillon, 1/4 teaspoon pepper, pepper flakes and garlic salt. Bring to a boil. Reduce the heat; simmer, uncovered, for 15-20 minutes.

Meanwhile, in a large skillet, saute onion and green

pepper in 2 tablespoons butter until tender; remove and keep warm. Sprinkle salt and remaining pepper over beef. In the same skillet, cook beef in remaining butter over medium-high heat until no longer pink. Spoon onto roll bottoms; top with cheese and onion mixture. Replace roll tops. Serve with au jus. **Yield:** 4 servings.

Cottage Cheese Salad

Prep/Total Time: 10 min.

I dress up cottage cheese with pecans and onions to make this savory side dish. It's a nice way to round out a sandwich lunch. I think it would also be good with chopped apples and walnuts, similar to a Waldorf salad.
—Karla Johnson, East Helena, Montana

✓ Uses less fat, sugar or salt. Includes Nutritional Analysis and Diabetic Exchanges.

    2 cups (16 ounces) cottage cheese
1/2 cup chopped green onions
1/4 to 1/2 cup chopped pecans
1/2 teaspoon minced garlic
1/4 teaspoon pepper
1/8 teaspoon salt

In a small bowl, combine all of the ingredients. Serve immediately. **Yield:** 5 servings.

Nutritional Analysis: 1/2 cup (prepared with fat-free cottage cheese and 1/4 cup pecans) equals 104 calories, 4 g fat (trace saturated fat), 4 mg cholesterol, 343 mg sodium, 5 g carbohydrate, 1 g fiber, 11 g protein. **Diabetic Exchanges:** 1-1/2 lean meat, 1 vegetable.

Malted Milk Ball Brownies

Prep: 15 min. Bake: 30 min. + cooling

You don't have to be a kid to love these yummy brownies! Using a purchased mix, I can whip up a big pan in a flash. Chopped malted milk balls in the batter and sprinkled on top make them special. —Mitzi Sentiff
Alexandria, Virginia

    1 package fudge brownie mix (13-inch
      x 9-inch pan size)
1-1/3 cups chopped malted milk balls, *divided*
    1 cup (6 ounces) semisweet chocolate chips
    2 tablespoons butter
    2 tablespoons milk
1/4 teaspoon vanilla extract

Prepare brownie batter according to package directions; stir in 1 cup malted milk balls. Spread into a greased 13-in. x 9-in. x 2-in. baking pan. Bake at 350° for 28-30 minutes or until a toothpick inserted 2 in. from an edge comes out with moist crumbs. Cool completely on a wire rack.

In a small saucepan, melt the chocolate chips and butter over low heat. Remove from the heat. Stir in the milk and vanilla extract. Spread the chocolate mixture over the brownies. Sprinkle with the remaining malted milk balls. Refrigerate the brownies for 10-15 minutes or until set. Cut into bars. **Yield:** 2 dozen.

Pea 'n' Crab Pasta Salad

(Pictured below)

Prep/Total Time: 30 min.

This pretty pasta salad from our Test Kitchen staff is jazzed up with crabmeat, spinach and peas. With crumbled feta cheese and just the right amount of Italian dressing, it makes a hearty side dish or a satisfying main course served with bread alongside.

✓ Uses less fat, sugar or salt. Includes Nutritional Analysis and Diabetic Exchanges.

2-1/2 cups uncooked medium pasta shells
2-1/2 cups fresh baby spinach
    1 package (10 ounces) frozen peas, thawed
1-1/2 cups imitation crabmeat
1/4 cup crumbled feta cheese
1/2 cup Italian salad dressing

Cook pasta according to package directions. Meanwhile, in a large bowl, combine the spinach, peas and crab. Drain pasta and rinse in cold water. Stir into spinach mixture. Sprinkle with feta cheese. Drizzle with dressing and toss to coat. **Yield:** 8 servings.

Nutritional Analysis: 1 cup (prepared with fat-free salad dressing) equals 198 calories, 2 g fat (1 g saturated fat), 13 mg cholesterol, 310 mg sodium, 35 g carbohydrate, 3 g fiber, 10 g protein. **Diabetic Exchanges:** 2 starch, 1 very lean meat, 1 vegetable.

Pea 'n' Crab Pasta Salad

Tomato Steak Sandwiches

(Pictured below)

Prep/Total Time: 15 min.

My husband and I came up with these open-faced sand-wiches when we didn't have much in the refrigerator. They've been a favorite ever since, particularly when we need a quick dinner. You can easily double the recipe when company drops by. —Tessa Edwards, Provo, Utah

- 3 plain bagels, split
- 6 tablespoons cream cheese
- 1 pound boneless beef sirloin steak, cut into thin strips
- 2 teaspoons vegetable oil
- 1/8 teaspoon salt
- Dash pepper
- 6 thick slices tomato
- 6 slices mozzarella cheese

Place bagels on an ungreased baking sheet; spread with cream cheese. Set aside. In a large skillet over medium heat, cook and stir beef in oil for 3-5 minutes or until no longer pink. Season with salt and pepper.

Using a slotted spoon, place beef on bagels. Top with tomato and mozzarella cheese. Broil 8 in. from the heat for 3-5 minutes or until cheese is melted and lightly browned. **Yield:** 6 servings.

Dilly Cucumber Salad

Dilly Cucumber Salad

(Pictured above)

Prep: 15 min. + chilling

This sweet and tangy side dish comes together in a snap. I often take this to church potlucks. It is so pretty and colorful with the red pepper and unpeeled cucumbers. —Mary Farley, Wasilla, Alaska

- 3 cups thinly sliced cucumbers
- 1 small sweet red pepper, julienned
- 1/2 cup chopped sweet onion
- 1/3 cup sugar
- 1/4 cup white wine vinegar
- 1-1/2 teaspoons salt
- 1 teaspoon dill seed

In a large bowl, combine all ingredients. Cover and refrigerate for at least 1 hour, stirring occasionally. **Yield:** 4 servings.

Blackened Chicken Salad

Prep/Total Time: 25 min.

I'm always in need of quick recipes. I like to serve this healthy salad with garlic cheese bread and peanut butter cookies for dessert. I stir up a big batch of the seasoning rub and keep it on hand, so I can start this salad in no time. —Tanya Brady, Montague, Michigan

- 2 teaspoons paprika
- 1 teaspoon onion powder
- 1 teaspoon garlic powder
- 1/2 teaspoon salt
- 1/2 teaspoon pepper

Tomato Steak Sandwiches

1/2 teaspoon dried oregano
1/2 teaspoon dried thyme
1/4 teaspoon cayenne pepper
1-1/2 pounds boneless skinless chicken breasts
1 package (10 ounces) Italian-blend salad greens
4 plum tomatoes, thinly sliced
1 medium sweet red pepper, julienned
1 cup seasoned salad croutons
1/2 to 3/4 cup salad dressing of your choice

Combine the seasonings; rub over chicken. Broil or grill, uncovered, over medium heat for 5-7 minutes on each side or until juices run clear.

On a serving platter or individual plates, arrange the salad greens, tomatoes and red pepper. Slice chicken; place over salad. Top with croutons and dressing. **Yield:** 4 servings.

Peas and Celery

Prep/Total Time: 15 min.

This recipe came with the first microwave we purchased, in the early '80s, and was one of the first vegetable recipes I tried. I loved the results and still prepare this side dish often. —Phyllis Groves, Ukiah, California

✓ Uses less fat, sugar or salt. Includes Nutritional Analysis and Diabetic Exchanges.

3 celery ribs, chopped
1/3 cup chopped onion
2 tablespoons water
2 tablespoons butter
1 package (10 ounces) frozen peas
1/4 teaspoon lemon-pepper seasoning

In a microwave-safe dish, combine the celery, onion, water and butter. Cover and microwave on high for 4-5 minutes. Stir in peas and lemon-pepper. Cover and microwave 4-6 minutes longer. Let stand for 4 minutes or until peas are tender. **Yield:** 4 servings.

Nutritional Analysis: 1/2 cup (prepared with reduced-fat butter) equals 90 calories, 3 g fat (2 g saturated fat), 10 mg cholesterol, 170 mg sodium, 12 g carbohydrate, 4 g fiber, 5 g protein. **Diabetic Exchange:** 1 starch.

Editor's Note: This recipe was tested in a 1,100-watt microwave.

Con Queso Spirals

(Pictured at right)

Prep/Total Time: 20 min.

This four-ingredient dish is a sure favorite no matter what the main course may be. Spicy Mexican cheese dip from the snack aisle creates a zippy coating for spiral pasta. —JoAnne Palmer, Mechanicsville, Maryland

2-1/2 cups uncooked spiral pasta
1 tablespoon butter
1 cup salsa con queso dip
Sour cream

Cook pasta according to package directions; drain. Place in a bowl; stir in butter until melted. Stir in con queso dip. Serve with sour cream. **Yield:** 4 servings.

Vegetable Turkey Hoagies

(Pictured below)

Prep/Total Time: 20 min.

Vegetable-flavored cream cheese dresses up these tasty turkey and sweet pepper sandwiches. A friend of mine often prepares them for picnic lunches. For variation, you can substitute deli chicken for the turkey. —Lauren Larson Orrville, Ohio

1 medium sweet yellow pepper, julienned
1 medium sweet red pepper, julienned
1 medium red onion, halved and thinly sliced
1 tablespoon olive oil
1/4 teaspoon salt
1/4 teaspoon pepper
2 loaves (8 ounces *each*) French bread, halved lengthwise
1/2 cup spreadable garden vegetable cream cheese
3/4 pound thinly sliced deli turkey

In a large skillet, saute peppers and onion in oil until tender. Stir in salt and pepper. Hollow out the top and bottom of loaves; spread cream cheese over cut sides. Top with turkey and sauteed vegetables. Cut in half. **Yield:** 4 servings.

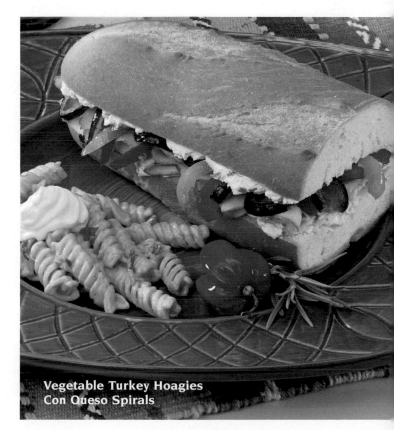

**Vegetable Turkey Hoagies
Con Queso Spirals**

⏱ *Fast, Delicious...and Nutritious*

COOKING HEALTHY doesn't have to be complicated and time-consuming, as the rapid recipes here prove.

If you're watching what you eat while keeping an eye on the clock, these light-but-fast foods are for you.

Choose from an array of delicious dishes that cut calories, fat, salt and sugar while reducing kitchen time. For dietary information about each recipe, just check the Nutritional Analysis and Diabetic Exchanges.

Anyone on a special diet—and even those who aren't—will enjoy this flavorful and nutritious fare.

(All the good-for-you foods in this book are flagged with a red checkmark in the indexes beginning on page 316.)

LIGHTER DELIGHTS. Pork 'n' Pea Pod Stir-Fry (p. 265) and Walnut Oat Brownies (p. 262).

Banana-Chip Oat Muffins

6 g fat (3 g saturated fat), 23 mg cholesterol, 174 mg sodium, 39 g carbohydrate, 3 g fiber, 4 g protein. **Diabetic Exchanges:** 2 starch, 1/2 fruit, 1/2 fat.

Walnut Oat Brownies

(Pictured on page 260)

Prep: 15 min. **Bake:** 25 min. + cooling

Oatmeal and wheat germ add a nutritious touch to these fudgy brownies. This recipe seems too good to be true, but these brownies really taste great. Use 1 cup plus 2 tablespoons of semisweet chocolate chips if you don't have six semisweet chocolate squares.
—Marilyn Yates
Roanoke, Virginia

       1/3 cup quick-cooking oats
       1/3 cup nonfat dry milk powder
       1/4 cup toasted wheat germ
       1/4 cup packed brown sugar
          2 tablespoons sugar
       1/2 teaspoon baking powder
       1/4 teaspoon salt
          6 squares (1 ounce *each*) semisweet chocolate
       1/4 cup butter
       1/2 cup egg substitute
       1/4 cup chopped walnuts
          1 teaspoon vanilla extract
   Confectioners' sugar, optional

In a large bowl, combine the first seven ingredients. In a microwave-safe bowl, melt chocolate and butter; cool slightly. Stir in the egg substitute, walnuts and vanilla. Stir into the dry ingredients.

Pour into an 8-in. square baking dish coated with nonstick cooking spray. Bake at 350° for 25-30 minutes or until a toothpick inserted near the center comes out clean. Cool on a wire rack. Dust with confectioners' sugar if desired. Cut into bars. **Yield:** 1 dozen.

Nutritional Analysis: 1 brownie equals 180 calories, 10 g fat (5 g saturated fat), 11 mg cholesterol, 145 mg sodium, 19 g carbohydrate, 2 g fiber, 5 g protein. **Diabetic Exchanges:** 2 fat, 1 starch.

Dilly Corn

(Pictured at right)

Prep/Total Time: 10 min.

Five items and a few minutes are all you need for this versatile side dish. I dress up frozen corn with dill weed and a little garlic powder for mild flavor that complements almost any main dish.
—Bernadette Bennett
Waco, Texas

          1 cup water
          1 teaspoon beef bouillon granules
   2-1/4 cups frozen corn
          3 teaspoons dill weed
          1 teaspoon garlic powder

In a small saucepan, bring water and bouillon to a boil. Stir in the corn, dill and garlic powder. Return to a boil. Reduce heat; cover and simmer for 3-4 minutes or until

All recipes in this chapter use less fat, sugar or salt and include Nutritional Analysis and Diabetic Exchanges.

Banana-Chip Oat Muffins

(Pictured above)

Prep: 25 min. **Bake:** 15 min.

These tender banana muffins are so full of chocolate chips that folks won't realize they're made with wholesome oats and whole wheat flour. I like to bake a batch to enjoy in the morning…or anytime.
—Kristine Sims
St. Joseph, Michigan

          1 cup quick-cooking oats
       3/4 cup all-purpose flour
       3/4 cup whole wheat flour
          2 teaspoons baking powder
       1/2 teaspoon baking soda
       1/8 teaspoon salt
          2 tablespoons butter, softened
       1/2 cup packed brown sugar
          3 medium ripe bananas, mashed
          1 egg
          2 tablespoons unsweetened applesauce
          1 teaspoon vanilla extract
       3/4 cup miniature semisweet chocolate chips

In a large bowl, combine the dry ingredients. In a small mixing bowl, beat butter and brown sugar until crumbly. Beat in the bananas, egg, applesauce and vanilla. Stir into dry ingredients just until moistened. Fold in chocolate chips.

Coat muffin cups with nonstick cooking spray or line with paper liners; fill three-fourths full. Bake at 350° for 15-20 minutes or until a toothpick comes out clean. Cool for 5 minutes before removing from pan to a wire rack. Serve warm. **Yield:** 1 dozen.

Nutritional Analysis: 1 muffin equals 218 calories,

corn is tender. Drain. **Yield:** 3 servings.

Nutritional Analysis: 2/3 cup equals 117 calories, 1 g fat (trace saturated fat), trace cholesterol, 204 mg sodium, 27 g carbohydrate, 3 g fiber, 4 g protein. **Diabetic Exchange:** 2 starch.

Turkey Sausage Jambalaya

(Pictured below)

Prep: 20 min. **Cook:** 20 min.

Creole cooking is delicious but frequently calls for lots of high-fat meats and oils. This is a spicy adaptation of an old favorite that is tasty, healthy and fast.
—*James McNaughton, Quincy, Florida*

- 3/4 pound reduced-fat smoked turkey sausage, cut into 1/4-inch slices
- 1/2 cup chopped onion
- 1/2 cup chopped green pepper
- 1 teaspoon minced garlic
- 1 tablespoon canola oil
- 1-1/2 cups water
- 1/2 cup uncooked long grain rice
- 1/4 teaspoon salt
- 1/4 teaspoon cayenne pepper
- 1/4 teaspoon hot pepper sauce
- 1 can (14-1/2 ounces) diced tomatoes with green chilies, undrained
- 1/4 pound uncooked medium shrimp, peeled and deveined

In a large saucepan, saute sausage, onion, green pepper and garlic in oil until vegetables are tender. Stir in the water, rice, salt, cayenne and hot pepper sauce. Bring to a boil. Reduce heat; cover and simmer for 15 minutes or until rice is tender. Add the tomatoes and shrimp; cook and stir until shrimp turn pink. **Yield:** 4 servings.

Nutritional Analysis: 1 cup equals 288 calories, 6 g fat (1 g saturated fat), 72 mg cholesterol, 1,311 mg sodium, 38 g carbohydrate, 3 g fiber, 18 g protein. **Diabetic Exchanges:** 2 starch, 2 lean meat, 1 vegetable.

Dilly Corn
Turkey Sausage Jambalaya

Cannellini Bean Salad

(Pictured below)

Prep/Total Time: 30 min.

This recipe has always been popular, particularly when served at potlucks. If you are crunched for time, instead of roasting the pepper yourself, use roasted red peppers sold in jars, often near the pickles and condiments.
—Alden Thornton, Warrenton, Oregon

- 1 large sweet red pepper
- 2 cans (15 ounces *each*) white kidney *or* cannellini beans, rinsed and drained
- 1 medium red onion, sliced and separated into rings
- 1/4 cup minced fresh basil
- 3 tablespoons red wine vinegar
- 2 tablespoons olive oil
- 1/4 teaspoon salt
- 1/4 teaspoon pepper

Cut red pepper in half; remove seeds. Place pepper halves cut side down on a rack in a broiler pan. Broil 4 in. from the heat until skin blisters, about 8 minutes. Immediately place pepper in a bowl; cover and let stand for 15-20 minutes. Peel off and discard charred skin. Cut pepper into strips; place in a large bowl. Add the beans, onion and basil.

In a jar with a tight-fitting lid, combine the vinegar, oil, salt and pepper; shake well. Pour over bean mixture; toss to coat. **Yield:** 5 servings.

Nutritional Analysis: 3/4 cup equals 190 calories, 6 g fat (1 g saturated fat), 0 cholesterol, 472 mg sodium, 26 g carbohydrate, 7 g fiber, 7 g protein. **Diabetic Exchanges:** 1-1/2 starch, 1 very lean meat, 1 fat.

Southwestern Chicken

(Pictured below)

Prep/Total Time: 20 min.

This simple six-ingredient recipe is so tasty, you won't believe it's also good for you. I like it because it is so quick to fix. It's just one way I add some of the flavors of the Southwest to lean chicken. —Roberta Freedman
Mesilla Park, New Mexico

- 2 teaspoons garlic powder
- 1 teaspoon chili powder
- 1/2 teaspoon salt
- 1/2 teaspoon paprika
- 4 boneless skinless chicken breast halves (4 ounces *each*)
- 2 teaspoons lime juice

In a small bowl, combine the garlic powder, chili powder, salt and paprika. Rub over both sides of chicken. In a large skillet coated with nonstick cooking spray, brown chicken on both sides; drizzle with lime juice. Cover and cook for 5-7 minutes or until chicken juices run clear. **Yield:** 4 servings.

Nutritional Analysis: 1 serving equals 130 calories, 3 g fat (1 g saturated fat), 63 mg cholesterol, 357 mg sodium, 2 g carbohydrate, trace fiber, 23 g protein. **Diabetic Exchange:** 3 lean meat.

Southwestern Chicken
Cannellini Bean Salad

Pork 'n' Pea Pod Stir-Fry

(Pictured on page 261)

Prep: 10 min. + marinating **Cook:** 15 min.

A spicy citrus sauce coats tender strips of pork and crisp snow peas in this speedy stir-fry. We like this dish extra spicy, so I use a tablespoon of red pepper flakes.
— *Jane Shapton, Tustin, California*

- 2 tablespoons reduced-sodium soy sauce
- 2 tablespoons honey
- 1-1/2 teaspoons minced fresh gingerroot
- 1/2 to 1 teaspoon crushed red pepper flakes
- 3/4 pound pork tenderloin, cut into 2-inch strips
- 2 teaspoons canola oil
- 1 tablespoon cornstarch
- 1/3 cup orange juice
- 2 tablespoons cider vinegar
- 1 pound fresh snow peas
- 2 teaspoons minced garlic
- 1 teaspoon grated orange peel

In a small bowl, combine the soy sauce, honey, ginger and pepper flakes. Place 3 tablespoons in a large re-sealable plastic bag; add the pork. Seal bag and turn to coat; refrigerate for 1 hour. Cover and refrigerate remaining marinade.

Drain and discard marinade from pork. In a large non-stick skillet or wok, stir fry pork in oil for 4-5 minutes or until no longer pink. Meanwhile, combine the cornstarch, orange juice, vinegar and reserved marinade; stir until blended. Remove pork and keep warm. In the same pan, stir-fry snow peas for 2-3 minutes or until crisp-tender. Stir in garlic and orange peel.

Stir cornstarch mixture and stir into pan. Bring to a boil; cook and stir for 1-2 minutes or until thickened. Return pork to the pan; heat through. **Yield:** 3 servings.
Nutritional Analysis: 1-1/3 cups equals 286 calories, 7 g fat (2 g saturated fat), 63 mg cholesterol, 354 mg sodium, 26 g carbohydrate, 4 g fiber, 28 g protein. **Diabetic Exchanges:** 3 lean meat, 2 vegetable, 1 fruit.

Tuna Shell Salad

Prep/Total Time: 25 min.

I created this light salad as a way to use tuna in dishes other than sandwiches. Mustard and dill enhance the flavor. — *Pat Kordas, Nutley, New Jersey*

- 1 package (7 ounces) small pasta shells
- 1 can (6 ounces) light water-packed tuna, drained and flaked
- 1/4 cup finely chopped onion
- 1 large carrot, shredded
- 3/4 cup reduced-fat mayonnaise
- 1/4 cup fat-free milk
- 1 tablespoon lemon juice
- 2 teaspoons prepared mustard
- 1 teaspoon dill weed
- 1/8 teaspoon pepper

Cook pasta according to the package directions; drain and rinse in cold water. In a salad bowl, combine the pas-

Banana Pudding Parfaits

ta, tuna, onion and carrot. In a small bowl, combine the remaining ingredients. Pour over the salad and toss to coat. Cover and chill until serving. **Yield:** 5 servings.
Nutritional Analysis: 1 cup equals 234 calories, 13 g fat (2 g saturated fat), 23 mg cholesterol, 445 mg sodium, 18 g carbohydrate, 1 g fiber, 12 g protein. **Diabetic Exchanges:** 2 fat, 1-1/2 lean meat, 1 starch.

Banana Pudding Parfaits

(Pictured above)

Prep: 15 min. + chilling

These sweet after-dinner treats are layered with fresh bananas, vanilla wafers and a creamy pudding mixture. Feel free to substitute fresh berries or a different flavor of sugar-free instant pudding. — *Margaret Wagner Allen Abingdon, Virginia*

- 3-1/3 cups cold fat-free milk
- 2 packages (1 ounce *each*) sugar-free instant vanilla pudding mix
- 2/3 cup fat-free sour cream
- 1/4 teaspoon vanilla extract
- 1 carton (8 ounces) frozen fat-free whipped topping, thawed, *divided*
- 32 reduced-fat vanilla wafers
- 3 medium ripe bananas, cut into 1/4-inch slices

In a bowl, whisk milk and pudding mix for 2 minutes. Let stand for 2 minutes. Whisk in sour cream and vanilla. Fold in three-fourths of whipped topping.

Set aside eight vanilla wafers for garnish. Place one wafer into each of eight parfait glasses; top with a third of the banana slices and pudding mixture. Repeat layers twice. Top with the remaining whipped topping. Refrigerate for at least 1 hour. Garnish with reserved vanilla wafers. **Yield:** 8 servings.
Nutritional Analysis: 1 serving equals 231 calories, 1 g fat (trace saturated fat), 5 mg cholesterol, 433 mg sodium, 46 g carbohydrate, 1 g fiber, 6 g protein.

Tasty Tuna Steaks

Prep/Total Time: 30 min.

Low-carb fans will love this easy tuna recipe from our Test Kitchen home economists. Marinated in red wine, soy sauce, ginger and garlic, these steaks are quick to fix on the stovetop and low in carbohydrates. Oriental vegetables or broccoli florets are excellent on the side.

- 1/3 cup dry red wine *or reduced-sodium beef broth*
- 1/3 cup reduced-sodium soy sauce
- 2 teaspoons minced fresh gingerroot
- 1 teaspoon minced garlic
- 4 tuna steaks (6 ounces *each*)
- 1 bay leaf
- 1 tablespoon olive oil

In a small bowl, combine the wine or broth, soy sauce, ginger and garlic. Pour into a large resealable plastic bag; add the tuna steaks and bay leaf. Seal bag and turn to coat; let stand for 15 minutes. Drain and discard marinade and bay leaf.

In a large skillet, cook tuna in oil over medium-high heat for 6-8 minutes on each side or until the fish flakes easily with a fork and is no longer pink. **Yield:** 4 servings.

Nutritional Analysis: 1 serving equals 224 calories, 5 g fat (1 g saturated fat), 77 mg cholesterol, 366 mg sodium, 1 g carbohydrate, trace fiber, 40 g protein. **Diabetic Exchanges:** 5 very lean meat, 1 fat.

Glazed Pork Medallions

(Pictured at right)

Prep/Total Time: 30 min.

When my husband was told he needed to lower his cholesterol, he was sure he'd never enjoy any good-tasting food again. He was surprised by this delicious entree. Sometimes we use pineapple marmalade instead of orange in the sauce.
—*Michele Flagel, Shellsburg, Iowa*

- 1 pork tenderloin (1-1/4 pounds)
- 1/4 teaspoon salt
- 1/3 cup reduced-sugar orange marmalade
- 2 teaspoons cider vinegar
- 2 teaspoons Worcestershire sauce
- 1/2 teaspoon minced fresh gingerroot
- 1/8 teaspoon crushed red pepper flakes

Cut pork into 1-in. slices and flatten to 1/4-in. thickness; sprinkle with salt. In a large nonstick skillet coated with nonstick cooking spray, cook pork in batches over medium-high heat until juices run clear. Reduce heat to low; return all meat to the pan. Combine the remaining ingredients; pour over the pork and turn to coat. Heat through. **Yield:** 4 servings.

Nutritional Analysis: 4 ounces cooked pork equals 200 calories, 5 g fat (2 g saturated fat), 79 mg cholesterol, 231 mg sodium, 9 g carbohydrate, trace fiber, 28 g protein. **Diabetic Exchanges:** 4 very lean meat, 1/2 fruit, 1/2 fat.

Grapefruit Spinach Salad

(Pictured at right)

Prep/Total Time: 15 min.

My mother-in-law prepared this for us during a visit. The fresh-tasting salad of spinach and grapefruit is lightly dressed with a sweet honey mixture. The recipe is so easy to put together, and we never have any leftovers.
—*Lee Ann Odell, Boulder, Colorado*

- 1 medium pink grapefruit
- 1 package (10 ounces) fresh spinach, torn
- 2 tablespoons chopped green onion
- 2 teaspoons cider vinegar
- 2 teaspoons olive oil
- 2 teaspoons honey
- 2 teaspoons prepared mustard

Cut grapefruit in half; with a sharp knife, cut around each section to loosen fruit, reserving juice. In a salad bowl, toss spinach, onion and grapefruit sections. In a jar with a tight-fitting lid, combine vinegar, oil, honey, mustard and reserved grapefruit juice; shake well. Drizzle over the salad and toss to coat. Serve immediately. **Yield:** 8 servings.

Nutritional Analysis: 1 cup equals 35 calories, 1 g fat (trace saturated fat), 0 cholesterol, 42 mg sodium, 6 g carbohydrate, 1 g fiber, 1 g protein. **Diabetic Exchange:** 1 vegetable.

Pudding Pumpkin Pie

(Pictured at right)

Prep: 15 min. + chilling

You don't have to spend all day whipping up a good-for-you dessert with this recipe. The nicely spiced pudding pie can be assembled in no time.
—*Sheila Roution Angleton, Texas*

- 1 egg white, beaten
- 1 reduced-fat graham cracker crust (8 inches)
- 1 cup cold fat-free milk
- 1 package (1-1/2 ounces) sugar-free instant vanilla pudding mix
- 1 can (15 ounces) solid-pack pumpkin
- 1 teaspoon pumpkin pie spice
- 1/2 teaspoon ground cinnamon
- 1/2 teaspoon ground nutmeg
- 1-1/2 cups reduced-fat whipped topping, *divided*

Brush egg white over crust. Bake at 375° for 5 minutes or until lightly browned. Cool on a wire rack.

In a large bowl, whisk milk and pudding mix. Stir in the pumpkin, pumpkin pie spice, cinnamon and nutmeg. Fold in 1 cup whipped topping. Pour into crust. Refrigerate for 4 hours or overnight.

Cut into slices; dollop with remaining whipped topping. Refrigerate leftovers. **Yield:** 8 servings.

Nutritional Analysis: 1 piece with 1 tablespoon whipped topping equals 180 calories, 5 g fat (3 g saturated fat), 1 mg cholesterol, 341 mg sodium, 29 g carbohydrate, 2 g fiber, 3 g protein. **Diabetic Exchanges:** 2 starch, 1 fat.

Pudding Pumpkin Pie
Grapefruit Spinach Salad
Glazed Pork Medallions

Three-Bean Chili
Spinach Chicken Pockets

Three-Bean Chili

(Pictured above)

Prep/Total Time: 30 min.

Hearty ingredients and zesty spices will make you forget that this chunky chili is good for you. It's loaded with taste—you'll never miss the meat! —Gail Rector-Evans
Hastings, Oklahoma

2-1/4 cups water
  1 can (16 ounces) kidney beans, rinsed and drained
  1 can (15-1/2 ounces) chili beans, undrained
  1 can (15 ounces) pinto beans, rinsed and drained
  1 can (15 ounces) tomato sauce
  1 can (14-1/2 ounces) no-salt-added stewed tomatoes
  1 can (6 ounces) tomato paste
  1 tablespoon chili powder
  1 teaspoon dried oregano
  1 teaspoon minced garlic
1-1/2 cups fresh *or* frozen corn
1-1/2 cups coarsely chopped yellow summer squash

In a Dutch oven, combine the first 10 ingredients. Bring to a boil. Reduce heat; simmer, uncovered, for 10 minutes. Add the corn and squash. Bring to a boil. Reduce heat; simmer 10 minutes longer or until squash is tender. **Yield:** 10 servings.

  Nutritional Analysis: 1 cup equals 236 calories, 1 g fat (trace saturated fat), 0 cholesterol, 722 mg sodium, 48 g carbohydrate, 13 g fiber, 12 g protein. **Diabetic Exchanges:** 2-1/2 starch, 2 vegetable.

Spinach Chicken Pockets

(Pictured above)

Prep/Total Time: 30 min.

The tender chicken mixture that's tucked into these pita pockets gets zip from cumin and has refreshing cucumber-and-yogurt flavor. A favorite at my house, this sandwich is great alone or served with soup or salad.
—Mitzi Sentiff
Alexandria, Virginia

3/4 pound boneless skinless chicken breast halves
1/2 cup reduced-fat plain yogurt
  2 tablespoons reduced-fat mayonnaise
  1 tablespoon Dijon mustard
1/4 teaspoon ground cumin
1/8 teaspoon cayenne pepper
  2 cups fresh baby spinach
1/2 cup chopped seeded cucumber
  2 green onions, sliced
  4 pita breads (6 inches), halved

In a large nonstick skillet coated with nonstick cooking spray, cook chicken over medium heat for 10-12 minutes on each side or until juices run clear. Remove; thinly slice chicken and cool.

  Meanwhile, in a small bowl, combine the yogurt,

mayonnaise, mustard, cumin and cayenne; set aside. In a large bowl, combine the spinach, cucumber, onions and chicken. Drizzle with yogurt mixture; toss to coat. Microwave pita breads for 15-20 seconds or until warmed. Fill each half with 1/2 cup chicken mixture. **Yield:** 4 servings.

Nutritional Analysis: 2 filled pita halves equals 317 calories, 6 g fat (1 g saturated fat), 51 mg cholesterol, 552 mg sodium, 39 g carbohydrate, 2 g fiber, 25 g protein. **Diabetic Exchanges:** 2-1/2 very lean meat, 2 starch, 1 vegetable, 1 fat.

Pistachio Fluff

Prep/Total Time: 10 min.

No one will suspect this creamy dessert is on the lighter side. You can whip up the colorful treat without much effort. —Lucia Johnson, Massena, New York

1-1/2 cups fat-free vanilla yogurt
   1 can (8 ounces) unsweetened crushed pineapple, undrained
   1 package (1 ounce) sugar-free instant pistachio pudding mix

In a small bowl, combine all ingredients. Refrigerate until serving. **Yield:** 5 servings.

Nutritional Analysis: 1/2 cup equals 75 calories, trace fat (trace saturated fat), 2 mg cholesterol, 280 mg sodium, 16 g carbohydrate, trace fiber, 3 g protein. **Diabetic Exchanges:** 1/2 fat-free milk, 1/2 fruit.

Blended Fruit Chiller

Prep/Total Time: 10 min.

This smoothie is great any time of the day. I especially like to serve it when my kids are in a finicky mood. —Kirsten Gunderson, Ottawa, Ontario

   3 cups (24 ounces) fat-free plain yogurt
   1 cup unsweetened pineapple juice, chilled
   1 cup frozen unsweetened strawberries
   1 medium ripe banana, frozen and sliced
1/2 cup fresh *or* canned unsweetened pineapple chunks
   3 tablespoons honey
   1 teaspoon vanilla extract

Place half of each ingredient in a blender; cover and process until blended. Repeat. **Yield:** 6 servings.

Nutritional Analysis: 1 cup equals 143 calories, trace fat (trace saturated fat), 3 mg cholesterol, 69 mg sodium, 34 g carbohydrate, 2 g fiber, 6 g protein. **Diabetic Exchanges:** 2 fruit, 1/2 fat-free milk.

Chocolate Swirl Cake

(Pictured at right)

Prep: 20 min. **Bake:** 35 min. + cooling

This tasty chocolate cake won't ruin your waistline. Pretty swirls of cream cheese dress it up while cherry pie fill-

ing provides moistness. Sometimes I add miniature chocolate chips for an extra-special treat. —Gail Maki
Marquette, Michigan

   1 package (18-1/4 ounces) chocolate fudge cake mix
   1 can (20 ounces) reduced-sugar cherry pie filling
   5 egg whites
   1 teaspoon vanilla extract
TOPPING:
   1 package (8 ounces) reduced-fat cream cheese
Sugar substitute equivalent to 1/3 cup sugar
   1/2 teaspoon vanilla extract
   2 egg whites

In a large bowl, combine the cake mix, pie filling, egg whites and vanilla just until moistened. Spread into a 13-in. x 9-in. x 2-in. baking dish coated with nonstick cooking spray; set aside.

In a small mixing bowl, beat the cream cheese, sugar substitute and vanilla. Add egg whites; beat on low speed just until combined. Spread over batter; cut through batter with a knife to swirl. Bake at 350° for 35-40 minutes or until a toothpick inserted near the center comes out clean and topping is set. Cool on a wire rack. Store in the refrigerator. **Yield:** 15 servings.

Nutritional Analysis: 1 piece equals 207 calories, 5 g fat (2 g saturated fat), 5 mg cholesterol, 350 mg sodium, 35 g carbohydrate, 1 g fiber, 5 g protein. **Diabetic Exchanges:** 1-1/2 starch, 1 fat, 1/2 fruit.

Editor's Note: This recipe was tested with Splenda No Calorie Sweetener.

Chocolate Swirl Cake

Warm Spinach Dip

(Pictured at right)

Prep/Total Time: 20 min.

I created this lighter version of a hot spinach dip after my husband and five children raved about a similar appetizer at a favorite restaurant. Besides vegetable dippers, serve it with reduced-fat tortilla chips, baked bagel chips or low-fat wheat crackers. —Debbie Marrone
Warner Robins, Georgia

  1 package (10 ounces) frozen chopped
     spinach, thawed and squeezed dry
  4 ounces fat-free cream cheese
1/2 cup shredded reduced-fat cheddar cheese
1/2 cup reduced-fat sour cream
  1 tablespoon spicy brown mustard
  1 teaspoon minced garlic
3/4 teaspoon hot pepper sauce
1/4 teaspoon salt
Assorted fresh vegetables

In a saucepan, combine the first eight ingredients. Bring to a boil over medium heat. Reduce heat; simmer, uncovered, for 7-8 minutes or until cheese is melted, stirring occasionally. Serve warm with vegetables. **Yield:** 2 cups.

Nutritional Analysis: 1/4 cup (calculated without vegetables) equals 64 calories, 3 g fat (2 g saturated fat), 11 mg cholesterol, 259 mg sodium, 4 g carbohydrate, 1 g fiber, 6 g protein. **Diabetic Exchanges:** 1 vegetable, 1/2 lean meat, 1/2 fat.

Avocado Turkey Wraps

(Pictured at right)

Prep/Total Time: 15 min.

These delicious sandwiches, prepared by our Test Kitchen staff, are perfect for late-summer picnics or brown-bag lunches. With sliced turkey, avocado and cheese, they'll add extra flavor to your family's noontime meal. If you like, replace the tomato slices on each wrap with a spoonful of well-drained chunky salsa.

  2 whole wheat tortillas (8 inches), warmed
  2 tablespoons fat-free mayonnaise
1/4 pound thinly sliced deli turkey
  8 thin slices tomato
  2 teaspoons finely chopped jalapeno pepper
1/4 cup shredded reduced-fat cheddar cheese
  2 teaspoons minced fresh cilantro
1/2 medium ripe avocado, peeled and thinly
     sliced

Spread tortillas with mayonnaise. Top each with turkey, tomato, jalapeno, cheese, cilantro and avocado. Roll up and cut in half. **Yield:** 2 servings.

Editor's Note: When cutting or seeding hot peppers, use rubber or plastic gloves to protect your hands. Avoid touching your face.

Nutritional Analysis: 1 wrap equals 279 calories, 13 g fat (4 g saturated fat), 37 mg cholesterol, 1,082 mg sodium, 31 g carbohydrate, 5 g fiber, 17 g protein. **Diabetic Exchanges:** 2 starch, 2 lean meat.

Veggie Chicken Skillet

Prep/Total Time: 30 min.

Almost everyone loves a good chicken dish, and this is one of the best I've tasted. It's simple and fast to prepare because everything cooks in the same skillet. I like to serve it with hot cooked rice. —Lisa Elizabeth Trudeau
Wikwemikong, Ontario

  8 boneless skinless chicken breast halves
     (4 ounces *each*)
  2 tablespoons cornstarch
  1 can (14-1/2 ounces) reduced-sodium chicken
     broth
  2 tablespoons Dijon mustard
  2 tablespoons honey
  2 cups fresh broccoli florets
  1 medium carrot, coarsely chopped
  1 medium onion, chopped
Dash cayenne pepper

In a large nonstick skillet coated with nonstick cooking spray, cook chicken over medium heat for 10-15 minutes or until juices run clear. Remove and keep warm. Combine the cornstarch, broth, mustard and honey until smooth; add to skillet. Bring to a boil; cook and stir for 2 minutes or until thickened.

Return chicken to the pan. Add the broccoli, carrot and onion. Sprinkle with cayenne. Reduce heat; cover and cook for 7-8 minutes or until vegetables are crisp-tender. **Yield:** 8 servings.

Nutritional Analysis: 1 chicken breast half with about 1/3 cup vegetables equals 169 calories, 3 g fat (1 g saturated fat), 63 mg cholesterol, 293 mg sodium, 10 g carbohydrate, 1 g fiber, 25 g protein. **Diabetic Exchanges:** 3 lean meat, 2 vegetable.

Caramel Apple Salad

Prep/Total Time: 15 min.

Kids of all ages will love the caramel apple taste of this easy-to-prepare salad, which could arguably be served as dessert. Salted peanuts nicely complement the pudding and whipped topping in this dish. It's very pretty with red apples or a combination of red and green apples.
—Dawn Harvey, Danville, Pennsylvania

   1 cup cold fat-free milk
   1 package (1 ounce) sugar-free instant
     butterscotch pudding mix
   2 cups reduced-fat whipped topping, *divided*
3-1/2 cups chopped unpeeled apples
 1/2 cup chopped salted peanuts

In a bowl, whisk the milk and pudding mix for 1 minute (mixture will be thick). Whisk in 1 cup whipped topping. Fold in the remaining topping. Fold in apples. Refrigerate until serving. Sprinkle with the peanuts. **Yield:** 6 servings.

Nutritional Analysis: 2/3 cup equals 177 calories, 6 g fat (1 g saturated fat), 1 mg cholesterol, 287 mg sodium, 26 g carbohydrate, 3 g fiber, 5 g protein. **Diabetic Exchanges:** 1 starch, 1 fruit, 1 fat.

Warm Spinach Dip
Avocado Turkey Wraps

Couscous Salad

(Pictured below)

Prep: 20 min. + chilling

I created this simple salad one weekend to bring to a friend's house, and everybody loved it. For extra flavor, dice up some reduced-fat pepperoni and add it to the salad.

—Debbie Graber, Eureka, Nevada

1-1/4 cups water
    1 cup uncooked couscous
    1/2 teaspoon salt
    1/2 cup fat-free Italian salad dressing
    3/4 cup chopped fresh mushrooms
    1 can (2-1/4 ounces) sliced ripe olives, drained
    1/2 cup diced cucumber
    1/3 cup *each* diced onion, green pepper and sweet red pepper

In a small saucepan, bring water to a boil. Stir in couscous and salt. Cover and remove from the heat; let stand for 5 minutes. Fluff with a fork. In a large bowl, combine the couscous, salad dressing, mushrooms, olives, cucumber, onion and peppers. Cover and refrigerate for 20 minutes. **Yield:** 6 servings.

Nutritional Analysis: 1/2 cup equals 147 calories, 2 g fat (trace saturated fat), 1 mg cholesterol, 580 mg sodium, 29 g carbohydrate, 2 g fiber, 5 g protein. **Diabetic Exchanges:** 1-1/2 starch, 1 vegetable.

Broiled Ginger Cod

Prep: 5 min. + marinating **Broil:** 15 min.

I think fish makes the easiest and healthiest of weeknight dinner entrees. Fresh ginger really perks up this moist broiled cod.   *—Carol Gaus, Itasca, Illinois*

    3/4 cup reduced-fat plain yogurt
    3 tablespoons lemon juice
    4 teaspoons minced fresh gingerroot
    2 teaspoons reduced-sodium soy sauce
    2 teaspoons minced garlic
    1 teaspoon ground coriander
    1 teaspoon ground cumin
    3 cod fillets (6 ounces *each*)
    2 tablespoons butter, melted, *divided*

In a small bowl, combine the first seven ingredients. Pour a third of the mixture into an 11-in. x 7-in. x 2-in. dish. Arrange cod fillets in a single layer over top. Spoon remaining yogurt mixture over fillets. Cover and refrigerate for 1-2 hours.

Using a slotted spoon, transfer fillets to a broiler pan coated with nonstick cooking spray. Drizzle with 1 tablespoon butter. Broil 4 in. from the heat for 6 minutes. Carefully turn fillets; brush with remaining butter. Broil 6-8 minutes longer or until fish flakes easily with a fork. **Yield:** 3 servings.

Nutritional Analysis: 1 serving equals 231 calories,

Couscous Salad

9 g fat (5 g saturated fat), 94 mg cholesterol, 254 mg sodium, 4 g carbohydrate, 1 g fiber, 32 g protein. **Diabetic Exchanges:** 4 very lean meat, 2 fat.

Grilled PB&J

Prep/Total Time: 20 min.

I enjoy peanut butter and jelly sandwiches so much, I turned them into a yummy breakfast treat reminiscent of stuffed French toast. I sometimes bake them in the oven, but cooking them in a skillet is quicker. —Sandi Tuttle
Hayward, Wisconsin

1/2 cup egg substitute
1/2 teaspoon vanilla extract
1/8 teaspoon ground cinnamon
  3 tablespoons reduced-fat peanut butter
  4 teaspoons raspberry jam
  4 slices light whole wheat bread

In a small bowl, combine the egg substitute, vanilla and cinnamon. Spread peanut butter and jam over two slices of bread; top with remaining bread. Brush sandwiches with egg substitute mixture.

In a large nonstick skillet coated with nonstick cooking spray, cook sandwiches over medium-high heat for 3-4 minutes on each side or until golden brown. **Yield:** 2 servings.

Nutritional Analysis: One sandwich equals 279 calories, 9 g fat (2 g saturated fat), 0 cholesterol, 493 mg sodium, 38 g carbohydrate, 7 g fiber, 17 g protein. **Diabetic Exchanges:** 2 starch, 2 lean meat, 1/2 fruit.

Chicken Salad Club

Prep/Total Time: 15 min.

My sister and I made this wonderfully light chicken salad for our sister-in-law's bridal shower, and it received rave reviews. It's easy to fix for a large crowd. It's also delicious on croissants or oatmeal bread. —Nan Janecke
Kalamazoo, Michigan

  3 cups shredded cooked chicken breast
3/4 cup chopped celery
  3 tablespoons chopped green onions
1/3 cup plus 1 tablespoon fat-free mayonnaise
1/3 cup plus 1 tablespoon fat-free plain yogurt
  2 tablespoons dried parsley flakes
  1 tablespoon lemon juice
1/2 teaspoon salt
1/4 teaspoon pepper
12 slices white bread *or* 6 hard rolls, split
  6 cooked bacon strips

In a large bowl, combine the chicken, celery and onions. Add the mayonnaise, yogurt, parsley, lemon juice, salt and pepper; mix well. Serve on bread with a strip of bacon. **Yield:** 6 servings.

Nutritional Analysis: 1 sandwich equals 315 calories, 9 g fat (2 g saturated fat), 67 mg cholesterol, 771 mg sodium, 29 g carbohydrate, 2 g fiber, 29 g protein. **Diabetic Exchanges:** 3-1/2 lean meat, 2 starch, 1 fat.

Very Berry Pie

Very Berry Pie

(Pictured above)

Prep: 15 min. + chilling

I came up with this creamy berry-filled pie when I needed a low-fat dessert for a get-together. My husband loves this pie and raves about how good it is.
—Becky Thompson, Maryville, Tennessee

1-3/4 cups reduced-fat whipped topping, *divided*
  1 reduced-fat graham cracker crust (8 inches)
  1 cup fresh raspberries
  1 cup fresh blueberries
Sugar substitute equivalent to 1 tablespoon sugar
  1 cup cold fat-free milk
  1 package (1 ounce) sugar-free instant white chocolate pudding mix

Spread 1/4 cup whipped topping into the crust. Combine berries and sugar substitute; spoon 1 cup over topping. In a bowl, whisk the milk and pudding mix for 2 minutes; let stand for 2 minutes or until soft-set. Spoon over berries. Spread with remaining whipped topping. Top with remaining berries. Refrigerate for 45 minutes or until set. **Yield:** 8 servings.

Nutritional Analysis: 1 piece equals 214 calories, 5 g fat (3 g saturated fat), 1 mg cholesterol, 259 mg sodium, 39 g carbohydrate, 2 g fiber, 2 g protein. **Diabetic Exchanges:** 1-1/2 fruit, 1 starch, 1 fat.

Editor's Note: This recipe was tested with Splenda No Calorie Sweetener.

Chapter 19

IF YOU COOK for just a few—and don't care for a lot of leftovers—you'll find these rapid recipes to be twice as nice!

That's because each delicious dish not only is fast to fix, it's sized right for two people. So you can enjoy quick home-cooked creations without filling your fridge with extras.

Choose from fabulous downsized recipes like Spicy Chicken Enchiladas, Potato Ham Chowder, Squash Ribbons and Blueberry Dessert Squares. You'll be amazed at how easy it is to prepare terrific fare with fewer servings.

Whether you want sandwiches, salads or a complete dinner menu, these cut-down dishes will prove doubly delightful.

DINNER DUO. Broccoli Cheese Crepes (p. 277) and Strawberry Avocado Salad (p. 279).

Stuffing-Coated Chicken

(Pictured below)

Prep: 10 min. **Bake:** 25 min.

Stuffing mix gives these moist chicken breasts a fast coating you'll both enjoy. I sometimes like to make them in my toaster oven. —Rosemary Dibble, Sandy, Utah

☑ Uses less fat, sugar or salt. Includes Nutritional Analysis and Diabetic Exchanges.

- 1 envelope individual serving cream of chicken soup mix
- 1/3 cup hot water
- 3/4 cup stuffing mix
- 2 boneless skinless chicken breast halves (4 ounces *each*)
- 1 tablespoon butter, melted

In a shallow bowl, stir the soup mix and water until blended. Place the stuffing mix in another shallow bowl. Dip the chicken in the soup mixture, then coat with stuffing. Place in an 8-in. square baking dish coated with nonstick cooking spray. Drizzle with butter. Bake, uncovered, at 375° for 25-30 minutes or until the juices run clear. **Yield:** 2 servings.

Nutritional Analysis: 1 serving (prepared with reduced-fat butter) equals 269 calories, 8 g fat (4 g saturated fat), 74 mg cholesterol, 913 mg sodium, 20 g carbohydrate, 1 g fiber, 27 g protein. **Diabetic Exchanges:** 3 lean meat, 1 starch.

Squash Ribbons

(Pictured below)

Prep/Total Time: 15 min.

These pretty vegetable ribbons shared by our Test Kitchen home economists are sure to dress up your dinner plate. Steamed and tossed with herbs, the curls of summer squash and zucchini make a healthy, versatile side dish.

☑ Uses less fat, sugar or salt. Includes Nutritional Analysis and Diabetic Exchanges.

- 1 small yellow summer squash
- 1 small zucchini
- 3 teaspoons butter, melted
- 1/4 teaspoon onion powder
- 1/4 teaspoon dried rosemary, crushed
- 1/8 teaspoon salt
- 1/8 teaspoon dried thyme
- 1/8 teaspoon pepper

With a vegetable peeler or metal cheese slicer, cut very thin slices down the length of each squash, making long ribbons. Place in a steamer basket in a saucepan over 1 in. of boiling water. Cover and steam for 2-3 minutes or until tender.

In a small bowl, combine the butter, onion powder, rosemary, salt, thyme and pepper. Add squash and toss to coat. **Yield:** 2 servings.

Nutritional Analysis: 3/4 cup (prepared with reduced-fat butter) equals 55 calories, 3 g fat (2 g saturated fat),

**Stuffing-Coated Chicken
Squash Ribbons**

10 mg cholesterol, 187 mg sodium, 6 g carbohydrate, 3 g fiber, 2 g protein. **Diabetic Exchanges:** 1 vegetable, 1/2 fat.

Fried Rice with Chicken

Prep/Total Time: 25 min.

I love fixing this recipe for my husband and me. Every time I make it, I try adding something new. I like to serve it with sweet-and-sour sauce.
—Susan Johnson
Rockford, Illinois

   3 bacon strips, diced
1/2 pound boneless skinless chicken breasts, cubed
   1 medium carrot, chopped
   1 celery rib, chopped
   2 eggs, beaten
1-1/2 cups cooked rice
   2 tablespoons soy sauce

In a large skillet, cook bacon over medium heat until crisp. Remove to paper towels. In the drippings, saute the chicken, carrot and celery until chicken juices run clear; remove and keep warm. In the same skillet, scramble eggs over medium heat, breaking into small pieces. Stir in the chicken mixture, rice, soy sauce and bacon. **Yield:** 2 servings.

Broccoli Cheese Crepes

(Pictured on page 274)

Prep: 30 min. + standing **Bake:** 5 min.

This recipe is perfect to prepare for a special brunch or light dinner for two. I tuck a cheesy mixture made with frozen chopped broccoli into tender homemade crepes.
—Jane Shapton, Tustin, California

   2 eggs
1/4 cup water
   6 tablespoons all-purpose flour
1/2 teaspoon salt
FILLING:
   2 tablespoons chopped onion
   1 tablespoon butter
   1 tablespoon all-purpose flour
   1 cup milk
   1 cup (4 ounces) shredded cheddar cheese, *divided*
   1 to 1-1/2 teaspoons Dijon mustard
   1 teaspoon Worcestershire sauce
1/4 teaspoon pepper
1/8 teaspoon salt
   2 cups frozen chopped broccoli, thawed

For batter, combine eggs, water, flour and salt in a blender. Cover and process until smooth; let stand for 15 minutes.

Meanwhile, in a small saucepan, saute the onion in butter until tender. Stir in flour until blended. Gradually stir in milk. Bring to a boil over medium heat, stirring constantly; cook and stir for 2 minutes or until slightly thickened. Reduce heat to low. Stir in 1/2 cup cheese,

Almond Apricot Bars

mustard, Worcestershire sauce, pepper and salt until cheese is melted. Stir in broccoli. Cover; keep warm.

Heat a lightly greased 8-in. nonstick skillet; pour 2 tablespoons batter into center of skillet. Lift and tilt pan to coat bottom evenly. Cook until top appears dry; turn and cook 15-20 seconds longer. Remove to a wire rack. Repeat with remaining batter, buttering skillet as needed.

Spoon about 1/2 cup filling down the center of each crepe; roll up. Place seam side down in an ungreased 11-in. x 7-in. x 2-in. baking dish. Sprinkle with remaining cheese. Bake, uncovered, at 350° for 5-7 minutes or until cheese is melted. **Yield:** 6 filled crepes.

Almond Apricot Bars

(Pictured above)

Prep: 15 min. **Bake:** 45 min. + cooling

Apricot jam provides the fruit flavor in this small pan of nutty dessert bars. They freeze well and are also good with seedless raspberry jam instead of apricot.
—Olga Wolkosky, Richmond, British Columbia

   2 cups vanilla *or* white chips, *divided*
1/2 cup butter, softened
1/2 cup sugar
   2 eggs
   1 teaspoon vanilla extract
   1 cup all-purpose flour
3/4 cup apricot jam
1/2 cup sliced almonds

In a microwave, melt 1 cup chips; set aside. In a large mixing bowl, cream butter and sugar. Add eggs, one at a time, beating well after each addition. Beat in melted chips and vanilla. Gradually beat in flour. Spread half of the batter into a greased 8-in. square baking dish. Bake at 325° for 15-20 minutes or until golden brown. Spread with jam.

Stir remaining chips into remaining batter. Drop by tablespoonfuls over jam; carefully spread over top. Sprinkle with almonds. Bake for 30-35 minutes or until golden brown. Cool completely on a wire rack. Cut into squares; cut squares in half. **Yield:** 1-1/2 dozen.

Herbed Lamb Chops
Veggie Stir-Fry

Herbed Lamb Chops

(Pictured above)

Prep/Total Time: 30 min.

This nicely seasoned lamb tastes marvelous whether sauteed on the stovetop or grilled on a hibachi. For a special meal, the chops are wonderful with parsley rice and lemon tarts. —Marion Lowery, Medford, Oregon

      1 teaspoon *each* dried thyme, oregano and
         rosemary, crushed
  1/2 teaspoon salt
  1/2 teaspoon ground coriander
  1/4 teaspoon pepper
Dash paprika
      4 lamb loin chops (about 1-1/4 inches thick)
  1/3 cup vegetable oil
  1/4 cup lemon juice
      3 bay leaves
      1 teaspoon grated lemon peel
      1 tablespoon butter, softened

In a small bowl, combine the seasonings; set aside 1/4 teaspoon. Rub remaining herb mixture over both sides of lamb chops. In a large resealable plastic bag, combine the oil, lemon juice, bay leaves and lemon peel. Add chops; seal bag and turn to coat. Let stand for 5 minutes; drain.

In a large skillet, brown the chops for 2 minutes on each side. Reduce heat to medium. Cover and cook for 4-6 minutes on each side or until the meat reaches desired doneness (for medium-rare, a meat thermometer should

read 145°; medium, 160°; well-done, 170°). Top the chops with butter and sprinkle with the reserved herb mixture. **Yield:** 2 servings.

Veggie Stir-Fry

(Pictured above)

Prep/Total Time: 15 min.

I stir-fry a medley of six vegetables to create this colorful side dish. It can even make a great meatless main course served on a bed of rice. Cook the rice while you're preparing the rest of this dish, and you'll have dinner in 15 minutes.
—Valerie Belley, St. Louis, Missouri

✓ Uses less fat, sugar or salt. Includes Nutritional Analysis and Diabetic Exchanges.

      2 teaspoons cornstarch
  1/2 cup cold water
      3 tablespoons soy sauce
      1 cup fresh broccoli florets
      1 medium carrot, thinly sliced
  1/2 small onion, julienned
      1 tablespoon vegetable oil
      1 cup shredded cabbage
      1 small zucchini, julienned
      6 large mushrooms, sliced
  1/2 teaspoon minced garlic
Hot cooked rice, optional

In a small bowl, whisk the cornstarch, water and soy sauce until smooth; set aside. In a large skillet or wok, stir-fry the broccoli, carrot and onion in oil for 5 minutes. Add the cabbage, zucchini, mushrooms and garlic. Stir-fry until vegetables are tender. Stir soy sauce mixture; add to skillet. Cook and stir until thickened. Serve with rice if desired. **Yield:** 2 servings.

Nutritional Analysis: 1 cup (prepared with reduced-sodium soy sauce; calculated without rice) equals 150 calories, 7 g fat (1 g saturated fat), 0 cholesterol, 939 mg sodium, 17 g carbohydrate, 5 g fiber, 6 g protein. **Diabetic Exchanges:** 3 vegetable, 1-1/2 fat.

Strawberry Avocado Salad

(Pictured on page 274)

Prep/Total Time: 15 min.

I blend together a sweet and tangy dressing to drizzle over this pretty salad. Substitute a little freshly grated onion instead of onion powder if you have an onion on hand. —Nancy Johnson, Laverne, Oklahoma

    2 tablespoons sugar
    2 tablespoons olive oil
    4 teaspoons honey
    1 tablespoon cider vinegar
    1 teaspoon lemon juice
1/4 teaspoon salt
1/4 teaspoon celery seed, crushed
1/4 teaspoon ground mustard
1/4 teaspoon paprika
1/8 teaspoon onion powder
    2 cups torn mixed salad greens
    1 medium ripe avocado, peeled and sliced
    6 medium fresh strawberries, sliced

In a small bowl, whisk the first 10 ingredients. Arrange greens on two salad plates; top with avocado and strawberries. Drizzle with the dressing. **Yield:** 2 servings.

California Pizzas

(Pictured at right)

Prep/Total Time: 20 min.

This is a delicious lunch or light dinner for a pair. Tortillas make the convenient crust for these crispy personal pizzas topped with fresh vegetables and cheese. —Sheila Martin, LaQuinta, California

✓ Uses less fat, sugar or salt. Includes Nutritional Analysis and Diabetic Exchanges.

1/2 cup chopped onion
1/2 cup chopped green pepper
    2 teaspoons canola oil
    2 flour tortillas (6 inches)
1/4 teaspoon dried oregano
1/8 teaspoon garlic powder
    1 medium tomato, sliced
1/2 cup shredded mozzarella cheese

In a small skillet, saute onion and green pepper in oil until tender. Place tortillas on an ungreased baking sheet.

Top with onion mixture, oregano, garlic powder, tomato and cheese. Bake at 400° for 8-10 minutes or until cheese is melted. Cut each pizza into four wedges. **Yield:** 2 servings.

Nutritional Analysis: 4 wedges (prepared with part-skim mozzarella) equals 245 calories, 13 g fat (3 g saturated fat), 16 mg cholesterol, 364 mg sodium, 23 g carbohydrate, 2 g fiber, 11 g protein. **Diabetic Exchanges:** 1-1/2 starch, 1-1/2 fat, 1 lean meat.

Celery Seed Vinaigrette

(Pictured below)

Prep/Total Time: 15 min.

I need just a few minutes to stir up this simple salad dressing for two. If you like, double the recipe so you'll have extra for later in the week. Leftover vinaigrette will keep in the refrigerator for about 3 days. —Edie Farm
Farmington, New Mexico

1/4 cup vegetable oil
    2 tablespoons cider vinegar
1-1/2 teaspoons sugar
1/2 teaspoon minced garlic
1/4 teaspoon salt
1/8 teaspoon celery seed
1/8 teaspoon ground mustard
1/8 teaspoon grated onion
Mixed salad greens

In a jar with a tight-fitting lid, combine the first eight ingredients; shake well. Serve over salad greens. **Yield:** about 1/4 cup.

Celery Seed Vinaigrette
California Pizzas

Breaded Sea Scallops

(Pictured below)

Prep/Total Time: 15 min.

I never liked seafood until my husband urged me to try scallops, and now I love them. He says my breaded version is the best he's ever had. I put them on paper towels to soak up the excess oil. —Martina Preston
Willow Grove, Pennsylvania

> 1 egg
> 1/3 cup mashed potato flakes
> 1/3 cup seasoned bread crumbs
> 1/4 teaspoon salt
> 1/8 teaspoon pepper
> 3/4 pound sea scallops
> 2 tablespoons butter
> 1 tablespoon vegetable oil

In a shallow bowl, beat the egg. In another bowl, combine the potato flakes, bread crumbs, salt and pepper. Dip scallops in egg, then roll in potato mixture.

In a large skillet, heat butter and oil over medium heat. Add scallops; cook for 4-5 minutes or until scallops are opaque and coating is golden brown, turning once. **Yield:** 2 servings.

Sesame Steamed Vegetables

(Pictured below)

Prep/Total Time: 15 min.

Broccoli grows abundantly during the long summer days here. I like to harvest it and freeze it along with julienned

Breaded Sea Scallops
Sesame Steamed Vegetables

carrots, so this is always ready to go. The two vegetables are wonderful together, and the judges at our state fair even awarded this dish a first prize. —Heidi Doudna
Fairbanks, Alaska

✓ Uses less fat, sugar or salt. Includes Nutritional Analysis and Diabetic Exchanges.

> 1-1/2 cups fresh broccoli florets
> 1 small carrot, julienned and cut into 2-inch pieces
> 1/4 cup sliced celery
> 3 tablespoons sliced water chestnuts
> 1 tablespoon water
> 1 tablespoon butter
> 1-1/2 teaspoons soy sauce
> 3/4 teaspoon sesame seeds, toasted

In a small saucepan, combine the broccoli, carrot, celery, water chestnuts, water, butter and soy sauce; bring to a boil. Cover and steam for 4-6 minutes or until vegetables are crisp-tender. Sprinkle with sesame seeds. **Yield:** 2 servings.

Nutritional Analysis: 2/3 cup (prepared with reduced-fat butter and reduced-sodium soy sauce) equals 68 calories, 4 g fat (2 g saturated fat), 10 mg cholesterol, 229 mg sodium, 8 g carbohydrate, 3 g fiber, 3 g protein. **Diabetic Exchanges:** 2 vegetable, 1/2 fat.

Potato Ham Chowder

Prep/Total Time: 30 min.

I find that homemade is always best, especially when it comes to soup. This rich dill-seasoned broth features hearty chunks of potatoes and ham. —Esther Danielson
Lake Arrowhead, California

✓ Uses less fat, sugar or salt. Includes Nutritional Analysis and Diabetic Exchanges.

> 3/4 cup cubed fully cooked ham
> 1/4 cup chopped onion
> 2 tablespoons chopped celery
> 1 tablespoon butter
> 1 cup chicken broth
> 1 cup cubed peeled potatoes
> 4 teaspoons all-purpose flour
> 1-1/3 cups 2% milk
> 1/4 teaspoon dill weed
> 1/8 teaspoon pepper

In a small saucepan, saute the ham, onion and celery in butter for 5 minutes or until ham is lightly browned and vegetables are tender. Add the broth and potatoes; bring to a boil. Reduce heat; cover and simmer for 15-20 minutes or until potatoes are tender.

In a small bowl, combine flour and milk until smooth; stir into chowder. Add dill and pepper. Bring to a boil, stirring constantly; cook for 1 minute or until thickened. **Yield:** 2 servings.

Nutritional Analysis: 1-1/2 cups equals 319 calories, 14 g fat (7 g saturated fat), 55 mg cholesterol, 1,286 mg sodium, 31 g carbohydrate, 2 g fiber, 18 g protein. **Diabetic Exchanges:** 2-1/2 lean meat, 2 starch, 1/2 fat.

Simple Squash and Sausage

Citrus Apple Crisp

Prep: 15 min. **Bake:** 35 min.

This smaller-sized crisp is sure to disappear as quickly at your home as it does at ours. We like it served warm with a little cream or a scoop of ice cream.
—Audrey Lanier, Amite, Louisiana

    4 cups chopped peeled tart apples (about 3
      large)
    2 tablespoons lemon juice
  1/2 cup raisins
  1/2 cup orange marmalade
    2 tablespoons all-purpose flour
  1/2 teaspoon ground cinnamon
    1 cup granola cereal with nuts

In a bowl, toss the apples and lemon juice. Add the raisins, marmalade, flour and cinnamon; stir to combine. Transfer to a greased 8-in. square baking dish. Sprinkle with granola. Bake, uncovered, at 350° for 35-40 minutes or until filling is bubbly. Serve warm. **Yield:** 6 servings.

Hearty English Muffins

Prep/Total Time: 20 min.

My husband and I enjoy these quick bites for breakfast before we start work on our dairy farm. Sometimes we top them with pizza sauce or a squirt of ketchup.
—Christine Weber, Palmerston, Ontario

    5 eggs, beaten
  1/2 cup shredded cheddar cheese

  1/2 teaspoon snipped chives
Salt and pepper to taste
    4 bacon strips
    2 English muffins, split and toasted

In a bowl, combine the eggs, cheese, chives, salt and pepper. Pour into a nonstick skillet; cook and stir over medium heat until eggs are completely set. Meanwhile, cut bacon strips in half widthwise; cook until crisp. Place two bacon pieces on each English muffin half; top with eggs. **Yield:** 2 servings.

Simple Squash and Sausage

(Pictured above)

Prep/Total Time: 20 min.

Dinner doesn't get any easier than this stovetop meal for two that I created one night. My husband insisted that I remember the colorful combination so that I could make it again. *—Lela Rauch, Oakland, Michigan*

  1/2 pound fully cooked smoked sausage, cut
      into 1/4-inch slices
    1 tablespoon olive oil
    1 medium zucchini, cut into 1/4-inch slices
    1 medium yellow summer squash, cut
      into 1/4-inch slices
    2 tablespoons apricot preserves

In a large skillet, saute sausage in oil until lightly browned; remove and keep warm. In the same skillet, saute the zucchini and yellow squash until crisp-tender. Return sausage to the pan. Stir in preserves. Cook and stir until heated through. **Yield:** 2 servings.

Spicy Chicken Enchiladas

Spicy Roast Beef Sandwiches

Prep/Total Time: 20 min.

Jalapenos add zip to this quick-to-assemble combo of roast beef and cheese. It's a good hot sandwich to eat in the car or to take to sporting events. —Shirley Wayne
Laguna Woods, California

> 2 teaspoons butter, softened
> 2 kaiser rolls, split
> 1/2 pound thinly sliced deli roast beef
> 2 slices Monterey Jack cheese
> 1 to 2 teaspoons canned diced jalapeno peppers

Spread butter over the cut sides of rolls. Layer beef, cheese and peppers on the bottom halves; replace tops. Wrap each sandwich in foil; place on an ungreased baking sheet. Bake at 350° for 10-15 minutes or until the cheese is melted. **Yield:** 2 servings.
   Editor's Note: When handling hot peppers, use rubber or plastic gloves to protect your hands. Avoid touching your face.

Portobello Melts

Prep/Total Time: 25 min.

We are always looking for satisfying vegetarian meals, and this one is packed with flavor. Large portobello mushrooms are marinated and topped with cheese, basil and tomatoes for these melts. They're especially good with garden tomatoes.
—Amy Smalley, Morehead, Kentucky

> 1/4 cup olive oil
> 2 tablespoons balsamic vinegar
> 1/2 teaspoon salt
> 1/2 teaspoon dried basil
> 2 large portobello mushrooms (1/2 pound)
> 6 fresh basil leaves
> 4 tomato slices
> 2 slices mozzarella cheese
> 2 slices Italian bread (1 inch thick)

In a large resealable plastic bag, combine the oil, vinegar, salt and dried basil. Remove and discard stems from mushrooms. Add mushroom caps to marinade; let stand for 5 minutes. Drain, reserving marinade.
   Place mushrooms, cap side down, on a greased broiler pan. Broil 4 in. from the heat for 3 minutes. Turn and broil 3-4 minutes longer or until tender. Top with basil leaves, tomato and cheese. Broil for 1 minute or until cheese is melted.
   Place bread on an ungreased baking sheet. Brush with reserved marinade. Broil 4 in. from the heat for 1 minute or until lightly toasted. Top with mushrooms. **Yield:** 2 servings.

Spicy Chicken Enchiladas

(Pictured above)

Prep/Total Time: 30 min.

Cooked chicken strips and canned enchilada sauce hurry along this zesty entree. I came up with it shortly after I got married. It's a delicious dinner for two that's easy to double for company. —Amy Dando, Endicott, New York

> 1 package (6 ounces) ready-to-use
>   Southwestern chicken strips
> 1-1/2 cups (6 ounces) shredded cheddar cheese,
>   *divided*
> 1 can (10 ounces) enchilada sauce, *divided*
> 1 cup refried beans
> 4 flour tortillas (7 inches), warmed
> 1 can (2-1/2 ounces) sliced ripe olives, drained
> Chopped tomato and shredded lettuce, optional

In a bowl, combine the chicken, 1 cup cheese and 1/2 cup enchilada sauce. Spread 1/4 cup refried beans down the center of each tortilla. Top with chicken mixture; roll up.
   Place in two ungreased small baking dishes. Top with the remaining enchilada sauce and cheese; sprinkle with olives. Cover and bake at 400° for 15-20 minutes or until heated through. Garnish with tomato and lettuce if desired. **Yield:** 2 servings.

Corn and Pea Medley

Prep/Total Time: 15 min.

Our Test Kitchen home economists sized this fresh-tasting side dish so it's perfect for a pair. Complete with a but-

tery dill sauce, it makes an ideal dinner accompaniment to nearly any main course.

✓ Uses less fat, sugar or salt. Includes Nutritional Analysis and Diabetic Exchanges.

1-1/2 cups fresh *or* frozen sugar snap peas
1/3 cup frozen corn
1 to 2 tablespoons chopped onion
2 teaspoons butter
3/4 teaspoon lemon juice
1/4 to 1/2 teaspoon dill weed
Pepper to taste

In a small saucepan, place 1 in. of water. Add peas and corn. Bring to a boil. Reduce heat; cover and simmer for 5-6 minutes or until peas are crisp-tender. Meanwhile, in another saucepan, saute onion in butter until tender. Stir in the lemon juice, dill and pepper. Drain peas and corn; add the onion mixture and stir to coat. **Yield:** 2 servings.

Nutritional Analysis: 1 cup (prepared with reduced-fat butter) equals 87 calories, 2 g fat (1 g saturated fat), 7 mg cholesterol, 33 mg sodium, 12 g carbohydrate, 3 g fiber, 3 g protein. **Diabetic Exchanges:** 2 vegetable, 1/2 fat.

Blueberry Dessert Squares

Prep: 10 min. **Bake:** 45 min.

This easy dessert will satisfy any sweet tooth. The recipe makes a smaller pan, but you will still have enough flavorful fruit bars to share...or to enjoy the next day. These squares are best served warm and topped with ice cream.
—Lori Halme, Battle Ground, Washington

1 cup all-purpose flour
1 cup quick-cooking oats
1 cup packed brown sugar
1/2 teaspoon salt
1/2 cup shortening
2-1/2 cups fresh *or* frozen blueberries
1/4 cup sugar

In a large bowl, combine the flour, oats, brown sugar and salt. Cut in shortening until crumbly. Press half of the mixture into a greased 9-in. square baking dish. Bake at 350° for 10 minutes or until brown around the edges.

Combine the blueberries and sugar; sprinkle over crust. Top with remaining oat mixture; press down gently. Bake 35-40 minutes longer or until golden brown. Serve warm. **Yield:** 9 servings.

Editor's Note: If using frozen blueberries, do not thaw.

Apricot-Pecan Mini Loaves

(Pictured at right)

Prep: 10 min. **Bake:** 45 min. + cooling

Chopped nuts and a hint of apricot make these little loaves a delightful treat. Instead of preparing two mini breads, you could bake just one loaf in a standard loaf pan.
—Nancy Foust, Stoneboro, Pennsylvania

2 tablespoons shortening
1 cup sugar
1 egg
1/2 cup milk
1/3 cup apricot baby food with mixed fruit
1-1/2 cups all-purpose flour
1/2 teaspoon baking soda
1/4 teaspoon salt
1/4 cup chopped pecans

In a small mixing bowl, cream shortening and sugar. Add the egg, milk and baby food. Combine the flour, baking soda and salt; gradually add to creamed mixture. Fold in pecans.

Transfer to two greased and floured 5-3/4-in. x 3-in. x 2-in. loaf pans. Bake at 350° for 45-50 minutes or until a toothpick inserted near the center comes out clean. Cool for 10 minutes before removing from pans to a wire rack. The loaves may be frozen for up to 3 months. **Yield:** 2 loaves.

Handy Kitchen Hints

- I've found that inexpensive paper plates make great covers for food in the microwave. They're easy to use, and the food doesn't stick to the plates.
—*Lara Dillon, Mt. Juliet, Tennessee*

- When beginning to cook a meal, I take out a dinner plate and set it on the counter as a "parking place" for measuring cups, measuring spoons, spatulas and any other utensils I might use. The plate is larger than a spoon rest, and it makes cleanup afterward a lot easier. —*Lynn Scheiderer, Morgan Hill, California*

Apricot-Pecan Mini Loaves

WHEN HUNGER HITS but dinnertime's still a long way off, you want something that'll satisfy appetites fast. You don't want to spend hours in the kitchen preparing it!

So count on the sensational snacks and appetizers offered here. From Sweet 'n' Crunchy Mix and Granola Banana Sticks to Chocolate Mint Wafers and Dilly Veggie Pizza, every delightful bite comes together in a snap to give you tasty munchies in no time flat.

Whether you need impressive hot hors d'oeuvres for company or no-bake goodies to tide the kids over until supper, you'll find fantastic foods that are guaranteed to please.

FUN FINGER FOODS. Granola Banana Sticks (p. 293), Italian Snack Mix (p. 290), PB&J Spirals (p. 286) and Bacon Nachos (p. 291).

Hot Lemon Artichoke Dip

Hot Lemon Artichoke Dip

(Pictured above)

Prep/Total Time: 15 min.

I found this recipe more than 15 years ago, and it has been requested every time I've been invited to a party. Since this dip is heated in the microwave instead of the oven, it can be ready to serve guests in mere minutes. —Robin Klawinski Eagle, Idaho

1/2 cup sour cream
1/2 cup mayonnaise
6 ounces brick cheese, shredded
1 can (14 ounces) artichoke hearts, rinsed, drained and coarsely chopped
1/2 cup grated Parmesan cheese
1/2 teaspoon grated lemon peel
1/8 teaspoon garlic powder
1/8 teaspoon white pepper
1 tablespoon minced fresh parsley
Crackers and fresh vegetables

In a 1-qt. microwave-safe serving bowl, combine sour cream and mayonnaise. Microwave, uncovered, on high for 1-2 minutes or until bubbly, stirring occasionally.

Stir in the brick cheese, artichokes, Parmesan cheese, lemon peel, garlic powder and pepper. Microwave on high for 3 minutes or until cheese is melted, stirring several times. Stir in parsley. Serve warm with crackers and vegetables. **Yield:** 2-1/3 cups.

Editor's Note: Reduced-fat or fat-free mayonnaise is not recommended for this recipe. It was tested in a 1,100-watt microwave.

Barbecue Chicken Bites

Prep/Total Time: 25 min.

Folks who enjoy the taste of barbecue will gobble up these tender chunks of chicken coated in crushed barbecue potato chips. They're a hit at home and at parties.
—Celena Cantrell, Eau Claire, Michigan

1 egg
2 tablespoons milk
4 cups barbecue potato chips, crushed
1/2 pound boneless skinless chicken breasts, cut into 1-1/2-inch cubes
Barbecue sauce

In a shallow bowl, whisk egg and milk. Place potato chips in another shallow bowl. Dip chicken in egg mixture, then roll in chips. Place in a single layer on a greased baking sheet. Bake at 400° for 10-15 minutes or until juices run clear. Serve with barbecue sauce. **Yield:** 4 servings.

Roast Beef Pinwheels

Prep/Total Time: 15 min.

You'll need just six ingredients to make these fast-to-fix pinwheels that are mildly seasoned with ranch dressing mix, garlic and green onions. Hearty and fun to eat, these roast beef snacks are a great way to ease your hunger until mealtime arrives. I like that I can prepare them ahead of time, too. —Randy Young, Shelbyville, Indiana

✓ Uses less fat, sugar or salt. Includes Nutritional Analysis and Diabetic Exchanges.

1 cup (8 ounces) sour cream
2 tablespoons ranch salad dressing mix
1/2 teaspoon minced garlic
1/4 cup finely chopped green onions
4 flour tortillas (10 inches)
1/2 pound thinly sliced deli roast beef

In a small bowl, combine sour cream, salad dressing mix and garlic. Stir in onions. Spread over tortillas; top with beef. Roll up tightly. Cut into 1-in. pieces; secure with toothpicks. Chill until serving. Discard toothpicks before serving. **Yield:** about 3 dozen.

Nutritional Analysis: 1 piece (prepared with reduced-fat sour cream and lean roast beef) equals 80 calories, 2 g fat (1 g saturated fat), 8 mg cholesterol, 300 mg sodium, 8 g carbohydrate, 1 g fiber, 5 g protein. **Diabetic Exchanges:** 1/2 starch, 1/2 lean meat.

PB&J Spirals

(Pictured on page 285)

Prep/Total Time: 30 min.

Kids young and old love these peanut butter and jelly treats that call for refrigerated crescent roll dough. They're

a fun snack for hungry youngsters to assemble; parents just have to help with the baking. Plus, they're easy to vary by using different nuts or jelly flavors.   —Lisa Renshaw
Kansas City, Missouri

- 1 tube (8 ounces) refrigerated crescent rolls
- 8 teaspoons creamy peanut butter
- 8 teaspoons grape jelly
- 1/4 cup chopped unsalted peanuts
- 2 tablespoons confectioners' sugar

Unroll crescent dough; separate into triangles. Spread 1 teaspoon each of peanut butter and jelly on the wide end of each triangle; sprinkle with peanuts. Roll up each from the wide end and place point side down 2 in. apart on an ungreased baking sheet. Curve ends to form a crescent shape.

Bake spirals at 375° for 11-13 minutes or until lightly browned. Dust with confectioners' sugar. Serve warm. **Yield:** 8 servings.

Mini Bagelizzas

Crispy Crab Rangoon

(Pictured below)

Prep/Total Time: 30 min.

My husband loved the appetizers we ordered at a Chinese restaurant so much that I was determined to make them at home. After two more trips to the restaurant to taste them again and about four home trials, I had them perfected.
—*Cathy Blankman, Warroad, Minnesota*

Crispy Crab Rangoon

- 1 package (3 ounces) cream cheese, softened
- 2 green onions, finely chopped
- 1/4 cup finely chopped imitation crabmeat
- 1 teaspoon minced garlic
- 16 wonton wrappers

Oil for frying
Sweet-and-sour sauce

In a small mixing bowl, beat cream cheese until smooth. Add the onions, crab and garlic; mix well. Place about 1-1/2 teaspoons in the center of each wonton wrapper. Moisten edges with water; fold opposite corners over filling and press to seal.

In an electric skillet, heat 1 in. of oil to 375°. Fry wontons for 1-2 minutes or until golden brown, turning once. Drain on paper towels. Serve with sweet-and-sour sauce. **Yield:** 16 appetizers.

Editor's Note: Fill wonton wrappers a few at a time, keeping the others covered until ready to use.

Mini Bagelizzas

(Pictured above)

Prep/Total Time: 25 min.

Garlic powder gives these speedy mini pizzas extra pizzazz. Not only are they so simple to make, but the ingredient list is easy on your pocketbook. Both my husband and our toddler love them.   —*Stephanie Klos-Kohr*
Moline, Illinois

- 8 miniature bagels, split
- 1 cup spaghetti sauce with miniature meatballs
- 32 slices pepperoni
- 3/4 teaspoon garlic powder
- 2 cups (8 ounces) shredded mozzarella cheese

Spread the cut sides of bagels with spaghetti sauce. Top each with two slices of pepperoni; sprinkle with garlic powder and cheese. Place on ungreased baking sheets. Bake at 350° for 15-20 minutes or until cheese is melted and bubbly. **Yield:** 8 servings.

duced-fat cheese and reduced-fat mayonnaise) equals 115 calories, 3 g fat (1 g saturated fat), 4 mg cholesterol, 258 mg sodium, 18 g carbohydrate, 1 g fiber, 4 g protein. **Diabetic Exchanges:** 1 starch, 1/2 fat.

Lemon Garlic Hummus

(Pictured at left)

Prep/Total Time: 10 min.

You'll need just five ingredients to blend together this smooth and creamy bean dip. We have it every Christmas Eve at our family party. It's delicious and quick to make.
—Kris Capener, Layton, Utah

  3/4 cup vegetable oil
    3 tablespoons lemon juice
    2 cups garbanzo beans *or* chickpeas, rinsed
      and drained
    2 teaspoons minced garlic
  1/2 teaspoon salt
Pita bread, cut into wedges

In a food processor, combine the oil, lemon juice, beans, garlic and salt; cover and process until smooth. Transfer to a small bowl. Serve with pita wedges. **Yield:** 1-1/2 cups.

Surprise Cheese Ball

Prep: 10 min. + chilling

Ramen noodles are the secret ingredient in this savory appetizer. It's wonderful to bring to school functions, church fellowships and family holiday gatherings.
—Phyllis Stanley, Avery, Texas

    1 cup (8 ounces) sour cream
    2 ounces cream cheese, softened
  1/2 cup chopped green onions
    1 package (3 ounces) chicken ramen noodles
  3/4 cup finely chopped pecans
  1/3 cup minced fresh parsley
Assorted crackers

In a small mixing bowl, combine the sour cream, cream cheese, onions and contents of seasoning mix from ramen noodles; beat until fluffy. Finely crush the noodles. Add the noodles and pecans to the cream cheese mixture; mix well.

Shape into a ball; roll in parsley. Cover and refrigerate for 2-3 hours. Remove from the refrigerator 15 minutes before serving. Serve with crackers. **Yield:** 1 cheese ball (2-1/2 cups).

Cheddar Bruschetta

(Pictured above)

Prep/Total Time: 30 min.

I always like to try bruschetta when we're eating out at a restaurant to see how it compares to my recipe—and I haven't found one that's better yet! It's a hit when I serve it to company or take it to potlucks and other gatherings. —Vicki Thompson Bristol, New Brunswick

✓ Uses less fat, sugar or salt. Includes Nutritional Analysis and Diabetic Exchanges.

  24 slices French bread (3/4 inch thick)
    2 medium tomatoes, seeded and chopped
  2/3 cup shredded cheddar cheese
  1/3 cup mayonnaise
  1/4 cup grated Parmesan cheese
    1 teaspoon dried oregano
  1/2 teaspoon dried basil
  1/2 teaspoon pepper

Place bread slices on ungreased baking sheets. Bake at 350° for 5 minutes on each side or until toasted. Meanwhile, in a small bowl, combine the remaining ingredients. Spread over toasted bread. Bake 8-10 minutes longer or until bubbly. Serve warm. **Yield:** 2 dozen.
Nutritional Analysis: 2 pieces (prepared with re-

Sweet 'n' Crunchy Mix

Prep/Total Time: 30 min.

My kids like snacks with a lot of crunch. So I combined a few of their favorite ingredients for this recipe, and it was an instant success. In fact, I've become famous in our neighborhood for this mix.
—Amy Briggs
Zimmerman, Minnesota

2-1/2 cups Rice Chex
2-1/2 cups Honey-Nut Cheerios
1 package (10 ounces) honey-flavored
    bear-shaped graham crackers
2 cups miniature pretzels
1/2 cup butter, melted
1/3 cup packed brown sugar
4-1/2 teaspoons ground cinnamon

In a large bowl, combine the first four ingredients. In a small bowl, combine the butter, brown sugar and cinnamon; pour over cereal mixture and toss to coat. Spread mixture into two ungreased 15-in. x 10-in. x 1-in. baking pans.

Bake at 275° for 10 minutes. Stir; bake 10 minutes longer. Store snack mix in an airtight container. **Yield:** about 1-1/2 quarts.

Veggie Appetizer Squares

Banana Shakes

(Pictured below)

Prep/Total Time: 10 min.

My husband is in the Army, and we're stationed about an hour from Tokyo. Our young children love any kind of ice cream, so they're always happy when I surprise them with these frosty shakes. Pop cups into the freezer for a few minutes if you like a thicker texture. Or use chocolate or strawberry ice cream instead. —Martha Miller
Camp Zama, Japan

1 cup half-and-half cream
4 cups vanilla ice cream, softened
1 medium banana, sliced
1/4 teaspoon banana extract

In a blender, combine all ingredients; cover and process until smooth. Pour into chilled glasses; serve immediately. **Yield:** 4 servings.

Banana Shakes

Veggie Appetizer Squares

(Pictured above)

Prep/Total Time: 30 min.

This tasty pizza will disappear in a hurry at your next gathering, so you may want to prepare two! It's a great snack or light supper, especially for warm summer days. I use refrigerated pizza crust to speed up preparation. —Mary Lynd
Minford, Ohio

1 tube (13.8 ounces) refrigerated pizza crust
1 package (8 ounces) cream cheese, softened
1/2 cup ranch salad dressing
1/2 teaspoon garlic powder
1/2 teaspoon dried parsley flakes
1/4 teaspoon salt
4 green onions, chopped
1-1/2 cups coarsely chopped fresh broccoli
1-1/2 cups coarsely chopped fresh cauliflower
1 medium carrot, finely chopped
1 celery rib, finely chopped
1/2 cup chopped green pepper
1-1/4 cups shredded pepper Jack cheese
1-1/4 cups shredded mozzarella cheese
1/2 cup shredded Parmesan cheese

Press pizza dough into a greased 15-in. x 10-in. x 1-in. baking pan. Bake at 400° for 6 minutes. Cool on a wire rack for 5 minutes. Meanwhile, in a small mixing bowl, beat the cream cheese, salad dressing, garlic powder, parsley and salt. Spread over crust. Top with the onions, broccoli, cauliflower, carrot, celery and green pepper. Sprinkle with cheeses. Bake for 10-15 minutes or until cheese is melted. **Yield:** 12-16 servings.

Tortellini Appetizers

Italian Snack Mix

(Pictured on page 285)

Prep/Total Time: 15 min.

This no-bake mixture can be put together in minutes and stores well in an airtight container. —Nancy Zimmerman
Cape May Court House, New Jersey

 8 cups Crispix
 4 cups sourdough pretzel nuggets
 3 tablespoons vegetable oil
1/4 cup grated Parmesan cheese
 1 tablespoon spaghetti sauce mix
 2 teaspoons garlic powder

In a 2-gal. resealable plastic bag, combine the cereal and pretzels. Drizzle with oil; seal bag and toss to coat. Combine the Parmesan cheese, spaghetti sauce mix and garlic powder; sprinkle over cereal mixture. Seal bag and toss to coat. **Yield:** about 3 quarts.

Chocolate Mint Wafers

Prep: 20 min. + standing

I created these thin mints for a cookie exchange, and everyone raved about them. They're often requested by my family and have become one of my daughter's favorites. To switch up the flavor, try using a different extract instead of peppermint. —Michelle Kester, Cleveland, Ohio

 4 ounces dark chocolate candy coating
1/8 to 1/4 teaspoon peppermint extract
18 to 24 vanilla wafers

Place candy coating in a microwave-safe bowl. Microwave, uncovered, on high for 30-60 seconds or until smooth, stirring every 15 seconds. Stir in extract. Dip wafers in coating; place on waxed paper until set. Store in an airtight container. **Yield:** about 1-1/2 dozen.
 Editor's Note: This recipe was tested in a 1,100-watt microwave.

Tortellini Appetizers

(Pictured above)

Prep: 20 min. **Bake:** 20 min. + cooling

The festive green and red of this appetizer make it a welcome addition to holiday buffets, and store-bought pesto cuts the preparation time. To hurry things along even more, I sometimes heat the garlic in a skillet rather than bake it. —Cheryl Lama, Royal Oak, Michigan

 4 garlic cloves, peeled
 2 tablespoons olive oil, *divided*
 1 package (10 ounces) refrigerated spinach
  tortellini
 1 cup mayonnaise
1/4 cup grated Parmesan cheese
1/4 cup milk
1/4 cup prepared pesto
1/8 teaspoon pepper
 1 pint grape tomatoes
26 frilled toothpicks

Place garlic cloves on a double thickness of heavy-duty foil; drizzle with 1 tablespoon oil. Wrap foil around garlic. Bake at 425° for 20-25 minutes or until tender. Cool for 10-15 minutes.
 Meanwhile, cook tortellini according to package directions; drain and rinse in cold water. Toss with remaining oil; set aside. In a small bowl, combine the mayonnaise, Parmesan cheese, milk, pesto and pepper. Mash garlic into pesto mixture; stir until combined.
 Alternately thread tortellini and tomatoes onto toothpicks. Serve with pesto dip. Refrigerate leftovers. **Yield:** about 2 dozen (1-1/2 cups dip).

Rye Ham Bites

Prep/Total Time: 30 min.

I came up with this recipe when looking for an appetizer to serve at a dinner party. These yummy bites—made of what I had in my refrigerator—got many compliments. —Darcy Kealy, Lincoln, Nebraska

 3 tablespoons butter, softened
30 slices snack rye bread
 1 package (8 ounces) cream cheese, softened
1/4 cup sour cream
 1 teaspoon garlic powder
1/4 teaspoon pepper
 1 cup diced fully cooked ham
 6 green onions, finely chopped
 1 can (2-1/4 ounces) chopped ripe olives,
  drained
3/4 cup shredded mozzarella cheese, *divided*
 2 tablespoons minced fresh parsley

Spread butter over one side of each slice of bread. Place buttered side up on two baking sheets. Broil 4 in. from the heat for 2-3 minutes or until lightly browned.

In a small mixing bowl, beat cream cheese, sour cream, garlic powder and pepper until smooth. Stir in ham, onions, olives, 1/4 cup mozzarella cheese and parsley. Spread a rounded tablespoonful over each slice of bread; sprinkle with remaining mozzarella. Broil 4 in. from the heat for 2-3 minutes or until cheese is melted. Serve warm. **Yield:** 2-1/2 dozen.

S'more Drops

(Pictured below)

Prep: 20 min. + cooling

I first tried these gooey treats in my sixth-grade home economics class. My friend and I would make them whenever we would get together. But we'd dig right in, not even bothering to wait for them to cool. We still reminisce about these indoor s'mores served with tall glasses of cold milk. —Diane Angell, Rockford, Illinois

>   4 cups Golden Grahams
> 1-1/2 cups miniature marshmallows
>   1 cup (6 ounces) semisweet chocolate chips
>   1/3 cup light corn syrup
>   1 tablespoon butter
>   1/2 teaspoon vanilla extract

In a large bowl, combine the cereal and miniature marshmallows; set aside. Place the chocolate chips, corn syrup and butter in a 1-qt. microwave-safe dish. Microwave, uncovered, on high for 1-2 minutes or until

Bacon Nachos

smooth, stirring every 30 seconds.

Stir in vanilla. Pour over cereal mixture and mix well. Drop by tablespoonfuls onto waxed paper-lined baking sheets. Cool. **Yield:** 2-1/2 dozen.

Editor's Note: This recipe was tested in a 1,100-watt microwave.

Bacon Nachos

(Pictured above and on page 284)

Prep/Total Time: 20 min.

These crispy nachos have always been a big hit in our house. Topped with kid-friendly ingredients like ground beef and cheddar cheese, they're sure to be requested by your family. They're also easy enough for older children to microwave by themselves. —Ruth Ann Bott Lake Wales, Florida

> 1/2 pound ground beef
>   4 cups tortilla chips
> 1/4 cup real bacon bits
>   2 cups (8 ounces) shredded cheddar cheese
> 1/2 cup guacamole dip
> 1/2 cup sour cream
> **Chopped tomatoes and green onions, optional**

In a small skillet, cook beef over medium heat until no longer pink; drain. Place the tortilla chips on a microwave-safe serving plate. Layer with the beef, bacon and cheese. Microwave, uncovered, on high for 1-2 minutes or until cheese is melted. Top with guacamole and sour cream. Sprinkle with tomatoes and onions if desired. **Yield:** 4-6 servings.

Editor's Note: This recipe was tested in a 1,100-watt microwave.

S'more Drops

Sweet Cheese Ball

1 can (4 ounces) mushroom stems and pieces, drained and chopped
1/3 cup chopped onion
24 slices pepperoni, chopped
1 can (8 ounces) pizza sauce
1 cup (4 ounces) shredded mozzarella cheese
Assorted crackers

Spread the cream cheese into an ungreased 9-in. microwave-safe pie plate. Top with the olives, mushrooms, onion, pepperoni, pizza sauce and mozzarella cheese. Microwave, uncovered, at 70% power for 7-10 minutes or until heated through and cheese is melted. Serve with crackers. **Yield:** 8-10 servings.

Editor's Note: This recipe was tested in a 1,100-watt microwave.

Pineapple Cheddar Spread

Prep/Total Time: 20 min.

I came across this easy idea when looking for something unique to impress guests. The slightly sweet spread received rave reviews from friends. Try it with celery sticks or crackers the next time you need a fast appetizer.
—Rebecca Pester, Beale Air Force Base, California

✓ Uses less fat, sugar or salt. Includes Nutritional Analysis and Diabetic Exchanges.

4 ounces cream cheese, softened
1/4 cup mayonnaise
1-1/2 teaspoons soy sauce
2 cups (8 ounces) shredded cheddar cheese
1 can (8 ounces) unsweetened crushed pineapple, drained
1/2 cup chopped almonds, toasted
1/4 cup finely chopped green pepper
2 tablespoons finely chopped green onion
Celery sticks

In a small mixing bowl, beat the cream cheese, mayonnaise and soy sauce until smooth. Beat in the cheddar cheese, pineapple, almonds, green pepper and onion. Serve with celery. **Yield:** 2-1/2 cups.

Nutritional Analysis: 1/4 cup (prepared with reduced-fat cream cheese, fat-free mayonnaise, reduced-sodium soy sauce and reduced-fat cheddar cheese) equals 150 calories, 11 g fat (5 g saturated fat), 25 mg cholesterol, 273 mg sodium, 7 g carbohydrate, 1 g fiber, 8 g protein. **Diabetic Exchanges:** 2 fat, 1/2 fruit.

Sweet Cheese Ball

(Pictured above)
Prep/Total Time: 10 min.

You'll need only a few items for this unique cheese ball. Coconut comes through in the cherry-flecked mixture that's coated in pecans. It looks pretty and tastes delicious served with apple slices, pineapple wedges or other fresh fruit. —*Melissa Friend, Oakland, Maryland*

2 packages (8 ounces *each*) cream cheese, softened
1/2 cup confectioners' sugar
2/3 cup flaked coconut
8 maraschino cherries, finely chopped
3/4 cup finely chopped pecans
Assorted fresh fruit

In a small mixing bowl, beat cream cheese and confectioners' sugar until smooth. Beat in the coconut and cherries. Shape into a ball; roll in pecans. Cover and refrigerate until serving. Serve with fruit. **Yield:** 1 cheese ball (3-1/2 cups).

Turkey Egg Rolls

Prep/Total Time: 30 min.

Coleslaw mix hurries along the preparation of these deep-fried egg rolls served with sweet-and-sour sauce. These elegant appetizers are as easy to make as they are to eat. —*Lucille Gendron, Pelham, New Hampshire*

1/2 pound ground turkey
2 cups coleslaw mix
1 tablespoon soy sauce
1/2 teaspoon ground ginger

Pepperoni Pizza Dip

Prep/Total Time: 15 min.

Folks will dig into this rich pizza-flavored dip. It's loaded with tasty toppings including pepperoni, mushrooms, olives and cheese, then warmed in the microwave.
—Donna Cajski, Milwaukee, Wisconsin

1 package (8 ounces) cream cheese, softened
1 can (4-1/4 ounces) chopped ripe olives, drained

1/4 teaspoon onion salt
1/4 teaspoon garlic powder
10 egg roll wrappers
Oil for deep-fat frying
Sweet-and-sour sauce

In a large skillet, cook turkey over medium heat until no longer pink; drain. Stir in the coleslaw mix, soy sauce, ginger, onion salt and garlic powder. Place 1/4 cup in the center of each egg roll wrapper. Fold bottom corner over filling; fold sides toward center. Moisten remaining corner of wrapper with water; roll up tightly to seal. Repeat.

In an electric skillet or deep-fat fryer, heat oil to 375°. Fry egg rolls, a few at a time, for 3-4 minutes or until golden brown, turning often. Drain the egg rolls on paper towels. Serve with the sweet-and-sour sauce. **Yield:** 10 egg rolls.

Cheese Fries

(Pictured below)

Prep/Total Time: 20 min.

I came up with this recipe after my daughter had cheese fries at a restaurant and couldn't stop talking about them. Now she can enjoy them at home. I like to put extra servings in foil packets, so they can be refrigerated and reheated in the oven for a quick snack. —Melissa Tatum
Greensboro, North Carolina

1 package (28 ounces) frozen steak fries
1 can (10-3/4 ounces) condensed cheddar cheese soup, undiluted
1/4 cup milk
1/2 teaspoon garlic powder

Granola Banana Sticks

1/4 teaspoon onion powder
Paprika

Arrange the steak fries in a single layer in two greased 15-in. x 10-in. x 1-in. baking pans. Bake at 450° for 15-18 minutes or until tender and golden brown.

Meanwhile, in a saucepan, combine the soup, milk, garlic powder and onion powder; heat through. Drizzle over fries; sprinkle with the paprika. **Yield:** 8-10 servings.

Granola Banana Sticks

(Pictured above and on page 284)

Prep/Total Time: 20 min.

My daughter and I won an award at our local fair for these healthy snacks. I like to prepare the ingredients ahead of time so our kids can assemble them when they get home from school. A crunchy alternative to the crushed granola bars is crisp rice cereal. —Diane Toomey
Allentown, Pennsylvania

1/4 cup peanut butter
2 tablespoons plus 1-1/2 teaspoons honey
4-1/2 teaspoons brown sugar
2 teaspoons milk
3 medium firm bananas
6 Popsicle sticks
2 crunchy oat and honey granola bars, crushed

In a small saucepan, combine the peanut butter, honey, brown sugar and milk; heat through.

Peel bananas and cut in half widthwise; insert a Popsicle stick into one end of each banana half. Spoon peanut butter mixture over bananas to coat completely. Sprinkle with granola. Serve immediately or place on a waxed paper-lined baking sheet and freeze. **Yield:** 6 servings.

Cheese Fries

Blue Cheese Crostini

Blue Cheese Crostini

(Pictured above)

Prep/Total Time: 15 min.

My sister-in-law gave me this great recipe, which includes two of my favorite ingredients—blue cheese and pear. Yum! —Kate Hilts, Grand Rapids, Michigan

>   4 ounces cream cheese, softened
>   3 tablespoons butter, softened
>   1 cup (4 ounces) crumbled blue cheese
>   1/4 cup finely chopped walnuts, toasted
>   15 slices French bread (1/2 inch thick), lightly toasted
>   1 medium ripe pear

In a small mixing bowl, beat the cream cheese and butter until smooth. Stir in blue cheese and walnuts. Spread evenly over toasted bread. Place on a baking sheet. Broil 3-4 in. from heat for 3-4 minutes or until cheese is bubbly. Core pear and cut into 30 thin slices. Place two pear slices on each of the crostini. Serve warm. **Yield:** 15 appetizers.

Hot Seafood Spread

Prep: 15 min. **Bake:** 50 min.

Bake this popular party dip in a pumpernickel or white round bread loaf. I often use canned crab instead of imitation crabmeat. —Linda Doll, St. Albert, Alberta

>   1 package (8 ounces) cream cheese, softened
>   2 cups (8 ounces) shredded cheddar cheese
>   1 cup mayonnaise
>   1 can (4-1/4 ounces) tiny shrimp, rinsed and drained
>   3/4 cup imitation crabmeat, chopped
>   1/2 cup chopped green onions
>   1/4 cup grated Parmesan cheese

>   2 teaspoons dill weed
>   2 teaspoons minced fresh parsley
>   1 round loaf (1-1/2 pounds) unsliced bread
>   Assorted fresh vegetables

In a mixing bowl, combine the first nine ingredients. Cut the top fourth off the loaf of bread; carefully hollow out bottom, leaving a 1/2-in. shell. Cube removed bread; set aside. Fill bread shell with seafood mixture. Place on an ungreased baking sheet. Cover top edges loosely with foil.

Bake at 350° for 25 minutes. Remove foil; bake 25-35 minutes longer or until crust is golden and spread is heated through. Serve with vegetables and bread cubes. **Yield:** 4 cups.

Editor's Note: Fat-free mayonnaise and cream cheese are not recommended for this recipe.

Kitchen-Sink Soft Tacos

Prep/Total Time: 15 min.

My kids invented this recipe by stirring some taco spice into leftover sloppy joes. Now, we make them with canned chili instead. They're excellent after school and as a quick lunch. —Darlene King, Estevan, Saskatchewan

>   1/2 cup uncooked instant rice
>   1 can (15 ounces) chili with beans
>   1 teaspoon taco seasoning
>   12 flour tortillas (6 inches), warmed
>   1 cup (4 ounces) shredded cheddar cheese

Cook rice according to package directions. Combine chili and taco seasoning in a microwave-safe bowl. Cover and microwave on high for 2-3 minutes or until heated through. Spoon rice and chili onto tortillas; sprinkle with cheese. Fold sides of each tortilla over filling. **Yield:** 6 servings.

Editor's Note: This recipe was tested in a 1,100-watt microwave.

Olive Cheese Ball

Prep/Total Time: 10 min.

If you like olives, you'll love this special cheese ball. I received the recipe from a friend many years ago and am always asked to make it. I like to prepare this ahead of time and refrigerate it for at least 3 hours. You can serve it with any snack cracker. —LaVerne Vinzant Catawba, Wisconsin

>   1 package (8 ounces) cream cheese, softened
>   1/2 cup butter, softened
>   1 can (4-1/2 ounces) chopped ripe olives, drained
>   1/2 cup chopped green onions
>   1 cup chopped walnuts
>   Assorted crackers

In a small mixing bowl, beat cream cheese and butter until smooth. Stir in the olives and onions. Shape into a ball; roll in walnuts. Cover and refrigerate until serving. Serve with crackers. **Yield:** 1 cheese ball (3 cups).

Garlic Oregano Dip

Prep/Total Time: 20 min.

This classic dip is fast and simple. I first had it at a party and always try to keep some on hand for snacking. We also like it with pumpernickel bread. —Sarah Vasques Milford, New Hampshire

> 1 cup mayonnaise
> 1 cup (8 ounces) sour cream
> 1 small red onion, chopped
> 1 teaspoon garlic powder
> 1 teaspoon dried oregano
> 1/4 teaspoon salt
> 1 round loaf (1 pound) unsliced sourdough bread
>
> Snack rye bread

In a bowl, combine the first six ingredients; cover and refrigerate. Meanwhile, cut the top third off the loaf of bread; carefully hollow out bottom, leaving a 1-in. shell. Cube removed bread and top of bread. Spoon dip into bread shell. Serve with bread cubes and snack rye. **Yield:** 1-3/4 cups.

Dilly Veggie Pizza

(Pictured below)

Prep: 20 min. **Bake:** 10 min. + cooling

This is one of my favorite ways to use up leftover chopped vegetables. It's a cinch to prepare, and you can change the mixture to match your kids' tastes. Always popular at special events, it tastes just as good the next day—if there's any left! —Heather Ahrens, Avon, Ohio

> 1 tube (8 ounces) refrigerated crescent rolls
> 1-1/2 cups vegetable dill dip

Dilly Veggie Pizza

Reuben Crescents

> 2 medium carrots, chopped
> 1 cup finely chopped fresh broccoli
> 1 cup chopped seeded tomatoes
> 4 green onions, sliced
> 1 can (2-1/4 ounces) sliced ripe olives, drained

Unroll crescent dough into one long rectangle. Press onto the bottom of a greased 13-in. x 9-in. x 2-in. baking pan; seal seams and perforations. Bake at 375° for 10-12 minutes or until golden brown. Cool completely on a wire rack.

Spread dip over crust; sprinkle with the carrots, broccoli, tomatoes, onions and olives. Cut into squares. Refrigerate leftovers. **Yield:** 15 servings.

Reuben Crescents

(Pictured above)

Prep/Total Time: 20 min.

If you like Reuben sandwiches, you're sure to like these quick-and-easy roll-ups. I sometimes serve them with a salad and fruit for a fast meal. —Dolores Hurtt Florence, Montana

> 1 tube (8 ounces) refrigerated crescent rolls
> 1 cup sauerkraut, rinsed, well drained and chopped
> 1 tablespoon Thousand Island salad dressing
> 4 slices process Swiss cheese, cut into 1/2-inch strips
> 8 thin slices deli corned beef

Separate crescent dough into eight triangles. Combine sauerkraut and salad dressing. Place two cheese strips across the short side of each triangle. Fold corned beef slices in half; place over cheese. Top with sauerkraut mixture. Roll up each from the short side. Place on an ungreased baking sheet. Bake at 375° for 10-15 minutes or until golden brown. **Yield:** 8 servings.

Chapter 21

☼ *On-the-Go Odds & Ends*

IF YOU LIKE to try a wide variety of recipes, you'll love this inspiring assortment. It features groups of theme-related creations, all on the quick-and-easy side so they'll fit your hectic schedule.

For fabulous fresh fare, make delicious dishes that take advantage of green beans, asparagus and apples. Or, whip up zippy salsas that are chock-full of garden-grown veggies and fruits.

When you need hearty home cooking, prepare mouth-watering meatball recipes that'll satisfy big appetites. Then top off the meal by blending creamy shakes that are sure to please.

During the holiday season, rely on the merry collection of Christmas cookies. And don't forget gifts of good cheer you can make in your kitchen.

MEATY MARVELS. Appetizer Meatballs, Meatball Vegetable Soup and Meatball Pizza (all recipes on pp. 302-303).

Cherry Malts

Caramel Chip Malts

(Pictured below)

Prep/Total Time: 5 min.

Our Test Kitchen home economists gave this chocolaty malt a hint of caramel. With its thick, creamy texture, it makes a speedy snack or creamy dessert.

    1 cup milk
    2 cups chocolate chip ice cream
1/2 cup caramel ice cream topping
    3 tablespoons chocolate malted milk powder

In a blender, combine milk, ice cream, caramel topping and chocolate malted milk powder; cover and process until blended. Pour into chilled glasses. **Yield:** 2 servings.

Orange Blueberry Shakes

(Pictured at right)

Prep/Total Time: 5 min.

A friend and I stumbled across this recipe when craving a good shake, but we substituted ingredients we had on hand. It turned out great! The citrus and berry taste in this cool beverage is so refreshing on a hot day.
          —Laura Gaskins, Erie, Colorado

1-1/4 cups strawberry ice cream
  3/4 cup vanilla ice cream
  2/3 cup orange juice
1-1/4 cups frozen unsweetened blueberries
    2 teaspoons sugar
Fresh strawberries, optional

Great Shakes

THERE'S NOTHING as refreshing as a frosty shake or mouth-watering malt when you're craving something cold and sweet on a warm day. But you don't need to head to the nearest ice cream parlor to enjoy one.

With the quick recipes here, you can blend a cool, creamy beverage in minutes. Then just sit back, relax and sip a special summer treat.

Cherry Malts

(Pictured above)

Prep/Total Time: 5 min.

White chocolate is a decadent addition to these malts from our Test Kitchen staff. For a fruitier malt, add frozen sweet cherries to the blender before processing.

    1 cup milk
    3 cups cherry ice cream
    3 tablespoons malted milk powder
    1 square (1 ounce) white baking chocolate, chopped

In a blender, combine milk, ice cream, malted milk powder and chocolate; cover and process until blended. Pour into chilled glasses. **Yield:** 2 servings.

Caramel Chip Malts

Orange Blueberry Shakes

Chilled Hot Chocolate

(Pictured below)

Prep/Total Time: 5 min.

You don't have to wait for cold weather before enjoying the rich taste of hot chocolate, thanks to this frosty version.
—Mary Tallman, Arbor Vitae, Wisconsin

✓ Uses less fat, sugar or salt. Includes Nutritional Analysis and Diabetic Exchanges.

1-1/2 cups warm water
    4 envelopes (1 ounce *each*) instant hot cocoa mix
    2 cups vanilla ice cream
1-1/2 cups half-and-half cream

In a blender, combine water and cocoa mix; cover and process until dissolved. Add ice cream and cream; cover and process for 30 seconds or until smooth. Pour into chilled mugs. **Yield:** 4 servings.

    Nutritional Analysis: 1-1/4 cups (prepared with sugar-free hot cocoa mix, fat-free half-and-half and reduced-fat frozen yogurt) equals 210 calories, 2 g fat (trace saturated fat), 4 mg cholesterol, 340 mg sodium, 37 g carbohydrate, 3 g fiber, 9 g protein. **Diabetic Exchanges:** 1-1/2 fat-free milk, 1 starch.

Creamy Berry Shakes
Chilled Hot Chocolate

In a blender, combine the first five ingredients; cover and process until smooth, stirring if necessary. Pour into chilled glasses. Garnish with strawberries if desired. **Yield:** 3 servings.

Creamy Berry Shakes

(Pictured at right)

Prep/Total Time: 10 min.

Fresh strawberries and raspberries provide the fruity flavor in this shake from our Test Kitchen staff. Use frozen fruit when fresh berries are not in season.

    2 cups milk
    2 cups vanilla ice cream
    2 cups fresh strawberries
    1 cup fresh raspberries
    2 tablespoons sugar
Whipped topping and additional raspberries, optional

In a blender, combine the first five ingredients; cover and process for 20 seconds or until smooth. Pour into chilled glasses. Garnish with whipped cream and additional raspberries if desired. **Yield:** 4 servings.

Lemony Shrimp 'n' Asparagus
Asparagus Ham Roll-Ups
Bacon-Wrapped Asparagus

Appetizing Asparagus

WITH a quick cooking time and lots of versatility, bright green asparagus spears offer crisp-tender texture and fresh taste. They're a great addition to fresh vegetable platters and also lend a bit of elegance to appetizers, salads, main dishes and more.

Here, you'll find asparagus in a tasty bacon side dish, cheesy ham wraps and a fabulous shrimp entree. Each recipe can be fixed in just a half hour...or less.

Lemony Shrimp 'n' Asparagus

(Pictured at left)

Prep/Total Time: 30 min.

This marvelous main dish cooks quickly in the microwave yet is special enough to serve to company. It's a pretty and tasty way to use your spring harvest of asparagus. An added bonus is the low calorie count. —Becky Von Seggern
Scribner, Nebraska

✓ Uses less fat, sugar or salt. Includes Nutritional Analysis and Diabetic Exchanges.

- 1 **pound fresh asparagus, trimmed and cut into 1-1/2-inch pieces**
- 1 **medium sweet red pepper, julienned**
- 1/2 **teaspoon minced garlic**
- 2 **tablespoons water**
- 3/4 **pound uncooked medium shrimp, peeled and deveined**
- 1/4 **cup soy sauce**
- 5 **teaspoons lemon juice**
- 1/2 **teaspoon grated lemon peel**
- 2 **teaspoons cornstarch**
- 1 **tablespoon cold water**

Hot cooked rice, optional

In a 2-qt. microwave-safe bowl, combine the asparagus, red pepper, garlic and water. Cover and microwave on high for 4 minutes. Add shrimp; cover and cook for 2 minutes or until the shrimp turn pink and asparagus is tender. With a slotted spoon, remove shrimp and vegetables; keep warm.

Add soy sauce, lemon juice and peel to the microwave dish. In a small bowl, combine the cornstarch and cold water until smooth. Stir into soy sauce mixture.

Microwave, uncovered, on high for 1-2 minutes or until thickened. Return the shrimp mixture to the bowl; toss to coat. Serve shrimp and vegetables with rice if desired. **Yield:** 4 servings.

Nutritional Analysis: 1 cup (prepared with reduced-sodium soy sauce; calculated without rice) equals 103 calories, 1 g fat (trace saturated fat), 126 mg cholesterol, 757 mg sodium, 7 g carbohydrate, 2 g fiber, 16 g protein. **Diabetic Exchanges:** 1-1/2 lean meat, 1 vegetable.

Editor's Note: This recipe was tested in a 1,100-watt microwave.

Asparagus Ham Roll-Ups

(Pictured at left)

Prep/Total Time: 10 min.

With tortillas and fresh asparagus spears, these wraps are a nice alternative to your typical ham and cheese sandwiches. You can replace the Swiss cheese with Brie or Camembert, then heat the sandwich in the oven or microwave until the cheese is melted. —Jillian Moseley-Williams
Barrie, Ontario

✓ Uses less fat, sugar or salt. Includes Nutritional Analysis and Diabetic Exchanges.

- 16 **fresh asparagus spears, trimmed**
- 1/4 **cup mayonnaise**
- 4 **flour tortillas (8 inches)**
- 4 **thin slices deli ham**
- 8 **slices Swiss cheese**

Place asparagus in a shallow microwave-safe dish; add 1/2 in. of water. Cover and microwave on high for 2 minutes or until crisp-tender. Drain and rinse in cold water. Spread 1 tablespoon of mayonnaise over each tortilla. Top each with one slice of ham, two slices of cheese and four asparagus spears; roll up. **Yield:** 4 servings.

Nutritional Analysis: 1 wrap (prepared with fat-free mayonnaise, lean ham and reduced-fat cheese) equals 305 calories, 12 g fat (5 g saturated fat), 27 mg cholesterol, 612 mg sodium, 31 g carbohydrate, 1 g fiber, 22 g protein. **Diabetic Exchanges:** 3 lean meat, 1-1/2 starch, 1 vegetable.

Editor's Note: This recipe was tested in a 1,100-watt microwave.

Bacon-Wrapped Asparagus

(Pictured at left)

Prep/Total Time: 30 min.

My husband and I cook dinner on the grill almost every night, and I love grilling asparagus for a side dish. I serve these bacon-wrapped spears with sliced fresh tomatoes to round out a wonderful meal. —Patricia Kitts
Dickinson, Texas

- 10 **fresh asparagus spears, trimmed**
- 1/8 **teaspoon pepper**
- 5 **bacon strips, halved lengthwise**

Place the asparagus on a sheet of waxed paper; coat with nonstick cooking spray. Sprinkle with the pepper; turn to coat. Wrap a bacon piece around each spear; secure ends with toothpicks. Grill, uncovered, over medium-low heat for 8-12 minutes or until the bacon is crisp, turning occasionally. Discard toothpicks. **Yield:** 2-3 servings.

Appetizer Meatballs
Meatball Vegetable Soup
Meatball Pizza

Marvelous Meatballs

A HEARTY MEAL is at your fingertips when you rely on rapid recipes that showcase meatballs.

Here, you'll find three ways to use convenient frozen meatballs. Try them as a nice change of pace from the typical meat topping on pizza...use them in place of ground beef in a filling soup...or dress them up with a flavorful sauce for an appealing appetizer.

And to serve your family super-fast kabobs, make a batch of homemade pork meatballs that take just minutes to cook in the microwave.

Appetizer Meatballs

(Pictured above)

Prep/Total Time: 30 min.

I made changes to a barbecue sauce recipe to suit my family's taste. When we needed a quick appetizer for a get-together, I used the sauce to jazz up prepared meatballs.
—Cheryl Crowson, Sundance, Wyoming

    2 cups ketchup
  1/2 cup water
  1/2 cup white vinegar
  1/2 cup honey
    2 tablespoons Worcestershire sauce
    1 tablespoon dried minced onion
  1/4 teaspoon pepper
Dash garlic powder
Dash cayenne pepper
    1 package (38 ounces) frozen fully cooked meatballs

In a Dutch oven, combine the first nine ingredients. Bring to a boil. Reduce heat; simmer, uncovered, for 15 minutes. Meanwhile, thaw meatballs in microwave according to package directions. Stir into sauce; heat through. **Yield:** about 6 dozen.

Meatball Vegetable Soup

(Pictured at left)

Prep/Total Time: 25 min.

This satisfying soup uses frozen meatballs and cooks on the stovetop in half an hour. Sometimes I double the recipe and simmer it in the slow cooker. —Marcia Piaskowski
Plantsville, Connecticut

  2/3 cup uncooked medium pasta shells
    4 cups chicken broth
    1 can (14-1/2 ounces) diced tomatoes, undrained
    1 can (10-1/2 ounces) condensed French onion soup, undiluted
  12 frozen fully cooked Italian meatballs, thawed and quartered
1-1/2 cups chopped fresh spinach
    1 cup frozen sliced carrots, thawed
  3/4 cup canned kidney beans, rinsed and drained
  3/4 cup garbanzo beans *or* chickpeas, rinsed and drained

Cook pasta according to package directions. Meanwhile, combine remaining ingredients in a Dutch oven or soup kettle. Bring to a boil. Reduce heat; cover and simmer for 15 minutes or until vegetables are tender. Drain pasta and stir into soup. **Yield:** 6-8 servings (about 2-1/2 quarts).

Meatball Pizza

(Pictured at left)

Prep/Total Time: 25 min.

I always keep meatballs and bread shell crusts in the freezer to make this pizza at the spur of the moment. Add a tossed salad and you have a delicious dinner.
—Mary Humeniuk-Smith, *Perry Hall, Maryland*

    1 prebaked Italian bread shell crust (14 ounces)
    1 can (8 ounces) pizza sauce
    1 teaspoon garlic powder
    1 teaspoon Italian seasoning
  1/4 cup grated Parmesan cheese
    1 small onion, halved and sliced
  12 frozen fully cooked Italian meatballs, thawed and halved
    1 cup (4 ounces) shredded mozzarella cheese
    1 cup (4 ounces) shredded cheddar cheese

Place the crust on an ungreased 12-in. pizza pan. Spread with pizza sauce; top with garlic powder, Italian seasoning, Parmesan cheese and onion. Arrange the meatball halves over top; sprinkle with cheeses. Bake at 350° for 12-17 minutes or until heated through and cheese is melted. **Yield:** 6-8 slices.

Pork Meatball Kabobs

Prep/Total Time: 30 min.

The first time I found out I could make kabobs in the microwave, I was thrilled because cooking on the grill can be a hassle for just two people. The sweet and tangy homemade meatballs are very easy and so tasty.
—Kitty Hernandez, *Chicago, Illinois*

    1 egg
  1/2 cup crushed chow mein noodles
    2 tablespoons plus 3/4 cup apple cider *or* juice, *divided*
    1 tablespoon soy sauce
  3/4 teaspoon ground ginger, *divided*
  3/4 pound ground pork
    1 medium green pepper, cut into 3/4-inch chunks
    1 medium sweet red pepper, cut into 3/4-inch chunks
  20 small fresh mushrooms
    2 teaspoons cornstarch
    3 tablespoons cider vinegar

In a bowl, combine egg, chow mein noodles, 2 tablespoons cider, soy sauce and 1/4 teaspoon ginger. Crumble pork over mixture; mix well. Shape into 20 meatballs.

On 10 soaked wooden skewers, alternately thread peppers and mushrooms; add one meatball to both ends of each skewer. Place in an ungreased 11-in. x 7-in. x 2-in. microwave-safe dish; set aside.

In a small microwave-safe bowl, combine the cornstarch, vinegar and remaining cider and ginger until smooth. Microwave, uncovered, on high for 3-4 minutes or until thickened, stirring every 30 seconds.

Pour 1/4 cup glaze over the kabobs. Loosely cover with waxed paper. Microwave on high for 6-8 minutes or until meat is no longer pink, turning and brushing with drippings every 2 minutes. Serve with remaining glaze. **Yield:** 3 servings.

Editor's Note: This recipe was tested in a 1,100-watt microwave.

All About Dutch Ovens

WHEN you want to prepare delicious *Quick Cooking* recipes like Appetizer Meatballs and Meatball Vegetable Soup, a Dutch oven is a handy item to have among the cookware in your kitchen.

A Dutch oven is a large covered pan that can be used both on the stovetop and in the oven. Dutch ovens were said to have originated with the Pennsylvania Dutch of the 1700s and were most likely made of cast iron.

Today, they can be made from a variety of different materials, such as aluminum, stainless steel, enameled steel and cast iron. They're great for cooking large quantities of food like pasta, soups and stews, and they can also be used for frying or braising meats.

Dutch ovens are available in a variety of sizes, but the average size is 5 quarts.

Greek Orzo Salad

Bountiful Beans

IF YOU want to jazz up everyday meals, green beans are a tasty menu addition. They're fabulous in salads, side dishes, entrees and more.

Although fresh green beans have a peak season of May to October, they're available year-round. Try one of these rapid reader recipes anytime, and your family is sure to enjoy beautiful beans!

Greek Orzo Salad

(Pictured above)

Prep/Total Time: 20 min.

I came up with this recipe in summer when my home-grown tomatoes were more plentiful than ever. The salad is a snap to prepare and simply sensational.
—Kelly Skahan, Springfield, Missouri

    4 quarts water
1-1/4 cups uncooked orzo pasta
    1 cup cut fresh green beans
    2 large tomatoes, seeded and chopped
  1/2 teaspoon lemon juice
  1/4 teaspoon grated lemon peel
  1/2 cup Greek vinaigrette

In a Dutch oven, bring water to a boil. Add orzo and cook for 5 minutes. Add beans; cook 4-5 minutes longer or until orzo and beans are tender.

Meanwhile, in a salad bowl, combine the tomatoes, lemon juice and lemon peel. Drain orzo and beans; rinse in cold water. Stir into tomato mixture. Drizzle with vinaigrette and toss to coat. Refrigerate until serving. **Yield:** 4-5 servings.

Green Bean Egg Salad

Prep: 30 min. + chilling

When I received this recipe from my mother-in-law, I discovered that it's a family-pleasing alternative to potato salad. Cook a large kettle of green beans for supper and use the leftovers the next day to fix this delicious dish. —Jane Gysbers Blaine, Minnesota

    1 pound fresh green beans, cut into 1-1/2-inch pieces
    3 hard-cooked eggs, chopped
  1/2 cup chopped sweet onion
  3/4 cup mayonnaise

3/4 teaspoon prepared mustard
3/4 teaspoon salt
1/8 to 1/4 teaspoon pepper

Place beans in a steamer basket. Place in a large saucepan over 1 in. of water. Bring to a boil; cover and steam for 8-10 minutes or until crisp-tender. Transfer to a bowl; cool. Add the eggs and onion.

In a small bowl, combine the mayonnaise, mustard, salt and pepper. Add to bean mixture and mix well. Cover and refrigerate for at least 2 hours before serving. **Yield:** 4-6 servings.

Savory Pork Supper

Bean and Carrot Salad

(Pictured below)

Prep/Total Time: 30 min.

Whenever I find a recipe full of vegetables that my family will eat, I'm a happy mom. My husband comes back for seconds when I serve this. The carrots and beans are great finger food for young kids. —Colleen Edelsward
Woodinville, Washington

✓ Uses less fat, sugar or salt. Includes Nutritional Analysis and Diabetic Exchanges.

    1/2 cup baby carrots, cut in half lengthwise
      2 cups cut fresh green beans
    1/4 cup chopped radishes
    1/4 cup chopped red onion
DRESSING:
      1 tablespoon lemon juice
  1-1/2 teaspoons olive oil
    1/2 teaspoon sugar
    1/2 teaspoon Dijon mustard
    1/4 teaspoon minced garlic
    1/8 teaspoon salt
    1/8 teaspoon ground cumin
  1-1/2 teaspoons sesame seeds, toasted

In a small saucepan, cook carrots in a small amount of boiling water for 4 minutes. Add the beans; cook 4-5 minutes longer or until vegetables are crisp-tender. Drain; chill in ice water. Drain and pat dry; place in a large bowl. Add the radishes and onion.

In a small bowl, whisk the lemon juice, oil, sugar, mustard, garlic, salt and cumin. Pour over bean mixture; toss to coat. Cover and refrigerate until serving. Sprinkle with sesame seeds. **Yield:** 4 servings.
    Nutritional Analysis: 2/3 cup equals 53 calories, 2 g fat (trace saturated fat), 0 cholesterol, 103 mg sodium, 8 g carbohydrate, 3 g fiber, 2 g protein. **Diabetic Exchange:** 2 vegetable.

Savory Pork Supper

(Pictured above)

Prep/Total Time: 30 min.

Fresh green beans and mushrooms are coated with a creamy rosemary-seasoned sauce, then served over pork chops and fettuccine in this skillet meal. It cooks quickly on the stovetop, so it's a nice family supper for busy weeknights. —Stephanie Moon, Nampa, Idaho

      4 boneless pork loin chops (4 ounces *each*)
      2 tablespoons vegetable oil
      1 tablespoon butter
  1-1/2 cups sliced fresh mushrooms
    1/2 pound fresh green beans, cut into 2-inch pieces
    1/4 teaspoon minced fresh rosemary
      1 can (10-3/4 ounces) condensed cream of mushroom soup, undiluted
      2 tablespoons water
    1/8 teaspoon pepper
      8 ounces uncooked fettuccine

In a large skillet, brown pork chops in oil and butter on each side; drain. Remove and keep warm. In the same skillet, saute the mushrooms, beans and rosemary for 2-3 minutes or until vegetables are tender. Stir in the soup, water and pepper; bring to a boil.

Top with pork chops. Reduce heat; cover and simmer for 10-15 minutes until pork juices run clear, stirring occasionally. Meanwhile, cook fettuccine according to package directions; drain. Serve with pork chops and top with sauce. **Yield:** 4 servings.

Bean and Carrot Salad

Autumn Apples

WHEN the time is ripe for picking apples as an addition to your family menu, turn to the bushel of appealing recipes here. Each one takes maximum advantage of this ever-popular, versatile fruit.

You'll find a wide range of appetizing apple dishes. Whether you're looking for an entree, side dish, beverage or dessert, you and your family are sure to find something irresistible.

Buttered Orange Cider

(Pictured below)

Prep/Total Time: 30 min.

On a cool day, this warm beverage offers comforting flavor. Plus, it simmers in a jiffy. If you have some leftover cider, use it instead of water when making lemon or orange gelatin. —Edna Hoffman, Hebron, Indiana

- 6 cups apple cider *or* juice
- 1/2 medium unpeeled navel orange, sliced
- 8 whole allspice
- 8 whole cloves
- 2 cinnamon sticks (3 inches)
- 1 orange peel strip (3 inches)
- 1/2 cup packed brown sugar
- 1/4 cup butter, softened
- 1/2 teaspoon ground cinnamon

In a large saucepan, combine the cider and orange slices. Place the allspice, cloves, cinnamon sticks and orange peel on a double thickness of cheesecloth; bring up corners of the cloth and tie with kitchen string to form a bag. Add to pan. Bring to a boil over medium heat. Reduce heat; simmer, uncovered, for 15-20 minutes.

In a small bowl, combine the brown sugar, butter and cinnamon. Discard spice bag. Ladle cider into mugs; dot with butter mixture. **Yield:** 6 servings.

Apple-Topped Biscuits

(Pictured below left)

Prep: 15 min. + standing **Bake:** 20 min.

This wonderful recipe is easy to double when you want to serve a crowd. It isn't hard to make the topping, but in a pinch, you can substitute canned apple pie filling.

- 3 cups sliced peeled tart apples
- 1/3 cup sugar
- 1 tablespoon quick-cooking tapioca
- 1-1/2 teaspoons lemon juice
- 1/2 teaspoon ground cinnamon
- 1/8 teaspoon salt
- 1/8 teaspoon ground nutmeg
- 1 tube (16.3 ounces) large refrigerated buttermilk biscuits

In a large saucepan, combine the apples, sugar, tapioca, lemon juice, cinnamon, salt and nutmeg. Let stand for 15 minutes. Cook over medium heat for 8-10 minutes or until apples are tender.

Transfer apple mixture to a greased 9-in. pie plate. Place biscuits over apples. Bake at 375° for 18-20 minutes or until biscuits are browned. Immediately invert onto a serving plate. **Yield:** 8 servings.

Apple Brie Quesadillas

Prep/Total Time: 30 min.

With onions, apples and cheese, these quesadillas are a surprising change from typical versions. I cut them into quarters and serve them for brunch with eggs and fruit. —Heather Kahn Gisi, San Dimas, California

- 2 medium onions, sliced
- 1/4 cup balsamic vinegar
- 1/8 teaspoon sugar
- 1/8 teaspoon dried thyme
- 1/8 teaspoon dried rosemary, crushed
- 1 tablespoon vegetable oil
- 4 flour tortillas (10 inches)
- 2 medium tart apples, sliced
- 8 ounces Brie *or* Camembert cheese, rind removed and quartered

In a skillet over medium heat, cook the onions, vinegar, sugar, thyme and rosemary in oil for 10 minutes or until onions are golden. Spoon the mixture over half of each tortilla; top with apples and cheese. Fold over. Cook on a griddle over medium heat for 2-3 minutes on each side or the until cheese is melted. **Yield:** 4 servings.

Buttered Orange Cider
Apple-Topped Biscuits

Luscious Apple Trifle

Prep/Total Time: 20 min.

I created this dessert using ingredients I had on hand. When I brought it to a church dinner, it was the first dessert to go. —Danette Bass, Hillrose, Colorado

- 2 cups cold milk
- 1 package (3.4 ounces) instant vanilla pudding mix
- 1 package (8 ounces) cream cheese, softened
- 1 carton (8 ounces) frozen whipped topping, thawed, *divided*
- 1 loaf (10-1/2 ounces) angel food cake, cut into 1-inch cubes
- 1 jar (12-1/4 ounces) butterscotch ice cream topping
- 3 medium red apples, chopped
- 1-1/2 teaspoons ground cinnamon

In a bowl, whisk milk and pudding mix for 2 minutes. Let stand for 2 minutes or until soft-set. In a large mixing bowl, beat cream cheese until smooth; beat in pudding. Fold in 1 cup whipped topping.

In a 3-qt. glass bowl, layer a third of cake cubes, a third of butterscotch topping, a third of apples, 1/2 teaspoon cinnamon and a third of cream cheese mixture. Repeat layers twice. Garnish with remaining whipped topping. Chill until serving. **Yield:** 12-14 servings.

Walnut Apple Rice

(Pictured at right)

Prep/Total Time: 25 min.

I've been making this delicious rice for years. It's easy to fix when you're in a hurry, and it goes well with pork. —Janice Mitchell, Aurora, Colorado

- 1 small onion, chopped
- 1 celery rib, chopped
- 2 tablespoons butter, softened
- 1 cup water
- 1 cup apple cider *or* juice
- 1 teaspoon salt
- 1/2 teaspoon ground cinnamon
- 2 cups uncooked instant rice
- 1 small red apple, chopped
- 1/2 cup chopped walnuts

In a large saucepan, saute onion and celery in butter for 3-4 minutes or until tender. Add the water, cider, salt and cinnamon; bring to a boil.

Stir in the rice, apple and walnuts. Cover and remove from the heat; let stand for 5 minutes. Fluff with a fork. **Yield:** 6 servings.

Apple Chutney Chops

(Pictured above right)

Prep/Total Time: 25 min.

When my husband and I lived in South Carolina for a year, some friends served this apple chutney. It tastes es-

Apple Chutney Chops
Walnut Apple Rice

pecially good in combination with rice and is also great over poultry or beef. Serve it hot or cold. —Cher Anjema, Brampton, Ontario

- 4 cups chopped peeled apples
- 1/2 cup golden raisins
- 1/2 cup honey
- 3 tablespoons cider vinegar
- 1/2 teaspoon salt
- 1/2 teaspoon ground ginger
- 1/2 teaspoon ground mustard
- 1/2 teaspoon curry powder
- 4 bone-in pork loin chops (1 inch thick)
- 1 tablespoon vegetable oil

For chutney, in a large saucepan, combine the apples, raisins, honey, vinegar, salt, ginger, mustard and curry. Bring to a boil. Reduce heat; simmer, uncovered, for 10-15 minutes or until apples are tender.

Meanwhile, in a large skillet, brown pork chops in oil over medium-high heat for 2-3 minutes on each side. Reduce heat; cook, uncovered, for 10-15 minutes or until juices run clear. Serve with chutney. **Yield:** 4 servings.

Summer Melon Salsa

Super Salsas

YOUR FAMILY will want to grab the chips and start snacking when they see these zippy salsas that are perfect for dipping...and can also be used in recipes that call for salsa.

Made with fresh vegetables, fruits and more, these fast dips outshine store-bought kinds by offering fabulous fresh taste and deliciously different flavors. So go ahead—spice up snack time!

Summer Melon Salsa

(Pictured above)

Prep/Total Time: 15 min.

I've been experimenting with lots of different fruit salsa recipes, and this one is so good. The refreshing blend of melons is complemented by a slight jalapeno kick. We like it with lime-flavored tortilla chips or over grilled chicken.
—Sue Gronholz, Beaver Dam, Wisconsin

✓ Uses less fat, sugar or salt. Includes Nutritional Analysis and Diabetic Exchanges.

  1/2 cup *each* cubed cantaloupe, honeydew and
      seedless watermelon
  1/4 cup chopped red onion
    1 jalapeno pepper, seeded and chopped
    2 tablespoons minced fresh cilantro
    1 tablespoon lime juice
  1/4 teaspoon pepper
  1/8 teaspoon salt
Tortilla chips

In a small bowl, combine the melons, onion, jalapeno, cilantro, lime juice, pepper and salt. Serve with chips. Refrigerate leftovers. **Yield:** 1-3/4 cups.

    Nutritional Analysis: 1/4 cup equals 15 calories, trace fat (trace saturated fat), 0 cholesterol, 45 mg sodium, 4 g carbohydrate, trace fiber, trace protein. **Diabetic Exchange:** Free food.

    Editor's Note: When cutting or seeding hot peppers, use rubber or plastic gloves to protect your hands. Avoid touching your face.

Avocado Salsa

Prep/Total Time: 20 min.

I combine tomatoes, onion and jalapeno with cilantro and avocado for a chunky salsa that is great with crunchy tortilla chips. Sometimes I use a few fresh green chilies instead of the jalapeno pepper, and I scoop the mixture over a green salad for a healthy and zesty dressing.
—Jamie Jeffers, Phoenix, Arizona

  3/4 pound plum tomatoes, cut into wedges
    1 small onion, cut into wedges
  1/4 cup lightly packed fresh cilantro leaves
    1 jalapeno pepper, seeded
  1/2 teaspoon minced garlic
  1/2 teaspoon salt
    1 large ripe avocado, peeled and diced
Tortilla chips

In a food processor, combine first six ingredients. Cover and pulse until coarsely chopped (do not overprocess); drain liquid. Transfer to a bowl; stir in avocado. Serve with chips. Refrigerate leftovers. **Yield:** about 2-1/2 cups.

    Editor's Note: When cutting or seeding hot peppers, use rubber or plastic gloves to protect your hands. Avoid touching your face.

Homemade Salsa

(Pictured at right)

Prep/Total Time: 20 min.

Almost every time I ask what I can bring to a party, I'm told to bring this crunchy, colorful salsa. For the best results, prepare and serve it on the same day.
—Mary Blott, Mukwonago, Wisconsin

✓ Uses less fat, sugar or salt. Includes Nutritional Analysis and Diabetic Exchanges.

    4 medium tomatoes, chopped and well drained
  1/2 cup chopped green onions
  1/2 cup chopped celery
  1/4 cup chopped green pepper
    1 tablespoon white wine *or* apple juice
    1 tablespoon cider vinegar
    1 tablespoon canola oil
    1 teaspoon mustard seed
  1/2 teaspoon salt
  1/4 teaspoon ground coriander
  1/8 teaspoon pepper
Tortilla chips

In a large bowl, combine tomatoes, onions, celery and green pepper. In a small bowl, whisk the wine or apple juice, vinegar, oil, mustard seed, salt, coriander and pepper; pour over vegetables and toss to coat. Serve with chips. Refrigerate leftovers. **Yield:** 2-1/2 cups.

 Nutritional Analysis: 1/4 cup equals 52 calories, 3 g fat (trace saturated fat), 0 cholesterol, 216 mg sodium, 6 g carbohydrate, 2 g fiber, 1 g protein. **Diabetic Exchanges:** 1 vegetable, 1/2 fat.

Peppy Peach Salsa

(Pictured below)

Prep/Total Time: 20 min.

Garden-fresh salsas are one of my favorite condiments. So when I saw a recipe for peach salsa in the newspaper, I couldn't think of anything that sounded better.
 —Jennifer Abbott, Moraga, California

 2 tablespoons lime juice
 1 tablespoon honey
1/2 teaspoon minced garlic
1/8 teaspoon ground ginger
 2 fresh peaches, peeled and diced
1/2 green serrano chili pepper, seeded and minced
1/2 red serrano chili pepper, seeded and minced
1/2 small yellow chili pepper, seeded and minced
 2 teaspoons minced fresh cilantro
Tortilla chips

In a small bowl, combine the lime juice, honey, garlic and ginger; let stand for 5 minutes. Stir in the peaches, peppers and cilantro. Serve with chips. Refrigerate leftovers. **Yield:** 1-1/4 cups.

 Editor's Note: When cutting or seeding hot peppers, use rubber or plastic gloves to protect your hands. Avoid touching your face.

Homemade Salsa
Peppy Peach Salsa

Confetti Cheese Salsa

(Pictured below)

Prep/Total Time: 20 min.

This creamy cheese dip is so quick and easy that it can be served in any season. But it's always a big hit at Fourth of July picnics. I never have to worry about covering the dish on the picnic table because the mixture disappears in no time.
—*Deidra Engle, Aledo, Illinois*

> 2 cups (8 ounces) finely shredded cheddar cheese
> 2 cups (8 ounces) shredded mozzarella cheese
> 2 large tomatoes, seeded and chopped
> 1 medium green pepper, diced
> 1 small cucumber, seeded and diced
> 1 small onion, chopped
> 1 bottle (8 ounces) ranch salad dressing
> 2 tablespoons salsa

Corn *or* tortilla chips

In a large bowl, combine the first six ingredients. Combine the salad dressing and salsa; pour over cheese mixture and toss gently. Serve with chips. Refrigerate leftovers. **Yield:** 7 cups.

Cranberry Onion Salsa

Prep/Total Time: 30 min.

Tucked into a basket with a bag of crunchy tortilla chips, a jar of this delicious homemade salsa makes an incredible edible gift. With only seven ingredients, it takes no time to make. This salsa also can be served warm as a condiment for pork or poultry.
—*Jamie Milligan*
Kimberley, British Columbia

> 1 can (8 ounces) crushed pineapple
> 1 cup chopped onion
> 1 teaspoon minced garlic
> 1/2 cup packed brown sugar
> 3 cups fresh *or* frozen cranberries
> 1 can (4 ounces) chopped green chilies
> 1/2 teaspoon hot pepper sauce

Drain pineapple, reserving juice; set pineapple aside. In a nonstick skillet coated with nonstick cooking spray, cook onion and garlic until tender. Stir in the brown sugar and reserved pineapple juice; cook and stir until sugar is melted.

Add the cranberries; cook and stir until mixture comes to a boil, cranberries pop and mixture is slightly thickened. Remove from the heat; stir in the chilies, hot pepper sauce and reserved pineapple. Transfer to a bowl; cool. Store in the refrigerator. **Yield:** about 3 cups.

Confetti Cheese Salsa

Christmas Cookies

WITH all the hustle and bustle of the season, do you think you don't have time to make trays of beautiful home-baked Christmas cookies? Think again!

The home economists in *Quick Cooking's* Test Kitchen came up with these time-saving treats that start with store-bought sugar cookie dough.

With only four tubes of refrigerated dough, you and your family can create all eight delightful varieties of cookies—from colorful candy canes to adorable elves.

That's 16 dozen treats, which is more than enough for munching…sharing…and giving as gifts! (Don't need so many? Use one or two tubes of dough and fix just a few of your favorites.)

The tempting treats are so much fun to decorate (and eat), they're sure to become an annual Christmas tradition—for you and yours.

Elf Cookies

Elf Cookies

(Pictured above right)

Prep: 45 min. **Bake:** 10 min.

A bright frosting glaze, colorful candies and well-placed almond slices turn these sugar cookie diamonds into a big batch of Santa's helpers for Christmas. Bake a batch of the adorable elves as a classroom treat or use a few to liven up each of your cookie trays.

- 1/2 **tube refrigerated sugar cookie dough, softened**
- 1/3 **cup all-purpose flour**
- 1-1/2 **cups confectioners' sugar,** *divided*
  - 3 **tablespoons milk,** *divided*
- 1/2 **teaspoon lemon extract,** *divided*
  - 6 **drops red food coloring,** *divided*
- 140 **milk chocolate M&M's (about 2/3 cup)**
- 56 **almond slices (about 4 teaspoons)**
- 56 **brown M&M miniature baking bits (about 1 tablespoon)**
- 28 **red M&M miniature baking bits (about 1-1/2 teaspoons)**

In a small mixing bowl, beat the sugar cookie dough and flour until combined. Roll out the dough on a lightly floured surface to 1/8-in. thickness. Cut with a floured 1-3/4-in. x 3-1/4-in. diamond cookie cutter. Place 2 in. apart on ungreased baking sheets. Bake at 350° for 7-9 minutes or until edges are golden brown. Remove to wire racks to cool.

For one batch of glaze, in a small bowl, combine 3/4 cup confectioners' sugar, 4-1/2 teaspoons milk and 1/4 teaspoon lemon extract. Remove 1 tablespoon glaze to another bowl. Tint the remaining glaze with 3 drops food coloring.

Working with one cookie at a time, spread red glaze over top half of cookie for the hat. Place one M&M at top for tassel and four M&M's across edge of glaze for hat brim. For ears, place two almond slices above M&M's on each end. Dip baking bits in plain glaze; place brown bits on cookie for eyes and a red bit for nose. Repeat with 13 more cookies.

Make second batch of glaze with remaining confectioners' sugar, milk, extract and food coloring. Decorate remaining cookies as before. **Yield:** 28 cookies.

Candy Cane Cookies

Prep: 25 min. **Bake:** 10 min.

Kids of all ages will want to pitch in when it comes time to shape these cute candy canes. With peppermint extract, the cookies taste as good as they look.

- 1/2 **tube refrigerated sugar cookie dough, softened**
- 2 **tablespoons all-purpose flour**
- 1/2 **teaspoon peppermint extract**
- 1/2 **teaspoon red food coloring**

In a large mixing bowl, beat the cookie dough, flour and extract until smooth. Divide dough in half; mix food coloring into one portion. Shape 1 teaspoon of white dough into a 6-in. rope. Shape 1 teaspoon of red dough into a 6-in. rope. Place ropes side by side; press together lightly and twist.

Place on an ungreased baking sheet; curve one end of cookie to form handle of cane.

Repeat with remaining dough, placing cookies 2 in. apart on baking sheets. Bake at 350° for 8-10 minutes or until set. Cool for 2 minutes before carefully removing to wire racks. **Yield:** 3 dozen.

Holiday Bells

Prep: 35 min. **Bake:** 10 min.

Our Test Kitchen home economists added all-purpose flour to the sugar cookie dough to make it easy to handle and shape these pecan-filled bells. Maraschino cherries provide a festive final touch as the bells' clappers.

     1/2 tube refrigerated sugar cookie dough,
          softened
     1/4 cup all-purpose flour
       1 tablespoon brown sugar
  2-1/4 teaspoons maraschino cherry juice
     1/2 teaspoon butter, softened
     1/4 cup finely chopped pecans
       5 red *or* green maraschino cherries, quartered

In a small mixing bowl, beat cookie dough and flour until combined. Roll out on a lightly floured surface to 1/8-in. thickness. Cut with a floured 2-1/2-in. round cookie cutter. Place 2 in. apart on ungreased baking sheets.

In a small bowl, combine brown sugar, cherry juice and butter. Stir in pecans. Place 1/2 teaspoonful in the center of each cookie. Shape into a bell by folding edges of dough to meet over filling; pinch edges together.

Place a piece of cherry at open end of each bell for clapper. Bake at 350° for 7-9 minutes or until edges are lightly browned. Immediately remove to wire racks. **Yield:** 1-1/2 dozen.

Raspberry Almond Strips

(Pictured below)

Prep/Total Time: 30 min.

Get ready to pour yourself a cup of tea, because you won't be able to resist sampling one of these treats. Almonds add taste and texture to the simple strips that are

Raspberry Almond Strips

jazzed up with raspberry pie filling and an easy powdered sugar drizzle.

     1/2 tube refrigerated sugar cookie dough,
          softened
     1/3 cup all-purpose flour
     1/4 cup finely chopped almonds
       3 tablespoons raspberry filling
     1/4 cup confectioners' sugar
  1-1/2 teaspoons milk
     1/8 teaspoon almond extract

In a small mixing bowl, beat the cookie dough, flour and almonds until combined. Roll into a 13-1/2-in. x 2-in. rectangle on an ungreased baking sheet. Using the end of a wooden spoon handle, make a 1/4-in.-deep indentation lengthwise down the center of rectangle. Bake at 350° for 5 minutes.

Spoon raspberry filling into the indentation. Bake 8-10 minutes longer or until lightly browned. Cool for 2 minutes. Remove to a cutting board; cut into 3/4-in. slices. Place on a wire rack. In a small bowl, combine the confectioners' sugar, milk and extract until smooth. Drizzle over warm cookies. **Yield:** 16 cookies.

Caramel Pecan Cookies

Prep: 15 min. **Bake:** 10 min. + standing

You're sure to impress guests with these showstopping treats. A golden sugar cookie is the base for an artful arrangement of creamy caramel, sweet chocolate and crunchy pecan halves.

     1/2 tube refrigerated sugar cookie dough
      24 caramels
       1 teaspoon heavy whipping cream
      64 pecan halves
       1 cup milk chocolate chips

Cut the sugar cookie dough into 1/4-in. slices. Place 2 in. apart on ungreased baking sheets. Bake at 350° for 8-10 minutes or until lightly browned. Remove to wire racks to cool.

In a 1-qt. microwave-safe bowl, combine caramels and cream. Microwave, uncovered, on high for 2 minutes, stirring once. Spoon onto the center of each cookie; arrange four pecan halves around caramel. In another microwave-safe bowl, melt chocolate chips; stir until smooth. Spoon over caramel. Let stand until set. **Yield:** 16 cookies.

Editor's Note: This recipe was tested in a 1,100-watt microwave.

Star Sandwich Cookies

Prep: 30 min. **Bake:** 10 min. + cooling

These dazzling sandwich cookies are sure to be the star of your holiday dessert tray. White chocolate and cream cheese form the sweet filling.

     1/2 tube refrigerated sugar cookie dough,
          softened
     1/3 cup all-purpose flour

Colorful Candy Bar Cookies

around each candy bar. Roll in colored sugar. Place 2 in. apart on parchment paper-lined baking sheets. Bake at 350° for 10-12 minutes or until edges are golden brown. Remove to wire racks. **Yield:** 2 dozen.

Dipped Spice Cookies

(Pictured below)

Prep: 25 min. **Bake:** 10 min. + standing

A hint of orange and a sprinkling of spices lend old-fashioned goodness to these delightful treats. The log-shaped cookies are dressed up with melted chocolate and chopped walnuts for a special look.

- 1/2 tube refrigerated sugar cookie dough, softened
- 1/2 cup all-purpose flour
- 1/4 cup packed brown sugar
- 1 tablespoon orange juice
- 3/4 teaspoon ground cinnamon
- 1/2 teaspoon ground ginger
- 1/2 teaspoon grated orange peel
- 1/2 cup semisweet chocolate chips
- 4 teaspoons shortening
- 1/4 cup finely chopped walnuts

In a small mixing bowl, beat the cookie dough, flour, brown sugar, orange juice, cinnamon, ginger and orange peel until combined. Shape teaspoonfuls of dough into 2-in. logs. Place 2 in. apart on ungreased baking sheets. Bake at 350° for 8-10 minutes or until edges are golden brown. Remove to wire racks to cool.

In a microwave-safe bowl, melt the chocolate chips and shortening; stir until smooth. Dip one end of each cookie into melted chocolate; sprinkle with walnuts. Place on waxed paper; let stand until set. **Yield:** about 3-1/2 dozen.

Red sugar, nonpareils *or* sprinkles
- 1 square (1 ounce) white baking chocolate
- 2 tablespoons cream cheese, softened
- 1 tablespoon butter, softened
- 4 drops red food coloring
- 1/2 cup confectioners' sugar

In a small mixing bowl, beat cookie dough and flour until combined. Roll out on a lightly floured surface to 1/8-in. thickness. Cut with a floured 2-3/4-in. star cookie cutter. Place 2 in. apart on ungreased baking sheets.

Decorate half of the cookies with red sugar. Bake at 350° for 7-9 minutes or until edges are golden brown. Remove to wire racks to cool.

In a microwave-safe bowl, melt white chocolate. Stir until smooth; cool. In a small mixing bowl, beat the cream cheese, butter and food coloring. Gradually beat in confectioners' sugar and melted chocolate until smooth. Spread over the bottoms of plain cookies; top with decorated cookies. Store in the refrigerator. **Yield:** about 1 dozen.

Colorful Candy Bar Cookies

(Pictured above)

Prep: 35 min. **Bake:** 10 min.

No one will guess that these sweet treats with a candy bar center start with store-bought dough. Roll them in colored sugar...or just dip the tops for even faster assembly. Instead of using miniature candy bars, you could slice regular-size bars into 1-inch pieces for the centers.

- 1/2 tube refrigerated sugar cookie dough, softened
- 1/4 cup all-purpose flour
- 24 miniature Snickers candy bars

Red and green colored sugar

In a small mixing bowl, beat cookie dough and flour until combined. Shape 1-1/2 teaspoonfuls of dough

Dipped Spice Cookies

Chocolate-Cherry Coffee Mix

Gifts From The Kitchen

HOMEMADE CREATIONS from your kitchen make some of the most heartwarming gifts during the holiday season. You'll find it's easy to delight loved ones with tasteful presents when you use the rapid recipes here.

So share marvelous mixes for fruit-and-nut muffins, candy-filled brownies and chocolaty coffee. By spending just a few minutes in the kitchen, you'll have delicious homemade gifts all wrapped up.

Chocolate-Cherry Coffee Mix

(Pictured above)

Prep/Total Time: 20 min.

*Cute ice cream cone-shaped packages of this flavored coffee mix are sure to delight friends and family. I want-*ed *something that both coffee and non-coffee drinkers would enjoy, so I added cherry flavoring to a mocha mix.*
—Jennifer Waters, Lubbock, Texas

    3 cups sugar
    2 cups confectioners' sugar
1-1/3 cups nondairy creamer
1-1/3 cups instant coffee granules
    1 cup baking cocoa
    1 envelope unsweetened cherry soft drink mix
    6 cups miniature marshmallows, *divided*
    6 teaspoons holiday sprinkles, *divided*
ADDITIONAL INGREDIENT (for each serving):
    1 cup hot milk

Combine the first six ingredients. Place 1 cup mix in a 12-in. disposable decorating bag. Fold corners of bag into the center and roll bag down; secure with transparent tape.

Place bag in a second disposable decorating bag. Top with 1 cup of marshmallows and 1 teaspoon of sprinkles. Gather and twist the top of the bag. Tie with ribbon. Repeat to make five more gift bags. Store in a cool dry place for up to 2 months. **Yield:** 6 gift bags (1 cup/8 servings per bag).

To prepare coffee: In a mug, dissolve 2 heaping tablespoons mix in hot milk; stir well. Top with marshmallows and sprinkles. **Yield:** 1 serving.

Cherry-Nut Muffin Mix

(Pictured below)

Prep: 15 min. **Bake:** 20 min.

Everyone will love having a warm-from-the-oven batch of these moist fruit-and-nut treats. To give this layered muffin mix as a gift, just print the directions for preparing the muffins and spiced butter on a holiday postcard and attach it to the jar with a festive ribbon.
—Marianne Clarke, Crystal Lake, Illinois

  2 cups all-purpose flour
  1 cup sugar
  1 teaspoon baking soda
  1 teaspoon ground cardamom
  1/2 to 1 teaspoon ground cloves
  1/2 cup dried cherries *or* cranberries
  1/2 cup chopped walnuts
ADDITIONAL INGREDIENTS:
  1 cup buttermilk
  1 egg
  1/2 cup butter, melted
CARDAMOM BUTTER:
  1/2 cup butter, softened
  1/4 cup confectioners' sugar
  1 teaspoon ground cardamom

In a small bowl, combine the flour, sugar and baking soda. In a 1-qt. glass container, layer the flour mixture, cardamom, cloves, cherries and walnuts, packing well between each layer. Cover and store in a cool dry place for up to 6 months. **Yield:** 1 batch (about 4 cups total).

To prepare muffins: Place mix in a large bowl. Combine the buttermilk, egg and butter; stir into mix just until moistened. Fill greased or paper-lined muffin cups three fourths full. Bake at 400° for 20-25 minutes

Sand Art Brownies

or until a toothpick comes out clean. Cool for 5 minutes before removing from pans to wire racks.

In a small mixing bowl, cream the butter, confectioners' sugar and cardamom until smooth. Store in an airtight container in the refrigerator. Soften just before serving with the muffins. **Yield:** 14 muffins (about 3/4 cup butter).

Sand Art Brownies

(Pictured above)

Prep: 15 min. **Bake:** 30 min. + cooling

A jar of this attractive layered mix produces a yummy batch of fudgy brownies that are dressed up with chocolate chips and M&M's. If you need a quick gift for a neighbor or teacher, this fills the bill—deliciously!
—Joan Hohwald, Lodi, New York

  1 cup plus 2 tablespoons all-purpose flour
  1/2 teaspoon salt
  1/2 teaspoon baking powder
  1/3 cup baking cocoa
  2/3 cup sugar
  2/3 cup packed brown sugar
  1/2 cup semisweet chocolate chips
  1/2 cup holiday milk chocolate M&M's
ADDITIONAL INGREDIENTS:
  3 eggs
  2/3 cup vegetable oil
  1 teaspoon vanilla extract

In a small bowl, combine the flour, salt and baking powder. In a 1-qt. glass container, layer the flour mixture, cocoa, sugar, brown sugar, chocolate chips and M&M's, packing well between each layer.

Cover; store in a cool dry place for up to 6 months. **Yield:** 1 batch (about 4 cups total).

To prepare brownies: In a large mixing bowl, beat the eggs, oil and vanilla. Add brownie mix and mix well. Pour into a greased 8-in. square baking dish. Bake at 350° for 26-28 minutes or until center is set (do not overbake). Cool on a wire rack. **Yield:** 16 servings.

Cherry-Nut Muffin Mix

General Recipe Index

This handy index lists every recipe by food category, major ingredient and/or cooking method, so you can easily locate recipes to suit your needs.

✓ Recipe includes Nutritional Analysis and Diabetic Exchanges

✓ *Recipe includes Nutritional Analysis and Diabetic Exchanges*

✓ Recipe includes Nutritional Analysis and Diabetic Exchanges

✓ Recipe includes Nutritional Analysis and Diabetic Exchanges

✓ *Recipe includes Nutritional Analysis and Diabetic Exchanges*

✓ *Recipe includes Nutritional Analysis and Diabetic Exchanges*

✓ Recipe includes Nutritional Analysis and Diabetic Exchanges

✓ Recipe includes Nutritional Analysis and Diabetic Exchanges

✓ Recipe includes Nutritional Analysis and Diabetic Exchanges

✓ *Recipe includes Nutritional Analysis and Diabetic Exchanges*

✓ Recipe includes Nutritional Analysis and Diabetic Exchanges

✓ Recipe includes Nutritional Analysis and Diabetic Exchanges

✓ Recipe includes Nutritional Analysis and Diabetic Exchanges

✓ *Recipe includes Nutritional Analysis and Diabetic Exchanges*

✓ Recipe includes Nutritional Analysis and Diabetic Exchanges

Alphabetical Index

This handy index lists every recipe in alphabetical order so you can easily find your favorite recipes.

✓Recipe includes Nutritional Analysis and Diabetic Exchanges

✓ Recipe includes Nutritional Analysis and Diabetic Exchanges

✓Glazed Pork Medallions, 266
Glazed Salmon, 205
Golden Diced Potatoes, 125
Graham Cracker Cookies, 230
Granola Banana Sticks, 293
Granola Trail Mix, 86
Grape Melon Medley, 32
✓Grapefruit Spinach Salad, 266
Greek Orzo Salad, 304
Green Bean Egg Salad, 304
Green Bean Turkey Bake, 112
Green Chili Tomato Soup, 88
Grilled Chicken Reubens, 192
Grilled Flank Steak Salad, 158
Grilled Honey-Ginger Corn, 50
✓Grilled PB&J, 273
Grilled Pork Chops, 156
Grilled Vegetable Medley, 126
✓Ground Beef Lo Mein, 107
Gumbo Joes, 242

H

Halloween Poke Cake, 31
Ham and Bean Soup, 180
Ham and Lentil Soup, 147
Ham 'n' Onion Gravy, 116
Ham 'n' Swiss with a Twist, 252
Ham Potato Puffs, 115
✓Ham with Creamed Vegetables, 59
Ham with Mixed Fruit, 45
Hamburger Supper, 197
Hard-Shell Ice Cream Sauce, 12
Hawaiian Deli Sandwiches, 256
Hearty Chicken Noodle Soup, 146
Hearty English Muffins, 281
Hearty Hash Brown Dinner, 144
Hearty Maple Beans, 246
Herbed Biscuit Knots, 74
Herbed Lamb Chops, 278
Herbed Potatoes and Veggies, 121
Herbed Rice, 123
Holiday Bells, 312
✓Homemade Salsa, 308
Homemade Turkey Soup, 114

Honey Fruit Salad, 168
Honey Lemon Cookies, 212
Honey-Mustard Turkey Breast, 74
Hot Corned Beef Buns, 26
Hot Diggity Dogs, 100
Hot Fruit Salad, 145
Hot Lemon Artichoke Dip, 286
Hot Seafood Spread, 294

I

Ice Cream Pretzel Cake, 156
Irish Creme Chocolate Trifle, 35
Irish Spud Strips, 26
Italian Chicken, 240
Italian Dipping Sticks, 92
Italian Sausage Hoagies, 155
Italian Snack Mix, 290
Italian Submarine, 32
✓Italian Turkey Skillet, 108

J

Jiffy Ground Pork Skillet, 236

K

Kidney Bean Coleslaw, 188
Kielbasa Biscuit Pizza, 114
Kielbasa with Baked Beans, 243
Kielbasa with Pasta, 202
Kielbasa with Veggies, 235
Kitchen-Sink Soft Tacos, 294

L

Lemon Angel Cake, 28
Lemon Angel Hair, 43
✓Lemon Blueberry Muffins, 136
✓Lemon-Butter Snow Peas, 120
✓Lemon Chicken and Peppers, 98
Lemon Corn and Zucchini, 127
Lemon Garlic Hummus, 288
✓Lemonade Chicken, 145
✓Lemony Shrimp 'n' Asparagus, 301
✓Lime Fruit Slushies, 32
Linguine Alfredo, 106
Loaded Tortillas, 83
Louisiana-Style Taco Soup, 100

Luncheon Chicken Salad, 116
Luscious Apple Trifle, 307

M

Mac 'n' Cheese Soup, 225
Macadamia Coconut Bars, 69
Macaroni Bean Salad, 190
Macaroni Bean Soup, 252
Macaroni Chicken Skillet, 234
✓Macaroni Vegetable Soup, 182
Malted Milk Ball Brownies, 257
✓Mandarin-Nut Tossed Salad, 86
Maple-Granola Trail Mix, 171
Maple Raisin Carrots, 65
Maple Syrup Pudding, 20
Marmalade-Glazed Carrots, 150
Marmalade Monkey Bread, 134
Marshmallow Witches, 30
✓Meat 'n' Potato Kabobs, 51
Meat Loaf Pie, 94
Meat Lover's Pizza Bake, 244
Meatball Pizza, 303
Meatball Vegetable Soup, 303
Mini Bagelizzas, 287
Mini Italian Biscuits, 141
Mint Cookie Candies, 211
Mint-Cream Fruit Topping, 175
✓Mixed Green Salad, 178
Monterey Turkey Omelet, 164
Mosaic Salad, 190
Mousse Tarts, 85
Mousse-Topped Pound Cake, 46
Mozzarella Beef Roll-Ups, 39
Mozzarella Wedges, 252
Mud Pie, 215
✓Mushroom Bean Medley, 55
Mushroom Cheese Bread, 139
Mushroom Oven Omelet, 206
Mushroom Romaine Salad, 42

N

Noel Cookie Gems, 34
Noodles with Broccoli, 58

O

Olive and Red Pepper Linguine, 129

✓ *Recipe includes Nutritional Analysis and Diabetic Exchanges*

Olive Cheese Ball, 294
One-Pot Pork Chops, 236
Onion Crescent Rolls, 48
Onion Meat Loaf, 148
Open-Faced Beef
    Sandwiches, 92
Orange Blueberry Shakes, 298
Orange Cranberry Bread, 138
✓Orange Dream Torte, 212
Orange-Glazed Chicken
    Wings, 62
Oregano-Swiss Bread
    Slices, 137
Oriental Chicken, 14
✓Oriental Shrimp Soup, 185
Owl Cookies, 231

P

Pancake Stack with
    Syrup, 164
✓Pantry Salsa, 230
Parmesan Couscous, 51
✓Parmesan Orange
    Roughy, 68
✓Pasta Beef Soup, 12
Pasta Sausage Supper, 53
Pastel Gelatin Salad, 95
Patriotic Cupcakes, 224
PB&J Spirals, 286
✓Pea 'n' Crab Pasta Salad, 257
Pea Salad, 82
Peach Coffee Cake, 166
✓Peach Strawberry
    Sundaes, 218
Peachy Tossed Salad, 189
Peanut Beef Stir-Fry, 239
Peanut Butter Cream
    Dessert, 226
Peanut Butter Eggs, 28
Peanut Lover's Pie, 218
Pear-Pecan Sausage
    Quiche,174
✓Peas and Celery, 259
Pecan Baked Apples, 59
Pecan Pancake Pizza, 172
Pecan Spinach Salad, 87
Pecan-Stuffed Waffles, 170
Pepper Artichoke
    Stromboli, 190
Pepper Pork Pockets, 189
Pepperoni Pizza Dip, 292
Peppy Peach Salsa, 309
Pesto Chicken 'n' Ravioli, 200
Pesto Minestrone, 178

Pierogi Supper, 240
Pineapple Berry Breeze, 218
Pineapple Carrot Salad, 76
✓Pineapple Cheddar
    Spread, 292
Pineapple Crunch, 210
Pineapple Sirloin
    Skewers, 159
Pinto Bean Chicken Soup, 103
Pistachio Cream Pie, 14
Pistachio Eclair Dessert, 161
✓Pistachio Fluff, 269
Pizza Burgers, 255
Pizza Dip, 152
Pizza Quesadillas, 88
Poached Orange Pears, 76
✓Pork 'n' Pea Pod Stir-Fry, 265
✓Pork Cabbage Saute, 196
Pork Chops Italiano, 58
Pork Chops with
    Sauerkraut, 148
Pork Cubes 'n' Stuffing, 235
Pork Meatball Kabobs, 303
Pork Noodle Soup, 116
Pork Vegetable Hero, 186
Portobello Melts, 282
✓Potato Ham Chowder, 280
Potluck Lasagna, 161
Pronto Beef and Rice, 204
Pronto Prosciutto Pasta, 199
✓Pudding Pumpkin Pie, 266
Pumpernickel Turkey
    Hero, 188
Pumpkin Cake Roll, 157
Pumpkin Coffee Cake, 140
Pumpkin Ginger Scones, 138
Pumpkin Pancakes, 167
Pumpkin Pie Dip, 80
Pumpkin Torte, 220

R

✓Raisin Sauce for Ham, 207
Raisin-Spice Snack Cake, 102
✓Ranch Pasta Salad, 16
Ranch Potato Salad, 65
Raspberry Almond Strips, 312
Raspberry Coconut Bars, 35
Raspberry Coconut
    Cookies, 214
Raspberry Cream Muffins, 133
Raspberry Lemon Torte, 218
Red Clam Sauce over
    Pasta, 234
Red-Hot Gelatin Salad, 74

Reuben Brunch Bake, 164
Reuben Crescents, 295
Ribbon Crispies, 214
Roast Beef Barbecue, 81
✓Roast Beef Pinwheels, 286
Rocky Ford Chili, 82
Rosemary Cheddar Bread, 135
Round Steak Sauerbraten, 154
Rustic Vegetarian Pizza, 96
Rye Ham Bites, 290

S

Salmon Linguine Alfredo, 199
Salmon Supper, 196
Salsa Sloppy Joes, 16
Sand Art Brownies, 314
Santa Pancakes, 229
Sauerkraut Slaw, 180
Sausage 'n' Sauerkraut, 243
Sausage Cheese Snacks, 181
✓Sausage Minestrone, 184
Sausage-Stuffed Squash, 197
Savory Cheese Bread, 12
Savory Pork Supper, 305
Scalloped Chicken
    Supper, 248
Scalloped Taters, 155
Scallops Alfredo, 240
Seafood Pitas, 94
✓Seasoned Potato Cubes, 54
Sesame Carrot Slices, 49
✓Sesame Steamed
    Vegetables, 280
Shortcut Shortcake, 103
Shredded Beef Nachos, 117
Shrimp and Ham Alfredo, 92
✓Shrimp Creole, 238
Simple Spinach Salad, 180
Simple Squash and
    Sausage, 281
Skillet Sausage Stuffing, 126
Skillet Shepherd's Pie, 239
Sloppy Dogs, 231
Sloppy Joes, 240
Smoked Beef Brisket, 151
S'more Drops, 291
Snowman Sugar Cookies, 93
Sour Cream Oven Omelet, 70
✓Sour Cream Salad
    Dressing, 62
Southern Pot Roast, 151
✓Southwestern Chicken, 264
✓Spanish Squash Medley, 122
Speedy Sausage Squares, 175

✓ *Recipe includes Nutritional Analysis and Diabetic Exchanges*

✓ *Recipe includes Nutritional Analysis and Diabetic Exchanges*